The Ultimate Egypt Travel (2025 Edition)

Everything You Need to Know - Top Attractions, Where to Eat, Best Places to Visit & Local Tips

Grace Bennett

Copyright Notice

No part of this book may be reproduced, written, electronic, recorded, or photocopied without written permission from the publisher or author.

The exception would be in the case of brief quotations embodied in critical articles or reviews and pages where permission is specifically granted by the publisher or author.

Although every precaution has been taken to verify the accuracy of the information contained herein, the author and publisher assume no responsibility for any errors or omissions. No liability is assumed for damages that may result from the use of the information contained within.

All Rights Reserved ©2025

The Ultimate Egypt Travel Guide 2025 Edition

TABLE OF CONTENTS

INTRODUCTION — 9

- Why Visit Egypt? — 10
- How to Use This Guide — 11
- Quick Facts — 12

CHAPTER 1: PLANNING YOUR TRIP — 15

- Best Time to Visit — 15
- Visa and Entry Requirements — 16
- Budgeting and Costs — 18
- The Ultimate Packing List for All Seasons — 20
- Major Airports — 22
- Train Travel from Neighboring Countries — 23
- Road Travel and Border Crossings — 25
- Ferry and Boat Travel — 27
- Bike or Walking — 29

CHAPTER 3: GETTING AROUND EGYPT — 31

- Public Transportation — 31
- Renting a Car — 33
- Taxis and Ride-Sharing — 35
- Biking — 37
- Walking and Hiking — 38
- Travel Passes & Cards — 40

CHAPTER 4: PRACTICAL INFORMATION — 43

- Language and Communication — 43
- Currency and Payments — 45
- Time Zone and Business Hours — 47
- Local Customs and Etiquette — 48
- Climate and Weather — 50
- Electricity and Plug Types — 52

CHAPTER 5: HEALTH AND SAFETY IN EGYPT — 53

- Healthcare — 53
- Medical Services — 55
- Emergency Services — 57
- Vaccinations and Health Precautions — 59
- Health Insurance and Medical Assistance — 61
- Food and Water Safety — 63

CHAPTER 6: CULTURAL ETIQUETTE AND CUSTOMS — 65

- General Etiquette — 65
- Dress Code — 67
- Public Behavior — 69
- Dining Etiquette — 71
- Customs and Traditions — 73
- Shopping and Bargaining — 75
- Behavior Towards Women — 77

CHAPTER 7: OUTDOOR ACTIVITIES — 81

- Desert Adventures — 81
- Nile River Activities — 83
- Beach and Water Sports — 86
- Hiking and Trekking — 89
- Historical and Archaeological Exploration — 92
- Wildlife and Nature — 95
- Cycling and Biking — 99

CHAPTER 8: SHOPPING IN EGYPT — 103

- Traditional Markets and Souks — 103
- Modern Shopping Malls — 104
- Unique Souvenirs — 106
- Jewelry and Accessories — 108
- Food and Spices — 110

CHAPTER 9: DINING AND NIGHTLIFE IN EGYPT — 113

- Traditional Egyptian Cuisine — 113
- Cafés and Bakeries — 123
- Bars and Lounges — 126

The Ultimate Egypt Travel Guide 2025 Edition

NIGHTCLUBS AND DANCE VENUES	**128**
TIPS FOR DINING AND NIGHTLIFE IN EGYPT	**131**

CHAPTER 10: CAIRO — 135

TOP 10 ATTRACTIONS & THINGS TO DO	**135**
ACCOMMODATION OPTIONS	**156**
LUXURY HOTEL	156
MID-RANGE HOTEL	167
BOUTIQUE HOTEL	175
DAY TRIP FROM CAIRO	**185**
THE PYRAMIDS OF GIZA	185
SAQQARA	187
MEMPHIS	189
ALEXANDRIA	191
AL MINYA	193
FAYOUM OASIS	195
ABU SIR	197
7-DAY ITINERARY FOR FIRST TIME TRAVELER	**199**
DAY 1: ARRIVAL AND ORIENTATION	199
DAY 2: GIZA PLATEAU AND PYRAMIDS	201
DAY 3: SAQQARA AND MEMPHIS	204
DAY 4: ISLAMIC CAIRO	207
DAY 5: COPTIC CAIRO AND LOCAL CULTURE	210
DAY 6: MODERN CAIRO AND RELAXATION	214
DAY 7: DAY TRIP TO ALEXANDRIA	218

CHAPTER 11: ALEXANDRIA — 223

TOP 10 ATTRACTIONS & THINGS TO DO	**223**
ACCOMMODATION OPTIONS	**246**
LUXURY HOTEL	246
MID-RANGE HOTEL	258
BOUTIQUE HOTEL	268
HOSTEL	278
DAY TRIP FROM ALEXANDRIA	**288**
CAIRO	288
SIWA OASIS	289
ROSETTA (RASHID)	290
MARSA MATROUH	291
BAHARIYA OASIS	293
FAIYUM	294
7-DAY ITINERARY FOR FIRST TIME TRAVELER	**297**

Day 1: Arrival and Introduction	297
Day 2: Historical Exploration	299
Day 3: Ancient Alexandria	301
Day 4: Day Trip to El Alamein	303
Day 5: Coastal Relaxation	305
Day 6: Cultural Immersion	307
Day 7: Leisure and Departure	309

CHAPTER 12: LUXOR — 311

Top 10 Attractions & Things to do	**311**
Accommodation Options	**336**
Luxury Hotel	336
Mid-Range Hotel	348
Boutique Hotel	359
Hostel	370
Day Trip from Luxor	**380**
Valley of the Queens	380
Edfu Temple	382
Kom Ombo Temple	383
Dendera Temple Complex	385
Aswan	386
Temple of Abydos	388
Hot Air Balloon Ride Over Luxor	390
7-day Itinerary for first time traveler	**392**
Day 1: Arrival in Luxor	392
Day 2: East Bank Exploration	394
Day 3: Valley of the Kings and Valley of the Queens	396
Day 4: Temple of Hatshepsut and Colossi of Memnon	398
Day 5: Dendera Temple Complex and Hot Air Balloon Ride	400
Day 6: Aswan Day Trip	402
Day 7: Relax and Depart	404

CHAPTER 13: CONCLUSION — 407

Tourist Information Centers	**407**
Useful Apps for travelers	**408**
Basic Egyptian Phrases	**411**
Final Tips and Recommendations	**412**

Grace Bennett

INTRODUCTION

Are you tired of cookie-cutter vacations that leave you feeling unfulfilled? Do you long for an adventure that combines ancient wonders with modern excitement? Are you overwhelmed by the thought of planning a trip to a country as rich in history and culture as Egypt? Do you worry about navigating a foreign land where you don't speak the language? Are concerns about safety holding you back from experiencing the vacation of a lifetime? Do you find yourself confused about the best time to visit or what to pack for Egypt's diverse climate? Are you unsure how to experience Egypt authentically without falling into tourist traps?

If you answered "yes" to any of these questions, you're in the right place. Welcome to "Egypt Unveiled: Your Ultimate Travel Companion," the comprehensive guide that will transform your Egyptian adventure from a daunting challenge into an unforgettable journey.

Egypt, the cradle of civilization, is a land where the past and present intertwine in a mesmerizing dance. From the iconic Pyramids of Giza to the bustling bazaars of Cairo, from the tranquil waters of the Nile to the coral-rich Red Sea, Egypt offers a tapestry of experiences that cater to every type of traveler.

But we understand that planning a trip to Egypt can be overwhelming. That's why we've created this guide – to take the guesswork out of your Egyptian adventure and replace it with confidence and excitement.

In the pages that follow, you'll find everything you need to know about visiting Egypt:

- Practical tips on when to visit, how to get there, and how to navigate the country
- Insider advice on staying safe and healthy while embracing local customs
- Comprehensive breakdowns of must-visit destinations, from Cairo to Luxor and beyond
- Curated itineraries for first-time visitors and seasoned travelers alike
- Recommendations for unforgettable experiences, from desert safaris to Nile cruises
- Guidance on shopping, dining, and nightlife to help you immerse yourself in Egyptian culture

Whether you're a history buff eager to walk in the footsteps of pharaohs, an adventure seeker ready to conquer the desert, or a culture enthusiast keen to experience modern Egyptian life, this guide has you covered.

So, are you ready to unravel the mysteries of Egypt? To stand in awe before ancient monuments, to lose yourself in colorful markets, to sail down the life-giving Nile? Then turn the page, and let your Egyptian odyssey begin. The land of the pharaohs awaits, and with this guide in hand, you're ready to explore it like never before.

Why Visit Egypt?

Egypt is a land where history comes alive and ancient wonders meet vibrant culture. Here's why you should consider adding Egypt to your travel bucket list:

Timeless Wonders: The Pyramids of Giza, the Sphinx, and the sprawling temples of Luxor offer an unparalleled glimpse into one of the world's most ancient civilizations. Walking among these colossal structures feels like stepping into the pages of a history book.

The Nile River: Known as the lifeblood of Egypt, the Nile offers breathtaking river cruises that allow you to experience Egypt from a unique perspective. From the lush banks of the river to the ancient ruins that line its shores, a Nile cruise is a journey through both history and natural beauty.

Grace Bennett

Rich Cultural Heritage: Egypt's history is not confined to the ancient past. The vibrant cities of Cairo and Alexandria are bustling with life, offering a blend of traditional markets, modern cafes, and a lively arts scene that reflects both the country's storied past and its contemporary culture.

Unique Experiences: Whether it's camel riding through the Sahara Desert, diving in the Red Sea's coral reefs, or exploring the bustling souks of Cairo, Egypt offers a range of experiences that are as diverse as they are unforgettable.

World-Class Museums: The Egyptian Museum in Cairo houses a vast collection of artifacts, including the treasures of Tutankhamun, providing insights into the grandeur of ancient Egypt and its influence on the world.

Cuisine and Hospitality: Egyptian cuisine, with its rich flavors and spices, offers a delightful culinary journey. From street food like koshari to elegant dining experiences, Egyptian food is a feast for the senses. Coupled with the renowned warmth and hospitality of the Egyptian people, your visit will be both delicious and welcoming.

Natural Beauty: Beyond the historic sites, Egypt's diverse landscapes—from the serene beaches of the Red Sea to the dramatic dunes of the Sahara—offer numerous opportunities for relaxation and adventure.

A Journey Through Time: Egypt is a living tapestry of human history, from ancient pyramids to modern marvels. Every corner tells a story, making it a destination where history is not just observed but experienced.

Whether you're captivated by ancient history, excited by cultural exploration, or simply seeking adventure, Egypt promises an unforgettable journey through one of the world's most fascinating destinations.

How to Use This Guide

This guide is designed to be your comprehensive companion for exploring Egypt, making your journey as enjoyable and stress-free as possible. Here's how to navigate and utilize the information effectively:

Start with the Basics: Begin with the introductory sections to get a general overview of Egypt, including why it's worth visiting and key quick facts. This will help you set the stage for your trip and understand the essentials before diving into more detailed planning.

Plan Your Trip: Move on to Chapter 1 to determine the best time to visit, understand visa requirements, budget effectively, and pack appropriately for the season. This chapter will lay the groundwork for your travel preparations, ensuring you're well-prepared before departure.

Travel Logistics: Chapter 2 covers the various ways to reach Egypt, from major airports to road and ferry options. Use this chapter to plan your arrival and transportation, so you can easily get from your home country to your Egyptian destination.

Getting Around: Once you're in Egypt, refer to Chapter 3 for information on local transportation options. Whether you're using public transit, renting a car, or navigating taxis and ride-sharing services, this chapter will help you get around efficiently.

Practical Information: Chapter 4 provides crucial details about language, currency, local customs, and other practical aspects of daily life in Egypt. This section will help you adapt to the local environment and make your interactions smoother.

Health and Safety: Chapter 5 addresses health precautions, medical services, and safety tips.

Review this section to ensure you're prepared for any health issues and understand the safety measures to take during your visit.

Cultural Etiquette: Chapter 6 is essential for understanding Egyptian customs and social norms. Knowing how to behave respectfully and appropriately will enhance your experience and interactions with locals.

Outdoor Adventures: For those looking to explore Egypt's natural beauty and engage in outdoor activities, Chapter 7 offers insights into desert adventures, Nile river activities, and other recreational options.

Shopping and Dining: Chapters 8 and 9 will guide you through the best places to shop for souvenirs and experience Egyptian cuisine and nightlife. Use these sections to discover local markets, unique gifts, and dining experiences.

Top Destinations: Chapters 10 through 12 provide detailed information on Egypt's top destinations, including Cairo, Alexandria, and Luxor. Each chapter includes attractions, accommodation options, day trips, and suggested itineraries to help you make the most of your visit to these key locations.

Final Tips and Resources: Conclude your preparation with Chapter 13, which includes essential tourist information centers, useful travel apps, basic Egyptian phrases, and final tips to ensure you have a smooth and enjoyable trip.

This guide is structured to be both a practical tool for planning and a valuable resource during your trip. By following the sections relevant to your needs and interests, you'll be well-equipped to navigate and enjoy all that Egypt has to offer.

Quick Facts

1. Location: Egypt is located in northeastern Africa, bordered by the Mediterranean Sea to the north, Libya to the west, Sudan to the south, and the Red Sea to the east. It also has a land bridge to the Sinai Peninsula, which connects it to Asia.

2. Capital City: Cairo

3. Official Language: Arabic

4. Currency: Egyptian Pound (EGP)

5. Time Zone: Egypt Standard Time (GMT+2)

6. Climate:

Summer (June to August): Hot and dry with temperatures often exceeding 40°C (104°F), especially in desert regions.

Winter (December to February): Mild and pleasant, with temperatures ranging from 10°C to 20°C (50°F to 68°F).

Spring and Autumn: Generally warm and comfortable, with less extreme temperatures.

7. Major Airports:

Cairo International Airport (CAI) – the main international gateway to Egypt.

Alexandria Borg El Arab Airport (HBE)

Luxor International Airport (LXR)

Aswan International Airport (ASW)

8. Electricity and Plug Types:

Voltage: 220V

Frequency: 50Hz

Plug Types: Mostly Type C and Type F (European-style plugs)

9. Important Numbers:

Emergency Services: 122

Tourist Police: 126

Local Dialing Code: +20

10. Entry Requirements:

Most visitors require a visa to enter Egypt. Check specific requirements based on your nationality and the type of visa needed.

Some nationalities may obtain a visa on arrival or apply for an e-visa.

11. Local Customs:

Egypt is a predominantly Muslim country, and Islamic practices influence local customs and daily life. Respect for religious practices and local traditions is important.

12. Health and Safety:

Vaccinations: Routine vaccines are recommended, and some travelers may need vaccines for hepatitis A, hepatitis B, and typhoid.

Health Precautions: Drink bottled or purified water to avoid waterborne illnesses.

13. Transportation:

Public Transit: Buses, metro (in Cairo), and trains are widely used.

Taxis and Ride-Sharing: Available in cities and major tourist areas.

Car Rental: Available but driving requires caution due to local traffic conditions.

14. Key Tourist Attractions:

The Pyramids of Giza

The Sphinx

The Egyptian Museum

Luxor Temple and Karnak Temple

The Valley of the Kings

These quick facts offer a snapshot of essential information to help you prepare for your trip to Egypt. For detailed planning, refer to the relevant sections in this guide.

Chapter 1: Planning Your Trip

Best Time to Visit

Choosing the right time to visit Egypt can significantly enhance your travel experience. Here's a breakdown of what to consider for each season:

Winter (December to February):

Weather: This is the most pleasant time to visit Egypt, especially in Cairo, Luxor, and Aswan. Daytime temperatures are mild, ranging from 15°C to 25°C (59°F to 77°F), while nights can be cooler. The weather is ideal for exploring ancient sites and enjoying outdoor activities.

Advantages: Comfortable temperatures make it perfect for sightseeing and outdoor excursions. This is also the peak tourist season, so you'll find most attractions well-maintained and tour services fully operational.

Considerations: Winter is the high season for tourism, so expect larger crowds and higher prices for accommodations and tours.

Spring (March to May):

Weather: Spring brings warmer temperatures, ranging from 20°C to 30°C (68°F to 86°F). The weather is generally pleasant, though it can start to get hot as summer approaches.

Advantages: Spring is a great time for sightseeing before the summer heat sets in. The landscapes are lush, especially in the Nile Delta and along the riverbanks.

Considerations: You may encounter some occasional sandstorms, particularly in the desert areas. Tourist crowds are slightly less than in winter, which can mean better availability and prices for accommodations.

Summer (June to August):

Weather: Summer in Egypt can be extremely hot, especially in inland areas like Cairo and Luxor, where temperatures can exceed 35°C (95°F) and sometimes reach 40°C (104°F). Coastal areas, such as Alexandria and the Red Sea resorts, are cooler but still warm.

Advantages: Fewer tourists during the summer months can lead to lower prices for flights and accommodations. The Red Sea resorts offer a great escape from the heat with opportunities for water sports and relaxation.

Considerations: The intense heat can make sightseeing uncomfortable, especially if you're not accustomed to high temperatures. It's important to stay hydrated and protect yourself from the sun.

Autumn (September to November):

Weather: Temperatures begin to cool down, ranging from 20°C to 30°C (68°F to 86°F). This is a transitional period with comfortable weather, making it a favorable time for travel.

Advantages: Autumn provides a nice balance of good weather and fewer crowds compared to winter. It's an excellent time for exploring Egypt's cultural and historical sites.

Considerations: Prices for travel and accommodation may start to rise as the season progresses, but they are generally lower than during the peak winter months.

Special Events and Festivals:

Ramadan: This Islamic holy month varies each year and can affect travel plans, as many businesses have reduced hours, and eating and drinking in public are restricted during daylight hours. However, experiencing Ramadan can provide unique cultural insights.

Eid Festivals: Following Ramadan, the Eid festivals (Eid al-Fitr and Eid al-Adha) are lively and festive times with special events and celebrations.

Overall, the best time to visit Egypt is during the cooler months of winter and spring, when the weather is most comfortable for sightseeing. However, if you're looking for lower prices and don't mind the heat, summer can also be a viable option, especially if you plan to focus on coastal and water-based activities.

Visa and Entry Requirements

Traveling to Egypt requires some preparation regarding visa and entry requirements. Here's a guide to help you navigate the process:

1. Visa Requirements

Tourist Visa:

Eligibility: Most travelers will need a tourist visa to enter Egypt. This includes citizens from countries such as the United States, Canada, the European Union, Australia, and many others.

Types:

Single Entry Visa: Allows one entry into Egypt and is typically valid for a stay of up to 30 days.

Multiple Entry Visa: Permits multiple entries within a certain period and can be valid for up to 90 days or more, depending on the applicant's needs.

Visa on Arrival:

Available at certain airports for travelers from select countries. This option is usually for a single-entry visa valid for 30 days. It's important to confirm eligibility with the nearest Egyptian embassy or consulate before traveling.

e-Visa:

Application: Travelers from eligible countries can apply for an e-visa online through the official Egyptian e-Visa Portal.

Process: Complete the online application form, upload required documents, and pay the visa fee. Processing typically takes a few days.

Advantages: The e-visa can be more convenient than obtaining a visa on arrival or through an embassy, allowing you to complete the process before you travel.

Visa Exemption:

Citizens of some countries may be exempt from needing a visa for short stays. This often applies to neighboring countries or those with specific bilateral agreements.

2. Required Documents

Passport: Must be valid for at least six months from the date of entry into Egypt.

Visa Application Form: Completed and signed, if applying through an embassy.

Passport-sized Photos: Typically required for visa applications.

Proof of Travel: This may include flight itineraries and hotel reservations.

Proof of Financial Means: Some visa applications may require proof that you can support yourself financially during your stay.

3. Visa Fees

Fees vary depending on nationality, visa type, and processing speed. It's advisable to check the latest fee structure on the official Egyptian embassy website or the e-Visa portal.

4. Entry Requirements

Health Requirements: As of the latest updates, COVID-19 vaccination and testing requirements may be in place. Check current health and travel advisories for any specific requirements or restrictions.

Customs Regulations: Be aware of customs regulations regarding items you can bring into

Egypt, such as certain types of medication and restricted goods.

5. Extending Your Stay

If you wish to stay longer than your visa allows, you can apply for an extension at the Egyptian Ministry of Interior or through local immigration offices. Extensions are typically granted for up to an additional 30 days.

6. Important Tips

Check for Updates: Visa requirements can change, so it's crucial to check the latest information from official sources or the Egyptian embassy or consulate in your home country.

Travel Insurance: Consider obtaining travel insurance that covers visa-related issues and medical emergencies.

Keep Copies: Make copies of your visa, passport, and other important documents in case of loss or theft.

By understanding these requirements and preparing accordingly, you can ensure a smoother entry into Egypt and start your adventure with confidence.

Budgeting and Costs

When planning a trip to Egypt, it's important to understand the potential costs involved to create a realistic budget. Here's a breakdown of typical expenses you might encounter:

1. Accommodation

Budget Hotels/Hostels: $20 to $50 per night. These options are basic but offer a good value, particularly in cities like Cairo and Alexandria.

Mid-Range Hotels: $50 to $100 per night. Comfortable hotels with additional amenities, often in prime locations.

Luxury Hotels: $100 to $300+ per night. High-end hotels with top-notch facilities, especially in tourist hotspots like Cairo, Luxor, and Sharm El Sheikh.

Resorts: $150 to $500+ per night. For all-inclusive resorts, particularly in Red Sea destinations, prices can be higher.

2. Food and Dining

Street Food: $2 to $5 per meal. Affordable and delicious options like koshari, falafel, and shawarma.

Casual Restaurants: $5 to $15 per meal. Typical dining spots where you can enjoy local dishes.

Mid-Range Restaurants: $15 to $30 per meal. Restaurants offering a mix of Egyptian and international cuisine.

High-End Restaurants: $30 to $75+ per meal. Fine dining experiences with a focus on gourmet cuisine.

3. Transportation

Public Transportation:

Metro: $0.30 to $0.50 per ride in Cairo.

Buses: $0.50 to $2 depending on distance and type.

Local Trains: $5 to $15 for journeys within major cities.

Taxis and Ride-Sharing:

Taxi Rides: $5 to $20 for short trips within cities.

Ride-Sharing: $3 to $10 for similar distances, depending on the app and demand.

Car Rental: $30 to $70 per day. Rates vary based on car type and rental company. Note that driving in Egypt may be challenging due to local traffic conditions.

Domestic Flights: $50 to $150. For traveling between major cities like Cairo, Luxor, and Aswan.

Nile Cruises: $150 to $300+ per night. Prices vary depending on the cruise length and luxury level.

4. Sightseeing and Activities

Historical Sites:

Pyramids of Giza: $10 to $25 for entry. Additional costs for guided tours or special access.

Luxor Temple and Karnak Temple: $10 to $20 for entry, with additional costs for guides.

Museums:

Egyptian Museum: $10 to $20 for entry, with extra charges for photography or guided tours.

New Grand Egyptian Museum: Admission prices may be higher as it's a new attraction.

Desert Tours: $50 to $150. Depending on the length and type of tour, including activities like camel riding and sandboarding.

Red Sea Activities:

Snorkeling/Diving: $30 to $100+ per trip. Prices depend on the type of excursion and equipment provided.

5. Miscellaneous Costs

Souvenirs and Shopping: $10 to $100+. Costs vary based on what you buy, from small trinkets to high-end items.

Tips and Gratuities: It's customary to tip service providers, with typical amounts being $1 to $5 for guides, drivers, and hotel staff.

6. Travel Insurance

Cost: $50 to $150 for a standard policy. Coverage for health, trip cancellations, and lost belongings.

7. Currency Exchange

Local Currency: Egyptian Pound (EGP). It's advisable to exchange some money before arrival or withdraw cash at local ATMs. Major credit cards are widely accepted in hotels and larger establishments.

Budgeting Tips

Plan Ahead: Research and book accommodations and activities in advance to secure better rates.

Local Dining: Eating at local restaurants and trying street food can significantly reduce food costs while offering an authentic experience.

Negotiate: Bargaining is common in markets and with some service providers. Always negotiate prices where appropriate.

Travel Off-Peak: Visiting during shoulder seasons (spring and autumn) can help you avoid high peak season prices.

The Ultimate Packing List for All Seasons

When preparing for a trip to Egypt, it's important to pack wisely to accommodate its diverse climate and varied activities. Here's a comprehensive packing list to ensure you're ready for all seasons:

1. Clothing

Lightweight and Breathable Fabrics: Cotton or linen shirts, blouses, and pants for comfort in hot weather.

Long-Sleeve Shirts and Pants: To protect against the sun and for cooler evenings.

Sun Protection Clothing: UPF-rated clothing can provide extra protection from the sun.

Comfortable Shoes: Walking shoes or sandals for exploring, plus closed-toe shoes for visiting historical sites.

Swimwear: Essential if you plan to visit the Red Sea or pool areas.

Light Jacket or Sweater: For cooler evenings, especially in winter or at higher altitudes.

Warm Layers: A fleece or insulated jacket if visiting during cooler months (especially in desert areas or higher altitudes).

Scarf or Shawl: Useful for covering shoulders when visiting religious sites and for extra warmth if needed.

Dress or Skirt: For dining out or more formal occasions.

Hat: Wide-brimmed for sun protection.

2. Accessories

Sunglasses: To protect your eyes from the strong sun.

Sunscreen: High SPF recommended to protect your skin from UV rays.

Reusable Water Bottle: Staying hydrated is crucial, especially in hot climates.

Travel Umbrella: Useful for both sun and unexpected rain.

Travel Pillow: For added comfort during long flights or drives.

Camera/Smartphone: For capturing your experiences. Don't forget chargers and extra batteries.

3. Toiletries and Personal Items

Basic Toiletries: Toothbrush, toothpaste, shampoo, conditioner, soap, and deodorant.

Medications: Any personal medications you need, plus a small first aid kit with basics like band-aids, pain relievers, and motion sickness tablets.

Moisturizer and Lip Balm: To combat dry air, especially in the desert.

Hand Sanitizer: Useful for hygiene on the go.

Bug Spray: Particularly if you plan to visit rural or marshy areas.

4. Travel Documents

Passport: Valid for at least six months beyond your travel dates.

Visa: Ensure you have the required visa and any necessary documentation.

Travel Insurance: Policy details and emergency contact numbers.

Flight Itinerary and Hotel Reservations: Printouts or digital copies.

Copies of Important Documents: For security and backup.

5. Electronics

Phone Charger: Plus any necessary adapters for Egyptian plug types (usually Type C or F).

Camera Accessories: Memory cards, batteries, and chargers.

Portable Power Bank: To keep your devices charged while on the go.

6. Miscellaneous

Travel Guidebook/Map: Useful for navigating and learning about local attractions.

Reusable Shopping Bag: Handy for shopping and reducing plastic use.

Travel Locks: For securing your luggage.

Notebook and Pen: For jotting down travel notes or journaling.

Seasonal Considerations

Summer (June to August):

Extra Sunscreen and Hats: To protect against intense heat.

Cooling Towels: To help stay cool during outdoor activities.

Winter (December to February):

Warmer Clothing: Especially if traveling to desert

areas or higher elevations where temperatures can drop.

Layering Pieces: Light layers to adjust to varying temperatures throughout the day.

Spring and Autumn (March to May, September to November):

Transitional Clothing: Light layers that can be added or removed as needed.

Major Airports

Egypt is served by several major international airports, making it relatively easy to reach various parts of the country. Here's an overview of the key airports:

Cairo International Airport (CAI)

Location: Cairo, the capital city.

Overview: Egypt's busiest and largest airport, handling the majority of international flights. It serves as a major hub for both domestic and international travel.

Facilities: Includes lounges, duty-free shops, restaurants, and car rental services.

Connections: Direct flights to and from most major cities around the world, as well as domestic flights to other parts of Egypt.

Alexandria Borg El Arab Airport (HBE)

Location: Near Alexandria, in the northwest of Egypt.

Overview: The second-largest airport in Egypt, serving the Alexandria area and the northern part of the country.

Facilities: Offers basic services including dining options, car rentals, and currency exchange.

Connections: Limited international flights compared to Cairo, but well-connected to major Egyptian cities.

Luxor International Airport (LXR)

Location: Luxor, a key tourist destination in southern Egypt.

Overview: Handles a significant number of tourists visiting the ancient sites in Luxor, such as the Valley of the Kings and Karnak Temple.

Facilities: Includes shops, dining options, and car rental services.

Connections: International flights mainly from Europe, with additional domestic connections.

Aswan International Airport (ASW)

Location: Aswan, in southern Egypt.

Overview: Primarily serves travelers heading to Aswan and the nearby Abu Simbel temples.

Facilities: Basic amenities including dining options and car rentals.

Connections: Limited international flights, mostly domestic connections with major cities like Cairo and Luxor.

Sharm El Sheikh International Airport (SSH)

Location: Sharm El Sheikh, a popular resort city on the Red Sea.

Overview: Serves the Red Sea resort area, known for its beaches, diving spots, and luxury resorts.

Facilities: Offers a range of services including shops, restaurants, and car rental.

Connections: International flights from various European cities and domestic connections.

Hurghada International Airport (HRG)

Location: Hurghada, another major Red Sea resort area.

Overview: Handles a large volume of tourists visiting the Red Sea resorts and diving sites.

Facilities: Includes dining, shopping, and car rental services.

Connections: International flights from Europe and other regions, along with domestic flights.

These airports provide access to Egypt's major cities and tourist destinations, facilitating both international and domestic travel.

Train Travel from Neighboring Countries

Traveling to Egypt by train from neighboring countries is a bit more complex compared to flying, as there are limited direct rail connections. However, there are some options for reaching Egypt by train with additional arrangements for crossing the border. Here's a guide to train travel from Egypt's neighboring countries:

1. From Sudan

Connection: There is no direct train service between Sudan and Egypt.

Alternative: You can travel by train from Khartoum, Sudan's capital, to the border town of Wadi Halfa. From Wadi Halfa, you can take a ferry across Lake Nasser to Aswan, Egypt.

Khartoum to Wadi Halfa: The train journey can be long and is operated by Sudan Railways.

Ferry: The ferry from Wadi Halfa to Aswan typically operates once a week and can be a multi-day journey.

2. From Libya

Connection: There are no direct train services between Libya and Egypt.

Alternative: Travel by train from Tripoli or Benghazi to the Libyan-Egyptian border. From the border, you will need to arrange for onward travel into Egypt, typically by bus or taxi.

Libya to Egypt Border: You will cross into Egypt through the Sallum border post.

Onward Travel: From Sallum, you can take a bus or taxi to Alexandria or Cairo, where you can access Egypt's domestic rail network.

3. From Israel

Connection: There is no direct train service between Israel and Egypt.

Alternative: You can travel by train from major Israeli cities like Tel Aviv or Haifa to the border town of Eilat. From Eilat, you can cross into Egypt through the Taba border post and continue by bus or taxi to Cairo or other destinations.

Israeli Cities to Eilat: Trains from Tel Aviv or Haifa to Eilat involve a combination of train and bus services.

Taba Border: Crossing the border into Egypt usually involves a bus or taxi ride to nearby towns.

4. From Jordan

Connection: There are no direct trains from Jordan to Egypt.

Alternative: Travel from Amman, Jordan, to the Aqaba port by bus or taxi. From Aqaba, you can take a ferry to Nuweiba, Egypt, and then travel by bus or train to other parts of Egypt.

Amman to Aqaba: Buses or taxis are available for this journey.

Ferry: The ferry from Aqaba to Nuweiba typically operates several times a week.

5. From Saudi Arabia

Connection: There is no direct train service from Saudi Arabia to Egypt.

Alternative: You would typically need to travel by air or consider a combination of train and ferry

The Ultimate Egypt Travel Guide 2025 Edition

services. One possible route is traveling by train to Jordan and then following the Jordan-Aqaba to Nuweiba route mentioned above.

Additional Considerations

Visa Requirements: Ensure you have the appropriate visa for Egypt before arriving at the border.

Travel Time: Train journeys and border crossings can be lengthy and require careful planning.

Reservations and Tickets: For train services within neighboring countries, make reservations in advance where possible, and confirm schedules, as services and timings may vary.

Local Transportation: Upon reaching Egyptian border towns or cities, be prepared to use local transportation to continue your journey into Egypt.

While direct train travel to Egypt is limited, using a combination of trains, ferries, and buses can provide an adventurous and scenic way to enter the country from neighboring regions.

Road Travel and Border Crossings

Traveling by road in Egypt and crossing borders can offer unique experiences, but it's important to be well-prepared. Here's what you need to know:

Road Travel Within Egypt

Road Conditions: Major highways and roads in Egypt are generally in good condition, especially around cities like Cairo, Alexandria, Luxor, and Hurghada. However, rural and desert roads may vary in quality. Be cautious of traffic and driving norms, as driving styles can be aggressive and traffic congestion is common in urban areas.

Rental Cars:

Availability: Rental services are widely available in major cities and airports.

Requirements: You'll need a valid international driving permit (IDP) along with your national driver's license. Traffic rules must be followed, and driving insurance is essential.

Local Driving: Traffic in cities can be chaotic, and road signs may not always be clear. Consider hiring a local driver if you're unfamiliar with Egyptian driving conditions.

Taxis and Ride-Sharing:

Taxis: Readily available in cities. It's advisable to agree on a fare before starting your journey or use a metered taxi.

Ride-Sharing Apps: Apps like Uber and Careem operate in major cities and can offer a more predictable fare and comfortable experience compared to traditional taxis.

Intercity Travel:

Buses: Several companies operate long-distance buses between major cities and tourist destinations. Options range from basic to luxury services.

Private Transfers: For more comfort and flexibility, consider booking a private transfer or tour operator service for intercity travel.

Border Crossings

If you plan to travel to or from Egypt by land, here's what you should know:

To/from Neighboring Countries:

Jordan: The main crossing point is at the Aqaba-Taba border. A ferry service operates between Nuweiba (Egypt) and Aqaba (Jordan). Ensure you have a visa for Jordan before crossing.

Israel: The main border crossing is at the Taba border. Travelers typically require a visa for Israel. Be prepared for security checks and visa requirements.

Libya: The border crossings between Egypt and

Libya are generally less frequented. Check current security and visa requirements, as they can vary.

Sudan: There are border crossings near Aswan, such as at Qustul. Verify visa requirements and travel advisories before crossing.

Visa Requirements:

Ensure you have the necessary visas for entry into neighboring countries before attempting to cross. Some crossings may require visas obtained in advance, while others might allow visa-on-arrival.

Travel Permits:

For traveling to remote or restricted areas within Egypt, such as the Sinai Peninsula, you might need special permits. These can be arranged through local authorities or tour operators.

Vehicle Documentation:

If you're driving your own vehicle or a rental car across borders, ensure you have the proper documentation, including vehicle registration, insurance, and any required permits.

Security and Safety:

Always check current travel advisories and safety information for border regions. Some areas may have heightened security concerns or travel restrictions.

General Tips for Road Travel and Border Crossings

Carry Copies: Keep photocopies of your passport, visa, and other important documents separate from the originals.

Travel Insurance: Ensure your insurance covers road travel and border crossings.

Local Currency: Carry some local currency for expenses at border crossings or in areas with limited banking facilities.

Road Safety: Follow local traffic laws, be cautious of road conditions, and always drive defensively.

Ferry and Boat Travel

Egypt's extensive coastline and its major rivers provide numerous opportunities for ferry and boat travel. Here's a guide to help you navigate these options:

1. Nile River Cruises

Overview: The Nile River is a major draw for tourists, offering scenic cruises between Cairo, Luxor, and Aswan. These cruises are a fantastic way to explore ancient temples and monuments along the river.

Types of Cruises:

Luxury Cruises: High-end vessels with spacious cabins, gourmet dining, and guided tours. Examples include the Oberoi Zahra and Sanctuary Sun Boat.

Mid-Range Cruises: Comfortable boats with decent amenities, often including guided excursions. Examples include the MS Farah and MS Royal Lotus.

Budget Cruises: More basic accommodations with fewer amenities, suitable for travelers looking for a more economical option.

Duration: Cruises typically range from 3 to 7 days, with itineraries that can include stops at major sites like the Valley of the Kings, Karnak Temple, and Abu Simbel.

Booking: It's advisable to book in advance, especially during peak tourist seasons. Tours can be arranged through travel agencies or directly with cruise operators.

2. Red Sea Ferries

Overview: Ferries operate across the Red Sea, connecting Egypt with destinations in Saudi Arabia and Jordan.

Major Routes:

The Ultimate Egypt Travel Guide 2025 Edition

Nuweiba to Aqaba: This route connects the Sinai Peninsula with Jordan. Ferries are available several times a week, and it's advisable to book tickets in advance.

Sharm El Sheikh to Aqaba: Another popular route to Jordan, with frequent services that cater to tourists.

Booking: Tickets can be purchased at the port, through travel agencies, or online for some routes. Check schedules and availability before traveling.

3. Lake Nasser Ferries

Overview: Lake Nasser, created by the Aswan High Dam, is a large man-made lake that offers opportunities for boat tours and cruises.

Popular Activities:

Cruises: Similar to Nile River cruises, but on Lake Nasser, offering views of temples and ruins submerged by the lake.

Private Boat Tours: For exploring specific areas of the lake or visiting archaeological sites such as Abu Simbel.

Booking: Arrange through local tour operators or at hotels in Aswan.

4. Local Ferries and Boats

Cairo:

Felucca Rides: Traditional sailboats offering a relaxing way to enjoy the Nile River. Popular for short trips and sunset cruises.

Public Ferries: Operate across the Nile, providing an affordable means of transportation between different parts of Cairo.

Alexandria:

Local Ferries: Connect various points along the coast and provide a scenic view of the Mediterranean.

Red Sea Resorts:

Boat Tours: Include snorkeling, diving, and leisure trips. Boats range from small private charters to larger group tours.

5. Practical Tips for Ferry and Boat Travel

Documentation: Ensure you have your passport and any required visas, especially for international ferry routes.

Booking: For popular routes, it's best to book in advance to secure your place, particularly during peak travel seasons.

Comfort: Bring essentials like sunscreen, a hat, and water, as conditions can be sunny and hot on the open water.

Health and Safety: Check for safety equipment on board and follow any instructions provided by the crew. If you're prone to seasickness, consider bringing medication.

Bike or Walking

Exploring Egypt by bike or on foot can offer a unique and immersive experience, allowing you to see the country's landscapes, historical sites, and local life up close. Here's a guide to help you make the most of these modes of travel:

1. Biking in Egypt

Popular Areas for Biking:

Cairo: Biking in Cairo can be challenging due to traffic congestion and road conditions. However, some areas like the Corniche along the Nile and certain parks offer safer biking paths.

Luxor: The city and its surroundings are more bike-friendly. Many tourists rent bikes to explore the West Bank's archaeological sites and the countryside.

Sharm El Sheikh: Offers bike rentals and scenic routes, including paths around the resort areas and through the desert.

Grace Bennett

Alexandria: Coastal promenades and parks provide pleasant routes for biking.

Bike Rentals:

Availability: Bike rentals are available in major tourist cities and resort areas. Look for local bike shops, hotels offering rentals, or organized bike tours.

Types: Options range from basic bicycles to mountain bikes and electric bikes.

Safety Tips:

Helmet: Always wear a helmet for safety.

Traffic Awareness: Be cautious of traffic, especially in busy urban areas. Follow local biking rules and stay alert.

Navigation: Use a map or GPS to navigate unfamiliar areas and plan routes in advance.

Organized Bike Tours:

Tours: Many cities offer guided bike tours that cover key attractions and provide local insights.

Booking: Arrange through local tour operators or travel agencies.

2. Walking in Egypt

Urban Walking:

Cairo: Walking in specific areas like Zamalek or along the Nile Corniche can be enjoyable. Be cautious of traffic and air quality, and consider walking tours for a guided experience.

Alexandria: The Corniche and historic neighborhoods offer pleasant walking routes.

Historical Sites:

Luxor and Aswan: Walking is a common way to explore the West Bank of Luxor, including the Valley of the Kings and other temples. Wear comfortable shoes and stay hydrated.

Pyramids of Giza: While the site is vast, walking around the pyramids and the Sphinx can be a rewarding experience. Camel or horse rides are also available.

Desert and Rural Walking:

Sinai Peninsula: Popular for hiking and walking in areas like the Sinai Desert and around Mount Sinai. Guided hikes are recommended for safety and navigation.

Faiyum Oasis: Offers scenic walking routes through natural landscapes and ancient sites.

Safety Tips:

Footwear: Wear comfortable, sturdy shoes suitable for various terrains.

Hydration: Carry water, especially when walking in hot or arid areas.

Sun Protection: Use sunscreen, wear a hat, and stay in shaded areas when possible.

Local Advice: Ask locals or guides for recommendations on safe walking routes and areas to avoid.

3. General Tips for Both Biking and Walking

Weather: Check the weather forecast and plan your activities accordingly. Avoid walking or biking during the hottest parts of the day, particularly in summer.

Health: Consider any health conditions that might affect your ability to walk or bike long distances, and prepare accordingly.

Local Customs: Respect local customs and dress codes, especially when visiting religious sites. Modest clothing is often required.

Navigation: Use reliable maps or GPS apps to navigate unfamiliar areas. Some regions may have limited signage.

Chapter 3: Getting Around Egypt

Public Transportation

Public transportation in Egypt offers an extensive network that connects major cities, tourist destinations, and rural areas. The system includes buses, metros, and trains, providing a range of options for getting around, each with its unique advantages and challenges. Understanding how to utilize these services can greatly enhance your travel experience, especially when exploring Egypt's rich history and vibrant culture.

Routes and Schedules

Egypt's public transportation routes cover extensive areas, making it relatively easy to travel between cities and key destinations.

Cairo Metro: The Cairo Metro is a fast and efficient way to navigate the city. It operates on several lines, connecting neighborhoods with major landmarks such as Tahrir Square, the Cairo Museum, and Giza. The metro runs from early morning until late at night, with frequent service during peak hours.

Buses: Buses operate throughout major cities and intercity routes. In Cairo, buses serve extensive routes, including both local and express services. Alexandria, Luxor, and other cities have their own bus systems. Long-distance buses connect cities like Cairo, Luxor, and Aswan. Companies such as GoBus and SuperJet offer services with various comfort levels.

Trains: Egypt's railway network is well-established, with trains running between Cairo and other major cities, including Alexandria, Luxor, and Aswan. The network includes both express trains and slower regional services. The trains are generally reliable but can be crowded, especially during peak travel times.

Ferries: In cities with significant water bodies, such as Cairo and Alexandria, ferries operate across the Nile and the Mediterranean Sea, offering scenic and practical travel options.

Limitations

While public transportation in Egypt is widespread, there are some limitations to be aware of:

Inconsistent Service: Bus and train schedules can be inconsistent, with delays not uncommon. For example, long-distance buses may not always adhere strictly to their schedules, and train services might experience delays due to various factors.

Crowding: During peak hours, particularly in Cairo, public transportation can be very crowded. The metro and buses may be packed, making travel uncomfortable, especially for tourists unfamiliar with local practices.

Language Barriers: English is not always widely spoken by public transportation staff. This can make navigating schedules and purchasing tickets challenging for non-Arabic speakers.

Limited Coverage: While major cities are well-served, some remote areas and tourist sites may not be easily accessible via public transportation. For instance, certain archaeological sites or desert areas might require additional travel arrangements.

Fares and Passes

Fares for public transportation in Egypt are relatively affordable, but the system's complexity can sometimes be a challenge:

Metro Fares: Cairo Metro fares are inexpensive, with a flat fee covering any distance on the network. Tickets can be purchased at stations or via rechargeable cards.

Bus Fares: Local bus fares are low, often costing less than a dollar. For long-distance buses, prices vary based on distance and service level. Tickets can be purchased at bus stations or online for some services.

Train Fares: Train fares are tiered based on class and distance. Local trains are cheaper, while express and sleeping trains are more expensive. Tickets should be purchased in advance, especially for popular routes.

Ferry Fares: Ferry fares are generally affordable, with prices varying based on the route and type of service. Tickets can be bought at the port or on board.

Pros

Public transportation in Egypt offers several advantages for tourists:

Cost-Effective: Public transportation is generally inexpensive compared to taxis or private hires, making it a budget-friendly option for exploring the country.

Extensive Network: The transportation network covers a wide range of areas, making it possible to reach many major attractions and cities without the need for private transport.

Cultural Experience: Using public transportation provides an opportunity to interact with locals and experience everyday life in Egypt, offering a more immersive travel experience.

Environmental Impact: Public transportation is more environmentally friendly compared to private car travel, reducing your carbon footprint while traveling.

Cons

Despite its benefits, there are some drawbacks to using public transportation in Egypt:

Comfort and Cleanliness: Public transportation, especially buses and trains, can be less comfortable and clean compared to private options. The facilities might not always meet Western standards.

Language and Navigation Challenges: Navigating the system can be difficult if you don't speak Arabic or if you're unfamiliar with local routes and schedules. This can lead to confusion and potential inconvenience.

Safety Concerns: While generally safe, crowded public transport can present pickpocket risks. It's important to remain vigilant and keep personal belongings secure.

Renting a Car

Renting a car in Egypt can be a convenient and flexible way to explore the country, especially if you plan to visit multiple destinations or venture off the beaten path. Here's a comprehensive guide to help you understand the benefits, options, and considerations for renting a car in Egypt.

Why Rent a Car?

Renting a car in Egypt provides several advantages:

Flexibility and Independence: A rental car allows you to create your own itinerary and travel at your own pace. This is particularly useful for exploring remote areas or sites not easily accessible by public transportation.

Convenience: Having a car gives you the freedom to visit less accessible attractions, such as desert oases or archaeological sites in remote locations. It can also be more convenient for managing your schedule and making spontaneous detours.

Comfort: Renting a car provides a private and comfortable space, especially for longer journeys. You can avoid the crowded and sometimes less comfortable conditions of public transportation.

Extended Reach: If you're planning to visit multiple cities or regions, renting a car can make it easier to travel between them without relying on bus or train schedules.

Rental Agencies

Several international and local car rental agencies operate in Egypt, providing a range of options for tourists:

International Agencies: Major global rental companies such as Hertz, Avis, Budget, and Europcar have offices in major cities and airports, offering a consistent level of service and a broad range of vehicles.

Local Agencies: Local rental agencies, such as Sixt Egypt and Cairo Rent A Car, can offer competitive rates and more personalized service. These agencies may also provide additional options and flexibility.

Booking: It's advisable to book your rental car in advance, especially during peak travel seasons. Reservations can be made online through the rental agency's website or through travel booking platforms.

Types of Vehicles

Rental agencies in Egypt offer a variety of vehicle types to suit different needs:

Economy Cars: Compact and fuel-efficient, these are ideal for city driving and short trips. They are usually the most affordable option.

SUVs and 4x4s: Suitable for more rugged terrain, including desert areas and off-road excursions. These vehicles offer greater comfort and capability for longer journeys and uneven roads.

Luxury Cars: For those seeking a more comfortable and stylish option, luxury cars provide a premium experience. These are often more expensive but offer higher comfort and amenities.

Minivans: Ideal for larger groups or families, minivans offer more space and comfort for extended trips.

Driving Tips

Driving in Egypt can be quite different from other countries, so here are some essential tips to ensure a safe and enjoyable experience:

Driving License: Ensure you have a valid international driving permit (IDP) in addition to your national driver's license. The IDP is recognized by Egyptian authorities and is often required for renting a car.

Traffic Conditions: Traffic in Egyptian cities can be chaotic, with aggressive driving styles and frequent congestion. Be prepared for unpredictable driving behavior and exercise caution.

Road Rules: Familiarize yourself with local traffic laws and regulations. While many rules are similar to international standards, there may be specific local practices to be aware of.

Navigation: Use a reliable GPS or mapping app to navigate, as road signs may not always be in English. Some areas may have limited signage, so having a good navigation system is crucial.

Safety: Keep your vehicle locked and valuables out of sight. Be cautious in crowded areas and secure your belongings to avoid theft.

Fuel: Fuel stations are widely available in cities and along major routes, but they may be less frequent in remote areas. Ensure you have enough fuel, especially if traveling to less populated regions.

Road Conditions: Be aware that road conditions can vary. While major highways are generally in good condition, rural and desert roads may be less well-maintained. Drive cautiously and be prepared for rough patches.

Parking: Parking in urban areas can be challenging. Look for designated parking areas and be aware of any local parking regulations to avoid fines or towing.

The Ultimate Egypt Travel Guide 2025 Edition

Taxis and Ride-Sharing

Taxis and ride-sharing services are popular and convenient ways to get around Egypt, especially in bustling cities like Cairo and Alexandria. Here's a detailed guide to help you navigate these options effectively:

Availability

Taxis: Taxis are widely available in major cities and tourist areas. You can hail a taxi on the street, find them at designated taxi stands, or book one through hotel concierge services. Taxis are also available at airports and train stations.

Ride-Sharing: Ride-sharing services such as Uber and Careem operate in several major cities, including Cairo, Alexandria, and Sharm El Sheikh. These services offer a convenient alternative to traditional taxis and are increasingly popular among both locals and tourists.

Cost

Taxis:

Metered Taxis: Taxis in Egypt often use meters, but it's a good practice to confirm this before starting your trip. Fares are relatively low compared to Western standards but can vary depending on the city and distance traveled. Prices can be higher during peak hours or if traveling long distances.

Negotiated Fares: In some cases, especially with non-metered taxis, you may need to negotiate the fare before starting the journey. It's advisable to agree on the fare upfront to avoid misunderstandings.

Ride-Sharing:

Fare Structure: Ride-sharing apps use a dynamic pricing model, which means fares can fluctuate based on demand, distance, and time of day. Prices are typically shown in the app before you confirm your ride.

Cost Comparison: Ride-sharing services are often more transparent and can be more cost-effective than traditional taxis, especially for longer trips or during peak hours.

When to Use

Taxis:

Short Trips: Ideal for short trips within cities or when public transportation is inconvenient.

Immediate Needs: Useful if you need immediate transportation and ride-sharing services are unavailable or experiencing high demand.

Limited Coverage: In areas where ride-sharing services might not be available or are less reliable.

Ride-Sharing:

Convenience: Offers door-to-door service and can be more reliable for planning routes and avoiding traffic.

Cost Transparency: Provides a clear fare estimate before you confirm the ride, making it easier to manage your budget.

Safety: Often includes features like driver ratings and in-app tracking, which can enhance safety.

Services Available

Taxis:

Standard Taxis: Basic vehicles that can vary in condition. Some may be older or less well-maintained.

Luxury Taxis: Higher-end options are available in major cities, providing a more comfortable experience.

Ride-Sharing:

Standard Rides: Basic service level with economy cars.

Premium Rides: Higher-end vehicles with additional comfort features.

Carpooling: Options for shared rides with other passengers, which can be more economical.

How to Use

Taxis:

Hailing a Taxi: Stand in a visible location on the street, and signal to approaching taxis. Check if the taxi is using a meter or negotiate the fare before getting in.

Booking by Phone: Some taxi companies offer phone booking services. You can call and request a taxi to your location.

Hotel and Airport Taxi Stands: Taxis are readily available at major hotels and airports. Hotel staff can assist with booking a taxi.

Ride-Sharing:

Download the App: Install Uber, Careem, or other ride-sharing apps on your smartphone. Sign up and enter your payment details.

Requesting a Ride: Open the app, enter your destination, and choose the type of ride you want. The app will match you with a nearby driver.

Payment: Payment is processed through the app, eliminating the need for cash. You'll receive a receipt via email or in the app.

Cost and Availability

Taxis: Costs are generally low, but they can vary based on distance, time of day, and whether the taxi is metered or negotiated. Availability is high in urban areas, but less so in rural or remote locations.

Ride-Sharing: Costs are competitive and transparent, with fares shown in the app before you book. Availability is high in major cities but may be limited in smaller towns or less frequented areas.

Biking

Bicycles are increasingly popular in Egypt, especially in urban areas and tourist destinations. The country's varied terrain—from busy city streets to serene desert paths—offers different biking experiences. While biking infrastructure is not as developed as in some other countries, many cities and tourist spots are becoming more bike-friendly, and bike rentals are available in key locations.

Why Bike?

Health and Fitness: Biking is a great way to stay active and healthy while traveling. It offers cardiovascular exercise and helps you maintain your fitness routine.

Eco-Friendly: Cycling is an environmentally friendly mode of transport, reducing your carbon footprint and contributing to a more sustainable travel experience.

Cost-Effective: Renting a bike is generally cheaper than using taxis or ride-sharing services for short distances. It can also be more economical than public transportation for certain trips.

Exploration: Biking allows you to explore at your own pace, discover hidden gems, and access areas that might be difficult to reach by car or public transport.

Local Interaction: Cycling through local neighborhoods and rural areas provides an opportunity to interact with residents and experience everyday life in Egypt more intimately.

Popular Routes

Cairo:

Nile Corniche: The riverbanks of the Nile offer a scenic route for cycling, with views of the river and Cairo's skyline. Parks and promenades along the Corniche are popular spots for biking.

Zamalek: This upscale district has quieter streets

and is more bike-friendly, making it ideal for leisurely rides.

Alexandria:

Corniche: The coastal Corniche in Alexandria offers a pleasant route with views of the Mediterranean Sea. It's a popular area for both locals and tourists to cycle along.

Luxor:

West Bank: The West Bank of Luxor is well-suited for biking, with many tourists using bicycles to visit the Valley of the Kings, Hatshepsut Temple, and other nearby sites. The relatively flat terrain makes for a comfortable ride.

Sharm El Sheikh:

Desert and Coastal Paths: The area around Sharm El Sheikh offers routes through the desert and along the coast, providing stunning views and a chance to explore less trafficked areas.

Faiyum Oasis:

Nature Trails: Known for its natural beauty, Faiyum offers scenic bike routes through the oasis and around Lake Qarun, ideal for nature enthusiasts.

Safety Considerations

Traffic Conditions:

Urban Areas: Traffic in cities like Cairo can be chaotic. Be prepared for aggressive driving and maintain high alertness. It's advisable to stick to designated bike paths or quieter streets whenever possible.

Rural Areas: Roads in rural areas may be less congested but can vary in quality. Watch out for uneven surfaces and occasional livestock or pedestrians.

Helmets: Always wear a helmet for safety. While helmets are not always provided by rental services, bringing your own or purchasing one locally is strongly recommended.

Visibility: Wear bright or reflective clothing to increase visibility, especially if you're biking in the early morning or late evening. Equip your bike with lights and reflectors to ensure you're seen by other road users.

Local Laws: Familiarize yourself with local biking regulations and road rules. In some areas, biking might not be permitted on certain roads, or there might be specific rules to follow.

Bike Condition: Ensure that the bike you rent is in good working condition. Check the brakes, tires, and gears before setting out. If you're renting from a local shop, inspect the bike thoroughly and report any issues before leaving.

Navigation: Use a map or GPS to navigate, as road signage might not always be in English. Plan your route in advance and be aware of your surroundings to avoid getting lost.

Hydration and Sun Protection: Carry water with you, especially on hot days. Use sunscreen and wear a hat or sunglasses to protect yourself from the sun.

Walking and Hiking

Walking and hiking in Egypt provide unique opportunities to explore the country's diverse landscapes, rich history, and vibrant culture. Whether you're interested in city walks, desert treks, or historical explorations, Egypt offers a range of experiences for outdoor enthusiasts. Here's a guide to help you make the most of walking and hiking during your visit.

Where to Walk

Cairo:

Nile Corniche: A pleasant place for a walk, offering views of the Nile River and Cairo's skyline. The Corniche is lined with cafes and parks, making it a popular spot for both locals and tourists.

Zamalek: This upscale district features leafy streets

and quiet areas ideal for a leisurely stroll. It's also home to several parks and cultural institutions.

Alexandria:

Corniche: The waterfront promenade offers beautiful views of the Mediterranean Sea and is a popular place for walking. It's a great spot to enjoy the sea breeze and explore the city's coastal charm.

Montazah Palace Gardens: A vast park with beautiful gardens and historic architecture, providing a peaceful setting for walking.

Luxor:

East Bank: Walk through the vibrant streets of Luxor, visiting markets and local attractions. The area around Karnak Temple and Luxor Temple is particularly interesting.

West Bank: Explore the quieter streets and rural areas of the West Bank, where you can visit ancient sites and enjoy a more tranquil environment.

Sharm El Sheikh:

Naama Bay: A bustling area with pedestrian-friendly streets, shops, and restaurants. It's a great place for a stroll in the evening.

Ras Mohammed National Park: For more adventurous walks, the park offers trails with stunning views of desert landscapes and coastal areas.

Desert Regions:

Siwa Oasis: Known for its stunning landscapes and unique salt lakes, Siwa offers various walking opportunities through the desert and oasis areas.

White Desert: Famous for its striking white rock formations, this area offers exceptional walking and hiking experiences.

What to See

Historical Sites: Many of Egypt's historical treasures are accessible by walking. Explore the temples of Luxor, the pyramids of Giza, and the ancient ruins of Alexandria on foot to fully appreciate their grandeur.

Natural Landscapes: Egypt's diverse landscapes include deserts, oases, and coastal areas. Enjoy the contrasting environments, from the lush greenery of oases to the stark beauty of the desert.

Local Life: Walking through local neighborhoods and markets provides insight into everyday life in Egypt. You'll encounter traditional crafts, local cuisine, and vibrant street scenes.

Cultural Attractions: Visit cultural landmarks such as museums, art galleries, and historic buildings. Walking around these sites allows for a deeper engagement with Egypt's rich heritage.

Best Trails

Mount Sinai: A popular hiking destination, known for its biblical significance and stunning sunrise views. The trail to the summit is challenging but rewarding, with spectacular vistas of the surrounding desert.

Valley of the Kings: While not a traditional hiking trail, walking through the Valley of the Kings and nearby tombs provides an incredible historical experience. Guided tours can enhance your visit.

Wadi Degla Protectorate: Located near Cairo, this nature reserve offers trails through rugged desert terrain, with opportunities to observe local flora and fauna.

Faiyum Oasis: Trails around Lake Qarun and the surrounding areas offer scenic walks through natural landscapes and ancient sites. The area is known for its birdwatching opportunities and picturesque views.

Ras Mohammed National Park: Offers several trails through desert and coastal landscapes, with opportunities to see diverse wildlife and marine life.

Safety Tips

Weather Awareness: Egypt's climate can be extremely hot, especially in the desert. Plan your walks and hikes for early morning or late afternoon to avoid the peak heat. Dress in light, breathable clothing and stay hydrated.

Footwear: Wear comfortable and sturdy walking shoes, especially for hiking. The terrain can vary from city pavements to rocky trails.

Sun Protection: Use sunscreen, wear a hat, and sunglasses to protect yourself from the sun. Carry water and take breaks in shaded areas to avoid dehydration and heat exhaustion.

Navigation: Ensure you have a reliable map or GPS for hiking trails. Some areas, especially in deserts, may lack clear signage. Inform someone of your plans and estimated return time if hiking in remote areas.

Wildlife: Be aware of local wildlife and avoid disturbing animals. In desert areas, watch out for snakes and other potential hazards.

Local Advice: Seek local advice on trail conditions, safety, and any potential risks. Tour guides or local experts can provide valuable insights and enhance your hiking experience.

Travel Passes & Cards

Travel passes and cards are designed to simplify your travel experience, offering a range of benefits including cost savings, convenience, and flexibility. They are particularly useful in major cities like Cairo and Alexandria, where navigating public transportation and accessing tourist sites can be challenging.

Public Transportation Passes

Cairo Metro Card:

Description: The Cairo Metro Card provides access to the city's metro system. It's a rechargeable card that can be topped up with various amounts.

Benefits: Offers a convenient way to pay for metro rides without needing cash. The card is used at entry and exit points in the metro stations.

Purchase: Available at metro stations. You can load credit onto the card at any station.

Bus Passes:

Description: While not as common, some bus services in Cairo and Alexandria offer passes for unlimited travel within specific periods (e.g., daily, weekly).

Benefits: Provides unlimited travel on the specified bus routes, which can be cost-effective for frequent travelers.

Purchase: Available at major bus stations and sometimes through local travel agencies.

Tourist Passes

Egyptian Museum Pass:

Description: This pass provides access to the Egyptian Museum in Cairo and may include entry to additional museums or archaeological sites.

Benefits: Offers savings on admission fees for multiple visits or combined sites.

Purchase: Available at the museum entrance or through authorized ticket vendors.

Luxor and Aswan Pass:

Description: This pass grants access to a range of historical sites in Luxor and Aswan, including temples, tombs, and museums.

Benefits: Provides discounted entry to multiple sites, making it a cost-effective option for exploring the area.

Purchase: Available at major ticket offices in Luxor and Aswan.

Sharm El Sheikh Pass:

Description: Offers access to various attractions in Sharm El Sheikh, including natural reserves and water parks.

Benefits: Can include discounted rates for multiple attractions, providing value for visitors planning to explore several sites.

Purchase: Available at tourist information centers and some hotels.

How to Use

Purchase: Most passes and cards can be purchased at designated sales points, including transportation hubs, tourist information centers, and online through official websites.

Activation: Some passes, like metro cards, require activation and initial loading of credit. Tourist passes may need to be validated at specific locations.

Usage: Simply present your card or pass at the entry points of transportation systems or attractions. For passes covering multiple attractions, be sure to check the included sites and any conditions or limitations.

Benefits

Cost Savings: Travel passes often provide significant savings compared to buying individual tickets for each journey or attraction.

Convenience: Passes and cards simplify the payment process, reducing the need to carry cash and making it easier to access various services and attractions.

Flexibility: With a travel pass or card, you can travel and explore at your own pace, with the freedom to hop on and off public transport or visit multiple attractions without additional purchases.

Considerations

Validity and Coverage: Ensure you understand the validity period and coverage of the pass or card. Some passes may be valid for specific periods or only cover certain routes or attractions.

Lost or Stolen Cards: Report lost or stolen travel cards to the issuing authority immediately. Replacement policies may vary, and it's important to protect your cards from unauthorized use.

Local Regulations: Familiarize yourself with any local regulations or restrictions associated with the use of passes and cards. Some passes may have specific usage rules or limitations.

Chapter 4: Practical Information

Language and Communication

Effective communication is key to a smooth and enjoyable travel experience in Egypt. Understanding the local language and communication practices will help you navigate daily interactions, ask for directions, and immerse yourself in Egyptian culture. Here's a detailed guide to language and communication in Egypt:

Language Overview

Official Language: The official language of Egypt is Arabic. Egyptian Arabic is the most widely spoken dialect, and while it has some unique features, it is generally understood across the Arab world.

English: English is commonly spoken in tourist areas, major cities, and among younger generations. It is often used in hotels, restaurants, and at popular tourist attractions. However, in more rural areas or local neighborhoods, English proficiency may be limited.

French and German: In some tourist spots and hotels, you may encounter French and German speakers, particularly in areas frequented by European tourists.

Basic Arabic Phrases

Greetings and Polite Expressions:

Hello: "Marhaban" (مرحبا) or "As-salamu alaykum" (عليكم السلام) – Peace be upon you.

Goodbye: "Ma'a as-salama" (مع السلامة) – Go with peace.

Please: "Min fadlik" (من فضلك) – Used when asking for something politely.

Thank you: "Shukran" (شكرا) – Thank you.

Yes: "Na'am" (نعم)

No: "La" (لا)

Basic Questions:

How much does this cost?: "Kam thaman hadha?" (كم ثمن هذا؟)

Where is the bathroom?: "Ayna al-hammam?" (أين الحمام؟)

Do you speak English?: "Hal tatakallam English?" (هل تتكلم إنجليزي؟)

Can you help me?: "Hal mumkin musa'adati?" (هل ممكن مساعدتي؟)

Communication Tips

Use Simple Language: If you don't speak Arabic fluently, use simple English and speak slowly. Many locals who understand some English will appreciate clear and straightforward communication.

Body Language: Non-verbal communication is essential. Gestures, facial expressions, and body language can help convey your message when words fail. However, be mindful of cultural norms and avoid gestures that might be considered rude.

Translation Apps: Smartphone apps like Google Translate can be very helpful. They can translate text and spoken words, and some apps even allow for offline use. Having a translation app on hand can be a valuable tool for overcoming language barriers.

Learn Key Phrases: Learning a few basic Arabic phrases can go a long way in showing respect and willingness to engage with the local culture. It's often appreciated by locals and can make your interactions more pleasant.

Local Etiquette: Understanding and respecting local customs and etiquette can enhance communication. For example, addressing people formally and with respect is important in Egyptian culture.

Local Communication Practices

Direct Communication: Egyptians generally appreciate direct communication, but it should be polite and respectful. Be clear about your needs and avoid ambiguous language.

Gestures and Expressions: Egyptians use a variety of hand gestures and facial expressions in communication. While many are universal, some may have specific cultural meanings. Observing local practices can help you understand these non-verbal cues.

Formal Address: Using titles and formal address is important, especially in professional or formal settings. Addressing people with titles such as "Mr." or "Ms." followed by their last name is a sign of respect.

Negotiation: In markets and shops, bargaining is common and expected. Approach negotiations with a friendly attitude and be prepared for a bit of back-and-forth. It's part of the shopping experience in Egypt.

Cultural Sensitivity

Respecting Differences: Egypt is a diverse country with a rich cultural heritage. Being sensitive to cultural and religious differences, and showing respect for local traditions, will enhance your interactions and help you build positive relationships.

Social Norms: Understand and follow local social norms, such as dress codes and behavior in religious sites. Being aware of these norms can prevent misunderstandings and ensure that your behavior is appropriate.

Currency and Payments

Understanding the currency and payment methods in Egypt is crucial for managing your budget and ensuring a smooth travel experience. Here's a comprehensive guide to help you navigate currency exchange, payment options, and financial considerations during your trip.

Currency

Official Currency: The official currency of Egypt is the Egyptian Pound (EGP), often symbolized as "£" or "E£". It is subdivided into 100 piastres.

Banknotes and Coins:

Banknotes: Common denominations include 1, 5, 10, 20, 50, 100, and 200 pounds. Banknotes are typically used for most transactions.

Coins: Less commonly used, but available in denominations of 1, 5, 10, 25, and 50 piastres, as well as 1 pound coins.

Currency Exchange

Exchange Rates: Currency exchange rates can fluctuate, so it's a good idea to check the current rate before exchanging money. Rates are available online or through financial news sources.

Where to Exchange:

Banks: Banks offer reliable exchange services. They are widely available in cities and towns, and offer competitive rates.

Currency Exchange Offices: Located in major tourist areas, airports, and shopping centers. They often have more flexible hours than banks.

Hotels: Many hotels offer currency exchange services, but rates might be less favorable than those at banks or exchange offices.

ATMs: ATMs are widely available in cities and major towns. Most ATMs accept international credit and debit cards. Be aware of transaction fees that your bank might charge for international withdrawals.

Credit and Debit Cards

Acceptance: Major credit and debit cards (such as Visa, MasterCard, and American Express) are widely accepted in hotels, restaurants, and larger shops. However, smaller businesses, local markets, and rural areas might not accept cards.

Notification: Inform your bank of your travel plans to avoid any issues with card usage due to fraud prevention measures.

Fees: Be aware of foreign transaction fees that your bank may charge. Some ATMs and merchants may also charge fees for card transactions.

Mobile Payments and Digital Wallets

Mobile Payment Services: Mobile payment systems like Apple Pay, Google Wallet, and Samsung Pay are gaining popularity in urban areas. However, they are not universally accepted, so it's wise to carry cash or cards as a backup.

Local Apps: In some cities, local digital payment apps and services are available. These might be useful for certain transactions, especially in urban and tourist areas.

Budgeting and Costs

Daily Expenses: Costs in Egypt can vary widely depending on the type of accommodation, dining choices, and activities. Budget travelers can manage with a modest amount of money, while luxury travelers will find higher costs in premium establishments.

Tipping: Tipping is customary in Egypt. In restaurants, a 10-15% tip is typical if service is not included. In taxis and other services, rounding up the fare or giving small amounts as tips is appreciated.

Safety and Security

Cash Security: Carry only the cash you need for daily expenses and use a money belt or secure pocket for safety. Avoid displaying large amounts of cash.

Banking Hours: Banks are generally open from Sunday to Thursday, with hours typically from 8:30 AM to 3:00 PM. Some banks may have extended hours in tourist areas.

Currency Exchange Scams: Be cautious of unofficial exchange services or individuals offering to exchange currency at unusually favorable rates. Stick to reputable banks or licensed exchange offices.

Time Zone and Business Hours

Understanding Egypt's time zone and business hours can help you plan your activities and manage your schedule effectively during your visit. Here's a detailed guide to help you navigate time and business practices in Egypt:

Time Zone

Standard Time: Egypt operates on Eastern European Time (EET), which is UTC+2 hours. This means that Egypt is 2 hours ahead of Coordinated Universal Time (UTC).

Daylight Saving Time: Egypt no longer observes daylight saving time. The country remains on UTC+2 year-round, so you won't need to adjust your clocks seasonally.

Business Hours

Government Offices:

Hours: Typically open from 8:00 AM to 3:00 PM, Sunday to Thursday. Government offices are generally closed on Fridays and Saturdays, which are the weekend days in Egypt.

Banks:

Hours: Most banks are open from 8:30 AM to 3:00 PM, Sunday to Thursday. Some banks, particularly in tourist areas, may have extended hours, including Saturday mornings.

Shops and Retail Stores:

Hours: Most shops open around 10:00 AM and close by 10:00 PM. Some smaller shops or those in local markets may have varying hours and could open earlier or close later. Retail stores generally operate from Sunday to Saturday, with a break on Friday afternoons.

Restaurants and Cafés:

Hours: Many restaurants and cafés open around 8:00 AM and close late into the evening, often around 11:00 PM or midnight. In tourist areas, some establishments may stay open 24 hours or have extended hours.

Tourist Attractions:

Hours: Major tourist sites such as museums, historical landmarks, and archaeological sites usually open from 9:00 AM to 5:00 PM. Hours can vary depending on the site and time of year. Some attractions might have extended hours or special evening openings.

Markets and Souks:

Hours: Traditional markets and souks (such as those in Cairo and Alexandria) typically operate from around 9:00 AM to 7:00 PM, with some stalls staying open later into the evening. Market hours can vary widely, so it's a good idea to check locally for specific opening times.

Weekend and Public Holidays

Weekend: The weekend in Egypt is Friday and Saturday. Friday is considered a holy day for Muslims, and many businesses may open later or close earlier on this day.

Public Holidays: Egypt observes several public holidays throughout the year, including:

Revolution Day (January 25)

Sinai Liberation Day (April 25)

Labor Day (May 1)

Eid al-Fitr: Marks the end of Ramadan, with dates varying each year based on the Islamic lunar calendar.

Eid al-Adha: An important Islamic holiday, with dates also varying each year.

Moulid El Nabi (Prophet Muhammad's Birthday): Date varies based on the Islamic calendar.

During public holidays, many businesses and government offices may be closed or operate with reduced hours. Tourist attractions might be busier than usual, especially around major Islamic holidays.

Local Customs and Etiquette

Understanding and respecting local customs and etiquette in Egypt will enhance your travel experience, help you navigate social interactions smoothly, and demonstrate your respect for Egyptian culture. Here's a comprehensive guide to local customs and etiquette in Egypt:

Greetings and Formalities

Greetings: Egyptians commonly greet each other with a handshake. Men typically shake hands with other men, while women may shake hands with men if initiated by the man. In more conservative settings, especially in rural areas, a nod or verbal greeting might be preferred by women.

Formal Address: Use polite forms of address, such as "Mr." or "Ms." followed by the person's last name. Titles and formal address show respect and are appreciated in both professional and casual settings.

Respect for Elders: Show particular respect to older individuals by using formal titles and addressing them with deference. This is an important aspect of Egyptian social etiquette.

Dress Code

Modesty: Dressing modestly is important, especially when visiting religious sites or more conservative areas. For women, this means covering shoulders and knees, and avoiding revealing or tight clothing. Men should avoid wearing shorts in formal settings or religious sites.

Religious Sites: When visiting mosques, women should cover their hair with a scarf and wear long, loose clothing. Men should dress modestly and remove their shoes before entering the prayer areas.

Casual Wear: In urban areas and tourist spots, casual attire is acceptable, but it's still a good idea to dress conservatively. Shorts and tank tops are generally acceptable in tourist areas and beach destinations.

Dining Etiquette

Sharing Meals: Meals are often shared family-style, and it's common for people to eat from the same dishes. It's polite to use the provided utensils or bread to scoop food, especially in informal settings.

Using the Right Hand: In traditional settings, it is customary to eat with the right hand only, as the left hand is considered unclean in many cultures. When passing food or items, use your right hand.

Tipping: Tipping (baksheesh) is customary in restaurants, cafes, and for services like taxis and porters. A tip of 10-15% is generally appreciated, although some places may include service charges in the bill.

Public Behavior

Respect and Decorum: Public displays of affection, such as hugging or kissing, are generally frowned upon, particularly in more conservative areas. It's best to keep interactions respectful and reserved.

Photography: Always ask for permission before photographing people, especially in rural or conservative areas. Some sites may have restrictions on photography, so look for signs or ask locals if in doubt.

Avoiding Sensitive Topics: Refrain from discussing sensitive topics such as politics, religion, and personal matters with people you have just met. Focus on neutral subjects like travel, culture, and general interests.

Social Norms

Hospitality: Egyptians are known for their hospitality and friendliness. It is common for hosts to offer refreshments or tea. If offered, it's polite to accept even if you're not hungry or thirsty.

Punctuality: While punctuality is appreciated in formal settings, in more relaxed social contexts, there can be a more flexible approach to time. However, it's still courteous to be on time for appointments and meetings.

Negotiating: In markets and souks, haggling over prices is a normal part of the shopping experience. Approach negotiations with a friendly attitude and be prepared for some back-and-forth.

Religious and Cultural Sensitivity

Respect for Religion: Egypt is predominantly Muslim, and Islamic practices and holidays play a significant role in daily life. Show respect for religious practices, such as prayer times and fasting during Ramadan. Avoid eating or drinking in public during daylight hours in Ramadan, and be mindful of the fasting customs.

Ramadan: During Ramadan, many restaurants and cafes may be closed during the day, and it's important to be discreet about eating and drinking in public. After sunset, there are special meals called iftar, where people break their fast together.

Shopping and Bargaining

Bargaining: In markets, bargaining is common and expected. Start with a lower offer and negotiate in a friendly manner. Be prepared to walk away if the price does not meet your expectations, as this can sometimes lead to a better offer.

Shopping Etiquette: When shopping in local stores, it's polite to greet the shopkeeper and show interest in their products. Be patient during transactions, as service may be slower than what you're accustomed to.

Climate and Weather

Egypt's climate and weather vary significantly depending on the region and the time of year. Understanding the climate can help you plan your trip, pack appropriately, and choose the best times to visit. Here's a comprehensive guide to Egypt's climate and weather:

Overview

General Climate: Egypt predominantly has a desert climate, characterized by hot, dry summers and mild, wet winters. Coastal areas along the Mediterranean have a more temperate climate, while the interior and southern parts experience more extreme temperatures.

Regional Climate Variations

Cairo and the Nile Delta:

Summer (June to August): Hot and dry, with temperatures often exceeding 35°C (95°F). Nights can be cooler but still warm.

Winter (December to February): Mild and pleasant during the day, with temperatures ranging from 14°C to 22°C (57°F to 72°F). Nights can be cool, dropping to around 10°C (50°F).

Spring and Autumn: Generally pleasant, with temperatures ranging from 20°C to 30°C (68°F to 86°F). These are ideal times to visit.

Luxor and Aswan:

Summer: Extremely hot, with temperatures often reaching 40°C (104°F) or higher. It can be very dry and sunny.

Winter: Warm and comfortable, with temperatures ranging from 15°C to 25°C (59°F to 77°F). Evenings can be cooler, so a light jacket might be needed.

Spring and Autumn: Very pleasant, with temperatures ranging from 20°C to 30°C (68°F to 86°F). Ideal for sightseeing and outdoor activities.

Red Sea Coast (e.g., Hurghada, Sharm El Sheikh):

Summer: Hot and sunny, with temperatures ranging from 30°C to 40°C (86°F to 104°F). The coastal breeze can provide some relief.

Winter: Mild and pleasant, with temperatures ranging from 15°C to 25°C (59°F to 77°F). Nights can be cooler but still comfortable.

Spring and Autumn: Generally warm and dry, with temperatures ranging from 20°C to 30°C (68°F to 86°F). Ideal for beach activities and water sports.

Mediterranean Coast (e.g., Alexandria):

Summer: Warm and humid, with temperatures ranging from 25°C to 35°C (77°F to 95°F). Coastal breezes can provide some cooling effect.

Winter: Mild and wetter compared to other regions, with temperatures ranging from 10°C to 20°C (50°F to 68°F). Rain is more common in winter.

Spring and Autumn: Pleasant and moderate, with temperatures ranging from 15°C to 25°C (59°F to 77°F). Good times to visit for moderate weather.

Weather Patterns

Rainfall: Egypt generally experiences low annual rainfall, with most precipitation occurring in the winter months (November to March). The Mediterranean coast receives more rain compared to the interior and southern regions, while the desert areas receive very little rainfall.

Humidity: Humidity levels are typically low in desert areas, making the dry heat more bearable. Coastal areas, particularly along the Mediterranean and Red Sea, can be more humid, especially in summer.

Sandstorms: In desert and interior regions, sandstorms can occur, particularly in the spring. These storms can reduce visibility and may impact outdoor activities. Check local weather reports for any warnings if you plan to visit during the sandstorm season.

Travel Tips

Packing: Pack light, breathable clothing for summer, especially if you're visiting the southern or desert regions. In cooler months, bring layers to accommodate temperature changes between day and night. For coastal areas, include a light jacket for cooler evenings.

Sun Protection: The sun can be intense, particularly during summer. Bring sunscreen, sunglasses, and a hat to protect yourself from sunburn. Stay hydrated by drinking plenty of water.

Timing: The best times to visit Egypt for pleasant weather are during the spring (March to May) and autumn (September to November). These seasons offer moderate temperatures and are ideal for sightseeing and outdoor activities.

Weather Preparedness: Check the local weather forecast before traveling to prepare for any extreme weather conditions or sandstorms, especially if you plan to explore desert areas.

Electricity and Plug Types

When traveling to Egypt, understanding the local electricity and plug types is crucial for a smooth and hassle-free trip. Here's what you need to know:

1. Voltage and Frequency

Voltage: The standard voltage in Egypt is 220V.

Frequency: The frequency is 50Hz.

Make sure your electronic devices are compatible with this voltage and frequency. If not, you may need a voltage converter or transformer to avoid damaging your equipment.

2. Plug Types

Egypt uses the following types of plugs:

Type C: This plug has two round pins and is commonly used throughout Europe and many other countries.

Type F: Similar to Type C but with two additional grounding clips on the sides. This type is also known as the Schuko plug and is used in several European countries.

Plug Shape and Pin Configuration:

Type C: Two round pins (4.0 mm diameter) spaced 19 mm apart.

Type F: Two round pins (4.8 mm diameter) with two grounding clips on the sides.

3. Adapters and Converters

If your devices use a different plug type or voltage:

Plug Adapter: You will need a plug adapter to fit your device's plug into the Egyptian socket. Adapters do not convert voltage.

Voltage Converter: If your device is not compatible with 220V, you will need a voltage converter to safely use your electronics.

4. Where to Find Adapters

Adapters and converters can be purchased at electronics stores, airports, or online retailers before you travel. It's a good idea to get them in advance to avoid any inconvenience upon arrival.

5. Safety Tips

Check Device Compatibility: Always check the specifications of your electronic devices to ensure they can handle the local voltage.

Use Quality Adapters: Invest in a high-quality adapter or converter to avoid potential damage to your devices.

Grace Bennett

Chapter 5: Health and Safety in Egypt

Healthcare

When traveling to Egypt, understanding the healthcare system and being prepared for medical needs is crucial for a safe and enjoyable trip. Here's a comprehensive guide to help you navigate healthcare in Egypt:

Healthcare System Overview

Public Healthcare:

Egypt has a public healthcare system that provides services at various levels, from local clinics to large hospitals. These facilities are generally affordable but may vary in quality.

Private Healthcare:

Many tourists opt for private healthcare facilities due to their higher standards and shorter wait times. Private hospitals and clinics are widespread in major cities like Cairo, Alexandria, and Luxor.

Medical Services

Hospitals and Clinics:

Major Hospitals: Large cities have well-equipped hospitals, such as Cairo's Kasr El Aini Hospital and Alexandria's Alexandria University Hospital. These facilities often have English-speaking staff and offer a wide range of medical services.

Private Clinics: Private clinics are available throughout Egypt, offering specialized care in areas like dentistry, dermatology, and general medicine. These clinics are often more comfortable and efficient than public facilities.

Pharmacies:

Pharmacies are readily available and well-stocked with over-the-counter medications. In larger cities, many pharmacists speak English. However, it's advisable to carry a basic medical kit with essential medications and prescriptions, especially if you need specific treatments.

Emergency Services

Emergency Numbers:

General Emergency: 122

Ambulance Service: 123

Fire Service: 180

Police: 122

Emergency Facilities:

Major hospitals and some private clinics have emergency departments equipped to handle urgent medical situations. If you require emergency care, don't hesitate to contact local emergency services or go directly to the nearest hospital.

Vaccinations and Health Precautions

Routine Vaccinations:

Ensure you are up-to-date on routine vaccinations such as measles, mumps, rubella, and tetanus.

Recommended Vaccinations for Egypt:

Hepatitis A: Recommended due to potential food and waterborne transmission.

Hepatitis B: Consider if you might have close contact with locals or require medical treatment.

Typhoid: Recommended if you plan to visit rural areas or have concerns about food hygiene.

Rabies: Consider if you plan to interact with animals or will be in remote areas.

Health Precautions:

Water Safety: Drink bottled or boiled water to avoid waterborne illnesses. Avoid ice in drinks if you're unsure about the water source.

Food Safety: Eat at reputable restaurants and avoid street food that may not meet hygiene standards.

Insect Protection: Use insect repellent to protect against mosquito bites, which can transmit diseases like malaria and dengue.

Health Insurance and Medical Assistance

Travel Insurance:

Purchase comprehensive travel insurance that covers medical expenses, emergency evacuation, and trip cancellation. Ensure that the policy covers health issues specific to Egypt.

Medical Assistance:

Most travel insurance policies include medical assistance services, such as locating healthcare providers and arranging medical evacuations if necessary. Familiarize yourself with the emergency contacts provided by your insurance provider.

Tips for Managing Healthcare Needs

Carry Essential Documents:

Bring a copy of your medical records, prescriptions, and any important health information. Keep these in a secure location separate from your primary belongings.

Know Your Medication:

If you take prescription medications, bring enough for the duration of your trip and keep them in their original packaging. It may be helpful to have a doctor's note or prescription in case you need to explain your medication to authorities or healthcare providers.

Understand Local Practices:

Familiarize yourself with the healthcare practices and etiquette in Egypt. For example, it's customary to address healthcare professionals politely and follow any advice given for treatments.

Medical Services

When traveling to Egypt, understanding the medical services available can help you manage health-related issues efficiently. Here's an in-depth look at the medical services you might need during your visit:

Types of Medical Facilities

Hospitals:

Public Hospitals: These facilities provide a range of services from emergency care to specialized treatments. While they are generally affordable, the quality and availability of services can vary. Large public hospitals in major cities include Kasr El Aini Hospital in Cairo and Alexandria University Hospital.

Private Hospitals: Known for higher standards of care and shorter wait times, private hospitals are often preferred by tourists. They offer a variety of services, including emergency care, surgical procedures, and specialized treatments. Notable private hospitals include Cairo's Gasser El Ghandour Hospital and Luxor's Luxor International Hospital.

Clinics:

General Clinics: Available throughout Egypt, these clinics provide routine care, minor treatments, and consultations. They are often less expensive and can handle common health issues.

Specialized Clinics: Many private clinics focus on specific fields such as dermatology, dentistry, and gynecology. They are equipped with specialized staff and equipment.

Pharmacies:

Pharmacies are widely available in urban and rural areas. They stock a variety of over-the-counter medications and basic health supplies. In major cities, many pharmacists can communicate in English. For prescription medications, a local prescription or doctor's note may be needed.

Accessing Medical Services

Finding a Medical Facility:

Hotel Recommendations: Many hotels can recommend nearby medical facilities or arrange for an English-speaking doctor.

Travel Insurance: Contact your travel insurance provider for recommendations on reputable healthcare facilities and assistance with medical services.

Emergency Care:

Emergency Numbers: Dial 122 for general emergencies, 123 for ambulances, and 180 for fire services.

Emergency Rooms: Major hospitals have emergency departments equipped to handle urgent medical situations. In case of an emergency, you can go directly to the nearest hospital or call for an ambulance.

Healthcare Quality and Standards

Quality of Care:

Public Facilities: Public hospitals may experience higher patient volumes and longer wait times. The quality of care can vary, so it's advisable to consider private options for more immediate and specialized care.

Private Facilities: Private hospitals and clinics generally offer higher standards of care, better facilities, and more personalized services. They may also have English-speaking staff and modern medical equipment.

Medical Staff:

Doctors: Many doctors in private hospitals and clinics are trained abroad and speak English. In public hospitals, English proficiency may vary, but staff are generally knowledgeable and professional.

Nurses and Support Staff: Both public and private hospitals employ qualified nurses and support staff who assist with medical care and patient management.

Medical Costs and Insurance

Cost of Care:

Public Hospitals: Typically more affordable, but the cost can still vary depending on the type of treatment and the facility's location.

Private Hospitals: Generally more expensive, but prices are transparent and services are often more comprehensive. It's a good idea to inquire about costs upfront.

Health Insurance:

Travel Insurance: Ensure your travel insurance covers medical expenses, including hospital stays, treatments, and emergency evacuations. Confirm that your policy provides coverage for healthcare services in Egypt.

Payment Methods: Many private facilities accept credit cards, but it's advisable to carry some cash as a backup. Public hospitals might require cash payments for certain services.

Health Precautions

Pre-Travel Preparation:

Vaccinations: Check with your healthcare provider for any recommended vaccinations before traveling to Egypt.

Medication: Bring any prescription medications you need, along with a doctor's note if necessary. Keep medications in their original packaging and carry them in your hand luggage.

During Your Stay:

Emergency Contacts: Keep a list of emergency contacts, including local hospitals and your insurance provider's helpline.

Local Health Issues: Be aware of common health issues in Egypt, such as food and waterborne illnesses, and take necessary precautions.

Emergency Services

When traveling to Egypt, knowing how to access emergency services is crucial for handling unexpected situations effectively. Here's a comprehensive guide on emergency services in Egypt:

Emergency Numbers

General Emergency Number:

122: This number connects you to emergency services for general assistance, including police, ambulance, and fire services.

Ambulance Service:

123: Use this number to request an ambulance for medical emergencies. It's advisable to provide clear information about your location and the nature of the emergency.

Fire Service:

180: Call this number in case of a fire or to report a fire emergency.

Police:

122: This number is also used to contact the police for assistance with crime or other law enforcement needs.

Emergency Facilities

Hospitals with Emergency Departments:

Public Hospitals: Major public hospitals have emergency departments equipped to handle urgent medical situations. Examples include Kasr El Aini Hospital in Cairo and Alexandria University Hospital.

Private Hospitals: Private hospitals offer emergency services with higher standards and shorter wait times. Examples include Gasser El Ghandour Hospital in Cairo and Luxor International Hospital in Luxor.

Clinics:

Some private clinics may offer emergency services, but for severe emergencies, it is usually better to go to a hospital with an emergency department.

What to Do in an Emergency

Immediate Actions:

Stay Calm: Try to remain calm to assess the situation clearly and communicate effectively.

Contact Emergency Services: Call the relevant emergency number and provide precise details about your location and the nature of the emergency.

Follow Instructions: Listen to and follow the instructions given by emergency operators or responders.

If You Need Medical Help:

Locate Nearest Hospital: If you cannot get through to emergency services, or if the situation requires immediate care, locate the nearest hospital with an emergency department.

Transport: If necessary, arrange for transport to the hospital. Many hotels can assist with arranging taxis or emergency transport.

Medical Insurance and Assistance

Travel Insurance:

Emergency Coverage: Ensure your travel insurance covers emergency medical services, including hospital stays, treatments, and evacuation if necessary.

Assistance Services: Contact your insurance provider for assistance in finding medical facilities, arranging payments, or handling emergency situations.

Insurance Providers:

Keep a list of your insurance provider's emergency contact numbers. Many travel insurance policies include 24/7 emergency assistance hotlines.

Language and Communication

Language Barrier:

English Speakers: Major hospitals and private clinics often have staff who speak English, but communication might be limited in public hospitals or rural areas.

Translator Services: Some hotels offer translation services or can assist in communicating with medical staff.

Safety Tips

Health Precautions:

Avoid Risky Areas: Be aware of your surroundings and avoid areas known for higher risks, such as poorly lit streets or unsafe neighborhoods.

Local Contacts: Keep a list of local contacts, including your hotel and any emergency services, in case you need assistance.

Documentation:

Carry Important Documents: Keep copies of your passport, travel insurance details, and emergency contacts with you at all times.

Emergency Kit:

Basic Supplies: Consider carrying a basic emergency kit that includes a first aid kit, necessary medications, and a list of medical conditions or allergies.

Contact Information for Embassies

Embassy Assistance:

Embassy Contacts: In case of serious emergencies or if you need help beyond medical services, contact your country's embassy or consulate in Egypt. They can provide assistance with legal issues, repatriation, and other emergencies.

Embassy Locations:

Cairo: The primary embassy for most countries is located in Cairo. Check the embassy's website for contact details and services offered.

Vaccinations and Health Precautions

When traveling to Egypt, taking appropriate health precautions and ensuring you have the necessary vaccinations can help protect you from illness and ensure a smooth trip. Here's a detailed guide on vaccinations and health precautions:

Recommended Vaccinations

Routine Vaccinations:

Routine Immunizations: Ensure that you are up-to-date on standard vaccinations such as measles, mumps, rubella (MMR), diphtheria, tetanus, and pertussis.

Travel-Specific Vaccinations:

Hepatitis A: Recommended for most travelers as it can be contracted through contaminated food and water.

Hepatitis B: Considered especially if you will have close contact with locals or plan to undergo medical procedures.

Typhoid: Recommended if you plan to visit rural areas or are concerned about food hygiene.

Rabies: Considered if you will be in close contact with animals or visiting remote areas where rabies may be more prevalent.

Other Vaccinations:

Cholera: May be recommended if you are traveling to areas with active cholera transmission or if you are at high risk.

Influenza: Seasonal flu vaccination is advised, particularly if traveling during flu season or if you are at higher risk of complications.

Health Precautions

Water and Food Safety:

Drinking Water: Drink only bottled or boiled water. Avoid ice cubes and raw food that might have been washed with tap water.

Food Safety: Eat well-cooked food and avoid street food that might not meet hygiene standards. Opt for reputable restaurants and avoid raw fruits and vegetables unless they can be peeled.

Personal Hygiene:

Hand Washing: Wash your hands frequently with soap and water, especially before eating. Use hand sanitizer when soap and water are not available.

Avoid Contact with Animals: To reduce the risk of rabies and other zoonotic diseases, avoid contact with stray animals and be cautious around pets.

Insect Protection:

Mosquitoes: Use insect repellent containing DEET to protect against mosquito bites, which can transmit diseases like malaria and dengue. Wear long-sleeved clothing and trousers, particularly in areas where mosquitoes are prevalent.

Sun Protection:

Sunscreen: Use sunscreen with high SPF to protect against sunburn. Egypt's climate can be very hot and sunny, so apply sunscreen regularly, especially if you are spending time outdoors.

Health Insurance:

Travel Insurance: Ensure you have comprehensive travel insurance that covers medical expenses, emergency evacuation, and trip cancellations. Confirm that your insurance covers health issues related to Egypt.

Medical Kit:

Basic Supplies: Carry a basic medical kit including medications for common issues like diarrhea, nausea, and headaches. Include any prescription medications you require, as well as a first aid kit.

Health Resources

Local Healthcare:

Hospitals and Clinics: Major cities like Cairo, Alexandria, and Luxor have reputable hospitals and clinics. For minor health issues or routine care, local pharmacies and clinics are also available.

Pharmacies: Pharmacies are widespread and offer over-the-counter medications and basic health supplies. Many pharmacists in urban areas speak English.

Emergency Contacts:

Emergency Services: Familiarize yourself with local emergency numbers (e.g., 122 for general emergencies, 123 for ambulances).

Embassy Assistance: If you experience a serious health issue, contact your country's embassy or consulate for assistance.

Pre-Travel Preparation

Consultation:

Travel Medicine Specialist: Before traveling, consult with a travel medicine specialist to discuss your specific health needs and get personalized recommendations.

Health Records: Bring copies of your medical records and any necessary prescriptions. Keep these documents in a secure place separate from your main belongings.

Travel Health Kit:

Prepare a Kit: Include items such as over-the-counter medications, first aid supplies, and any necessary prescription medications. Consider packing a thermometer and a digital thermometer for monitoring your health.

Health Insurance and Medical Assistance

When traveling to Egypt, having appropriate health insurance and knowing how to access medical assistance are crucial for ensuring a safe and smooth experience. Here's a comprehensive guide to help you navigate health insurance and medical assistance during your trip:

Health Insurance

Types of Coverage:

Travel Health Insurance:

Emergency Medical Coverage: Includes coverage for medical expenses incurred due to illness or injury while traveling. This typically covers hospital stays, doctor visits, medications, and sometimes emergency dental care.

Emergency Evacuation: Covers the cost of evacuation to the nearest suitable medical facility or repatriation to your home country if necessary.

Trip Cancellation or Interruption: Reimburses you for non-refundable trip costs if you need to cancel or cut short your trip due to a covered medical emergency.

Comprehensive Travel Insurance:

Full Coverage: Includes not only medical expenses but also protection against other travel issues such as trip delays, lost luggage, and theft. This type of insurance provides a broader range of protection.

Choosing a Policy:

Coverage Limits: Ensure that the policy offers sufficient coverage limits for medical expenses and emergency evacuation. Check the maximum coverage amounts and any exclusions.

Pre-existing Conditions: Verify whether pre-existing medical conditions are covered. Some policies may exclude or offer limited coverage for pre-existing conditions.

Network Providers: Check if the insurance provider has a network of healthcare providers or preferred hospitals in Egypt to streamline the claims process.

Medical Assistance Services

Emergency Assistance:

Insurance Assistance Hotlines: Most travel insurance policies provide 24/7 emergency assistance hotlines. These can help you find local medical facilities, arrange for emergency services, and handle claims.

Medical Evacuation: If you need to be evacuated due to a serious health issue, your insurance provider will coordinate the logistics and cover the costs, including air ambulance services if required.

Finding Medical Care:

Hotel Concierge Services: Many hotels offer concierge services that can assist with finding reputable medical facilities and arranging transportation to hospitals or clinics.

Local Recommendations: Contact your insurance provider or embassy for recommendations on reliable hospitals and clinics.

Payment and Claims:

Direct Billing: Some hospitals and clinics may offer direct billing arrangements with insurance companies. Confirm this in advance to avoid out-of-pocket expenses.

Paying Upfront: In cases where direct billing is not available, you may need to pay for medical services upfront and submit a claim to your insurance provider for reimbursement. Keep all receipts and documentation related to the treatment.

Preparing for Medical Needs

Pre-Travel Preparations:

Health Records: Bring copies of important medical records, including details of any chronic conditions, allergies, and medications. Having these on hand can be crucial in case of an emergency.

Medication: Carry enough prescription medication for the duration of your trip, along with a copy of the prescription and a doctor's note if needed. Pack medications in their original packaging and keep them in your hand luggage.

Emergency Contacts:

Insurance Contact Information: Keep the contact details of your insurance provider's emergency hotline in a readily accessible place.

Local Emergency Contacts: Have a list of local emergency numbers, including hospital and ambulance services, as well as contact details for your country's embassy or consulate in Egypt.

Additional Tips

Travel Health Kit:

Basic Supplies: Pack a travel health kit that includes over-the-counter medications for common issues (e.g., pain relievers, anti-diarrheal medication), a first aid kit, and any specific health items you may need.

Health and Safety Precautions:

Follow Health Guidelines: Adhere to health guidelines such as drinking safe water, eating properly, using insect repellent, and practicing good hygiene to prevent illness.

Emergency Plan:

Have a Plan: Familiarize yourself with the steps to take in case of an emergency, including how to contact your insurance provider and where to seek medical help.

Food and Water Safety

Ensuring food and water safety is crucial when traveling to Egypt to avoid common illnesses and have a pleasant trip. Here's a comprehensive guide to help you stay safe:

Water Safety

Drinking Water:

Bottled Water: Drink only bottled water from reputable brands. Ensure the seal is intact before purchasing. This is the safest option for avoiding waterborne diseases.

Boiled Water: If bottled water is not available, boil tap water for at least one minute to kill any harmful pathogens. However, this is less convenient than buying bottled water.

Avoiding Ice:

Ice Cubes: Avoid ice cubes in drinks, as they may be made from contaminated tap water. Opt for drinks without ice to minimize risk.

Checking Water Quality:

Local Advice: Ask locals or hotel staff about the quality of tap water. In many tourist areas, bottled water is widely available and recommended.

Food Safety

Eating Out:

Reputable Restaurants: Dine at well-established restaurants and cafes with good hygiene practices. Popular tourist spots and high-end establishments are generally safer.

Street Food: Be cautious with street food. While it can be tempting, it's often harder to gauge food hygiene and preparation standards. If you do try street food, choose vendors with high turnover and good sanitation practices.

Food Preparation:

Cooked Food: Prefer well-cooked foods as cooking kills most pathogens. Avoid raw or undercooked meat, seafood, and eggs.

Peelable Fruits: Opt for fruits and vegetables that you can peel yourself, such as bananas and oranges. Avoid raw salads or unpeeled fruits that might have been washed with contaminated water.

Food Hygiene:

Observe Hygiene Practices: Check if the restaurant or food vendor follows good hygiene practices. This includes proper food handling, cleanliness of utensils, and overall sanitation.

Personal Hygiene: Wash your hands frequently with soap and water, especially before eating. Use hand sanitizer when soap and water are not available.

Common Foodborne Illnesses

Symptoms:

Common Symptoms: Foodborne illnesses can cause symptoms such as nausea, vomiting, diarrhea, abdominal pain, and fever. Symptoms may appear within hours or days after consuming contaminated food or water.

When to Seek Medical Help:

Persistent Symptoms: If you experience severe or persistent symptoms, such as prolonged diarrhea, high fever, or signs of dehydration (e.g., excessive thirst, dry mouth, reduced urination), seek medical attention promptly.

Health Precautions

Travel Health Kit:

Medication: Carry medications to treat common digestive issues, such as anti-diarrheal tablets, antacids, and rehydration salts. Having these on hand can help manage mild symptoms and prevent dehydration.

Rehydration:

Oral Rehydration Salts (ORS): Use ORS to rehydrate if you experience diarrhea. These are available in pharmacies and can help replace lost fluids and electrolytes.

Avoiding Risky Foods:

Caffeine and Alcohol: Limit caffeine and alcohol intake, as they can exacerbate dehydration and digestive issues.

Local Health Resources

Pharmacies:

Availability: Pharmacies are widely available and can provide medications for common ailments. Many pharmacists in urban areas speak English and can offer advice.

Medical Facilities:

Hospitals and Clinics: Major cities have hospitals and clinics where you can seek treatment if you experience foodborne illness or other health issues.

Additional Tips

Consulting Locals:

Local Recommendations: Ask locals or hotel staff for recommendations on safe dining options and any specific food safety tips for the area you're visiting.

Cultural Considerations:

Local Cuisine: Familiarize yourself with local cuisine and common practices. Understanding what to expect can help you make informed choices about what to eat and drink.

Chapter 6: Cultural Etiquette and Customs

General Etiquette

Understanding and respecting local customs is essential for a positive travel experience. Here's a detailed look at general etiquette in Egypt to help you navigate social interactions smoothly:

Greetings and Social Interactions

Warm Greetings:

Handshakes: Handshakes are common when greeting someone, especially among men. A firm but gentle handshake is customary. When greeting someone of the opposite sex, it's polite to wait for the other person to extend their hand first.

Verbal Greetings: Common phrases include "As-salamu alaykum" (Peace be upon you) and "Wa alaykum as-salam" (And upon you be peace). Using these greetings shows respect for local customs.

Personal Space: Egyptians value personal space but are generally warm and friendly. Maintain an appropriate distance during conversations and avoid standing too close.

Addressing People:

Titles: Use formal titles and honorifics such as "Mr." (Sayyid) or "Mrs." (Sayyida) followed by the person's surname. It's a sign of respect to address someone using their proper title, especially in formal settings.

Respect for Religion and Religious Practices

Observing Prayer Times:

Respect Prayer Times: Egypt is predominantly Muslim, and prayer times are observed five times a day. During prayer times, it is respectful to maintain quiet in public places and avoid disrupting those who are praying.

Respecting Religious Sites:

Mosques: When visiting mosques, follow the local customs, such as removing your shoes before entering the prayer area and being quiet and respectful. It is also customary to dress modestly and avoid physical contact in prayer areas.

Public Behavior:

Respect for Religious Beliefs: Be respectful of Islamic practices and beliefs. Avoid discussing sensitive religious topics or making negative comments about religion.

Dining Etiquette

Sharing Meals:

Hospitality: Egyptians are known for their hospitality. When invited to someone's home, it is polite to accept their offer and try the food. Compliment the host on their cooking and express gratitude for their hospitality.

Eating Practices: Meals are often shared from a common dish. Use your right hand for eating, as the left hand is considered impolite in social contexts. Forks and knives are used for cutting, but many Egyptians use their fingers for eating bread and certain dishes.

Offering and Receiving:

Offering Food: It is customary to offer food and drinks to guests. When offered, it's polite to accept at least a small amount, even if you are not very hungry.

Public Behavior and Etiquette

Queuing and Patience:

Queueing: While queueing is becoming more common, it's important to be patient and wait your turn, especially in public places like banks or service counters.

Public Conduct:

Moderation: Public displays of affection are generally frowned upon. Maintain modest behavior in public spaces, and avoid loud or disruptive conduct.

Tipping: Tipping is a common practice in Egypt. It is customary to leave a small tip for service staff in restaurants, hotels, and taxis. Round up the bill or leave 10-15% of the total amount as a tip.

Respect for Local Customs

Visiting Homes:

Shoes: Remove your shoes before entering someone's home. It is considered a sign of respect and cleanliness.

Gifts: When visiting someone's home, it is a nice gesture to bring a small gift, such as sweets or flowers, to show appreciation for their hospitality.

Photography:

Permission: Always ask for permission before photographing people, especially in rural areas or at religious sites. Some areas may have restrictions on photography, so be mindful of local rules and sensitivities.

Behavior Towards Women:

Respect Personal Space: Be respectful and mindful of personal space, particularly towards women. Avoid physical contact and adhere to local customs regarding interactions.

Business Etiquette

Meetings and Communication:

Punctuality: Arriving on time for meetings and appointments is important, although there may be some flexibility in more informal settings.

Formal Communication: Use formal titles and address business associates with respect. Building personal relationships is important in business dealings, so take time to engage in polite conversation before discussing business matters.

Dress Code

When visiting Egypt, dressing appropriately is important for respecting local customs and ensuring comfort in various settings. Here's a detailed guide on the dress code to help you navigate your attire during your trip:

General Guidelines

Modesty:

Cultural Norms: Egypt is a predominantly Muslim country, and modesty is highly valued in both social and religious contexts. Dress modestly to respect local customs and avoid drawing unnecessary attention.

Covering Shoulders and Knees: Both men and women should aim to cover their shoulders and knees. This is especially important when visiting religious sites, public places, and rural areas.

Comfort and Practicality:

Weather Considerations: Egypt's climate can be extremely hot and dry, particularly in the summer months. Opt for light, breathable fabrics such as cotton or linen to stay comfortable.

Layers: Consider wearing layers that can be added or removed as needed, especially if you plan to visit air-conditioned indoor locations or travel between regions with varying temperatures.

Dress Code for Specific Settings

Religious Sites:

Mosques: When visiting mosques, it's important to dress conservatively. For women, this means wearing long skirts or trousers and long-sleeved tops. A headscarf is usually required for women entering mosques. Men should wear long trousers and shirts with sleeves.

Churches: Similar to mosques, modest attire is expected in churches. Women should cover their shoulders, and both men and women should avoid wearing shorts.

Public Areas and Cities:

Casual Attire: In cities like Cairo and Alexandria, casual yet modest attire is appropriate. Women can wear dresses or skirts with long sleeves, or pants with blouses. Men can wear long trousers with shirts or polo shirts.

Beachwear: Swimwear is acceptable at the beach or poolside but should not be worn in public areas away from these locations. Cover up with a sarong, cover-up, or shorts and a T-shirt when leaving the beach.

Restaurants and Hotels:

Smart Casual: For dining in nicer restaurants or staying in upscale hotels, smart casual attire is recommended. This could include collared shirts or blouses, long trousers or skirts, and closed-toe shoes.

Evening Wear: Some high-end establishments may have a more formal dress code for evening dining. In such cases, dressing up slightly with a smart outfit or dress can be appropriate.

Outdoor Activities:

Comfortable Clothing: For activities such as sightseeing, hiking, or desert excursions, wear comfortable and practical clothing. Light, long-sleeved shirts and trousers will protect you from the sun and sand. Don't forget a wide-brimmed hat and sunglasses.

Specific Tips for Women

Headscarves:

Voluntary Use: While it's not mandatory for women to wear a headscarf outside of religious sites, it can be a sign of respect in certain settings and is advisable when visiting religious or traditional areas.

Fashion Choices:

Avoid Revealing Clothing: Avoid clothing that is too tight or revealing. Opt for garments that cover your arms and legs, and choose modest necklines.

Specific Tips for Men

Appropriate Attire:

Avoid Shorts: In urban areas and formal settings, it's best to avoid wearing shorts. Long trousers are more appropriate and respectful in most situations.

Shirts with Sleeves: Wear shirts with sleeves rather than sleeveless tops to maintain a respectful appearance.

General Dress Tips

Cultural Sensitivity:

Respect Local Customs: Even if you're in tourist areas, it's courteous to dress in a way that reflects respect for local cultural and religious practices.

Adjusting to Local Norms: Observe how locals dress and adapt your attire accordingly. In more tourist-heavy areas, you may find a wider range of attire, but maintaining modesty remains a general guideline.

Public Behavior

Understanding and adhering to local social norms is essential for a respectful and enjoyable visit to Egypt. Here's a detailed guide on public behavior to help you navigate social interactions and customs:

Respect for Personal Space

Physical Proximity:

Appropriate Distance: Maintain a respectful distance when interacting with others, especially in public spaces. Avoid standing too close, as personal space is valued.

Avoiding Touch: Public displays of affection, such as hugging or holding hands, are generally discouraged. Respect personal boundaries, particularly in more conservative areas.

Conduct in Public Spaces

Noise Levels:

Moderation: Keep noise levels down in public places, such as public transport, restaurants, and public areas. Loud conversations or disruptive behavior can be seen as impolite.

Mobile Phones: Use mobile phones discreetly and avoid talking loudly. If you need to make a call, step away from crowds to minimize disruption.

Behavioral Norms:

Respectful Attitude: Be polite and considerate towards others. Maintain a calm demeanor, even in situations where you might feel frustrated or stressed.

Queueing: Practice patience and respect when queuing. Although queuing may not always be strictly observed, waiting your turn is a sign of good manners.

Interaction with Locals

Politeness:

Courtesy: Use polite phrases and gestures, such as "please" (min fadlak) and "thank you" (shukran). Showing appreciation for services and hospitality is always appreciated.

Conversation Topics: Avoid discussing sensitive topics such as politics, religion, or personal beliefs unless you are familiar with the context and comfortable with the discussion.

Cultural Sensitivity:

Respecting Customs: Be aware of and respect local customs and traditions. Avoid behaviors or language that could be perceived as disrespectful or offensive.

Interactions with Women: Approach interactions with women respectfully. In more conservative areas, avoid direct physical contact and be mindful of local social norms regarding gender interactions.

Public Decorum

Dress and Appearance:

Modesty: Dress modestly in public, adhering to local dress codes. Even in casual settings, avoid wearing clothing that is too revealing or suggestive.

Cleanliness: Maintain cleanliness and tidiness in public areas. Dispose of litter properly and use public restrooms with respect for hygiene practices.

Dining Etiquette:

Public Eating: In urban areas, it's generally acceptable to eat in public. However, in more traditional or rural areas, eating in public may be less common and should be approached with discretion.

Sharing Meals: When invited to a meal, it is polite to try the food offered, even if only a small amount. Compliment the host and express gratitude for their hospitality.

Use of Public Transportation

Behavior on Transport:

Respectful Conduct: Maintain respectful behavior on public transport. Offer your seat to the elderly, pregnant women, or those with disabilities if necessary.

Queues and Seating: Follow any queuing practices and be mindful of reserved seating areas. Keep personal belongings tidy and avoid occupying more space than necessary.

Photography and Filming

Permission:

Ask Before Taking Photos: Always ask for permission before photographing people, especially in rural areas or at religious sites. Respect any restrictions on photography and be aware of signs indicating where photography is prohibited.

Cultural Sites: Be mindful of local customs and rules regarding photography at cultural or religious sites. Some areas may have specific regulations to preserve their sanctity.

Dealing with Conflicts

Conflict Resolution:

Calm Approach: Handle conflicts or disagreements calmly and politely. Avoid raising your voice or displaying anger in public settings.

Seek Help if Needed: If you encounter serious issues or need assistance, approach local authorities, hotel staff, or your embassy for support.

Dining Etiquette

Dining in Egypt offers a rich cultural experience, with its own set of customs and etiquette. Understanding these norms can enhance your experience and help you navigate social meals with ease. Here's a detailed guide on dining etiquette in Egypt:

Invited to a Meal

Accepting Invitations:

Gracious Acceptance: If you receive an invitation to a meal, it's polite to accept, even if you're not very hungry. This is a gesture of respect and appreciation for the host's hospitality.

Bringing a Gift: It is customary to bring a small gift, such as sweets, fruit, or flowers, when visiting someone's home for a meal. This gesture shows appreciation for their hospitality.

Arrival Time:

Punctuality: Arriving on time is important, but being a little late (about 10-15 minutes) is generally acceptable. If you're running late, inform your host if possible.

At the Table

Seating Arrangements:

Follow the Host: Wait for the host to indicate where you should sit. In many cases, the host will guide you to your place at the table.

Position: Men and women might be seated separately, especially in more traditional settings. Follow the lead of your host regarding seating arrangements.

Table Manners:

Use of Hands and Utensils: While many meals in Egypt are eaten with the hands (particularly bread and certain dishes), utensils are used for other foods. Use your right hand for eating, as the left hand is considered impolite in social contexts.

Sharing Dishes: Meals are often served family-style with shared dishes. Take small portions and use the serving utensils provided. Avoid using your own utensils to serve food from communal dishes.

Eating Customs

Starting the Meal:

Wait for the Host: Wait for the host to begin the meal or offer a blessing before starting. This is a sign of respect and follows traditional customs.

Bread: Bread is a staple in Egyptian meals and is often used to scoop up food. It's considered a crucial part of the meal, so don't waste it.

Eating Process:

Small Portions: Take small portions of each dish to avoid overloading your plate. It's better to go back for more if you're still hungry.

Compliments: Compliment the host on the meal. Egyptians take pride in their cooking, and positive feedback is always appreciated.

Drinking and Toasting

Beverages:

Water and Soft Drinks: Bottled water, soft drinks, and traditional beverages like tea and hibiscus juice are commonly served. It's polite to accept a drink if offered.

Alcohol: In more conservative settings, alcohol might not be served or might be less commonly consumed. If alcohol is served, handle it discreetly and respectfully. In social settings where alcohol is present, toasting with a simple "cheers" (in Arabic, "saha") is appropriate.

After the Meal

Expressing Gratitude:

Thank You: Thank your host for the meal and express your appreciation. A simple "shukran" (thank you) is appropriate.

Offering to Help: If the meal is at someone's home, offer to help with clearing the table or washing dishes. Even if your offer is declined, it's a polite gesture.

Leaving the Table:

Wait for the Host: Wait for the host to indicate that the meal is over before leaving the table. This shows respect and attentiveness to the host's lead.

Special Considerations

Dietary Restrictions:

Inform in Advance: If you have dietary restrictions or allergies, inform your host in advance. Egyptians are generally accommodating, but advance notice helps ensure suitable options are available.

Cultural Sensitivity:

Avoiding Certain Foods: In more traditional or religious settings, avoid foods or behaviors that may be considered disrespectful, such as eating pork or drinking alcohol, if you're unsure of the host's preferences.

Dining in Restaurants

Tipping:

Service Charge: A service charge (usually 10-12%) is often included in the bill. If not, it is customary to leave a tip of around 10-15% of the total bill for good service.

Behavior:

Politeness: Maintain polite behavior and dress appropriately for the type of restaurant you're visiting. Follow the same general table manners as you would when dining in someone's home.

Customs and Traditions

Egypt's rich history and diverse cultural influences have shaped a unique set of customs and traditions. Understanding these can enrich your experience and help you navigate social interactions with respect. Here's a comprehensive guide to key customs and traditions in Egypt:

Social Customs

Hospitality:

Warm Welcome: Egyptians are renowned for their hospitality. When visiting someone's home, expect a warm welcome and generous offers of food and drink. It's polite to accept these offers, even if only a small amount.

Guest Protocol: If invited to someone's home, it is customary to bring a small gift, such as sweets or fruit, as a token of appreciation.

Greetings:

Traditional Greetings: Use "As-salamu alaykum" (Peace be upon you) as a common greeting. The response is "Wa alaykum as-salam" (And upon you be peace). This shows respect and acknowledges the local customs.

Handshakes and Gestures: Handshakes are common, especially among men. When greeting women, wait for them to extend their hand first, or use a nod or verbal greeting if unsure.

Religious Practices

Islamic Traditions:

Prayer Times: Muslims pray five times a day. Be respectful during these times by maintaining quiet and avoiding disruptions. Prayer times vary, so check local schedules if you need to plan around them.

Ramadan: During the month of Ramadan, Muslims fast from dawn until sunset. It's considerate to avoid eating or drinking in public during daylight hours. Many restaurants and hotels provide discreet areas for non-fasting guests.

Christian Traditions:

Coptic Christianity: Egypt is also home to Coptic Christians, who have unique customs. Attend services or events with respect for their traditions, and be aware of Christian holidays and festivals.

Festivals and Celebrations

Eid al-Fitr:

End of Ramadan: Eid al-Fitr marks the end of Ramadan and is celebrated with communal prayers, festive meals, and giving of gifts. It's a time of joy and family gatherings.

Eid al-Adha:

Festival of Sacrifice: Eid al-Adha commemorates the willingness of Ibrahim (Abraham) to sacrifice his son. The festival involves the slaughter of livestock, and the meat is shared with family, friends, and those in need.

Sham El-Nessim:

Spring Festival: Celebrated on the first day of spring, Sham El-Nessim is a traditional Egyptian holiday marked by picnics, eating salted fish, and spending time outdoors.

Coptic Christmas and Easter:

Religious Observances: Coptic Christmas (January 7) and Easter are significant holidays with special church services, family gatherings, and traditional foods.

Daily Life and Social Norms

Dining Etiquette:

Sharing Meals: Meals are often shared from communal dishes. Use your right hand for eating and take small portions. It's respectful to compliment the host on the meal.

Dress Code:

Modesty: Dress modestly, particularly when visiting religious sites or rural areas. Cover shoulders and knees, and avoid overly revealing clothing.

Public Behavior:

Politeness: Maintain a polite and respectful demeanor in public. Avoid loud or disruptive behavior and be considerate of others' personal space.

Customs Related to Family Life

Family Structure:

Family Importance: Family is central to Egyptian life, with strong ties between relatives. Extended families often live close together and maintain close-knit relationships.

Marriage Traditions:

Arranged Marriages: While arranged marriages are less common among younger generations, family involvement in marital decisions is still significant. Weddings are often large and elaborate celebrations.

Customs in Rural Areas

Traditional Practices:

Local Traditions: Rural areas may have distinct customs and traditions that differ from urban practices. Be observant and respectful of local ways of life, which might include traditional farming practices, crafts, and festivals.

Respect for Elders:

Honor and Respect: In rural areas, showing respect to elders is particularly emphasized. It's customary to greet and address older individuals with additional politeness.

Language and Communication

Language Use:

Arabic: Arabic is the official language, and knowing a few basic phrases can be helpful. Greetings and polite expressions in Arabic are appreciated and show respect for the culture.

Non-Verbal Communication:

Body Language: Be aware of non-verbal communication. For example, gestures that are acceptable in other cultures may not be understood the same way in Egypt.

Shopping and Bargaining

Shopping in Egypt is an engaging experience that blends traditional practices with modern convenience. Understanding local shopping customs and bargaining techniques will help you make the most of your shopping adventures. Here's a comprehensive guide to shopping and bargaining in Egypt:

Types of Shopping Venues

Traditional Markets (Souks):

Variety of Goods: Souks are bustling markets where you can find a wide array of goods, from spices and textiles to jewelry and souvenirs. Popular markets include Cairo's Khan El Khalili and Alexandria's Souk El-Tawfiq.

Atmosphere: These markets offer an authentic Egyptian experience with lively atmospheres, vibrant colors, and the opportunity to interact directly with local vendors.

Modern Shopping Malls:

Convenience: Modern malls, such as Cairo's City Stars and Mall of Arabia, provide a more familiar shopping experience with international brands, food courts, and entertainment options.

Pricing: Prices in malls are usually fixed, and there is less room for bargaining compared to traditional markets.

Specialty Shops:

Crafts and Artisans: Look for specialty shops that sell traditional crafts, such as handmade carpets, pottery, and textiles. These shops often offer high-quality goods and a more personalized shopping experience.

Bargaining Etiquette

Understanding Bargaining:

Common Practice: Bargaining is a common and expected practice in traditional markets and some smaller shops. It's seen as part of the shopping experience rather than a sign of disrespect.

Fixed Prices: In modern malls and some upscale shops, prices are fixed, and bargaining is generally not practiced.

How to Bargain:

Start Low: Begin by offering a price lower than what you're willing to pay. This allows room for negotiation and helps you reach a mutually acceptable price.

Be Polite: Approach bargaining with a friendly and respectful attitude. Smile and engage in light conversation to build rapport with the vendor.

Know When to Stop: If a vendor is firm on their price and you're not satisfied, it's acceptable to politely decline and walk away. Vendors may be more willing to negotiate if they see you are genuinely interested.

Cultural Sensitivity:

Respectful Negotiation: While bargaining is expected, it's important to be respectful. Avoid aggressive or confrontational tactics, and be mindful of cultural norms regarding negotiation.

Commonly Purchased Items

Souvenirs and Gifts:

Traditional Items: Popular souvenirs include papyrus scrolls, Egyptian perfumes, alabaster statues, and traditional jewelry. These items reflect Egypt's rich history and culture.

Spices and Herbs: Egypt is known for its spices and herbs, such as cumin, coriander, and mint. Purchasing spices from local markets can be a flavorful memento of your trip.

Clothing and Textiles:

Traditional Garments: Consider buying traditional Egyptian garments like galabeyas (long robes) or shawls. These items are not only practical but also offer a unique insight into local fashion.

Textiles: Look for high-quality textiles and fabrics, including embroidered linens and carpets, which are often handmade and feature intricate designs.

Payment Methods

Cash and Cards:

Cash: Cash is commonly used in traditional markets and smaller shops. Carry enough local currency (Egyptian pounds) for transactions, and be prepared for small denominations.

Credit/Debit Cards: Most modern stores, malls, and larger establishments accept credit and debit cards. However, it's always a good idea to carry some cash for smaller purchases or in more remote areas.

Currency Exchange:

Exchanging Money: Currency exchange services are available at banks, hotels, and exchange bureaus. Ensure you're familiar with current exchange rates and avoid exchanging money on the street.

Shopping Tips

Research and Compare:

Price Comparison: Before making a purchase, compare prices across different vendors to ensure you're getting a fair deal. This is particularly useful in markets where prices can vary.

Check Quality: Inspect items carefully for quality and authenticity, especially when buying souvenirs or artisanal products. Look for certification or provenance if available.

Be Prepared for Crowds:

Busy Markets: Markets can be crowded and bustling, especially during peak hours. Be prepared for a lively atmosphere and potential crowds.

Respect Local Customs:

Local Practices: Be aware of and respect local customs and practices when shopping. For example, removing your shoes before entering certain shops may be customary.

Behavior Towards Women

Understanding cultural norms around gender interactions is crucial when visiting Egypt. Social practices and expectations regarding behavior towards women can differ significantly from those in other parts of the world. Here's a detailed guide to help you navigate these cultural nuances respectfully:

General Attitudes and Respect

Respectful Interaction:

Politeness: Show respect towards women in both public and private settings. This includes using polite language, avoiding overly familiar behavior, and maintaining a courteous demeanor.

Physical Contact: Avoid physical contact with women unless you are sure it is welcomed. This includes handshakes, which might not be extended by women to men in more conservative settings. Wait for the woman to initiate contact or follow their lead.

Public Spaces:

Personal Space: Be mindful of personal space and avoid standing too close to women in public areas. Respect their comfort and privacy.

Avoiding Stares: Refrain from staring or making unsolicited comments. Respect for personal dignity is important in maintaining a respectful interaction.

Dress Code and Modesty

Appropriate Attire:

Modesty: Both men and women are expected to dress modestly, particularly in more conservative areas. For women, this generally means covering shoulders, cleavage, and knees. In religious or rural settings, more conservative dress may be expected.

Public Behavior: When in public spaces, dress modestly to avoid drawing undue attention. Women should consider wearing clothing that aligns with local norms and shows respect for cultural practices.

Religious and Traditional Settings:

Religious Sites: When visiting religious sites, women should dress more conservatively. In mosques and some churches, it's customary to cover the head with a scarf and wear long skirts or trousers and long-sleeved tops.

Interaction in Social and Professional Settings

Workplace Behavior:

Professionalism: In professional settings, treat female colleagues with the same respect and professionalism you would offer male colleagues. Avoid any form of gender-based discrimination or biased behavior.

Meetings and Discussions: In meetings or discussions, give women equal opportunity to contribute and ensure their voices are heard. Respect their viewpoints and expertise.

Social Situations:

Social Gatherings: At social events, follow the lead of your hosts and be sensitive to local customs regarding interactions between men and women. Social norms may dictate certain behaviors, such as seating arrangements or interaction patterns.

Handling Gender-Specific Situations

Transportation and Public Areas:

Separate Spaces: In some public transportation systems and spaces, there may be separate areas for women. Respect these designations and follow local guidelines regarding their use.

Queues and Seating: When using public transport, offer seats to women, especially if they are elderly or pregnant. This gesture is a sign of respect and consideration.

Dining and Social Interactions:

Mixed-Gender Settings: In restaurants or social settings where men and women are present together, follow local practices and norms. Avoid any behavior that might be perceived as inappropriate or disrespectful.

Cultural Sensitivity and Awareness

Understanding Local Norms:

Cultural Variations: Be aware that cultural norms regarding gender interactions can vary between urban and rural areas. Urban settings may be more liberal, while rural or conservative areas may adhere to stricter norms.

Learning from Locals: Observe and learn from local practices and behaviors. If in doubt, follow the lead of local women or seek guidance from your hosts or guides.

Communication:

Respectful Language: Use respectful language when addressing or referring to women. Avoid making assumptions or stereotypes based on gender.

Listening and Engagement: Engage in conversations with women in a respectful manner, listening actively and valuing their contributions.

Handling Uncomfortable Situations

Appropriate Responses:

Addressing Unwanted Attention: If you or a woman you are with encounters unwanted attention or behavior, calmly and politely address the situation or seek assistance from local authorities if necessary.

Seeking Assistance: If you feel unsure about how to behave or need guidance, don't hesitate to ask local contacts or guides for advice.

Chapter 7: Outdoor Activities

Desert Adventures

Egypt's deserts offer an incredible range of outdoor adventures, from thrilling dune bashing to serene stargazing. With vast expanses of sand, unique geological formations, and ancient archaeological sites, the Egyptian deserts provide a diverse and captivating experience for adventurers. Here's an extensive guide to desert adventures in Egypt:

1. Popular Desert Regions

The Western Desert:

Siwa Oasis: Known for its unique landscapes, historical sites, and natural springs, Siwa Oasis is a popular destination. Activities include exploring ancient ruins, bathing in natural springs, and enjoying the picturesque sand dunes.

Bahariya Oasis: Famous for its black and white desert landscapes, Bahariya Oasis offers various adventures such as exploring the Crystal Mountain, the Black Desert, and the ancient tombs in the Valley of the Golden Mummies.

The Sinai Desert:

Mount Sinai: A prominent site for both hiking and spiritual exploration, Mount Sinai is renowned for its sunrise and sunset views. The hike to the summit is challenging but offers rewarding panoramic vistas.

Saint Catherine's Monastery: Located in the Sinai Peninsula, this ancient monastery is set against the backdrop of rugged desert mountains and offers a historical and spiritual experience.

The Eastern Desert:

Wadi Rum: Known for its dramatic red sandstone mountains and expansive desert landscapes, Wadi Rum offers a classic desert adventure experience with opportunities for rock climbing, camel trekking, and jeep safaris.

2. Desert Activities

Sand Dune Adventures:

Dune Bashing: Experience the thrill of off-roading over sand dunes in a 4x4 vehicle. Guided dune bashing tours take you across the undulating dunes of the desert, providing an adrenaline-pumping experience.

Sandboarding: Glide down the sandy slopes on a sandboard, similar to snowboarding but on sand. Sandboarding is a fun and exhilarating activity suitable for all skill levels.

Camel Trekking:

Traditional Ride: Explore the desert landscape on a camel, a traditional mode of transportation. Camel treks can range from short rides to multi-day excursions, offering a unique way to experience the desert's beauty.

Cultural Experience: Interact with local Bedouin guides during your trek, gaining insight into their traditional way of life and customs.

Hiking and Trekking:

Mount Sinai: Hike to the summit of Mount Sinai for a breathtaking sunrise or sunset view. The trek takes you through rugged terrain and offers a chance to experience the spiritual significance of the mountain.

Wadi Rum Trails: Explore the trails in Wadi Rum, including options for both short hikes and longer treks. The stunning rock formations and vast desert scenery make for memorable hikes.

Stargazing:

The Ultimate Egypt Travel Guide 2025 Edition

Clear Skies: The desert's clear skies and minimal light pollution create perfect conditions for stargazing. Enjoy the stunning night sky and observe constellations, planets, and shooting stars.

Bedouin Camps: Many desert tours include an overnight stay in a Bedouin camp, where you can relax under the stars and experience traditional Bedouin hospitality.

Exploring Ancient Sites:

Siwa Oasis Ruins: Visit the ancient Temple of the Oracle, where Alexander the Great is said to have sought guidance. Explore the ruins of traditional mud-brick architecture and historical sites.

Valley of the Golden Mummies: Discover the archaeological wonders of Bahariya Oasis, including well-preserved mummies and ancient tombs. The valley offers a glimpse into Egypt's rich history and desert burial practices.

Photography and Scenic Tours:

Landscape Photography: Capture the stunning desert landscapes, including dramatic dunes, rocky formations, and unique natural features. The changing light and colors of the desert provide excellent opportunities for photography.

Scenic Jeep Tours: Enjoy guided jeep tours that take you to the most picturesque and interesting locations in the desert. These tours often include visits to geological formations, natural springs, and cultural landmarks.

3. Practical Tips for Desert Adventures

Preparation:

Hydration: The desert climate is extremely dry, so stay hydrated by drinking plenty of water. Carry additional water supplies, especially if you're heading into remote areas.

Sun Protection: Protect yourself from the sun by wearing sunscreen, sunglasses, and a wide-brimmed hat. Lightweight, long-sleeved clothing can also help shield your skin from the sun's rays.

Safety:

Guided Tours: Opt for guided tours or excursions with experienced operators who are familiar with desert conditions. This ensures your safety and enhances your experience.

Navigation: Be aware of your surroundings and stick to marked trails or guided routes. Desert landscapes can be disorienting, so it's essential to have a reliable guide or navigation system.

Equipment:

Appropriate Gear: Wear sturdy hiking boots for trekking and comfortable clothing suited for desert conditions. Bring essential gear such as a map, compass, or GPS device if exploring independently.

Camping Gear: If planning an overnight stay in the desert, ensure you have appropriate camping equipment, including a tent, sleeping bag, and cooking supplies.

Cultural Respect:

Local Customs: Respect local Bedouin customs and traditions. Engage with local guides and communities with sensitivity and appreciation for their way of life.

Environment: Be mindful of the environment by following Leave No Trace principles. Avoid disturbing wildlife and preserve the natural beauty of the desert.

Nile River Activities

The Nile River, often referred to as the lifeline of Egypt, is a central feature of the country's landscape and culture. Stretching over 6,600 kilometers, it offers a variety of activities that allow travelers to explore its historical, cultural, and natural wonders. Here's a comprehensive guide to Nile River activities:

Grace Bennett

1. Nile Cruises

Luxury Cruises:

Classic Itinerary: Luxury Nile cruises typically operate between Luxor and Aswan, covering major archaeological sites such as the Valley of the Kings, Karnak Temple, and Philae Temple. These cruises often include guided tours, fine dining, and luxurious accommodations.

Duration: Cruises usually last between 3 to 7 days, providing ample time to explore key attractions along the river. The longer cruises might extend to Cairo or other destinations.

Felucca Rides:

Traditional Sailing: Feluccas are traditional wooden sailing boats that offer a more intimate and serene experience on the Nile. These small, typically wind-powered boats provide a leisurely way to enjoy the river and its surroundings.

Sunset and Sunrise Cruises: Felucca rides are ideal for enjoying the Nile's tranquil beauty at sunset or sunrise. The experience is peaceful and offers great opportunities for photography.

2. Historical and Cultural Tours

Temple Visits:

Karnak Temple: Located in Luxor, Karnak Temple is one of Egypt's most impressive religious sites. A cruise often includes guided tours to explore its massive halls, obelisks, and statues.

Philae Temple: Situated on an island in Lake Nasser, Philae Temple is dedicated to the goddess Isis. Accessible by boat, it is renowned for its beautifully preserved reliefs and stunning location.

Valley of the Kings:

Royal Tombs: The Valley of the Kings, near Luxor, is famous for its rock-cut tombs of pharaohs and nobles. Explore the elaborate tombs, including those of Tutankhamun and Ramses VI, with guided tours arranged through cruise packages.

Aswan High Dam:

Engineering Marvel: The Aswan High Dam is a key modern landmark on the Nile. Tours offer insights into its construction and its impact on Egypt's agriculture and economy.

3. Outdoor and Adventure Activities

Fishing:

Sport Fishing: The Nile offers opportunities for sport fishing, particularly for species like Nile perch. Local guides can assist with fishing trips and provide equipment.

Catch-and-Release: Practice catch-and-release fishing to preserve the river's ecosystem and ensure sustainable fishing practices.

Kayaking and Canoeing:

Paddle Adventures: Kayaking and canoeing on the Nile provide a more active way to experience the river. Rent a kayak or canoe for a few hours or a full day to explore quieter stretches of the river and observe wildlife.

Bird Watching:

Avian Species: The Nile is home to a diverse range of bird species, including egrets, herons, and kingfishers. Bring binoculars and a bird guide to spot and identify various species along the riverbanks.

4. Cultural Experiences

Local Villages:

Village Visits: Many Nile cruises include visits to traditional villages where you can experience local culture, crafts, and daily life. Interact with villagers, enjoy traditional music and dance, and learn about local customs.

Agriculture: Observe traditional farming practices along the riverbanks, where the fertile soil supported by the Nile's annual inundation sustains agriculture.

The Ultimate Egypt Travel Guide 2025 Edition

Local Cuisine:

Dining Experiences: Sample traditional Egyptian dishes during river cruises or at local restaurants. Enjoy dishes like koshari, falafel, and fresh Nile fish, often prepared with ingredients sourced from the river region.

5. Relaxation and Scenic Enjoyment

Riverfront Walks:

Scenic Strolls: Take leisurely walks along the riverbanks in cities like Luxor and Aswan. Enjoy the scenic views, local flora, and bustling riverfront activity.

Photography:

Capturing Beauty: The Nile offers numerous opportunities for photography, from the dramatic landscapes and historical monuments to the daily life along the river. Early morning and late afternoon provide the best lighting for capturing stunning images.

6. Practical Tips for Nile River Activities

Best Time to Visit:

Climate Considerations: The best time to visit is during the cooler months from October to April. The summer months can be extremely hot, particularly in Upper Egypt.

Health and Safety:

Stay Hydrated: Ensure you drink plenty of water and use sunscreen to protect against the sun. Be cautious with food and drink to avoid digestive issues.

Cultural Sensitivity:

Respect Local Customs: Dress modestly, especially when visiting religious sites or local villages. Be respectful of local traditions and practices.

Booking and Tours:

Book in Advance: Nile cruises and specialized tours can be popular, so book in advance to secure your preferred dates and options. Look for reputable operators and read reviews to ensure a high-quality experience.

Beach and Water Sports

Egypt is not only known for its historical monuments and desert landscapes but also for its stunning coastline and crystal-clear waters. The country's beaches, particularly along the Red Sea and the Mediterranean, offer a paradise for water sports enthusiasts and those looking to relax by the sea. Here's an extensive guide to beach and water sports activities in Egypt:

1. Top Beach Destinations

The Red Sea Coast:

Sharm El Sheikh: Known as a premier diving destination, Sharm El Sheikh offers beautiful beaches, luxury resorts, and world-class water sports facilities. It's ideal for both relaxation and adventure.

Hurghada: Another major destination on the Red Sea, Hurghada is famous for its wide range of water sports, vibrant nightlife, and family-friendly beaches. It's also a gateway to various diving spots.

Dahab: A laid-back town with a bohemian vibe, Dahab is perfect for those seeking a more relaxed beach experience. It's also a top destination for diving, snorkeling, and windsurfing.

The Mediterranean Coast:

Alexandria: Egypt's second-largest city, Alexandria, offers a blend of historical sites and beautiful Mediterranean beaches. While it's more urban, you can still find spots for swimming and water sports.

Marsa Matruh: Known for its white sandy beaches and calm turquoise waters, Marsa Matruh is a favorite summer destination for Egyptians. It's great for swimming, sunbathing, and water sports.

Sinai Peninsula:

Nuweiba: Located in the Sinai Peninsula, Nuweiba offers tranquil beaches, crystal-clear waters, and a more secluded atmosphere. It's ideal for snorkeling and diving.

2. Water Sports Activities

Scuba Diving:

Red Sea Diving: The Red Sea is one of the top diving destinations in the world, famous for its vibrant coral reefs, diverse marine life, and excellent visibility. Popular dive sites include Ras Mohammed National Park, the Thistlegorm wreck, and the Straits of Tiran.

Courses and Certifications: Many dive centers in Sharm El Sheikh, Hurghada, and Dahab offer PADI courses and certifications, ranging from beginner to advanced levels. Experienced divers can also enjoy technical diving and deep-sea expeditions.

Snorkeling:

Coral Reefs: For those who prefer to stay closer to the surface, snorkeling is a fantastic way to explore the underwater world of the Red Sea. Sites like the Blue Hole in Dahab and Giftun Island in Hurghada offer easy access to vibrant coral reefs and a variety of marine species.

Day Trips: Many resorts and tour operators offer snorkeling day trips to nearby reefs, often combined with boat cruises and beach visits.

Windsurfing and Kitesurfing:

Dahab: Known for its consistent winds and shallow lagoons, Dahab is a top spot for windsurfing and kitesurfing. The town hosts international competitions and offers lessons for all levels.

El Gouna: Located near Hurghada, El Gouna is another popular destination for kitesurfing, with wide beaches and excellent wind conditions. The town's upscale resorts also cater to water sports enthusiasts.

Sailing and Boat Cruises:

Nile River Cruises: While not a beach activity, Nile cruises offer a serene sailing experience along one of the world's most famous rivers. These cruises often include stops at historical sites and temples.

Red Sea Cruises: Enjoy sailing along the Red Sea coast with options ranging from luxury yachts to traditional wooden boats. These cruises often include stops for snorkeling, diving, and beach picnics.

Parasailing:

Bird's Eye View: Experience the thrill of parasailing along the Red Sea coast, where you can enjoy panoramic views of the beaches, coral reefs, and surrounding landscapes from high above the water.

Popular Spots: Sharm El Sheikh and Hurghada are the most popular spots for parasailing, with many operators offering tandem flights.

Jet Skiing and Water Skiing:

Adrenaline Rush: For a high-speed adventure, jet skiing and water skiing are popular activities along the Red Sea and Mediterranean coasts. Rentals are available at most major beach resorts.

Safety First: Ensure you are aware of the safety regulations and guidelines provided by operators, especially if you are new to these sports.

Paddleboarding and Kayaking:

Calm Waters: Paddleboarding and kayaking are great ways to explore Egypt's calm coastal waters. They're especially popular in areas like El Gouna and along the quieter beaches of the Sinai Peninsula.

Eco-Friendly Exploration: These activities allow you to quietly navigate the waters, making them ideal for exploring marine life and enjoying the natural surroundings without disturbing the environment.

3. Relaxation and Beach Activities

Sunbathing and Swimming:

Pristine Beaches: Egypt's beaches, particularly along the Red Sea, are known for their soft sand and clear, warm waters, perfect for swimming and sunbathing. Resorts often provide sun loungers, umbrellas, and beachside service.

Family-Friendly Spots: Many beaches are family-friendly, with shallow waters and gentle waves, making them ideal for children and less confident swimmers.

Beach Volleyball and Games:

Active Fun: Many resorts and public beaches offer facilities for beach volleyball, soccer, and other beach games. These activities are a great way to stay active while enjoying the sun and sea.

Spa and Wellness:

Beachside Relaxation: After a day of water sports, unwind with a massage or wellness treatment at one of the many beachside spas. Resorts in Sharm El Sheikh and Hurghada offer a range of spa services, often incorporating local ingredients and techniques.

4. Practical Tips for Beach and Water Sports Activities

Best Time to Visit:

Ideal Conditions: The best time for beach and water sports in Egypt is between October and April, when the weather is warm but not overly hot, and the water conditions are optimal.

Safety Precautions:

Marine Life: While the Red Sea is generally safe for swimming, it's important to be aware of the local marine life. Some species, like jellyfish and certain types of coral, can be harmful if touched. Always listen to the guidance of local instructors and guides.

Sun Protection: The Egyptian sun can be intense, so always use a high-SPF sunscreen, wear a hat and sunglasses, and stay hydrated. Consider bringing reef-safe sunscreen to protect the marine environment.

Equipment and Rentals:

Quality Gear: Ensure that you rent equipment from reputable operators who maintain their gear to high safety standards. If you're diving or snorkeling, check that the equipment is well-fitted and in good condition.

Personal Gear: If you have your own snorkeling gear, it's a good idea to bring it along for comfort and familiarity. Some travelers also bring their own wetsuits, especially if visiting during the cooler months.

Environmental Responsibility:

Respect the Reef: When diving or snorkeling, avoid touching the coral or disturbing marine life. The reefs are delicate ecosystems that can be easily damaged.

Sustainable Tourism: Choose eco-friendly operators and be mindful of your environmental impact. Reduce plastic use, avoid littering, and follow any local guidelines aimed at preserving the natural beauty of Egypt's beaches and waters.

Hiking and Trekking

Egypt, known primarily for its ancient monuments and vast deserts, also offers some of the most remarkable hiking and trekking experiences in the Middle East. From the rugged mountains of the Sinai Peninsula to the lush oases of the Western Desert, Egypt's diverse landscapes provide ample opportunities for adventure seekers. Here's an extensive guide to hiking and trekking in Egypt:

1. Top Hiking and Trekking Destinations

Mount Sinai (Gebel Musa):

Religious Significance: Mount Sinai is perhaps the most famous trekking destination in Egypt, known for its religious significance to Christians, Jews, and Muslims. According to tradition, this is where Moses received the Ten Commandments.

The Trail: The trek to the summit, which stands at 2,285 meters, is a popular pilgrimage. The two main routes are the Camel Path (Siket Sayidna Musa), a gentler but longer route, and the Steps of Repentance (Siket Sayidna Musa), a steeper and more challenging ascent via 3,750 stone steps.

Sunrise and Sunset Treks: Many hikers choose to climb at night to reach the summit by sunrise, enjoying the breathtaking views as the sun rises over the surrounding mountains. Sunset treks are also popular, offering equally stunning views.

The White Desert:

Unique Landscapes: Located in the Farafra Oasis in the Western Desert, the White Desert is known for its surreal landscapes of chalk rock formations that have been shaped by wind erosion over millennia. These formations, resembling giant mushrooms, icebergs, and other shapes, create a mesmerizing environment for trekking.

Camping and Hiking: Treks in the White Desert often involve camping under the stars, providing a unique experience of the desert's silence and beauty. Day hikes explore the main formations and the surrounding dunes.

The Black Desert:

Volcanic Terrain: Also located near Bahariya Oasis, the Black Desert is characterized by its volcanic hills and black-topped mountains. The landscape is dotted with black volcanic stones, creating a stark contrast to the white sands of the nearby White Desert.

Day Treks: Short hikes allow visitors to explore the hills and take in the panoramic views of this unique landscape. Some tours combine visits to both the White and Black Deserts.

St. Catherine's Monastery and Surrounding Peaks:

Historical and Spiritual Trekking: Located at the base of Mount Sinai, St. Catherine's Monastery is one of the oldest working monasteries in the world. Treks in this area often start or end at the monastery, providing a blend of historical and spiritual exploration.

Surrounding Peaks: In addition to Mount Sinai, there are other peaks in the region worth exploring, such as Gebel Katherina (Egypt's highest peak at 2,629 meters) and Gebel Abbas Basha. These treks offer more challenging routes with fewer crowds and equally stunning views.

The Coloured Canyon:

Natural Wonder: Located near Nuweiba in the Sinai Peninsula, the Coloured Canyon is famous for its narrow, winding passages and the vibrant colors of its rock walls, which range from deep reds and purples to yellows and oranges.

Moderate Trek: The trek through the Coloured Canyon is of moderate difficulty, involving some scrambling over rocks. The route is relatively short, making it accessible for most hikers while offering a visually stunning experience.

Wadi Degla:

Urban Escape: Situated near Cairo, Wadi Degla Protectorate is a popular spot for those looking to escape the city and enjoy a day hike. The wadi, or valley, offers a stark, rocky landscape with some interesting geological features.

Easy to Moderate Hikes: The trails in Wadi Degla are relatively easy, making them suitable for beginners or families. It's a great spot for a quick hike or a picnic.

2. Practical Tips for Hiking and Trekking in Egypt

Best Time to Hike:

The Ultimate Egypt Travel Guide 2025 Edition

Ideal Seasons: The best time for hiking in Egypt is during the cooler months, from October to April. During this period, temperatures are mild, making outdoor activities more enjoyable. Summers can be extremely hot, particularly in desert areas.

Timing Your Trek: For sunrise or sunset treks, plan your start time carefully to ensure you reach key vantage points at the right time. Night treks are common on Mount Sinai to avoid the daytime heat and to catch the sunrise.

Safety Considerations:

Guided Tours: For most desert treks, particularly in remote areas like the White Desert or Sinai, it's advisable to go with an experienced guide. They can navigate the terrain, ensure your safety, and provide insights into the local environment.

Hydration: The desert environment is very dry, so carrying enough water is essential. Hydrate frequently, even if you don't feel thirsty. Electrolyte drinks can also help maintain hydration levels.

Equipment and Gear:

Footwear: Wear sturdy, comfortable hiking boots with good ankle support. The terrain can be rocky and uneven, so proper footwear is crucial.

Clothing: Dress in layers, as temperatures can vary significantly between day and night, especially in the desert. Lightweight, moisture-wicking fabrics are ideal for daytime, while warmer layers are needed for nighttime.

Sun Protection: Use a high-SPF sunscreen, wear a wide-brimmed hat, and sunglasses to protect against the intense sun. Consider bringing a scarf or bandana to cover your face from dust and sand.

Backpack Essentials: Carry a small daypack with essentials such as water, snacks, a first-aid kit, a flashlight or headlamp (for early morning or evening hikes), a map or GPS device, and a camera.

Cultural Respect:

Local Customs: When trekking near villages or religious sites, dress modestly out of respect for local customs. Be mindful of your behavior, particularly in culturally significant areas.

Leave No Trace: Practice responsible trekking by leaving no trace. Pack out all your trash, avoid disturbing wildlife, and stick to marked trails to preserve the natural environment.

Camping:

Overnight Treks: If your trek includes camping, ensure you have the right gear, including a tent, sleeping bag, and cooking supplies. Many guided tours provide camping equipment, but it's important to confirm this in advance.

Stargazing: The clear desert skies offer incredible stargazing opportunities. Bring a star chart or a stargazing app to make the most of the experience.

Permits and Regulations:

Protected Areas: Some trekking areas, such as the St. Catherine region, require permits or have specific regulations. Always check in advance and obtain any necessary permissions.

Guided Requirements: In certain areas, particularly near borders or in protected zones, hiring a local guide might be mandatory. They can help with navigation and ensure you follow local regulations.

3. Unique Trekking Experiences

Desert Expeditions:

Extended Treks: For the more adventurous, consider multi-day desert expeditions that explore deeper into Egypt's vast desert regions. These treks might involve camel support for carrying supplies, with nights spent under the stars in traditional Bedouin camps.

Cultural Immersion: These longer treks often provide opportunities to interact with local Bedouin communities, learning about their way of life, traditional knowledge, and survival skills in the desert environment.

Historical Routes:

Pilgrimage Trails: Some treks in Egypt follow ancient pilgrimage routes, providing a unique blend of physical challenge and spiritual reflection. These routes often connect significant religious sites, offering a deeper understanding of the region's history and culture.

Trekking for Conservation:

Eco-Treks: Participate in eco-trekking experiences that focus on conservation and sustainable tourism. These treks often involve education on local ecosystems and efforts to preserve Egypt's natural heritage.

Historical and Archaeological Exploration

Egypt, often referred to as the "Cradle of Civilization," is a treasure trove of historical and archaeological wonders that span thousands of years. From the iconic pyramids to lesser-known ancient temples and tombs, Egypt offers an unparalleled journey through time. Here's an in-depth guide to exploring the historical and archaeological sites of this fascinating country.

1. Iconic Sites

The Pyramids of Giza:

Overview: The Pyramids of Giza, located on the outskirts of Cairo, are the most recognizable symbols of ancient Egypt. The complex includes three main pyramids—those of Khufu (Cheops), Khafre (Chephren), and Menkaure—as well as the Great Sphinx.

Khufu's Pyramid (Great Pyramid): The largest of the three, Khufu's Pyramid, is one of the Seven Wonders of the Ancient World and the only one still in existence. Visitors can enter the pyramid's interior, though the passageways are narrow and not recommended for those with claustrophobia.

The Great Sphinx: Adjacent to the pyramids, the Great Sphinx is a massive limestone statue with the body of a lion and the head of a pharaoh, believed to represent King Khafre.

The Valley of the Kings:

Location: Situated near Luxor, the Valley of the Kings is a royal burial ground for pharaohs of the New Kingdom (1550-1070 BCE).

Famous Tombs: Among the 60-plus tombs, the most famous is that of Tutankhamun, discovered by Howard Carter in 1922. The tomb is renowned for its riches and the well-preserved state of the artifacts found within.

Tomb Architecture: The tombs are carved deep into the limestone mountains and are decorated with intricate paintings that depict scenes from the afterlife, according to ancient Egyptian beliefs.

Karnak Temple Complex:

Overview: Located in Luxor, the Karnak Temple Complex is one of the largest religious structures ever built. It served as the principal place of worship for the god Amun-Ra.

Notable Features: The complex is famous for its Hypostyle Hall, a vast room filled with towering columns, some of which are over 20 meters tall. The Avenue of Sphinxes, which once connected Karnak to Luxor Temple, is another highlight.

Sacred Lake: The complex also features a sacred lake, which was used by priests for purification rituals.

Abu Simbel Temples:

Location: These temples are located near the southern border of Egypt with Sudan, along the banks of Lake Nasser.

Ramses II: The two temples at Abu Simbel were built by Pharaoh Ramses II in the 13th century BCE. The larger temple is dedicated to Ramses himself, while the smaller one is dedicated to his queen, Nefertari.

Relocation: The temples were relocated in the 1960s to avoid being submerged by the waters of Lake Nasser, following the construction of the Aswan High Dam. This was one of the most remarkable feats of archaeological engineering.

2. Lesser-Known Gems

Saqqara:

Step Pyramid of Djoser: Located just south of Cairo, Saqqara is home to the Step Pyramid of Djoser, the earliest colossal stone building in Egypt and the precursor to the more familiar pyramids of Giza.

Mastaba Tombs: The site also features a number of mastaba tombs, which are flat-roofed, rectangular structures that served as burial places for early Egyptian nobility.

The Temple of Hatshepsut:

Location: This mortuary temple is located at Deir el-Bahari, near the Valley of the Kings.

Architectural Marvel: Built into the cliffs of the Theban Mountains, the Temple of Hatshepsut is known for its unique terraced design and its alignment with the winter solstice.

Queen Hatshepsut: The temple honors Hatshepsut, one of Egypt's few female pharaohs, and is decorated with scenes depicting her divine birth and trade expeditions to the land of Punt.

The Temple of Philae:

Location: Situated on Agilkia Island near Aswan, the Temple of Philae is dedicated to the goddess Isis.

Rescue from Submersion: Like Abu Simbel, the temple was relocated to avoid submersion due to the construction of the Aswan High Dam.

Sound and Light Show: The temple is particularly famous for its evening sound and light show, which tells the story of Isis and Osiris through dramatic illuminations and narration.

The Tombs of the Nobles:

Location: Found in several locations across Egypt, including Luxor and Aswan, these tombs belong to high-ranking officials and nobles of ancient Egypt.

Detailed Paintings: Unlike the tombs of the pharaohs, the Tombs of the Nobles often contain more intimate and detailed scenes of daily life, giving insights into the lives, occupations, and beliefs of ancient Egyptians.

3. Archaeological Exploration Tips

Engaging with Local Guides:

Expert Insights: Hiring a knowledgeable local guide can greatly enhance your experience. Guides can provide detailed explanations of the sites, the history behind them, and the significance of various symbols and structures.

Language: While many guides speak English, it's beneficial to confirm their language skills in advance to ensure clear communication.

Photography Guidelines:

Permits: Some sites require a photography permit, especially if you wish to take photos inside tombs or temples. Always check the regulations beforehand.

Respect for the Sites: Flash photography is generally prohibited in areas with delicate wall paintings, as it can cause long-term damage. Use a high ISO setting and stabilize your camera to capture images in low light.

Best Times to Visit:

Early Morning or Late Afternoon: To avoid the crowds and the intense midday heat, it's best to visit popular sites like the Pyramids of Giza, Karnak, or the Valley of the Kings early in the morning or late in the afternoon.

Seasonal Considerations: The cooler months from October to April are ideal for exploring Egypt's archaeological sites. During this period, temperatures are more comfortable, especially in the desert regions.

Respecting Cultural Norms:

Modest Dress: When visiting religious sites, it's important to dress modestly out of respect for local customs. This typically means covering shoulders and knees.

Behavioral Etiquette: While exploring these ancient sites, always be respectful of the environment. Avoid touching or climbing on the monuments, as they are fragile and irreplaceable.

Exploration Beyond the Crowds:

Less-Visited Sites: While major sites like Giza and Luxor attract large numbers of tourists, consider visiting lesser-known locations like Abydos or Dendera for a more tranquil experience.

Day Trips: Many of Egypt's archaeological sites are accessible via day trips from major cities. Plan your itinerary to include some of these excursions for a more comprehensive exploration of the country's ancient history.

4. The Role of Archaeological Discoveries

Ongoing Excavations:

New Finds: Egypt continues to be a focal point for archaeological research, with new discoveries being made regularly. These finds often shed new light on ancient practices, beliefs, and daily life.

Public Engagement: Some sites, like the excavation at the Serapeum in Saqqara or the tomb of Seti I in the Valley of the Kings, have seen recent restorations and are now open to the public, offering fresh insights and experiences.

Museums and Exhibitions:

Egyptian Museum (Cairo): Located in Cairo, the Egyptian Museum houses an extensive collection of artifacts, including the treasures of Tutankhamun. A visit here is essential for understanding the broader context of Egypt's ancient history.

Grand Egyptian Museum (Giza): Expected to open soon, the Grand Egyptian Museum will be the largest archaeological museum in the world, featuring an unprecedented array of ancient Egyptian artifacts, many of which will be on public display for the first time.

Luxor Museum: This smaller museum offers a well-curated collection of artifacts from the Luxor region, including some items from the tomb of Tutankhamun and the royal cachette found at Deir el-Bahari.

5. Planning Your Archaeological Exploration

Itinerary Considerations:

Multi-Day Passes: For sites in the Luxor region, consider purchasing a multi-day pass that allows access to several sites, including the Valley of the Kings, the Karnak and Luxor Temples, and the Valley of the Queens.

Guided Tours: Many tour companies offer specialized archaeological tours that include expert guides, transportation, and sometimes exclusive access to restricted sites.

Accommodation Near Sites:

Luxor and Aswan: Both cities offer a range of accommodations from luxury hotels to budget-friendly options. Staying near the archaeological sites allows for early starts and less travel time.

Cairo: For exploring the Pyramids of Giza and nearby sites, staying in the Giza district or central Cairo provides easy access.

Wildlife and Nature

While Egypt is often celebrated for its ancient monuments and bustling cities, it also offers rich and diverse natural environments. From the vibrant ecosystems of the Nile River to the unique desert landscapes and marine life of the Red Sea, Egypt is home to an array of wildlife and natural wonders. This guide will take you through some of the best places to experience Egypt's wildlife and natural beauty.

1. Protected Areas and National Parks

Ras Mohammed National Park:

Location: Situated at the southern tip of the Sinai Peninsula, near the city of Sharm El Sheikh, Ras Mohammed is Egypt's first and most famous national park.

Marine Biodiversity: The park is renowned for its vibrant coral reefs, which are among the best-preserved in the world. The waters teem with marine life, including over 1,000 species of fish, sea turtles, dolphins, and sometimes even whale sharks.

Terrestrial Wildlife: On land, the park features mangroves, salt marshes, and a variety of desert flora. Wildlife such as foxes, gazelles, and numerous bird species can also be spotted.

Wadi El Gemal National Park:

Location: Situated on the Red Sea coast, south of Marsa Alam, Wadi El Gemal (Valley of the Camels) is a vast area that combines marine and desert ecosystems.

Marine Life: The coastal area is known for its rich marine biodiversity, including coral reefs, sea turtles, and the elusive dugong, a marine mammal similar to the manatee.

Desert Wildlife: The park's inland areas are home to Bedouin communities and a range of desert animals, such as Nubian ibex, hyrax, and various bird species, including the Egyptian vulture.

White Desert National Park:

Location: Located in the Farafra Oasis in the Western Desert, the White Desert is famous for its otherworldly landscapes of chalk rock formations.

Unique Geology: The white chalk formations, sculpted by wind and sand over millennia, resemble abstract sculptures and create a surreal, lunar-like landscape.

Desert Flora and Fauna: The park is home to desert-adapted wildlife, including fennec foxes, desert hares, and various reptiles. The flora is sparse but includes hardy shrubs and acacias.

Gebel Elba National Park:

Location: This remote and relatively unknown park is located in Egypt's southeast corner, near the border with Sudan.

Biodiversity Hotspot: Gebel Elba is a biodiversity hotspot, featuring a mix of desert, savannah, and mountainous ecosystems. It is home to unique species like the African wild ass, Barbary sheep, and a variety of endemic plants.

Birdwatching: The park is a prime location for birdwatchers, with many migratory species passing through, as well as resident species like the Lappet-faced vulture and the Verreaux's eagle.

Lake Nasser:

Location: Created by the construction of the Aswan High Dam, Lake Nasser is one of the largest artificial lakes in the world, stretching into both Egypt and Sudan.

Fish and Birdlife: The lake is rich in fish species, making it a popular spot for fishing. Birdwatchers can also find a variety of species, especially in the southern reaches of the lake, where migratory birds stop to rest.

Crocodiles and Reptiles: Lake Nasser is one of the few places in Egypt where Nile crocodiles can still be found in significant numbers.

2. Marine Life and Coral Reefs

The Red Sea:

World-Class Diving: The Red Sea is one of the world's premier destinations for scuba diving and snorkeling, offering crystal-clear waters, vibrant coral reefs, and an abundance of marine life.

Notable Diving Spots: Popular diving spots include the Blue Hole in Dahab, the Thistlegorm wreck near Sharm El Sheikh, and the reefs around the Brother Islands.

Marine Species: Divers and snorkelers can expect to see a wide variety of marine life, including parrotfish, lionfish, moray eels, rays, and various species of sharks. The reefs are also home to colorful corals and sponges, providing a stunning underwater landscape.

Dolphin and Whale Watching:

Dolphin Spots: Areas like Marsa Alam and the Dolphin House Reef (Sha'ab Samadai) are known for their resident populations of spinner dolphins, which can often be seen in large pods.

Seasonal Sightings: While dolphins can be seen year-round, certain times of the year offer better chances of spotting other marine mammals, such as whales and whale sharks.

3. Desert Wildlife

Western Desert Oases:

Oasis Ecosystems: The oases of the Western Desert, such as Siwa, Bahariya, and Farafra, are pockets of life in an otherwise arid environment. These areas support a variety of plants, including date palms, olive trees, and other crops cultivated by local communities.

Desert Fauna: The desert surrounding the oases is home to wildlife such as the fennec fox, desert hedgehogs, and various lizards. Bird species like sandgrouse and larks are also common.

Sinai Desert:

Mountainous Terrain: The Sinai Peninsula features a diverse landscape of mountains, wadis (valleys), and desert plains. This area is home to unique wildlife, including the Sinai leopard (now critically endangered), Nubian ibex, and the desert fox.

Bedouin Culture: The indigenous Bedouin tribes of Sinai have lived in harmony with the desert for centuries. Their knowledge of the land, plants, and animals is invaluable for understanding the desert ecosystem.

4. Birdwatching in Egypt

Migratory Birds:

Flyway Location: Egypt is situated on one of the world's major bird migration routes, making it an excellent destination for birdwatching. During the spring and autumn migration seasons, millions of birds pass through Egypt.

Wetland Reserves: Areas like the Nile Delta, Lake Qarun, and the Wadi El Rayan Protected Area are prime spots for observing migratory waterbirds, such as pelicans, flamingos, and various species of herons and egrets.

Resident Bird Species:

Desert Birds: The deserts of Egypt are home to several resident bird species adapted to arid conditions, including the sand partridge, the greater hoopoe lark, and the brown-necked raven.

Nile River Birds: The banks of the Nile River support a variety of birdlife, including kingfishers, hoopoes, and bee-eaters. The river is also a habitat for waterfowl such as geese, ducks, and herons.

5. Conservation Efforts

Environmental Challenges:

Threats to Biodiversity: Egypt's wildlife and natural habitats face challenges from habitat loss, climate change, pollution, and human encroachment.

Overfishing, coral reef degradation, and the illegal wildlife trade are also significant concerns.

Conservation Initiatives: Both governmental and non-governmental organizations are working to protect Egypt's natural heritage. Conservation efforts include the establishment of protected areas, habitat restoration projects, and public awareness campaigns.

Sustainable Tourism:

Eco-Tourism: Sustainable tourism practices are encouraged in Egypt to minimize the environmental impact of tourism on fragile ecosystems. Eco-lodges, responsible diving practices, and community-based tourism initiatives are some examples of how visitors can contribute to conservation.

Responsible Wildlife Viewing: Tourists are encouraged to observe wildlife respectfully, keeping a safe distance and not disturbing the animals. This helps ensure that wildlife habitats remain undisturbed and that animals do not become habituated to human presence.

6. Practical Tips for Wildlife and Nature Exploration

Guided Tours:

Expert Knowledge: Joining a guided tour with an experienced naturalist or local guide can greatly enhance your understanding of Egypt's wildlife and natural environments. Guides can help spot wildlife that you might otherwise miss and provide insights into the behavior and ecology of different species.

Safety Considerations: When exploring desert or marine environments, it's important to follow safety guidelines, such as staying hydrated, using sun protection, and ensuring you have the proper equipment for activities like diving or trekking.

Best Times to Visit:

Seasonal Variations: The best time for wildlife and nature exploration in Egypt generally aligns with the cooler months, from October to April. This period is ideal for desert excursions, birdwatching, and marine activities, as temperatures are more comfortable and wildlife is more active.

Respecting the Environment:

Leave No Trace: Practice responsible tourism by leaving no trace of your visit. Avoid littering, stay on designated paths, and refrain from touching or disturbing plants and animals.

Support Conservation: Consider supporting local conservation efforts, whether by donating to conservation projects, participating in eco-friendly tours, or choosing accommodations that prioritize sustainability.

Cycling and Biking

Exploring Egypt by bicycle offers a unique and immersive way to experience the country's diverse landscapes, from bustling cities to serene deserts and coastal roads. Cycling allows travelers to connect more closely with the environment, enjoy a slower pace of travel, and visit places that are often inaccessible by car. Whether you're a casual rider or an avid cyclist, Egypt has a variety of routes and experiences to offer.

1. Urban Cycling: Exploring Cities by Bike

Cairo:

Challenges: Cycling in Cairo can be challenging due to heavy traffic, chaotic driving habits, and limited cycling infrastructure. However, there are opportunities for urban cycling in quieter neighborhoods or during off-peak hours.

Key Areas: Zamalek Island is one of the more cyclist-friendly areas in Cairo, with its tree-lined streets and relatively low traffic. The area around the Nile Corniche also offers scenic views, especially during early mornings or late afternoons.

Cairo Critical Mass: This is a monthly event where cyclists gather to ride through the streets of Cairo, promoting cycling as a mode of transportation and raising awareness about cyclist safety.

Alexandria:

Seaside Rides: Alexandria offers more relaxed cycling opportunities, especially along the Corniche, the city's coastal road that stretches along the Mediterranean Sea. The relatively flat terrain and scenic views make it a pleasant ride.

Historical Exploration: Cycling through Alexandria allows you to explore its rich history, from the ancient Library of Alexandria to the modern Bibliotheca Alexandrina, as well as the city's various historical districts.

Luxor:

Cycling Amongst Temples: Luxor is a fantastic city for cycling, particularly because many of its major attractions, such as the Karnak Temple and the Valley of the Kings, are relatively close to each other. Cycling between these sites offers a leisurely and convenient way to explore the city's ancient history.

Nile-side Rides: Cycling along the Nile in Luxor provides stunning views of the river and surrounding countryside. Early morning or late afternoon rides are particularly enjoyable, with cooler temperatures and softer light.

2. Desert Biking: An Adventure in the Sands

Sinai Peninsula:

Mountainous Terrain: The rugged terrain of the Sinai Peninsula offers challenging and rewarding cycling routes. The mountains, valleys, and wadis (dry riverbeds) create a stunning backdrop for any cycling adventure.

Popular Routes: One of the most popular routes is from St. Catherine's Monastery to Dahab, which combines a mix of road and off-road cycling. The route offers dramatic views of the desert and mountains, passing through Bedouin villages and historic sites.

Safety Tips: Due to the harsh conditions and remote locations, it's advisable to cycle in a group and with a guide who is familiar with the terrain. Adequate preparation, including sufficient water, food supplies, and appropriate gear, is essential.

Western Desert Oases:

Oasis Routes: Cycling through the Western Desert's oases, such as Siwa, Bahariya, and Farafra, offers a unique experience of riding through verdant islands in a sea of sand. These oases are connected by long stretches of desert roads, making for an epic cycling journey.

Siwa Oasis: Siwa, in particular, is a popular destination for cyclists. The flat terrain, coupled with the oasis's palm groves, salt lakes, and ancient ruins, provides a fascinating landscape to explore by bike. Cycling is one of the main modes of transport in Siwa, and many locals and visitors use bikes to get around.

Crossing the Desert: For more adventurous cyclists, there are routes that traverse the Western Desert between the oases. These routes are challenging due to the extreme heat, long distances, and lack of facilities, so proper planning and experience are crucial.

3. Coastal Cycling: Along the Red Sea

Red Sea Coast:

Scenic Routes: The Red Sea coast offers some of the most scenic cycling routes in Egypt. The coastal road from Hurghada to Marsa Alam is particularly popular, with its stunning views of the Red Sea on one side and the rugged mountains of the Eastern Desert on the other.

Diving and Cycling: Combining cycling with diving or snorkeling is a great way to experience the Red Sea. Many resorts along the coast offer bike rentals, allowing you to explore the area at your own pace and discover secluded beaches and coves.

Best Time to Cycle: The best time for cycling along the Red Sea is during the cooler months, from October to April, when temperatures are more manageable, especially if you plan to cycle long distances.

4. Practical Tips for Cycling in Egypt

Choosing the Right Bike:

Type of Bike: Depending on your route, you may need a road bike for smoother city and coastal rides or a mountain bike for rougher terrain, especially in the desert and mountainous areas.

Renting vs. Bringing Your Own: While it is possible to rent bikes in major cities and tourist areas, serious cyclists may prefer to bring their own bike to ensure they have the right equipment. If renting, make sure to inspect the bike thoroughly and ensure it's suitable for the type of terrain you'll be covering.

Safety Considerations:

Traffic Awareness: In urban areas, be mindful of the traffic, which can be unpredictable. Wearing a helmet is essential, and using lights or reflective gear at night is highly recommended.

Hydration and Nutrition: Egypt's hot climate means that staying hydrated is crucial, especially when cycling in the desert. Carry enough water and snacks to sustain you during your ride, as facilities can be sparse, especially in remote areas.

Navigation: GPS devices or maps are essential for desert and long-distance rides, as signposts may be scarce, and it's easy to get lost in the expansive landscapes.

Local Customs and Etiquette:

Respect Local Culture: In more conservative areas, such as rural villages and small towns, dress modestly, and be respectful of local customs. This includes avoiding cycling through sensitive areas or during religious events without prior knowledge.

Interacting with Locals: Egyptians are generally very welcoming, and cyclists often receive friendly greetings from locals. It's common for people, especially in rural areas, to offer help or even invite you for tea or a meal.

Cycling Events and Tours:

Organized Tours: Several companies offer guided cycling tours in Egypt, ranging from city tours to multi-day desert adventures. These tours often provide bikes, support vehicles, and guides, making it easier to explore challenging routes.

Cycling Events: Egypt hosts a few cycling events and races throughout the year, such as the "Tour d'Egypte" and various local bike marathons, which attract both local and international participants.

5. Environmental Impact and Responsible Cycling

Eco-Friendly Travel:

Sustainable Tourism: Cycling is one of the most environmentally friendly ways to explore Egypt. By choosing to cycle, you reduce your carbon footprint and contribute to sustainable tourism practices.

Respect Nature: Whether cycling through urban areas, deserts, or along the coast, always respect the environment. Avoid littering, stick to designated paths, and be mindful of the natural surroundings.

Supporting Local Communities:

Local Economy: Cycling allows you to connect more directly with local communities. Support small businesses by staying in locally-owned accommodations, eating at local restaurants, and purchasing souvenirs from local artisans.

Chapter 8: Shopping in Egypt

Traditional Markets and Souks

Historical Significance

Ancient Trade Hubs: Egypt has been a center of trade for thousands of years, with markets and souks forming the backbone of its economy. Historically, these markets were the places where traders from Africa, the Middle East, and Asia exchanged goods, contributing to Egypt's wealth and cultural diversity.

Preservation of Tradition: Many of Egypt's traditional markets have been in existence for centuries, such as the famous Khan El Khalili bazaar in Cairo, established in the 14th century. These markets have preserved traditional methods of commerce, including haggling and bartering, which are still practiced today.

Variety of Goods

Handicrafts and Souvenirs: Traditional markets in Egypt are renowned for their array of handmade goods, including intricately woven carpets, brassware, jewelry, and leather products. These items often reflect Egypt's rich cultural heritage, with designs and techniques passed down through generations.

Spices and Perfumes: Egyptian markets are also famous for their spices, herbs, and perfumes. Vendors offer a sensory experience, with stalls brimming with colorful spices and aromatic oils. Many tourists and locals alike visit these souks to buy traditional Egyptian fragrances, such as musk and jasmine.

Textiles and Clothing: Cotton, a significant Egyptian product, is often sold in traditional markets. From fine cotton sheets to intricately embroidered galabiyas (traditional robes), the textile offerings in Egyptian souks are diverse and of high quality.

Cultural Experience

Social Interaction: Shopping in Egyptian souks is not just a commercial activity; it is a social experience. Vendors often engage in lengthy conversations with customers, offering tea or coffee as they discuss the quality and price of goods. This interaction is a key aspect of Egyptian hospitality.

Haggling as an Art: Haggling is a common practice in these markets and is considered an art form. The process of negotiating the price is often light-hearted and playful, with both the buyer and seller enjoying the interaction. For many, this is an essential part of the shopping experience in Egypt.

Architecture and Atmosphere: The architecture of traditional souks adds to their charm. Narrow alleyways, arched entrances, and the hustle and bustle of people contribute to a unique atmosphere that transports visitors back in time.

Key Markets and Souks

Khan El Khalili (Cairo): Perhaps the most famous souk in Egypt, Khan El Khalili is a labyrinth of narrow streets filled with shops selling everything from jewelry to antiques. It is a must-visit for anyone interested in traditional Egyptian crafts and souvenirs.

Aswan Souk (Aswan): Known for its Nubian influence, the Aswan Souk offers a variety of goods, including Nubian handicrafts, spices, and traditional clothing. It is less hectic than Cairo's markets but equally rich in culture.

Luxor Market (Luxor): Located near some of Egypt's most famous ancient sites, the Luxor Market offers a mix of goods, including alabaster carvings, papyrus, and pharaonic-themed souvenirs.

Challenges and Modernization

Modern Competition: Traditional markets in Egypt face competition from modern shopping malls and online retailers. However, they continue to thrive due to their cultural significance and the unique experience they offer.

Preservation Efforts: There are ongoing efforts to preserve these traditional markets, ensuring that they remain a vital part of Egypt's cultural heritage. This includes initiatives to maintain the traditional craftsmanship that is at the heart of these markets.

These traditional markets and souks in Egypt offer a shopping experience rich in culture, history, and social interaction, making them an essential part of any visit to the country.

Modern Shopping Malls

Introduction to Modern Shopping Malls

Over the past few decades, Egypt has seen a significant rise in the development of modern shopping malls, particularly in major cities like Cairo, Alexandria, and Giza. These malls offer a stark contrast to traditional markets and souks, providing a more contemporary shopping experience that caters to a wide range of consumer needs and preferences.

Variety of Retail Options

International Brands: Modern shopping malls in Egypt house a variety of international brands, making them a go-to destination for consumers looking for global fashion, electronics, and lifestyle products. Brands such as Zara, H&M, Apple, and Nike have prominent outlets in these malls.

Local Retailers: In addition to international names, many malls also feature stores from local retailers, offering Egyptian-made goods ranging from fashion to home décor. This blend of local and international options provides a diverse shopping experience.

Luxury Shopping: Some of Egypt's modern malls, like Cairo Festival City Mall and Mall of Egypt, include sections dedicated to luxury shopping, with high-end brands like Gucci, Louis Vuitton, and Rolex attracting affluent consumers.

Entertainment and Leisure

Cinemas and Theaters: Most modern shopping malls in Egypt are equipped with state-of-the-art cinemas, offering the latest movies, including international blockbusters and local films. Some malls also feature theaters for live performances and events.

Family Entertainment: Malls often include family-friendly entertainment options, such as indoor amusement parks, arcades, and children's play areas. For example, Mall of Egypt is home to Ski Egypt, Africa's first indoor ski resort, offering a unique leisure experience.

Dining Options: Food courts in modern malls offer a wide array of dining choices, from fast food to fine dining. International chains like McDonald's, Starbucks, and KFC sit alongside popular local eateries, providing options for every taste and budget.

Convenience and Accessibility

Location and Accessibility: Modern malls are strategically located in key urban areas, often near residential neighborhoods, making them easily accessible for both locals and tourists. They are typically well-connected by public transportation and offer ample parking facilities.

One-Stop Shopping Experience: The convenience of finding everything under one roof is a major draw for shoppers. Malls often include supermarkets, pharmacies, electronics stores, fashion outlets, and service centers, allowing visitors to complete multiple tasks in a single visit.

Specialized Services: Many malls offer specialized services such as beauty salons, fitness centers, and banking facilities, making them a hub for various lifestyle needs.

Architectural Design and Ambience

Modern Architecture: The architectural design of these malls is often a blend of modern aesthetics with functional spaces. They are designed to provide a comfortable and visually appealing environment, with spacious walkways, ample natural light, and contemporary décor.

Seasonal Decorations: During holidays and festivals, malls are often elaborately decorated, enhancing the shopping experience and attracting more visitors. Events like Christmas, Ramadan, and Eid see malls adorned with lights, ornaments, and themed displays.

Challenges and Competition

Competition with Traditional Markets: While modern malls offer a different experience, they compete with traditional markets and souks, especially for tourists seeking a cultural shopping experience. However, each caters to different segments of the market.

Economic Fluctuations: Egypt's economy has seen fluctuations that impact consumer spending power. Malls have had to adapt by offering more promotions, discounts, and affordable luxury options to maintain foot traffic.

Sustainability Concerns: As awareness of environmental issues grows, there is increasing pressure on malls to adopt sustainable practices, such as energy-efficient designs and waste reduction programs. Some newer malls are incorporating green spaces and environmentally friendly technologies in their construction and operation.

Notable Shopping Malls in Egypt

Cairo Festival City Mall: Located in New Cairo, this mall is one of the largest in Egypt, featuring over 300 stores, a large food court, and an IKEA store. It also hosts a variety of events and festivals throughout the year.

Mall of Egypt: Situated in 6th of October City, this mall is famous for its entertainment options, including Ski Egypt, a cinema complex, and a family entertainment center. It also has a wide selection of international and local retail outlets.

City Stars Mall: One of the oldest and most iconic malls in Cairo, City Stars offers a mix of shopping, dining, and entertainment, including a multiplex cinema, indoor amusement park, and a wide range of stores.

Modern shopping malls in Egypt have become key destinations for both locals and tourists, offering a comprehensive and convenient shopping experience that combines retail, entertainment, and leisure. These malls represent the evolving landscape of consumer culture in Egypt, balancing modernity with tradition.

Unique Souvenirs

Papyrus Scrolls

Ancient Art Form: Papyrus is one of the most iconic souvenirs from Egypt, as it was the material used by ancient Egyptians for writing. Genuine papyrus is made from the papyrus plant, which grows along the Nile.

Artistic Designs: Modern papyrus scrolls often feature reproductions of ancient Egyptian art, including hieroglyphics, scenes from the Book of the Dead, and depictions of gods and pharaohs. They make for beautiful wall art and a meaningful keepsake.

Cartouche Jewelry

Personalized Jewelry: A cartouche is an oval-shaped hieroglyphic nameplate that was used by pharaohs. Today, you can buy jewelry, such as necklaces and bracelets, with a cartouche that can be personalized with your name or a loved one's name in hieroglyphics.

Material Options: Cartouches are available in a variety of materials, including gold, silver, and copper. This makes them both a unique and customizable souvenir that carries a deep connection to ancient Egyptian culture.

Alabaster Carvings

Handcrafted Art: Alabaster is a soft stone that has been used in Egypt for centuries to create beautiful carvings. In modern times, skilled artisans craft vases, statues, and lamps from alabaster, each with a unique, translucent quality.

Traditional and Modern Designs: You can find alabaster carvings in both traditional Egyptian designs, such as replicas of ancient statues, and more contemporary styles, making them versatile souvenirs for different tastes.

Perfume Oils

Fragrant Tradition: Egypt has a long history of creating perfumes, and you can find a wide range of pure essential oils in local markets and specialized perfume shops. These oils are often sold in beautifully crafted glass bottles, making them both a sensory and visual treat.

Popular Scents: Some of the most popular scents include lotus, jasmine, and musk. Many shops will also allow you to create your own custom blend, offering a truly personalized souvenir.

Khan El Khalili Lanterns

Handmade Lanterns: These colorful metal lanterns, known as "fanoos," are a staple of Egyptian markets, especially in the famous Khan El Khalili bazaar in Cairo. They are typically handcrafted and decorated with intricate patterns.

Cultural Significance: These lanterns are traditionally used during the month of Ramadan but are also popular as decorative items. They come in various sizes and styles, ranging from small tea light holders to large statement pieces.

Nubian Handicrafts

Cultural Artifacts: Nubian crafts, which reflect the rich cultural heritage of the Nubian people from southern Egypt, include colorful textiles, baskets, and pottery. These items are often vibrant and decorated with geometric patterns.

Unique Designs: The bright colors and unique designs make Nubian handicrafts stand out. They are typically available in Aswan and other southern parts of Egypt, offering a distinctive souvenir option.

Egyptian Cotton Products

High-Quality Textiles: Egyptian cotton is renowned worldwide for its exceptional quality. Souvenirs made from this luxurious material include bed linens, towels, and clothing such as galabiyas (traditional robes).

Soft and Durable: These products are prized for their softness, durability, and comfort. Egyptian cotton items are a practical and luxurious souvenir that you can enjoy for years.

Miniature Pyramids and Sphinxes

Iconic Replicas: Miniature replicas of the Pyramids of Giza and the Sphinx are among the most popular souvenirs in Egypt. These items are often made from stone, metal, or resin, and come in various sizes.

Symbolic Value: These replicas serve as a tangible reminder of Egypt's ancient wonders and are perfect for display at home or in the office.

Scarab Beetles

Ancient Symbol: The scarab beetle was a powerful symbol in ancient Egyptian culture, representing rebirth and protection. Today, scarab amulets and jewelry are popular souvenirs.

Variety of Forms: Scarabs can be found in various materials, including stone, metal, and faience (glazed ceramic). They are often used in rings, necklaces, and small decorative items.

Egyptian Spices

Culinary Souvenirs: Egypt's markets are filled with aromatic spices such as cumin, coriander, and saffron. These spices are a great way to bring a taste of Egypt back home.

Herbal Teas: In addition to spices, you can also find traditional herbal teas like hibiscus (karkade), which is a popular drink in Egypt. These are often sold in colorful packaging, making them an attractive gift.

These unique souvenirs not only offer a piece of Egypt to take home but also carry the rich cultural and historical significance of this ancient land. Whether you're looking for something personal, decorative, or practical, Egypt's markets and shops provide a treasure trove of memorable items.

Jewelry and Accessories

Gold Jewelry

Ancient Craftsmanship: Egypt is famous for its gold jewelry, a tradition that dates back to the time of the pharaohs. The ancient Egyptians were master goldsmiths, and this legacy continues today with intricate designs that often draw inspiration from ancient motifs.

Pharaonic Designs: Many gold pieces feature symbols from ancient Egypt, such as the ankh (symbol of life), the Eye of Horus (protection), and depictions of gods and goddesses. These pieces are not only beautiful but also carry deep symbolic meanings.

Quality and Craftsmanship: Egyptian gold jewelry is known for its high quality, often crafted in 18-karat or 21-karat gold. The craftsmanship is detailed, with artisans skilled in creating delicate filigree work, engraving, and inlay.

Silver Jewelry

Affordable Elegance: Silver jewelry is also widely available and is a popular choice for those looking for elegant yet affordable accessories. Egyptian silver often features intricate designs and is sometimes adorned with semi-precious stones.

Bedouin and Nubian Styles: Silver jewelry from Egypt often incorporates traditional Bedouin or Nubian designs, characterized by bold geometric patterns and the use of coins or beads. These styles reflect the rich cultural diversity of Egypt.

Cartouche Jewelry

Personalized Pieces: One of the most popular types of jewelry in Egypt is the cartouche, a pendant or bracelet featuring an oval-shaped nameplate inscribed with hieroglyphics. Tourists can have their names or a loved one's name inscribed in ancient Egyptian script, creating a personalized and meaningful piece.

Materials: Cartouches are typically made from gold, silver, or a combination of both, and can be simple or elaborately decorated. They serve as a unique memento of your visit to Egypt.

Beaded Jewelry

Handcrafted Designs: Beaded jewelry is another popular accessory in Egypt, often made by local artisans. These pieces are crafted using a variety of materials, including glass beads, semi-precious stones, and metals.

Colorful and Vibrant: Beaded necklaces, bracelets, and earrings are often colorful and vibrant, reflecting traditional Egyptian and Nubian designs. They are perfect for adding a touch of Egyptian flair to your wardrobe.

Ethnic Jewelry

Bedouin and Nubian Crafts: Egypt's Bedouin and Nubian communities are known for their distinctive jewelry styles. Bedouin jewelry often features large, bold pieces made of silver, adorned with coins, bells, and colored stones. Nubian jewelry, on the other hand, is known for its colorful beading and intricate designs, often incorporating symbols of fertility and protection.

Handcrafted Authenticity: These pieces are typically handmade, offering a unique and authentic accessory that connects you with Egypt's diverse cultural heritage.

Turquoise and Lapis Lazuli

Semi-Precious Stones: Turquoise and lapis lazuli are two semi-precious stones with deep historical roots in Egypt. These stones were highly prized by the ancient Egyptians and were often used in jewelry and amulets.

Symbolic Meanings: Turquoise symbolizes protection and good fortune, while lapis lazuli was associated with royalty and wisdom. Jewelry featuring these stones is not only beautiful but also carries a rich history and symbolism.

Leather Accessories

Handcrafted Leather Goods: In addition to jewelry, Egypt is known for its high-quality leather products. Handcrafted leather belts, wallets, bags, and sandals are popular items, often made by skilled artisans using traditional methods.

Unique Designs: Many leather accessories feature embossed patterns or are decorated with brass and silver accents, giving them a distinct Egyptian touch.

Kohl Eyeliner

Traditional Beauty Product: Kohl, a traditional eyeliner used in Egypt since ancient times, is still widely used today. It is made from ground minerals and is believed to have protective properties, as well as being a cosmetic product.

Authentic Packaging: When purchased in Egypt, kohl often comes in ornate, traditional containers made of wood or metal, making it a unique and practical souvenir.

Handmade Scarves and Shawls

Textile Art: Scarves and shawls are popular accessories in Egypt, often made from high-quality materials like cotton, silk, or wool. They are usually handwoven or hand-dyed, featuring traditional patterns and vibrant colors.

Versatile and Stylish: These accessories are both stylish and functional, suitable for both casual and formal wear. They make for a versatile souvenir that can be worn year-round.

Brass and Copper Accessories

Decorative and Wearable: Brass and copper are commonly used in Egyptian jewelry and accessories, often shaped into intricate designs that reflect traditional patterns. Items such as bracelets, rings, and cufflinks made from these metals are popular for their warm tones and unique appearance.

Symbolic Motifs: These accessories often feature motifs like the scarab beetle, lotus flower, or ankh, which are iconic symbols in Egyptian culture.

Egypt offers a rich array of jewelry and accessories that blend ancient traditions with modern styles. Whether you're looking for something luxurious, personalized, or culturally significant, you're sure to find the perfect piece to remember your journey.

Food and Spices

Egyptian Spices

Aromatic and Flavorful: Egyptian markets are brimming with a variety of spices that are integral to the country's cuisine. These spices make for perfect souvenirs as they bring the authentic flavors of Egypt to your kitchen.

Popular Spices:

Cumin: A staple in Egyptian cooking, cumin is used in many dishes, including ful medames (fava beans) and koshari. It has a warm, earthy flavor that enhances the taste of stews and soups.

Coriander: Both ground coriander and coriander seeds are widely used in Egyptian cuisine. Coriander adds a citrusy, slightly sweet flavor to dishes and is often used in spice blends.

Sumac: This tangy, lemony spice is made from ground sumac berries. It is often sprinkled over salads, grilled meats, and vegetables, adding a refreshing tartness.

Hibiscus (Karkade): Dried hibiscus flowers are used to make a popular Egyptian drink known as karkade. The flowers have a tart, cranberry-like flavor and can also be used in teas and infusions.

Dukkah: A traditional Egyptian spice blend made from ground nuts (usually hazelnuts), sesame seeds, coriander, cumin, and salt. It is often used as a dip with bread and olive oil or sprinkled over salads and roasted vegetables.

Halawa (Halva)

Sweet Sesame Treat: Halawa, known internationally as halva, is a dense, sweet confection made from ground sesame seeds (tahini) and sugar. It often contains nuts, chocolate, or vanilla for added flavor.

Varieties: Egyptian halawa comes in different forms, including plain, swirled with chocolate, or mixed with pistachios. It's a rich, sweet treat that makes for a delightful souvenir.

Dates and Dried Fruits

Natural Delicacies: Egypt is one of the largest producers of dates in the world, and they are an integral part of the local diet. Egyptian dates are sweet, rich, and often sold in beautifully packaged boxes, making them an ideal gift.

Popular Varieties:

Siwa Dates: Known for their soft texture and intense sweetness, Siwa dates are a favorite in Egypt. They are often enjoyed on their own or stuffed with nuts.

Medjool Dates: Larger and more succulent, Medjool dates are prized for their caramel-like flavor and are considered a delicacy.

Dried Fruits: Other dried fruits such as figs, apricots, and raisins are also popular in Egyptian markets. These fruits are often used in traditional dishes or enjoyed as a healthy snack.

Egyptian Tea and Coffee

Traditional Beverages: Tea and coffee play a significant role in Egyptian culture. Bringing home a packet of Egyptian tea or coffee allows you to savor a part of the daily life in Egypt.

Koshary Tea: A strong, black tea commonly enjoyed throughout Egypt, usually served with a lot of sugar and sometimes with mint. It's perfect for those who appreciate a robust, flavorful tea.

Egyptian Coffee (Ahwa): Egyptian coffee, also known as "ahwa," is similar to Turkish coffee. It is finely ground and brewed strong, often flavored with cardamom. Coffee in Egypt is more than just a drink; it's a social ritual, often enjoyed slowly in the company of friends.

Tahini

Versatile Sesame Paste: Tahini is a creamy paste made from ground sesame seeds and is a key ingredient in many Middle Eastern dishes, including hummus and baba ghanoush. It has a rich, nutty flavor and is also used as a condiment or in desserts like halawa.

High Quality: Egyptian tahini is known for its high quality and smooth texture. A jar of this versatile ingredient makes for a practical and delicious souvenir.

Molokhia

Green Leafy Soup Base: Molokhia is a popular Egyptian dish made from the leaves of the jute plant. The dried leaves are ground into a fine powder and used to make a thick, flavorful soup. This unique ingredient can be difficult to find outside of Egypt, making it a special culinary souvenir.

Traditional Use: The soup is typically served with rice or bread and flavored with garlic and lemon, offering a taste of traditional Egyptian home cooking.

Egyptian Sweets

Baklava: A popular pastry made of layers of filo dough, filled with chopped nuts, and sweetened with honey or syrup. Egyptian baklava often has a touch of rose or orange blossom water, adding a distinct flavor.

Basbousa: A semolina cake soaked in sweet syrup, often garnished with almonds or coconut. It is a moist and sweet dessert that is loved across Egypt.

Konafa: Made with thin strands of dough (like shredded phyllo), konafa is usually filled with cheese, nuts, or cream, and soaked in sugar syrup. It's a delicious, rich dessert with a crisp exterior and soft, sweet filling.

Spice Blends

Foul Medames Spice Mix: This spice blend is specifically used for preparing foul medames, one of Egypt's most popular dishes made from fava beans. The mix typically includes cumin, garlic, lemon, and olive oil, providing the essential flavors for this traditional breakfast dish.

Egyptian Curry Powder: Egyptian-style curry powder is a blend of spices including turmeric, cumin, coriander, and black pepper. It is milder than Indian curry powder but adds a warm, aromatic flavor to stews and rice dishes.

Olive Oil

High-Quality Oil: Olive oil is another staple in Egyptian cuisine, used in cooking and as a dressing. Egyptian olive oil is known for its rich, fruity flavor and is often sold in beautifully crafted bottles.

Culinary and Health Benefits: Beyond its culinary uses, Egyptian olive oil is also valued for its health benefits, making it a thoughtful and useful gift.

These food items and spices from Egypt not only allow you to recreate traditional Egyptian dishes at home but also make for unique and flavorful souvenirs. Whether you're a foodie or just looking to bring back a taste of your travels, these items are sure to remind you of Egypt's rich culinary heritage.

Chapter 9: Dining and Nightlife in Egypt

Traditional Egyptian Cuisine

1. **Koshari**

Koshari is often considered Egypt's national dish and a culinary symbol of the country. It's a hearty, satisfying meal beloved by locals and a must-try for visitors seeking to experience authentic Egyptian cuisine. Koshari combines a variety of textures and flavors in a single dish, reflecting the rich and diverse culinary traditions of Egypt.

Main Ingredients

Rice: The base of the dish, providing a fluffy, neutral foundation.

Lentils: Typically brown or black lentils, adding a protein boost and a hearty texture.

Pasta: Usually small pasta shapes like elbow macaroni, contributing to the dish's filling nature.

Chickpeas: Cooked chickpeas are sprinkled on top for additional protein and a slightly nutty flavor.

Tomato Sauce: A spiced tomato sauce, often flavored with garlic and cumin, adds a tangy and aromatic element.

Crispy Onions: Fried onions are used as a crunchy topping, adding both flavor and texture.

Garlic Vinegar Sauce: A garlic-infused vinegar sauce is drizzled over the dish for an extra layer of tanginess.

Optional Toppings: Some variations might include extra herbs or hot sauce for added flavor.

Where to Try Koshari in Egypt

Local Eateries and Street Food Stalls: For an authentic experience, try Koshari at local eateries or street food stalls where the dish is often made fresh daily. These spots typically serve some of the most flavorful and traditional versions of Koshari.

Famous Koshari Restaurants:

Abou Tarek: Located in Cairo, this restaurant is renowned for its Koshari and has been serving the dish for decades. It's often recommended by locals and travelers alike.

Koshary El Tahrir: Another popular spot in Cairo, known for its consistent quality and traditional preparation of Koshari.

Koshary Cairo: Known for its classic Koshari and a range of other Egyptian dishes, this restaurant is well-regarded for both flavor and service.

Local Souks and Markets: Markets like Khan El Khalili in Cairo have several vendors offering Koshari, allowing you to enjoy the dish while exploring the vibrant market atmosphere.

What Makes Koshari Special?

Flavor Harmony: Koshari is a unique blend of flavors and textures—savory rice and lentils, tangy tomato sauce, crunchy fried onions, and the aromatic garlic vinegar sauce all combine to create a well-balanced and satisfying meal.

Cultural Significance: It's a dish that reflects Egyptian culinary traditions and is often enjoyed during family gatherings and special occasions. Its widespread popularity and affordability make it a staple of Egyptian street food culture.

Nutritional Balance: Koshari provides a balanced mix of carbohydrates, protein, and fiber, making it both filling and nutritious. Its combination of lentils, chickpeas, and rice ensures a hearty and sustaining meal.

Tips for Enjoying Koshari

Customize Your Sauce: Adjust the amount of garlic vinegar sauce and hot sauce (if available) to suit your taste. The sauce is essential for adding a tangy kick to the dish.

Mix Thoroughly: For the best experience, mix all the components together before eating. This allows the flavors to meld and ensures that each bite has a balance of ingredients.

Pair with Refreshments: Koshari can be quite filling, so it pairs well with a refreshing drink such as a chilled mint tea or ayran (a yogurt-based drink).

Try Different Variations: While traditional Koshari is delicious, don't hesitate to explore regional variations or different toppings if available. Some places might offer additional ingredients or slight tweaks to the classic recipe.

Embrace the Experience: Enjoy Koshari in a local setting to fully appreciate its cultural context. Whether you're eating at a street stall or a well-known restaurant, taking in the local atmosphere will enhance your culinary experience.

2. Ful Medames

Ful medames is a traditional Egyptian dish made from fava beans that holds a special place in Egyptian cuisine. It is often considered a staple breakfast food, but it can be enjoyed at any time of the day. Known for its simplicity and hearty nature, ful medames is both nutritious and satisfying, embodying the essence of Egyptian home cooking.

Main Ingredients

Fava Beans: The primary ingredient, these beans are cooked until tender and then seasoned to create a flavorful base.

Garlic: Minced or crushed garlic adds depth of flavor to the dish.

Lemon Juice: Freshly squeezed lemon juice provides a tangy contrast and enhances the overall flavor.

Olive Oil: Adds richness and a smooth texture.

Cumin: A common spice in Egyptian cooking, cumin imparts a warm, earthy flavor.

Salt and Pepper: Basic seasonings to taste.

Optional Toppings:

Chopped Tomatoes: Adds freshness and additional flavor.

Chopped Onions: Provides a crunchy texture and a hint of sharpness.

Parsley: For a fresh and vibrant touch.

Pickles: Often served on the side, pickles add a tangy contrast.

Where to Try Ful Medames in Egypt

Local Breakfast Spots: Ful medames is a popular breakfast dish, so look for local cafes and eateries that serve traditional Egyptian breakfasts. These spots often offer freshly made ful medames with a variety of toppings.

Street Food Stalls: Street vendors frequently sell ful medames, often served in a pita bread or as part of a larger meal. These stalls provide an authentic and casual dining experience.

Famous Restaurants:

El Darb El Ahmar: Located in Cairo, this restaurant is known for its traditional Egyptian dishes, including a well-regarded ful medames.

Abou El Sid: With multiple locations in Cairo, this restaurant is celebrated for its classic Egyptian dishes, including a flavorful ful medames.

Felfela: A popular restaurant in Cairo offering a range of traditional Egyptian dishes, including ful medames, known for its consistent quality and traditional preparation.

What Makes Ful Medames Special?

Historical Significance: Ful medames has ancient roots and is mentioned in various historical texts. It has been a staple of Egyptian cuisine for centuries, reflecting the country's agricultural history and culinary traditions.

Nutritional Value: The dish is rich in protein, fiber, and essential nutrients, making it a healthy and filling option. Fava beans are known for their high nutrient content, including iron, potassium, and vitamins.

Versatility: Ful medames can be customized with various toppings and seasonings, allowing for a range of flavors and presentations. It's versatile enough to be adapted to different tastes and dietary preferences.

Tips for Enjoying Ful Medames

Mix Thoroughly: Before eating, mix the ful medames well with the olive oil, lemon juice, and spices. This ensures that the flavors are well combined and each bite is flavorful.

Add Toppings: Experiment with different toppings to enhance the dish. Fresh chopped tomatoes, onions, parsley, and pickles can add layers of flavor and texture.

Pair with Bread: Ful medames is traditionally served with Egyptian bread, such as baladi bread or pita. The bread is perfect for scooping up the beans and making the meal more filling.

Accompany with Sides: Ful medames is often served with additional sides like eggs, cheese, or salad. These sides can complement the dish and create a more complete meal.

Try Variations: Some regional variations include additional spices or ingredients. Feel free to try different versions to experience the diversity of ful medames preparations.

3. Mahshi

Mahshi is a cherished Egyptian dish consisting of vegetables stuffed with a flavorful mixture of rice, herbs, and sometimes meat. It's a traditional dish often served during special occasions, family gatherings, and celebrations. Mahshi reflects the rich and diverse culinary traditions of Egypt, combining aromatic spices and fresh ingredients to create a comforting and satisfying meal.

Main Ingredients

Vegetables: The most common vegetables used for stuffing in Mahshi include:

Zucchini: Tender and flavorful when cooked.

Bell Peppers: Adds a sweet and crunchy texture.

Eggplants: Absorbs flavors well and becomes tender.

Grape Leaves: Traditionally used for stuffing, offering a unique taste and texture.

Rice: The base of the stuffing mixture, usually combined with various seasonings and herbs.

Ground Meat (optional): Often beef or lamb, mixed with rice and spices for added richness and flavor.

Tomato Paste: Provides a tangy base for the stuffing mixture and enhances the overall flavor.

Herbs and Spices: Includes parsley, dill, mint, cumin, cinnamon, and black pepper, adding aromatic and complex flavors.

Onions: Sauteed to add sweetness and depth to the stuffing mixture.

Tomatoes: Sometimes used in the cooking liquid or as a topping to add flavor and moisture.

Where to Try Mahshi in Egypt

Local Restaurants: Many traditional Egyptian restaurants offer Mahshi on their menu. Look for places known for authentic Egyptian cuisine to enjoy a well-prepared version of the dish.

Family-run Eateries: Smaller, family-owned restaurants or cafes often serve Mahshi, prepared according to traditional recipes and techniques.

Specialty Dishes: Some restaurants and eateries are renowned for their Mahshi. For example:

Abou El Sid: Known for its traditional Egyptian dishes, including Mahshi, served with authenticity and care.

El Darb El Ahmar: Offers a variety of traditional Egyptian dishes, including Mahshi, in a traditional setting.

Felfela: A popular spot in Cairo known for its classic Egyptian fare, including Mahshi.

What Makes Mahshi Special?

Rich Flavor Profile: The combination of seasoned rice, fresh herbs, and optional meat creates a complex and flavorful filling. The vegetables or grape leaves absorb the flavors during cooking, making each bite delicious.

Cultural Significance: Mahshi is a dish often associated with special occasions and family gatherings. Its preparation can be labor-intensive, making it a dish that brings people together and is shared during important meals.

Versatility: Mahshi can be adapted to different tastes and dietary preferences. Variations might include different vegetables, spices, or the inclusion of meat, making it a versatile and customizable dish.

Tips for Enjoying Mahshi

Try Different Fillings: Experiment with various types of vegetables and fillings to discover your favorite combination. Some variations might include additional ingredients like nuts or dried fruits.

Pair with Side Dishes: Mahshi pairs well with traditional Egyptian sides such as salad, yogurt, or a simple cucumber and tomato dish. These sides complement the rich flavors of Mahshi and balance the meal.

Enjoy with Sauces: Some people like to drizzle a bit of yogurt or a tomato-based sauce over their Mahshi for added flavor and creaminess.

Savor the Cooking Liquid: The cooking liquid, often flavored with tomato paste and spices, can be enjoyed as a sauce or broth. It adds an extra layer of flavor to the stuffed vegetables.

Be Patient with Cooking: Mahshi requires a longer cooking time to ensure that the vegetables are tender and the flavors are well-developed. Patience during the cooking process ensures a more flavorful and satisfying dish.

4. Molokhia

Molokhia is a beloved dish in Egyptian cuisine, known for its distinctive flavor and rich history. Made from the leaves of the jute plant, Molokhia is a hearty, green stew that has been a staple in Egyptian households for centuries. It is often served as a comforting main course, especially during colder months or special occasions.

Main Ingredients

Molokhia Leaves: The key ingredient, Molokhia leaves (also known as jute leaves), are finely chopped and used to create the base of the stew. They have a slightly mucilaginous (slimy) texture when cooked, which contributes to the dish's unique consistency.

Garlic: Minced or chopped garlic is sautéed to add depth and flavor to the stew.

Onions: Often sautéed with garlic to create a flavorful base.

Chicken or Beef: Typically used as the main protein in the stew. The meat is cooked separately and then added to the Molokhia, providing additional flavor and richness.

Chicken Broth: The cooking liquid for the Molokhia, adding richness and depth to the stew.

Lemon Juice: Adds a tangy contrast to the savory flavors of the stew.

Spices: Common spices include coriander, cumin, and black pepper. These spices enhance the overall flavor of the dish.

Optional Toppings: Some variations include additional ingredients like toasted pine nuts or fried onions for added texture and flavor.

Where to Try Molokhia in Egypt

Local Restaurants: Many traditional Egyptian restaurants serve Molokhia, often as part of a larger meal. Look for places specializing in Egyptian cuisine for an authentic experience.

Family-Run Eateries: Smaller, family-owned restaurants or cafes are known for serving homemade Molokhia, prepared according to traditional recipes.

Famous Restaurants:

Abou El Sid: Known for its classic Egyptian dishes, including Molokhia, prepared with care and authenticity.

El Darb El Ahmar: Offers a range of traditional Egyptian dishes, including a flavorful Molokhia.

Koshary El Tahrir: Known for its traditional fare, this restaurant often includes Molokhia as part of its menu.

What Makes Molokhia Special?

Unique Texture: The mucilaginous texture of Molokhia is distinctive and sets it apart from other stews. This texture comes from the natural properties of the jute leaves and adds a unique mouthfeel to the dish.

Cultural Significance: Molokhia has deep roots in Egyptian culinary traditions and is often associated with family gatherings and special occasions. It reflects the rich agricultural history of Egypt, where jute plants have been cultivated for centuries.

Nutritional Benefits: Molokhia leaves are highly nutritious, rich in vitamins (such as A, C, and K), minerals, and antioxidants. The dish is both comforting and healthful, offering a range of nutritional benefits.

Tips for Enjoying Molokhia

Pair with Rice or Bread: Molokhia is commonly served with rice or Egyptian bread (baladi bread). The rice or bread complements the stew and helps to soak up the flavorful broth.

Adjust the Consistency: Molokhia can vary in consistency from a thick stew to a more soupy texture. Adjust the amount of broth according to your preference, and be aware that traditional Molokhia is often quite thick.

Try with Lemon: A squeeze of fresh lemon juice enhances the flavor of Molokhia, balancing the richness and adding a tangy contrast.

Enjoy with Sides: Molokhia is often served alongside other traditional Egyptian dishes such as salad, pickles, or yogurt. These sides provide additional flavors and textures to complement the stew.

Savor the Flavor: The depth of flavor in Molokhia comes from the slow cooking process and the combination of spices. Take your time to enjoy the rich, savory taste and the aromatic garlic and spices.

5. Egyptian Pita Bread (Eish Baladi)

Eish Baladi, often referred to as Egyptian pita bread, is a fundamental element of Egyptian cuisine. This traditional flatbread is characterized by its round shape, airy texture, and slightly chewy consistency. Eish Baladi is a versatile bread that accompanies a wide variety of Egyptian dishes, from savory stews and salads to kebabs and dips.

Main Ingredients

Flour: The primary ingredient, typically all-purpose flour or a combination of whole wheat and white flour, which gives the bread its structure.

Water: Hydrates the flour and helps form the dough.

Yeast: Causes the dough to rise, creating the signature airy pockets within the bread.

Salt: Adds flavor to the dough.

Optional Additions: Some recipes might include a bit of sugar or olive oil to enhance flavor and texture.

Where to Try Eish Baladi in Egypt

Local Bakeries: Traditional bakeries throughout Egypt often specialize in Eish Baladi. These bakeries produce freshly baked bread daily, and the aroma of baking bread is a common feature in Egyptian neighborhoods.

Markets and Street Stalls: Street vendors and market stalls often sell Eish Baladi, providing a convenient and authentic option for enjoying this staple bread.

Restaurants: Many Egyptian restaurants serve Eish Baladi as a standard accompaniment to meals. It's commonly found in both casual eateries and more formal dining establishments.

What Makes Eish Baladi Special?

Cultural Importance: Eish Baladi is more than just a bread; it's a cultural symbol and an integral part of everyday Egyptian life. It has been a staple in Egyptian cuisine for centuries, reflecting the country's agricultural and culinary traditions.

Texture and Versatility: The bread's slightly chewy texture and the ability to form pockets make it perfect for dipping, stuffing, or wrapping around various fillings. This versatility enhances its role as a fundamental part of Egyptian meals.

Freshness: Eish Baladi is best enjoyed fresh out of the oven when it's still warm and soft. The bread's freshness contributes to its delightful texture and flavor.

Tips for Enjoying Eish Baladi

Pair with Traditional Dishes: Eish Baladi is commonly served with dishes like ful medames, koshari, and molokhia. It's also great for scooping up dips such as hummus or baba ganoush.

Use as a Wrap: The bread's pocket-like structure makes it ideal for wrapping around various fillings, from grilled meats and vegetables to salads and spreads.

Store Properly: If you have leftovers, store Eish Baladi in an airtight container or plastic bag to keep it fresh. It can be reheated in the oven or on a skillet to restore its soft texture.

Experiment with Toppings: Try toasting the bread and adding toppings like olive oil, za'atar, or cheese for a simple yet flavorful snack.

Enjoy Warm: For the best experience, enjoy Eish Baladi warm. You can briefly heat it in the oven or on a skillet to refresh its texture and flavor.

Cafés and Bakeries

Egyptian cafés and bakeries offer a unique blend of traditional and modern flavors, reflecting the country's rich culinary heritage and vibrant contemporary scene. Whether you're looking for a cozy spot to enjoy a leisurely coffee or a bakery to savor freshly baked goods, Egypt has a diverse range of options to explore. Here are five top cafés and bakeries that stand out for their quality, ambiance, and delightful offerings:

1. El Abd Patisserie (Cairo)

Overview: Founded in 1952, El Abd Patisserie is a legendary name in Cairo, renowned for its exquisite pastries, cakes, and traditional Egyptian sweets. With several branches across the city, it has become a beloved institution for locals and tourists alike.

Highlights:

Baklava: El Abd is famous for its rich and flaky baklava, made with layers of crisp pastry, chopped nuts, and a sweet syrup.

Knafeh: A traditional Middle Eastern dessert made from shredded phyllo dough and sweet cheese, topped with syrup and pistachios.

Traditional Cakes: The patisserie offers a variety of cakes, including sponge cakes and cheesecakes, often adorned with beautiful decorations.

Ambiance: The main branch in Downtown Cairo features a classic and elegant interior, with glass display cases showcasing the bakery's finest creations. It's a great place for a casual coffee break or to pick up gifts and treats.

Must-Try:

Fruit Tart: A colorful and fresh tart topped with seasonal fruits and a light custard.

Mango Mousse: A creamy and tropical dessert that is perfect for a light treat.

2. Birdcage Café (Cairo)

Overview: Located in the upscale Zamalek neighborhood, Birdcage Café offers a chic and modern atmosphere with a focus on high-quality coffee and gourmet pastries. It has quickly become a favorite among Cairo's café culture enthusiasts.

Highlights:

Artisan Coffee: Birdcage takes pride in its expertly brewed coffee, with a selection of single-origin beans and various brewing methods.

Pastries and Croissants: The café offers a range of

freshly baked pastries, including buttery croissants and unique creations like matcha éclairs.

Breakfast Options: Their breakfast menu features a selection of dishes, from avocado toast to shakshuka.

Ambiance: The café's interior combines modern design with a cozy feel, featuring stylish furnishings, bright decor, and a relaxed atmosphere. It's an ideal spot for both casual meetings and leisurely brunches.

Must-Try:

Matcha Croissant: A delicious twist on the classic croissant, filled with creamy matcha custard.

Iced Coffee: Perfectly balanced and refreshing, ideal for a hot Cairo day.

3. La Poire (Cairo)

Overview: La Poire is a renowned patisserie and café chain in Cairo, known for its elegant pastries, cakes, and a wide range of savory options. Established in 1990, it has built a reputation for quality and sophistication.

Highlights:

Eclairs: La Poire's éclairs are a must-try, filled with rich cream and topped with a glossy glaze.

Opera Cake: A luxurious layered cake with coffee, chocolate, and almond flavors.

Savory Options: The café also offers a selection of savory pastries and sandwiches, perfect for a light lunch.

Ambiance: La Poire's locations feature a refined and upscale atmosphere, with stylish decor and comfortable seating. It's a popular choice for afternoon tea or celebratory treats.

Must-Try:

Opera Cake: A rich and flavorful cake with layers of coffee-soaked sponge and chocolate ganache.

Mini Quiches: Delicious bite-sized savory treats that pair perfectly with coffee.

4. Maison Thomas (Cairo)

Overview: Maison Thomas, located in the upscale neighborhood of Zamalek, is renowned for its French-style pastries, gourmet pizzas, and elegant atmosphere. Established in 1922, it has a long-standing reputation for quality and tradition.

Highlights:

French Pastries: The bakery offers a range of French pastries, including croissants, tarts, and éclairs.

Pizza: Maison Thomas is also famous for its thin-crust pizzas, made with high-quality ingredients and traditional techniques.

Desserts: Their selection of desserts includes classic French options like crème brûlée and mousse au chocolat.

Ambiance: The café features a charming and sophisticated ambiance, with classic French decor and a relaxed atmosphere. It's a great spot for a leisurely lunch or a special dessert.

Must-Try:

Tarte Tatin: A caramelized apple tart that is a true French classic.

Chocolate Eclair: Filled with rich chocolate cream and topped with a glossy glaze.

5. Baker & Spice (Cairo)

Overview: Baker & Spice is a modern bakery and café chain that offers a wide range of artisanal bread, pastries, and gourmet coffee. With multiple locations across Cairo, it has become a popular choice for high-quality baked goods and a relaxed café experience.

Highlights:

Artisan Bread: The bakery is known for its freshly baked bread, including sourdough, baguettes, and focaccia.

Pastries and Cookies: Baker & Spice offers a selection of sweet treats, including cookies, cakes, and tarts.

Salads and Sandwiches: Their menu also features fresh salads and gourmet sandwiches, perfect for a light meal.

Ambiance: The café's modern and airy design, with clean lines and natural light, creates a welcoming and comfortable environment. It's an excellent place for breakfast, lunch, or an afternoon coffee.

Must-Try:

Sourdough Bread: Freshly baked with a tangy flavor and chewy texture.

Cinnamon Roll: Warm and gooey, with a generous amount of cinnamon and icing.

Bars and Lounges

Egypt's nightlife scene offers a vibrant mix of bars and lounges where locals and visitors alike can unwind, socialize, and enjoy a variety of drinks in stylish settings. From upscale lounges with stunning city views to laid-back bars with live music, Egypt's top bars and lounges cater to diverse tastes and preferences. Here's a guide to some of the best spots across Cairo, Alexandria, and other key cities:

1. Cairo Jazz Club (Cairo)

Overview: Cairo Jazz Club is a staple in Cairo's nightlife scene, renowned for its live music performances and eclectic atmosphere. Established in 2002, it's a favorite among both locals and tourists who appreciate good music and a lively ambiance.

Highlights:

Live Music: The club features a range of live performances, including jazz, blues, and local bands, offering an authentic musical experience.

Cocktails: A well-curated cocktail menu with creative concoctions and classic favorites.

Atmosphere: An intimate setting with a laid-back vibe, perfect for enjoying music and conversation.

Ambiance: With its cozy interior and stylish decor, Cairo Jazz Club provides an inviting environment for music lovers. The venue's focus on quality performances and a relaxed atmosphere makes it a great spot for a night out.

Must-Try:

Signature Cocktails: Try one of their signature cocktails or request a custom mix based on your preferences.

Local Bands: Enjoy performances by local jazz and blues bands, offering a taste of Cairo's vibrant music scene.

2. Sky Lounge (Cairo)

Overview: Sky Lounge, located on the rooftop of the Kempinski Nile Hotel, offers breathtaking views of the Nile River and Cairo's skyline. It's an upscale venue known for its sophisticated ambiance and premium drinks.

Highlights:

Panoramic Views: Stunning vistas of the Nile and the city, especially beautiful at sunset and night.

Fine Dining: A menu that includes gourmet appetizers, sushi, and tapas.

Cocktail Selection: An extensive cocktail menu featuring both classic and innovative drinks.

Ambiance: Sky Lounge combines elegance with comfort, providing a luxurious setting for enjoying drinks and light bites. The sophisticated decor and panoramic views make it an ideal choice for a special evening.

Must-Try:

Signature Cocktails: Explore their creative cocktail

menu, including options like the Nile Sunset or Cairo Breeze.

Gourmet Tapas: Sample their selection of gourmet appetizers and tapas for a complete experience.

3. The Roof Bar (Alexandria)

Overview: The Roof Bar at the Four Seasons Hotel Alexandria offers a chic and relaxed atmosphere with panoramic views of the Mediterranean Sea. It's a popular spot for both sunset drinks and late-night lounging.

Highlights:

Sea Views: Spectacular views of the sea and Alexandria's coastline.

Craft Cocktails: A diverse cocktail menu with a focus on craft and artisanal drinks.

Chilled Vibes: A laid-back setting ideal for enjoying a drink with friends or a romantic evening.

Ambiance: The Roof Bar features modern decor with comfortable seating and a relaxed vibe, making it perfect for a casual yet upscale night out. The stunning sea views add a touch of romance to the experience.

Must-Try:

Mediterranean Cocktails: Enjoy cocktails inspired by Mediterranean flavors.

Seafood Tapas: Pair your drinks with a selection of fresh seafood tapas.

4. Le Gourmet (Cairo)

Overview: Located in the heart of Cairo, Le Gourmet is a sophisticated bar and lounge known for its refined atmosphere and high-quality beverages. It's a popular choice for those seeking a more upscale drinking experience.

Highlights:

Elegant Setting: A stylish and refined interior with comfortable seating and an upscale atmosphere.

Premium Drinks: A selection of fine wines, high-end spirits, and expertly crafted cocktails.

Gourmet Menu: A menu of gourmet appetizers and light bites to complement your drinks.

Ambiance: Le Gourmet's elegant design and attention to detail create a luxurious setting for enjoying premium drinks. The bar's focus on quality and sophistication makes it a top choice for a classy night out.

Must-Try:

Signature Wines: Explore their selection of fine wines from around the world.

Gourmet Bites: Pair your drinks with gourmet appetizers like truffle-infused dishes and artisanal cheeses.

5. Cairo Opera House Rooftop Bar (Cairo)

Overview: The Cairo Opera House Rooftop Bar offers a unique blend of cultural ambiance and modern luxury. Situated atop the Cairo Opera House, it provides a chic environment with stunning views of Cairo's skyline.

Highlights:

Cultural Vibes: Enjoy a sophisticated atmosphere that reflects the cultural richness of the Cairo Opera House.

Elegant Cocktails: A selection of well-crafted cocktails and premium spirits.

Cultural Events: Occasionally hosts cultural and artistic events, adding a special touch to your visit.

Ambiance: With its elegant decor and panoramic views, the Cairo Opera House Rooftop Bar offers a refined and cultural experience. The sophisticated setting and connection to the arts make it a distinctive choice for a night out.

Must-Try:

Opera-Themed Cocktails: Enjoy cocktails inspired by the themes of opera and classical music.

Cultural Events: Attend one of their special events or performances for an enriched experience.

Nightclubs and Dance Venues

Egypt's nightlife scene extends beyond bars and lounges to include a vibrant array of nightclubs and dance venues. From high-energy dance floors to stylish clubs with top DJs, Egypt offers a dynamic nightlife experience for those looking to dance the night away. Here's a guide to some of the top nightclubs and dance venues across Cairo, Alexandria, and other key cities:

1. Cairo Jazz Club 610 (Cairo)

Overview: Cairo Jazz Club 610, a newer addition to the Cairo nightlife scene, builds on the success of the original Cairo Jazz Club. Located in the upscale 6th of October City, it's known for its energetic atmosphere, live music, and DJ sets.

Highlights:

Live Performances: Features live music from local bands and international acts, spanning genres from jazz to electronic.

DJ Nights: Hosts regular DJ nights with a mix of electronic, house, and popular music.

Themed Events: Organizes themed parties and special events, adding a unique twist to the nightlife experience.

Ambiance: With a modern and stylish design, Cairo Jazz Club 610 offers a spacious dance floor, comfortable seating areas, and an overall lively vibe. The venue's focus on quality music and dynamic events makes it a popular choice for night owls.

Must-Try:

Themed Nights: Check out their schedule for themed nights and special events.

Signature Cocktails: Enjoy a selection of creative cocktails crafted to complement the energetic atmosphere.

2. Saeed's Club (Cairo)

Overview: Saeed's Club is a well-established nightclub in Cairo known for its vibrant nightlife and diverse music offerings. It's a popular destination for both locals and tourists looking to enjoy a night of dancing and entertainment.

Highlights:

Varied Music: Offers a range of music genres, from Arabic hits to international dance tracks.

Dance Floors: Features multiple dance floors, each with its own musical focus.

VIP Areas: Provides exclusive VIP areas for a more private and luxurious experience.

Ambiance: Saeed's Club boasts a large and energetic space with a high-energy atmosphere. The club's modern design, combined with its extensive music selection, makes it a go-to spot for a lively night out.

Must-Try:

Dance Floors: Explore different dance floors to experience a variety of music genres.

VIP Service: Opt for VIP service for a premium experience with added comforts.

3. The First Nile Boat (Cairo)

Overview: The First Nile Boat is a unique nightclub situated on a boat floating on the Nile River. It offers a combination of scenic views, lively music, and a sophisticated nightlife experience.

Highlights:

River Views: Enjoy stunning views of the Nile while dancing and socializing.

Live Music and DJs: Features live music performances and DJ sets with a mix of local and international styles.

Elegant Setting: The boat's elegant design and decor create a refined yet lively atmosphere.

Ambiance: The First Nile Boat offers a unique setting with panoramic river views and a chic, modern interior. The combination of great music and a scenic location makes it a standout choice for a night out in Cairo.

Must-Try:

River Views: Take advantage of the boat's location for stunning nighttime views of the Nile.

Signature Drinks: Enjoy expertly crafted cocktails and premium beverages.

4. Jewel Nightclub (Cairo)

Overview: Jewel Nightclub is a high-end venue known for its luxurious design, top-notch sound system, and vibrant atmosphere. Located in Cairo's upscale neighborhoods, it attracts a stylish crowd seeking an upscale nightlife experience.

Highlights:

Luxurious Design: Features opulent decor, including chandeliers, plush seating, and a grand dance floor.

International DJs: Hosts performances by renowned international DJs, ensuring top-quality music and entertainment.

VIP Tables: Offers exclusive VIP tables and private areas for a more intimate and premium experience.

Ambiance: Jewel Nightclub's extravagant design and sophisticated vibe create a glamorous setting for a night out. The club's focus on high-end service and top-tier entertainment makes it a premier destination for those looking to indulge.

Must-Try:

International DJs: Experience live sets from acclaimed DJs and enjoy the club's high-energy atmosphere.

VIP Tables: Book a VIP table for an exclusive experience with enhanced service and comfort.

5. El Borde (Alexandria)

Overview: El Borde is a trendy nightclub in Alexandria known for its modern design, lively atmosphere, and diverse music offerings. It's a popular spot for both dancing and socializing, attracting a youthful and energetic crowd.

Highlights:

Varied Music: Offers a mix of international dance hits, local music, and themed party nights.

Stylish Interior: Features a contemporary and stylish interior with vibrant lighting and decor.

Themed Parties: Hosts regular themed parties and special events, adding excitement to the nightlife experience.

Ambiance: El Borde combines a modern design with an energetic atmosphere, making it a hotspot for nightlife in Alexandria. The club's focus on varied music and themed events ensures a dynamic and engaging experience.

Must-Try:

Themed Parties: Attend one of their themed parties for a unique and memorable night out.

Signature Cocktails: Enjoy a range of creative cocktails and drinks tailored to the club's lively ambiance.

Tips for Dining and Nightlife in Egypt

Navigating Egypt's dining and nightlife scene can be a delightful adventure, offering a rich array of experiences from traditional cuisine to modern entertainment. To help you make the most of your time in Egypt, here are some essential tips for dining and enjoying the nightlife:

Dining Tips

Embrace Local Cuisine:

Explore Traditional Dishes: Don't miss the chance to try Egyptian staples like koshari (a hearty mix of rice, lentils, and pasta), molokhia (a green leafy stew), and stuffed pigeons.

Street Food: Sample street food from local vendors. Popular options include falafel, shawarma, and kebabs. Ensure the vendor follows proper hygiene practices.

Understand Meal Times:

Lunch: Typically served between 1 PM and 3 PM.

Dinner: Usually starts around 8 PM, but many restaurants open later.

Restaurant Etiquette:

Reservations: For popular restaurants or high-end dining, making a reservation in advance is advisable.

Tipping: A service charge is often included in the bill, but it's customary to leave a small additional tip (around 5-10% of the total bill) for good service.

Check for Alcohol:

Alcohol Availability: Not all restaurants and cafes serve alcohol. Look for licensed establishments or those in major tourist areas.

Alcohol with Meals: Some traditional restaurants might not serve alcohol, so check beforehand if you wish to enjoy a drink with your meal.

Dining Customs:

Sharing Food: Egyptian meals are often shared family-style, so be prepared to enjoy dishes communally.

Eating with Hands: It's common to eat certain foods, like bread or falafel, with your hands. Using utensils is also acceptable for other dishes.

Respect Local Dietary Practices:

Ramadan: During the holy month of Ramadan, many restaurants and cafes may close during the day and open later in the evening. Be respectful and avoid eating or drinking in public during fasting hours.

Nightlife Tips

Dress Appropriately:

Dress Code: Many upscale clubs and bars have a formal dress code. Smart casual or semi-formal attire is often required, especially in high-end venues.

Comfortable Footwear: If you plan to dance, wear comfortable shoes as some clubs have extensive dance floors.

Safety First:

Travel in Groups: For safety, it's advisable to go out in groups, especially late at night.

Use Reputable Transport: Arrange transportation through reliable services or apps, rather than hailing taxis off the street.

Respect Local Customs:

Public Behavior: Public displays of affection should be minimal, as Egypt is a conservative country. Keep behavior respectful and modest.

Photography: Avoid taking photos in nightclubs and bars unless you have permission, as this can be frowned upon.

Understand the Venue:

Music and Vibe: Check the type of music and atmosphere of a venue before heading out. Some places focus on live performances, while others may have DJ sets and dance floors.

Entry Fees: Some nightclubs and bars have cover charges, especially for special events or high-profile DJs. Be prepared for these additional costs.

Enjoy Local Drinks:

Try Local Beverages: In addition to international drinks, try local favorites like freshly squeezed juices, or traditional beverages such as karkade (hibiscus tea).

Cocktails and Spirits: Many bars offer creative cocktails and a selection of international spirits. Explore local twists on classic cocktails.

Know the Legal Drinking Age:

Legal Age: The legal drinking age in Egypt is 21. Be prepared to show ID if requested.

Cultural Sensitivities

Respect Local Values:

Conservative Culture: Egypt is predominantly conservative, so dress modestly and behave respectfully in public spaces.

Gender Dynamics: Be mindful of cultural norms regarding interactions between men and women.

Local Language:

Language: While many places in tourist areas will have English-speaking staff, learning a few basic Arabic phrases can enhance your dining and nightlife experience.

Stay Hydrated and Safe:

Hydration: Drink plenty of bottled water to stay hydrated, especially if consuming alcohol.

Health Precautions: Be cautious with the type of food and drinks you consume to avoid foodborne illnesses.

Top Destinations in Egypt

Chapter 10: Cairo

Top 10 Attractions & Things to do

1. **The Pyramids of Giza**

The Pyramids of Giza, one of the most iconic landmarks in the world, are a must-visit attraction for anyone traveling to Cairo. Located on the Giza Plateau, these ancient structures have fascinated historians, archaeologists, and tourists for centuries. The complex includes the Great Pyramid of Giza, the Pyramid of Khafre, and the Pyramid of Menkaure, along with the Sphinx, making it a treasure trove of ancient Egyptian history and architecture.

History

Great Pyramid of Giza: Built for Pharaoh Khufu (also known as Cheops) around 2580–2560 BCE, this pyramid is the largest and oldest of the three. It was originally 146.6 meters (481 feet) high and was the tallest man-made structure in the world for over 3,800 years.

Pyramid of Khafre: Constructed for Khufu's son, Pharaoh Khafre, around 2570 BCE. Slightly smaller than the Great Pyramid, it retains some of its original casing stones at the top, which give it a distinctive appearance.

Pyramid of Menkaure: The smallest of the three pyramids, built for Pharaoh Menkaure around 2510 BCE. It stands at 65 meters (213 feet) and is accompanied by three smaller queen's pyramids.

The Great Sphinx: Located near the pyramids, the Sphinx is a colossal limestone statue with the body of a lion and the head of a Pharaoh, believed to represent Khafre. It is thought to have been constructed during the same period as the pyramids.

Location

Address: Giza Plateau, Giza Governorate, Cairo, Egypt.

Coordinates: 29.9792° N latitude, 31.1342° E longitude.

Accessibility: The site is located approximately 9 kilometers (5.6 miles) southwest of Cairo city center, making it easily accessible by car or public transportation.

Opening and Closing Hours

Hours of Operation:

Daytime: Generally from 8:00 AM to 4:00 PM, with extended hours in the peak tourist season.

Night Visits: Occasionally available during special events or shows, but standard visits are during daytime hours.

Ticket Booth: Closes about 30 minutes before the site itself closes.

Top Things to Do

Explore the Pyramids: Walk around and enter the pyramids (where allowed) to appreciate their grandeur and learn about their construction and history.

Visit the Great Sphinx: Admire this enigmatic statue and explore the surrounding area for great photo opportunities.

Camel and Horse Rides: Experience a traditional camel or horse ride around the Giza Plateau for a unique perspective of the pyramids and desert landscape.

Visit the Solar Boat Museum: Located near the Great Pyramid, this museum houses the reconstructed Khufu ship, which was discovered buried near the pyramid and is believed to have been used for the Pharaoh's journey in the afterlife.

Take a Guided Tour: Engage a knowledgeable guide to enrich your visit with detailed historical and cultural insights about the pyramids and surrounding monuments.

Enjoy the Sound and Light Show: Attend the evening sound and light show (if available) to experience a dramatic presentation of the history of the pyramids through visual and audio effects.

Practical Information

Tickets: Tickets can be purchased at the entrance. Prices vary based on nationality and whether you plan to enter the interior of the pyramids. Additional tickets are required for special areas like the Solar Boat Museum.

Guides and Tours: Available on-site or through various tour operators in Cairo. Consider booking in advance to ensure availability.

Facilities: There are basic facilities such as restrooms and souvenir shops at the site. However, amenities are limited, so plan accordingly.

Tips for Visiting

Wear Comfortable Clothing: The site involves a lot of walking and climbing, so wear comfortable shoes and clothing suited for hot and sunny weather.

Stay Hydrated: Bring plenty of water, as the desert climate can be very dry and hot.

Sun Protection: Use sunscreen, a hat, and sunglasses to protect yourself from the strong sun.

Respect Local Customs: Dress modestly and follow local customs and rules, especially when interacting with local guides or taking photographs.

Avoid Peak Times: Visit early in the morning or late in the afternoon to avoid the crowds and heat. The site can become very crowded, especially during peak tourist seasons.

Bring Cash: Some smaller purchases or tips might require cash, as not all vendors accept cards.

Be Cautious with Vendors: There are many vendors around the site selling souvenirs and offering rides.

Be prepared to negotiate prices and be cautious of overzealous sellers.

2. The Egyptian Museum

The Egyptian Museum in Cairo is one of the world's most important museums dedicated to ancient Egyptian artifacts. It houses an extensive collection of over 120,000 items, showcasing the rich history and culture of ancient Egypt. From the treasures of Tutankhamun to mummies and statues of pharaohs, the museum offers an unparalleled glimpse into Egypt's past.

History

Established: The museum was founded in 1835 by the Egyptian government under the patronage of Muhammad Ali Pasha, who was keen on preserving Egypt's ancient heritage.

Location: The museum was originally housed in a building near the old Cairo University before moving to its current location in Tahrir Square in 1902.

Architectural Design: The current museum building was designed by French architect Marcel Dourgnon and reflects the architectural style of the early 20th century, with its grand facade and impressive interiors.

Location

Address: Tahrir Square, Downtown Cairo, Egypt.

Coordinates: 30.0479° N latitude, 31.2357° E longitude.

Accessibility: Located in the heart of Cairo, the museum is easily accessible by car, taxi, or public transportation. The central location makes it a convenient stop for visitors exploring the city.

Opening and Closing Hours

Hours of Operation:

Daytime: Typically from 9:00 AM to 5:00 PM daily. Extended hours or special openings may occur during peak tourist seasons.

Friday: Often closed or may have reduced hours; check ahead as schedules can vary.

Ticket Booth: Closes about 30 minutes before the museum itself closes.

Top Things to Do

Tutankhamun Gallery: Marvel at the treasures of Tutankhamun, including his famous gold mask, jewelry, and other artifacts discovered in his tomb.

Royal Mummy Room: View the mummies of ancient Egyptian royalty and learn about the mummification process and burial practices.

Statues and Sculptures: Admire the impressive statues of pharaohs and deities, including the iconic statue of Ramses II.

Papyrus Collection: Explore ancient papyrus scrolls with hieroglyphics, offering insights into ancient Egyptian writing and literature.

Jewelry and Artifacts: Examine the elaborate jewelry, amulets, and daily-life artifacts that provide a glimpse into the luxury and daily routines of ancient Egyptians.

Temporary Exhibitions: Check out temporary exhibitions that feature special collections or thematic displays related to Egyptian history and culture.

Practical Information

Tickets: Available for purchase at the museum entrance. Prices vary for local and international visitors. Additional fees may apply for special exhibitions or the Royal Mummy Room.

Guided Tours: Available in various languages, providing in-depth information and context about the exhibits. Consider booking a tour in advance or hiring a guide on-site.

Facilities: The museum offers amenities such as restrooms, a gift shop, and a café. However, facilities can be basic, so plan accordingly.

Tips for Visiting

Arrive Early: To avoid the crowds and fully enjoy the exhibits, try to arrive early in the morning.

Wear Comfortable Shoes: The museum is large, and you will be doing a lot of walking. Comfortable footwear is essential.

Stay Hydrated: Bring a bottle of water, as exploring the museum can be quite extensive.

Respect Museum Rules: Follow the museum's guidelines regarding photography and handling of exhibits. Some areas, like the Royal Mummy Room, may have restrictions.

Plan Your Visit: Prioritize key exhibits you want to see and consider taking a guided tour for a more comprehensive experience.

Check for Updates: Verify opening hours and any special events or temporary exhibitions before your visit to ensure you don't miss out on anything interesting.

3. The Citadel of Saladin

The Citadel of Saladin, also known as the Cairo Citadel, is a historic Islamic fortress located in Cairo, Egypt. This imposing structure was built in the 12th century by the Muslim leader Salah ad-Din (Saladin) to defend Cairo from Crusader attacks. The Citadel is not only a key historical landmark but also a significant architectural achievement, offering panoramic views of the city and a glimpse into Cairo's medieval past.

History

Construction: The Citadel was begun in 1176 AD by Saladin as a strategic military fortification to protect Cairo from the Crusaders. The fortress was expanded and modified over the centuries by various rulers, including the Mamluks and Ottomans.

Historical Significance: The Citadel played a crucial role in Cairo's history, serving as a seat of government and residence for the ruling dynasties. It was also the site of numerous historical events and battles.

Location

Address: Salah Salem Street, Cairo, Egypt.

Coordinates: 30.0274° N latitude, 31.2603° E longitude.

Accessibility: Located on a hill in central Cairo, the Citadel is easily reachable by car or taxi. It's situated approximately 3 kilometers (1.8 miles) southeast of the Egyptian Museum and Tahrir Square.

Opening and Closing Hours

Hours of Operation:

Daytime: Typically from 8:00 AM to 5:00 PM daily.

Extended Hours: Occasionally available during peak tourist seasons or special events.

Ticket Booth: Closes about 30 minutes before the Citadel itself closes.

Top Things to Do

Explore the Citadel's Walls: Walk along the fortress walls for panoramic views of Cairo and an understanding of its defensive architecture.

Visit the Mosque of Muhammad Ali: Also known as the Alabaster Mosque, this mosque is a prominent feature of the Citadel and an excellent example of Ottoman architecture. It offers stunning interiors and sweeping views from its domes and minarets.

Tour the National Military Museum: Located within the Citadel, this museum showcases a collection of military artifacts and provides insights into Egypt's military history.

Discover the Mosque of Al-Nasir Muhammad: Another significant mosque within the Citadel complex, known for its beautiful architecture and historical importance.

Explore the Sultan al-Nasir Muhammad Complex: Includes the mosque, a palace, and a madrasa (Islamic school), reflecting the architectural style of the Mamluk period.

Practical Information

Tickets: Entrance fees apply. Tickets can be purchased at the main gate. There may be additional fees for specific areas or museums within the Citadel.

Guided Tours: Available on-site or through various tour operators in Cairo. A guide can provide valuable historical context and enhance your visit.

Facilities: The Citadel has basic facilities such as restrooms, a souvenir shop, and a café. However, amenities may be limited, so plan accordingly.

Tips for Visiting

Wear Comfortable Shoes: The Citadel involves walking on uneven terrain and climbing stairs. Comfortable footwear is essential.

Stay Hydrated: Bring a bottle of water, especially during the hotter months, as the Citadel is spread out and exploring can be physically demanding.

Respect Local Customs: Dress modestly, particularly when visiting religious sites like the Mosque of Muhammad Ali.

Plan Your Visit: Allow sufficient time to explore the various sites within the Citadel. Consider starting early in the day to avoid the midday heat and crowds.

Photography: Be mindful of photography rules, especially in religious and museum areas. Some sites may have restrictions on taking photos.

Check for Updates: Verify opening hours and any potential closures or special events before your visit to ensure a smooth experience.

4. Khan El Khalili Bazaar

Khan El Khalili is one of Cairo's most famous and historic bazaars, offering an immersive experience into the heart of Egyptian commerce and culture. Established in the 14th century during the Mamluk era, the bazaar is renowned for its bustling atmosphere, diverse range of goods, and traditional architecture. It remains a vibrant hub for both locals and tourists seeking to explore Egypt's rich history and vibrant marketplace culture.

History

Origins: Khan El Khalili was founded in 1382 by the Mamluk Sultan Barquq. Originally, it was a caravanserai, a type of inn for travelers and merchants. Over the centuries, it evolved into a bustling commercial center.

Historical Significance: The bazaar played a crucial role in Cairo's trade and commerce, serving as a major trading post along ancient trade routes. Its historical importance is reflected in its preserved architecture and continued use as a marketplace.

Location

Address: El Khalili, Cairo, Egypt.

Coordinates: 30.0455° N latitude, 31.2618° E longitude.

Accessibility: Situated in the heart of Islamic Cairo, the bazaar is accessible by car, taxi, or public transportation. It's a short distance from other historical sites like the Al-Azhar Mosque and the Citadel of Saladin.

Opening and Closing Hours

Hours of Operation:

Daily: Typically from 9:00 AM to 10:00 PM. However, individual shop hours may vary, and the market is generally more vibrant in the late morning and early evening.

Friday: Some shops may close for Friday prayers, typically from around 1:00 PM to 2:00 PM.

Top Things to Do

Shop for Souvenirs: Explore the myriad of shops selling traditional Egyptian goods, including handcrafted jewelry, textiles, spices, perfumes, and souvenirs. Popular items include intricately designed lamps, carpets, and traditional clothing.

Enjoy Traditional Food: Sample local street food and traditional dishes at various eateries and food stalls within the bazaar. Popular options include falafel, kebabs, and freshly squeezed juices.

Visit Historical Sites: Check out nearby historic sites such as the Al-Azhar Mosque and the Sultan Al-Ghuri Complex. These sites offer insights into Cairo's rich Islamic heritage.

Experience Local Culture: Take in the lively atmosphere of the bazaar, with its bustling streets, street performers, and traditional craftspeople.

Relax in a Traditional Coffeehouse: Enjoy a coffee or tea at one of the traditional coffeehouses (ahwa) in the area. El-Fishawy Café is a renowned spot where you can experience authentic Egyptian café culture.

Practical Information

Currency: Egyptian pounds (EGP) are used, and many shops accept cash. Credit cards may be accepted in some larger shops or restaurants.

Bargaining: Bargaining is a common practice in Khan El Khalili. It's expected and can be a fun part of the shopping experience. Start by negotiating the price and be prepared for back-and-forth discussions.

Safety: The bazaar is generally safe for tourists, but be mindful of your belongings in the crowded areas. Watch out for pickpockets and keep your valuables secure.

Tips for Visiting

Wear Comfortable Clothing: The bazaar involves a lot of walking and navigating through narrow, crowded streets. Comfortable clothing and footwear are essential.

Stay Hydrated: Cairo can be quite hot, so carry water with you and stay hydrated, especially if you're visiting during the hotter months.

Practice Patience: The bazaar can be crowded and busy. Take your time to explore and enjoy the lively environment.

Respect Local Customs: Dress modestly and be respectful of local customs and practices. This is especially important when entering religious sites or interacting with local vendors.

Ask for Directions: Khan El Khalili is a maze of alleys and streets. Don't hesitate to ask for directions if you get lost, and consider using a map or GPS for better navigation.

Visit in the Evening: The bazaar is particularly lively in the late afternoon and evening. This is when the market comes alive with activity and vendors.

5. Al-Azhar Mosque

Al-Azhar Mosque, one of Cairo's most significant religious and historical landmarks, is renowned for its architectural splendor and its role as a major center of Islamic scholarship. Established in 970 AD, it is not only one of the oldest mosques in Cairo but also a leading institution of Islamic learning and culture.

History

Founding: Al-Azhar Mosque was founded by the Fatimid caliph Al-Mu'izz li-Din Allah in 970 AD. It was originally built as a place of worship and a center for Islamic education.

Historical Significance: Over the centuries, Al-Azhar has played a crucial role in Islamic scholarship and education. It is home to Al-Azhar University, which was established in 975 AD and is one of the oldest continually operating universities in the world. The mosque and university have been central to the development of Islamic jurisprudence, theology, and philosophy.

Location

Address: Al-Azhar Street, Islamic Cairo, Cairo, Egypt.

Coordinates: 30.0454° N latitude, 31.2615° E longitude.

Accessibility: Situated in the heart of Islamic Cairo, Al-Azhar Mosque is easily accessible by car, taxi, or public transportation. It is near other historic sites such as Khan El Khalili Bazaar and the Citadel of Saladin.

Opening and Closing Hours

Hours of Operation:

Prayer Times: The mosque is open for prayers five times a day, with specific hours for each prayer. The exact times can vary based on the time of year and local schedules.

Visitor Hours: Generally, non-worshipping visitors are allowed to enter during non-prayer times, typically from 9:00 AM to 5:00 PM. However, access may be restricted during prayer times or religious events.

Friday: The mosque is especially busy during Friday prayers (Jumu'ah), which take place around midday. Visitors are advised to plan their visit around these times.

Top Things to Do

Explore the Mosque's Architecture: Admire the mosque's stunning architectural features, including its grand domes, minarets, and intricate decoration. The mosque combines various architectural styles from different periods.

Visit Al-Azhar University: If possible, explore the university's surrounding areas. The university's libraries and study halls have been centers of Islamic learning for centuries.

Experience the Courtyards: Wander through the mosque's courtyards and gardens, which provide a serene atmosphere and showcase traditional Islamic design elements.

Learn About Islamic History: Take the opportunity to learn about the history of Islamic scholarship and education through the mosque's historical significance and its role in the broader context of Islamic civilization.

Practical Information

Dress Code: Modest dress is required for both men and women. Women should cover their heads with a scarf, and both genders should wear clothing that covers the arms and legs.

Guided Tours: Consider hiring a local guide for a deeper understanding of the mosque's history and architecture. Tours can provide valuable insights and context.

Facilities: Basic facilities are available, including restrooms. There are also shops and cafes nearby for refreshments.

Tips for Visiting

Respect Prayer Times: Be mindful of prayer times when visiting. The mosque can be closed to tourists during these times, so plan your visit accordingly.

Be Respectful: As a functioning place of worship, it is important to be respectful of those praying and observing religious practices. Maintain a quiet demeanor and avoid disruptive behavior.

Bring Identification: Carry a form of identification, as it may be required for entry or registration purposes.

Photography: Photography may be restricted inside the mosque, especially during prayer times. Always ask for permission before taking photos, and be respectful of signage and local guidelines.

Plan Ahead: Check the mosque's visiting hours and any special events or closures before your visit to ensure a smooth experience.

6. The Cairo Tower

The Cairo Tower, an iconic modern structure in the heart of Cairo, stands as a symbol of the city's post-independence era. Completed in 1961, the tower offers stunning panoramic views of Cairo and the Nile River, making it a popular destination for both locals and tourists. With its unique design and strategic location, the Cairo Tower provides a different perspective on Egypt's bustling capital.

History

Construction: The Cairo Tower was built between 1956 and 1961, during the presidency of Gamal Abdel Nasser. It was designed by Egyptian architect Naoum Shebib and was intended to symbolize the country's modernity and independence.

Design: The tower's design is inspired by the lotus flower, an important symbol in ancient Egyptian culture. The structure is made of reinforced concrete and stands out due to its distinctive cylindrical shape and latticework.

Location

Address: Gezira Island, Zamalek, Cairo, Egypt.

Coordinates: 30.0456° N latitude, 31.2247° E longitude.

Accessibility: Located on Gezira Island in the Nile River, the Cairo Tower is easily accessible by car, taxi, or public transportation. It's situated in the Zamalek district, a notable area for dining and leisure.

Opening and Closing Hours

Hours of Operation:

Daytime: Typically from 9:00 AM to 11:00 PM daily.

Extended Hours: May be available during peak tourist seasons or special events.

Ticket Booth: Closes about 30 minutes before the tower itself closes.

Top Things to Do

Enjoy the Panoramic Views: Take the elevator to the observation deck for breathtaking views of Cairo, the Nile River, and the surrounding landscape. The tower provides an excellent vantage point for photography and sightseeing.

Dine at the Restaurant: Visit the revolving restaurant located at the top of the tower for a meal with a view. The restaurant offers a variety of international and local dishes and provides a unique dining experience as it slowly rotates.

Visit the Lower Observation Deck: If you prefer a more stationary view, the lower observation deck offers great sights without the rotation.

Explore the Surroundings: After visiting the tower, take a stroll around Gezira Island and enjoy the nearby parks, cafes, and shops.

Practical Information

Tickets: Available for purchase at the entrance. Prices vary for adults and children, and additional fees may apply for access to the restaurant or special observation decks.

Facilities: The tower has basic amenities, including restrooms, a gift shop, and dining options. The revolving restaurant provides a unique dining experience with views of the city.

Guided Tours: While the tower itself doesn't typically offer guided tours, you can find local tour operators who include a visit to the Cairo Tower in their city tours.

Tips for Visiting

Visit During Sunset: For the most spectacular views, plan your visit around sunset. The changing colors of the sky and city lights provide a memorable experience.

Dress Comfortably: Wear comfortable clothing and shoes, as you'll be spending time walking and standing in line.

Check for Special Events: The tower occasionally hosts special events or private functions, which might affect visitor access. Check in advance to avoid any disruptions to your visit.

Be Prepared for Security Checks: Expect to undergo security screenings at the entrance, as with many major tourist attractions in Cairo.

Stay Hydrated: Carry a bottle of water with you, especially if you're visiting during the hotter months.

7. The Hanging Church (Saint Virgin Mary's Coptic Orthodox Church)

The Hanging Church, officially known as Saint Virgin Mary's Coptic Orthodox Church, is one of Cairo's most ancient and significant Christian sites. Located in the Coptic Cairo district, this church is renowned for its unique architecture and historical importance in the Coptic Christian tradition. It is named "Hanging" because it is built on top of the southern gate of the old Roman Babylon Fortress, giving it a distinctive elevated appearance.

History

Founding: The church's origins date back to the 3rd century AD, though the current structure was established in the 7th century under the Patriarch Abraham. It has undergone several renovations and expansions over the centuries.

Historical Significance: The Hanging Church is one of the oldest Coptic churches in Egypt and has been a major center of Coptic Christianity. It was a key site for the Coptic community during the early Islamic period and played a significant role in preserving Coptic traditions and theology.

Location

Address: Coptic Cairo, Old Cairo, Cairo, Egypt.

Coordinates: 30.0291° N latitude, 31.2355° E longitude.

Accessibility: Located in the Coptic Cairo area, it is easily accessible by car, taxi, or public transportation. It's situated near other important Coptic sites, such as the Coptic Museum and the Church of Saint Sergius and Bacchus.

Opening and Closing Hours

Hours of Operation:

Daily: Typically from 9:00 AM to 4:00 PM. The church may close during midday prayers.

Friday: May have different hours due to religious services; it's advisable to check in advance.

Special Services: The church hosts various religious services and events, which may affect visitor access.

Top Things to Do

Admire the Architecture: Explore the church's unique architectural features, including its wooden ceiling, intricately carved icons, and ancient frescoes. The church's design reflects traditional Coptic art and architecture.

Visit the Iconostasis: The church's iconostasis (the screen separating the altar from the nave) is adorned with beautifully painted icons depicting various saints and biblical scenes.

Explore the Relics: View significant relics and artifacts, including the remains of Saint George and other important Coptic figures, which are displayed within the church.

Experience the Historical Setting: Walk around the church's elevated position and enjoy the view of the surrounding ancient Roman ruins and historical architecture of Coptic Cairo.

Practical Information

Dress Code: Modest attire is required for entry. Women should cover their heads with a scarf, and both men and women should wear clothing that covers their shoulders and knees.

Photography: Photography may be restricted inside the church, especially during services. Always ask for permission before taking photos and respect any signage regarding photography.

Facilities: The church has basic facilities, including restrooms. Nearby Coptic Cairo also offers various cafes and shops for refreshments.

Tips for Visiting

Respect Religious Practices: The Hanging Church is an active place of worship. Be mindful of ongoing services and avoid disrupting prayers or religious ceremonies.

Allow Time to Explore: The church and its surroundings offer rich historical and cultural insights. Allow yourself plenty of time to explore and appreciate the site's significance.

Hire a Local Guide: For a more in-depth understanding of the church's history and significance, consider hiring a local guide who can provide context and answer any questions you might have.

Check for Service Times: Be aware of the church's service schedule to plan your visit around any potential closures or restricted access during religious services.

Stay Hydrated: Carry a bottle of water, particularly if visiting during the warmer months, as exploring can be physically demanding.

8. The Coptic Museum

The Coptic Museum in Cairo is dedicated to preserving and showcasing the rich heritage of Egypt's Coptic Christian community. Established in 1908, it houses one of the world's most comprehensive collections of Coptic art and artifacts, spanning over 1,400 years of history. The museum offers a deep dive into the artistic and cultural contributions of the Coptic Christians to Egyptian history.

History

Founding: The Coptic Museum was founded by Marcus Simaika Pasha, a prominent Coptic scholar and activist, with the aim of preserving Coptic art and heritage.

Historical Significance: The museum's collection highlights the development of Coptic art and culture from the early Christian period through the Islamic era. It plays a crucial role in understanding the influence of Coptic Christianity on Egyptian civilization.

Location

Address: Coptic Cairo, Old Cairo, Cairo, Egypt.

Coordinates: 30.0289° N latitude, 31.2370° E longitude.

Accessibility: Located in the heart of Coptic Cairo, the museum is easily reachable by car, taxi, or public transportation. It's near other important Coptic sites, such as the Hanging Church and the Church of Saint Sergius and Bacchus.

Opening and Closing Hours

Hours of Operation:

Daily: Typically from 9:00 AM to 4:00 PM. The museum is closed on Fridays and certain public holidays.

Extended Hours: May be available during peak tourist seasons or special events.

Ticket Booth: Closes about 30 minutes before the museum itself closes.

Top Things to Do

Explore the Collections: Admire the extensive collection of Coptic artifacts, including ancient manuscripts, textiles, sculptures, and religious icons. Key exhibits include early Christian manuscripts, intricate woodwork, and Coptic pottery.

View the Mummy Portraits: See the famous Coptic Fayum mummy portraits, which are exquisite examples of Roman-era Egyptian art depicting the deceased.

Visit the Gilded Iconography: Examine the museum's collection of gilded icons and religious art that illustrate the development of Coptic iconography and artistry.

Tour the Museum's Architecture: Appreciate the museum's own historical architecture, which blends elements of traditional Coptic design with modern museum functionality.

Practical Information

Tickets: Available for purchase at the museum entrance. Prices vary for local and international visitors. Group tickets and guided tours can also be arranged.

Facilities: The museum offers basic amenities including restrooms, a gift shop, and a small café. Facilities may be limited, so plan accordingly.

Guided Tours: Consider hiring a local guide or joining a tour for in-depth explanations of the exhibits and historical context.

Tips for Visiting

Check for Updates: Verify the museum's opening hours and any special events or temporary exhibitions before your visit to ensure a smooth experience.

Dress Modestly: As with other religious and historical sites, modest attire is recommended. Ensure your shoulders and knees are covered.

Photography: Photography policies may vary. Always ask for permission before taking photos, and respect any restrictions on photographing exhibits.

Allow Plenty of Time: The museum houses a vast collection. Allow sufficient time to fully explore the exhibits and appreciate the intricate details of Coptic art and history.

Stay Hydrated: Carry a bottle of water, particularly if visiting during the hotter months, as the museum's extensive displays involve a lot of walking.

9. The Giza Plateau Solar Boat Museum

The Giza Plateau Solar Boat Museum, located near the Great Pyramids of Giza, is a museum dedicated to preserving and showcasing one of the most remarkable archaeological finds of the 20th century: the Khufu solar boat. The museum offers a fascinating insight into ancient Egyptian maritime practices and the significance of the solar boat in the context of royal funerary rituals.

History

Discovery: The solar boat was discovered in 1954 by the Egyptian archaeologist Kamal el-Mallakh in a pit near the Great Pyramid of Giza. The boat dates back to the 26th century BCE and was believed to have been used in the afterlife by Pharaoh Khufu (also known as Cheops).

Purpose: The boat was intended to transport the pharaoh to the afterlife, reflecting the ancient Egyptian belief in the sun god Ra and the importance of the boat in religious ceremonies. The solar boat symbolizes the journey of the deceased in the afterlife.

Location

Address: Giza Plateau, Giza, Egypt.

Coordinates: 29.9773° N latitude, 31.1324° E longitude.

Accessibility: Located on the Giza Plateau, the museum is easily accessible from the nearby pyramids. It is well-connected by car or taxi, and guided tours often include a stop at the museum.

Opening and Closing Hours

Hours of Operation:

Daily: Typically from 9:00 AM to 5:00 PM.

Extended Hours: Occasionally available during peak tourist seasons or special events.

Ticket Booth: Closes about 30 minutes before the museum itself closes.

Top Things to Do

Explore the Solar Boat: View the meticulously restored solar boat, which is displayed in a specially designed hall. The boat is made of cedar wood and measures about 43.6 meters (143 feet) in length. The museum provides detailed information about its construction and significance.

Learn About Ancient Egyptian Maritime Practices: Discover how ancient Egyptians used boats in both religious and practical contexts, and learn about their advanced shipbuilding techniques.

View Interactive Exhibits: Engage with interactive displays and multimedia presentations that offer insights into the history and significance of the solar boat and its role in ancient Egyptian culture.

Practical Information

Tickets: Tickets can be purchased at the entrance of the museum. Prices may vary for local and international visitors. It's often included in a combined ticket for the Giza Plateau area.

Facilities: The museum has basic amenities, including restrooms, a gift shop, and a small café. Facilities may be limited, so plan accordingly.

Guided Tours: Consider hiring a local guide or joining a tour to gain deeper insights into the historical and cultural context of the solar boat.

Tips for Visiting

Check for Updates: Verify the museum's opening hours and any potential closures before your visit to ensure a smooth experience.

Dress Comfortably: Wear comfortable clothing and footwear, as exploring the Giza Plateau can involve a lot of walking.

Stay Hydrated: Carry a bottle of water, especially if visiting during the hotter months, as it can get quite warm on the plateau.

Photography: Photography policies may vary. Always ask for permission before taking photos, especially of the exhibits.

Combine with Other Visits: The Solar Boat Museum is often visited in conjunction with the Great Pyramids and other sites on the Giza Plateau. Plan your itinerary to make the most of your visit to this historic area.

10. The Opera House

The Cairo Opera House, officially known as the Egyptian Opera House, is the premier venue for performing arts in Cairo. Located in the heart of the city, this architectural marvel is a center for music, ballet, opera, and other cultural events. It plays a vital role in Egypt's cultural landscape, offering a space for both international and local artists to showcase their talents.

History

Construction: The original Cairo Opera House was built in 1869 to celebrate the opening of the Suez Canal and was designed by the Italian architect Pietro Avoscani. It was demolished in 1971. The current building, a modern reconstruction, opened in 1988 and was designed by the Japanese architect Kenzo Tange.

Cultural Significance: The new Cairo Opera House represents a modern era of cultural renaissance in Egypt. It continues the legacy of promoting high-quality performing arts and serves as a hub for cultural exchange.

Location

Address: El Gezira, Zamalek, Cairo, Egypt.

Coordinates: 30.0595° N latitude, 31.2243° E longitude.

Accessibility: Located on Gezira Island in the Nile River, the Cairo Opera House is easily reachable by car, taxi, or public transportation. It is situated in the Zamalek district, a notable area for its cultural and artistic establishments.

Opening and Closing Hours

Hours of Operation:

Box Office: Typically open from 10:00 AM to 7:00 PM, though hours may vary depending on performance schedules.

Performances: Vary by day and event. Evening performances usually start around 8:00 PM.

Ticket Sales: Tickets can be purchased at the box office or online through the opera house's official website.

Top Things to Do

Attend a Performance: Experience a variety of performances, including opera, ballet, classical music concerts, and traditional Egyptian music. Check the schedule for upcoming events and performances.

Explore the Architecture: Admire the building's modern architectural design, including its striking facade and spacious interiors. The design combines traditional elements with contemporary aesthetics.

Visit the Museum: The Cairo Opera House complex includes a museum showcasing memorabilia from past performances and historical figures in the performing arts.

Dine at the Restaurants: Enjoy a meal at one of the opera house's dining options, which offer a range of cuisine and provide a great place to relax before or after a performance.

Practical Information

Tickets: Available for purchase at the box office or online. Prices vary depending on the performance and seating category. Booking in advance is recommended for popular shows.

Facilities: The opera house features modern facilities, including restrooms, a gift shop, and dining options. There are also VIP lounges and special seating arrangements for certain performances.

Dress Code: While there is no strict dress code, smart casual attire is recommended for attending performances.

Tips for Visiting

Check the Schedule: Visit the Cairo Opera House's official website or contact the box office to check the performance schedule and book tickets in advance.

Arrive Early: Arriving early allows you to find parking, explore the venue, and find your seat without rush.

Plan Transportation: Traffic around the opera house can be busy, especially during performance times. Plan your transportation and allow extra time to reach the venue.

Respect Performance Etiquette: Silence mobile phones and avoid talking during performances to ensure a pleasant experience for all attendees.

Explore the Area: The Zamalek district, where the opera house is located, has a range of cafes, shops, and cultural sites. Take some time to explore the neighborhood.

Accommodation Options

Luxury Hotel

Experience the ultimate in comfort and elegance with Egypt's luxury hotels. From opulent suites overlooking the Nile to stunning beachfront resorts, these high-end accommodations offer world-class amenities, exceptional service, and breathtaking views. Whether you're exploring ancient wonders or relaxing by the pool, luxury hotels in Egypt provide a perfect blend of sophistication and relaxation, ensuring an unforgettable stay. Indulge in fine dining, rejuvenating spas, and personalized service that will make your Egyptian vacation truly extraordinary.

Top 5 Luxury Hotel

1. The Nile Ritz-Carlton, Cairo

The Nile Ritz-Carlton, Cairo is a premier luxury hotel situated in the heart of Cairo. Renowned for its exceptional service, sophisticated design, and stunning views of the Nile River, this hotel offers an opulent retreat for discerning travelers. It blends contemporary luxury with traditional Egyptian charm, making it a popular choice for both leisure and business visitors.

Grace Bennett

Location (Address & Proximity)

Address: 1113 Corniche El Nil, Cairo, Egypt

Proximity: The hotel is strategically located on the banks of the Nile, offering breathtaking river views. It's situated in the central district of Cairo, making it easily accessible to major attractions such as the Egyptian Museum, Tahrir Square, and the historic Khan El Khalili bazaar. The Cairo International Airport is about a 30-minute drive away.

Highlights

Stunning Views: The Nile Ritz-Carlton offers panoramic views of the Nile River and Cairo's skyline.

Luxurious Accommodations: The rooms and suites are elegantly furnished with high-end amenities, providing a plush and comfortable stay.

Dining Options: The hotel features several dining venues, including fine dining restaurants, a rooftop bar, and cafes, catering to a range of culinary preferences.

Spa and Wellness

The Ritz-Carlton Spa: The spa offers a comprehensive menu of treatments designed to rejuvenate and relax. Facilities include private treatment rooms, a sauna, a steam room, and a relaxation lounge. The spa uses premium products and offers therapies inspired by both local and international traditions.

Bars

Nile Lounge: Located on the hotel's rooftop, this bar provides an elegant setting with panoramic views of the Nile. It's an ideal spot for evening cocktails and light bites.

The Pool Bar: Located near the outdoor pool, it offers refreshing drinks and light snacks in a casual atmosphere.

Events and Conferences

Meeting Facilities: The hotel has a range of versatile meeting and conference spaces, including large ballrooms and smaller meeting rooms equipped with the latest technology.

Event Planning: The experienced events team provides comprehensive services, from planning and catering to audio-visual support, ensuring successful and memorable events.

Basic Facilities and Amenities

Swimming Pool: An outdoor pool with a sun deck and views of the Nile.

Fitness Center: A fully equipped gym with state-of-the-art exercise machines and personal training services.

Business Center: Equipped with office amenities for business travelers, including high-speed internet and meeting rooms.

Concierge Services: Assistance with travel arrangements, local recommendations, and reservations.

Opening and Closing Hours

Check-in: Typically from 3:00 PM

Check-out: By 12:00 PM

Restaurants and Bars: Operating hours vary by venue, but generally, breakfast is served from 6:00 AM to 10:00 AM, lunch from 12:00 PM to 3:00 PM, and dinner from 7:00 PM to 11:00 PM. The bars often remain open until late evening.

Price

Room Rates: Prices can vary significantly depending on the season, room type, and booking time. On average, rates range from $300 to $600 per night. Premium suites and special packages may cost more.

Pros

Prime Location: Central location with easy access to key attractions.

Exceptional Service: Renowned for its attentive and personalized service.

Luxury Accommodations: Spacious rooms with high-end amenities and décor.

Diverse Dining Options: A variety of dining experiences within the hotel.

Beautiful Views: Stunning vistas of the Nile River and Cairo skyline.

Cons

Cost: It is a high-end luxury hotel, and the rates may be steep for some travelers.

Traffic: Cairo's traffic congestion can affect travel times to and from the hotel.

Noise: Being in a central location, some rooms might experience city noise.

Local Tips

Explore Nearby Attractions: Take advantage of the hotel's location to visit nearby landmarks like the Egyptian Museum and Tahrir Square.

Use Hotel Transfers: For convenience and safety, consider using the hotel's transfer services rather than navigating Cairo's busy streets on your own.

Dress Code: Some of the hotel's dining venues may have a dress code, so it's a good idea to check in advance.

Currency Exchange: While the hotel offers currency exchange services, it might be beneficial to also exchange money at local banks for better rates.

2. Four Seasons Hotel Cairo at Nile Plaza

The Four Seasons Hotel Cairo at Nile Plaza is a luxury hotel that epitomizes opulence and sophistication. Located along the Nile River, this hotel offers a perfect blend of modern comfort and traditional Egyptian style. Known for its exceptional service and attention to detail, it caters to both leisure and business travelers seeking a premium experience in Cairo.

Location (Address & Proximity)

Address: 1089 Corniche El Nile, Garden City, Cairo, Egypt

Proximity: The hotel is situated in the upscale Garden City district, right on the Nile's edge. It's conveniently close to major attractions such as the Egyptian Museum, Tahrir Square, and the historic Khan El Khalili bazaar. Cairo International Airport is approximately a 30-minute drive away.

Highlights

Spectacular Nile Views: Many rooms and suites offer sweeping views of the Nile River, enhancing the overall experience.

Luxurious Accommodations: The hotel boasts elegantly appointed rooms and suites with high-end amenities and stylish décor.

Culinary Excellence: Offers an array of dining options, including renowned restaurants and bars, providing diverse culinary experiences.

Spa and Wellness

The Spa at Four Seasons: The hotel features a full-service spa offering a variety of treatments designed for relaxation and rejuvenation. Facilities include private treatment rooms, a sauna, a steam room, and a relaxation area. Treatments range from traditional massages to advanced skincare therapies.

Bars

Nile Plaza Lounge: This upscale lounge offers an elegant setting with views of the Nile. It's perfect for enjoying afternoon tea or evening cocktails.

Pool Bar: Located adjacent to the outdoor pool, it serves refreshing beverages and light snacks in a relaxed atmosphere.

Events and Conferences

Meeting Facilities: The hotel provides extensive meeting and event facilities, including spacious ballrooms and smaller conference rooms. Each venue is equipped with the latest technology and can be customized for various types of events.

Event Planning: The dedicated events team offers comprehensive planning services to ensure successful and memorable gatherings, from corporate meetings to social events.

Basic Facilities and Amenities

Swimming Pool: An outdoor pool with panoramic views of the Nile and a sun deck.

Fitness Center: A state-of-the-art gym featuring a wide range of exercise equipment and personal training options.

Business Center: Equipped with modern business amenities, including high-speed internet and meeting rooms.

Concierge Services: Provides assistance with travel arrangements, local recommendations, and special requests.

Opening and Closing Hours

Check-in: Typically from 3:00 PM

Check-out: By 12:00 PM

Restaurants and Bars: Opening hours for dining venues generally include breakfast from 6:30 AM to 10:30 AM, lunch from 12:30 PM to 3:00 PM, and dinner from 7:00 PM to 11:00 PM. Bars may open later in the evening.

Price

Room Rates: Prices vary based on the season, room type, and booking period. Typically, rates range from $350 to $700 per night, with higher rates for suites and special packages.

Pros

Prime Location: Situated in a prestigious area with easy access to major Cairo attractions.

Exceptional Service: Known for attentive and personalized service from the staff.

Luxurious Rooms: Spacious and well-appointed rooms with stunning views of the Nile.

Diverse Dining Options: A variety of dining and bar experiences to suit different tastes.

Top-Notch Facilities: Comprehensive spa, fitness, and business facilities.

Cons

High Cost: The luxury experience comes at a premium price, which may be high for some travelers.

Traffic: Cairo's traffic can sometimes lead to delays when traveling to and from the hotel.

Busy Area: The central location may mean more noise from the city, although soundproofing in the rooms generally mitigates this.

Local Tips

Explore the Area: Take advantage of the hotel's location to visit nearby attractions like the Egyptian Museum and the bustling Khan El Khalili bazaar.

Hotel Transfers: Consider using the hotel's transfer services for convenience and safety in navigating Cairo's busy streets.

Dining Reservations: Make reservations for the hotel's popular dining venues in advance, especially during peak times.

Local Currency: While the hotel provides currency exchange services, exploring local banks may offer better rates.

3. Sofitel Legend Old Cataract Aswan

The Sofitel Legend Old Cataract Aswan is a historic luxury hotel that embodies the grandeur of a bygone era while offering modern amenities and

The Ultimate Egypt Travel Guide 2025 Edition

unparalleled service. Located on the banks of the Nile, this iconic hotel is celebrated for its stunning architecture, historical significance, and picturesque setting. It provides a unique blend of French colonial charm and Egyptian heritage, making it a captivating choice for travelers seeking a luxurious experience in Aswan.

Location (Address & Proximity)

Address: Abtal El Tahrir Street, Aswan, Egypt

Proximity: The hotel is situated on the banks of the Nile River, offering spectacular views and easy access to key attractions such as the Philae Temple, Abu Simbel, and the Nubian Museum. It's also close to the Aswan High Dam and other historical sites in the region. The Aswan International Airport is approximately a 20-minute drive away.

Highlights

Historic Charm: The hotel is renowned for its historic significance and colonial architecture, reflecting its rich heritage.

Spectacular Nile Views: Many rooms and public areas offer breathtaking views of the Nile River.

Elegant Accommodations: The hotel combines classic design with modern comforts, providing a luxurious and unique experience.

Spa and Wellness

Sofitel Spa: The spa offers a range of treatments designed for relaxation and rejuvenation. Facilities include private treatment rooms, a sauna, a steam room, and a relaxation area. The spa menu features both traditional and contemporary therapies using high-quality products.

Bars

The Terrace: A sophisticated spot offering panoramic views of the Nile and the surrounding landscape. It's a perfect place to enjoy afternoon tea or evening cocktails in a relaxed setting.

The Bar: Located in the heart of the hotel, this bar provides an elegant environment for enjoying a variety of drinks and light snacks.

Events and Conferences

Meeting Facilities: The hotel offers a range of meeting and event spaces, including elegantly appointed rooms and ballrooms suitable for conferences, weddings, and other special occasions.

Event Planning: The dedicated events team provides comprehensive services to ensure successful and memorable events, from planning and coordination to catering and technical support.

Basic Facilities and Amenities

Swimming Pool: The hotel features an outdoor pool with stunning views of the Nile and lush gardens.

Fitness Center: A well-equipped gym offering various exercise machines and personal training services.

Business Center: Provides essential business services, including high-speed internet, printing, and meeting facilities.

Concierge Services: Assists with travel arrangements, local recommendations, and special requests.

Opening and Closing Hours

Check-in: Typically from 3:00 PM

Check-out: By 12:00 PM

Restaurants and Bars: Dining venues usually serve breakfast from 6:30 AM to 10:30 AM, lunch from 12:30 PM to 3:00 PM, and dinner from 7:00 PM to 11:00 PM. The bars generally open later in the evening.

Price

Room Rates: Rates vary depending on the season, room type, and booking time. Typically, prices range from $250 to $600 per night, with premium suites and special packages costing more.

Pros

Historic Significance: The hotel's rich history and colonial architecture offer a unique and enchanting atmosphere.

Luxurious Accommodations: Elegant rooms and suites with stunning Nile views and modern amenities.

Prime Location: Conveniently situated near major attractions and historical sites in Aswan.

Exceptional Service: Renowned for attentive and personalized service from the staff.

Beautiful Setting: Gorgeous views of the Nile and lush gardens enhance the overall experience.

Cons

Price: The luxury experience comes with a high price tag, which may not be affordable for all travelers.

Age of Property: While charming, the historic nature of the hotel may come with some limitations compared to more modern facilities.

Traffic: Being a popular destination, the hotel and surrounding area can sometimes experience congestion.

Local Tips

Explore Nearby Attractions: Take advantage of the hotel's location to visit iconic sites like Philae Temple and the Nubian Museum.

Use Hotel Transfers: For convenience and safety, consider using the hotel's transfer services when traveling to and from the airport or other attractions.

Dress Code: Some dining venues within the hotel may have a dress code, so it's advisable to check in advance.

Currency Exchange: The hotel offers currency exchange services, but local banks might provide better rates.

4. The St. Regis Cairo

The St. Regis Cairo is a five-star luxury hotel renowned for its opulent accommodations, sophisticated design, and impeccable service. Situated on the banks of the Nile River, the hotel combines classic elegance with modern comforts, offering a refined experience in the heart of Cairo. With its exquisite decor, exceptional dining options, and premium amenities, The St. Regis Cairo caters to both leisure and business travelers seeking a high-end retreat.

Location (Address & Proximity)

Address: 1191 Corniche El Nil, Cairo, Egypt

Proximity: The hotel is ideally located along the Nile River, providing picturesque river views and easy access to major Cairo attractions. It's close to landmarks such as the Egyptian Museum, Tahrir Square, and the bustling Khan El Khalili bazaar. Cairo International Airport is approximately a 30-minute drive from the hotel.

Highlights

Elegant Design: The hotel's interiors reflect a blend of classic and contemporary design, featuring luxurious furnishings and sophisticated decor.

Nile Views: Many of the rooms and public areas offer stunning views of the Nile River, enhancing the overall guest experience.

Luxurious Accommodations: Rooms and suites are thoughtfully designed with high-end amenities and plush furnishings to ensure maximum comfort.

Spa and Wellness

Iridium Spa: The hotel's spa offers a range of treatments aimed at relaxation and rejuvenation. Facilities include private treatment rooms, a sauna, a steam room, and a relaxation lounge. The spa uses premium products and offers various therapies, including massages and skincare treatments.

Bars

The St. Regis Bar: This elegant bar is known for its sophisticated ambiance and extensive selection of cocktails, fine wines, and light bites. It's a great place to unwind and socialize in style.

The Roof Bar: Located on the rooftop, this bar provides breathtaking views of the Nile and Cairo's skyline. It's an ideal spot for evening cocktails and casual gatherings.

Events and Conferences

Meeting Facilities: The hotel offers a range of versatile event spaces, including grand ballrooms and smaller meeting rooms, all equipped with the latest technology for conferences and events.

Event Planning: The St. Regis Cairo provides comprehensive event planning services, from initial planning and coordination to catering and technical support, ensuring successful and memorable events.

Basic Facilities and Amenities

Swimming Pool: The hotel features an outdoor pool with panoramic views of the Nile, complemented by a sun deck and comfortable loungers.

Fitness Center: A state-of-the-art gym is available, featuring a variety of exercise equipment and options for personal training.

Business Center: Provides essential services such as high-speed internet, printing, and meeting facilities for business travelers.

Concierge Services: Offers assistance with travel arrangements, local recommendations, and special requests to enhance the guest experience.

Opening and Closing Hours

Check-in: Typically from 3:00 PM

Check-out: By 12:00 PM

Restaurants and Bars: The dining venues generally serve breakfast from 6:30 AM to 10:30 AM, lunch from 12:30 PM to 3:00 PM, and dinner from 7:00 PM to 11:00 PM. Bars typically open in the late afternoon and remain open until late evening.

Price

Room Rates: Rates can vary based on the season, room type, and booking time. On average, prices range from $300 to $700 per night, with higher rates for suites and special packages.

Pros

Prime Location: Centrally located with stunning Nile views and close proximity to major attractions.

Luxurious Rooms: Elegant and well-appointed accommodations with modern amenities.

Exceptional Service: Renowned for its high level of personalized service and attention to detail.

Diverse Dining Options: A range of high-quality dining and bar experiences within the hotel.

Beautiful Setting: Breathtaking views of the Nile River and Cairo's skyline.

Cons

High Cost: The luxury experience comes at a premium, which may not be affordable for all travelers.

Traffic: Cairo's traffic congestion can affect travel times to and from the hotel.

Noise: Being in a central location, some rooms might experience city noise, though soundproofing is generally effective.

Local Tips

Explore the City: Take advantage of the hotel's central location to visit nearby landmarks such as the Egyptian Museum and Khan El Khalili.

Hotel Transfers: Utilize the hotel's transfer services for convenience and safety in navigating Cairo's busy streets.

Dining Reservations: Make reservations for the hotel's dining venues in advance, particularly during peak periods.

Currency Exchange: The hotel offers currency exchange services, but local banks may provide better rates.

5. Marriott Mena House, Cairo

The Marriott Mena House, Cairo is a historic luxury hotel located at the foot of the Great Pyramids of Giza. Known for its rich history, stunning views, and elegant accommodations, this iconic hotel offers a unique blend of traditional Egyptian charm and modern comfort. It provides an exceptional experience for visitors seeking both luxury and proximity to one of the world's most famous landmarks.

Location (Address & Proximity)

Address: Mena House Pyramids, Giza, Cairo, Egypt

Proximity: The hotel is situated directly adjacent to the Giza Plateau, offering unrivaled views of the Great Pyramids and the Sphinx. It is a short drive from other Cairo attractions such as the Egyptian Museum and Khan El Khalili. Cairo International Airport is about a 45-minute drive away.

Highlights

Pyramid Views: The hotel offers some of the best views of the Great Pyramids of Giza, making it a prime location for experiencing this world-famous landmark.

Historic Atmosphere: The hotel's design reflects its rich history, with traditional Egyptian decor and architecture that transport guests to a bygone era.

Luxurious Accommodations: The rooms and suites are elegantly furnished, blending modern amenities with classic charm.

Spa and Wellness

Wellness Center: The hotel features a wellness center with a range of services, including massages and treatments designed to promote relaxation and well-being. Facilities may include a sauna and a steam room.

Bars

The Great Pyramid Bar: Located with views of the Pyramids, this bar is an ideal spot for enjoying a variety of cocktails and light snacks while taking in the stunning surroundings.

Palms Bar: A more casual option offering a selection of drinks and refreshments in a relaxed setting.

Events and Conferences

Meeting Facilities: The hotel offers a variety of meeting and event spaces, including large ballrooms and smaller meeting rooms. These spaces are equipped with modern technology and can be configured for various types of events.

Event Planning: The dedicated events team assists with planning and executing conferences, weddings, and other special events, ensuring a smooth and memorable experience.

Basic Facilities and Amenities

Swimming Pool: An outdoor pool with views of the Pyramids and a spacious sun deck.

Fitness Center: A well-equipped gym offering a range of exercise equipment and personal training services.

Business Center: Provides essential services for business travelers, including high-speed internet, printing, and meeting rooms.

Concierge Services: Assists with travel arrangements, local recommendations, and special requests to enhance guests' stay.

Opening and Closing Hours

Check-in: Typically from 3:00 PM

Check-out: By 12:00 PM

Restaurants and Bars: Dining venues generally serve breakfast from 6:30 AM to 10:30 AM, lunch from 12:30 PM to 3:00 PM, and dinner from 7:00 PM to 11:00 PM. Bars usually open in the late afternoon and remain open until late evening.

Price

Room Rates: Prices vary based on the season, room type, and booking time. On average, rates range from $200 to $500 per night, with premium suites and special packages costing more.

Pros

Unmatched Location: Directly adjacent to the Pyramids of Giza, offering unparalleled views and easy access to the site.

Historic Charm: Rich historical ambiance combined with luxurious modern amenities.

Luxurious Accommodations: Elegant rooms and suites with high-end furnishings and amenities.

Exceptional Views: Breathtaking views of the Pyramids from many parts of the hotel.

Unique Experience: Offers a unique blend of history, luxury, and proximity to one of the world's most iconic landmarks.

Cons

Cost: The luxury experience comes with a premium price, which may be high for some travelers.

Distance from Downtown: The hotel is a bit farther from central Cairo, which can mean longer travel times to other city attractions.

Traffic: Traffic congestion in Cairo can affect travel times to and from the hotel.

Local Tips

Explore the Pyramids: Take full advantage of the hotel's proximity to the Pyramids by visiting early in the morning or later in the evening to avoid the heat and crowds.

Use Hotel Services: Consider using the hotel's organized tours or guides for a more comprehensive experience of the Giza Plateau and surrounding areas.

Dining Reservations: Make reservations in advance for dining venues, especially during peak tourist seasons.

Currency Exchange: The hotel offers currency exchange services, but local banks might provide better rates.

Mid-Range Hotel

Mid-range hotels in Egypt provide a perfect balance of comfort, convenience, and affordability. These accommodations offer well-appointed rooms, reliable amenities, and a central location, making them an excellent choice for travelers who want quality without breaking the bank. Enjoy a comfortable stay with essential services and a warm atmosphere, ensuring a pleasant experience while exploring Egypt's remarkable destinations.

Top 5 Mid-Range Hotel

1. Steigenberger Hotel El Tahrir Cairo

The Steigenberger Hotel El Tahrir Cairo is a mid-range hotel that offers a blend of comfort, convenience, and value in one of Cairo's most central locations. Positioned near key cultural and historical attractions, this hotel provides a welcoming environment for both leisure and business travelers. With modern amenities, a central location, and a focus on quality service, it represents a well-rounded choice for travelers seeking a reliable and comfortable stay in Cairo.

Location (Address & Proximity)

Address: 12 Mohamed Mazhar Street, Garden City, Cairo, Egypt

Grace Bennett

Proximity: Located in the upscale Garden City district, the hotel is within walking distance of Tahrir Square and the Egyptian Museum. It's also close to other attractions like the Cairo Opera House and the historic Khan El Khalili bazaar. Cairo International Airport is about a 30-minute drive away.

Highlights

Central Location: Positioned in a prime area with easy access to major Cairo attractions and cultural landmarks.

Modern Comfort: Offers comfortable and well-appointed rooms with modern amenities, providing a pleasant stay for guests.

Value for Money: Provides a good balance of quality and affordability, making it a popular choice for mid-range travelers.

Spa and Wellness

Wellness Facilities: The hotel includes basic wellness facilities such as a fitness center for guests looking to maintain their exercise routines. However, it does not have a full-service spa.

Bars

Lounge Bar: The hotel features a lounge bar where guests can enjoy a selection of drinks and light refreshments in a relaxed setting. It's an ideal spot for unwinding after a day of sightseeing or meetings.

Events and Conferences

Meeting Rooms: The hotel offers several meeting and event spaces suitable for business meetings, conferences, and social events. These rooms are equipped with standard audiovisual technology and can be arranged to accommodate various event sizes.

Event Planning: The hotel's events team assists with planning and organizing events, providing support for everything from setup to catering.

Basic Facilities and Amenities

Dining: The hotel's restaurant offers a variety of dining options, including breakfast, lunch, and dinner, with both local and international cuisine available.

Business Center: Provides essential business services such as high-speed internet access, printing, and meeting room facilities.

Fitness Center: A well-equipped gym for guests to stay active during their stay.

Concierge Services: Assists with local recommendations, travel arrangements, and special requests to enhance the guest experience.

Opening and Closing Hours

Check-in: Typically from 3:00 PM

Check-out: By 12:00 PM

Restaurants and Bars: The restaurant usually serves breakfast from 6:30 AM to 10:30 AM, lunch from 12:30 PM to 3:00 PM, and dinner from 7:00 PM to 10:30 PM. The lounge bar's hours vary but typically open in the late afternoon and remain open until late evening.

Price

Room Rates: Rates for a stay at the Steigenberger Hotel El Tahrir Cairo typically range from $100 to $200 per night, depending on the season, room type, and booking period. This pricing positions it firmly in the mid-range category.

Pros

Prime Location: Central location with easy access to major attractions and cultural sites in Cairo.

Comfortable Rooms: Modern and comfortable accommodations that provide good value for money.

Value for Money: Offers a good balance of quality and affordability for mid-range travelers.

Efficient Service: Known for attentive and friendly service from the staff.

Cons

Limited Wellness Options: Lacks a full-service spa, which may be a drawback for guests seeking extensive wellness facilities.

Basic Amenities: Some amenities and services may be more basic compared to higher-end luxury hotels.

Traffic: Being in a busy area, traffic congestion can sometimes affect travel times to and from the hotel.

Local Tips

Explore Nearby Attractions: Take advantage of the hotel's central location to visit nearby landmarks such as the Egyptian Museum and Tahrir Square.

Use Hotel Services: Consider utilizing the hotel's concierge services for local recommendations and travel arrangements.

Dining: The local area has a variety of dining options; ask the concierge for recommendations if you want to explore beyond the hotel's restaurant.

Traffic Considerations: Plan your travels around Cairo's traffic patterns to make the most of your time in the city.

2. Pyramisa Cairo Hotel

The Pyramisa Cairo Hotel offers a mid-range option for travelers seeking comfort and practicality in the bustling capital of Egypt. Known for its value-for-money accommodations and central location, this hotel provides a solid choice for both leisure and business travelers. With a range of amenities and services designed to meet the needs of its guests, the Pyramisa Cairo Hotel is a reliable choice for a comfortable stay in Cairo.

Location (Address & Proximity)

Address: 60 Giza Street, Cairo, Egypt

Proximity: Located in the Giza district, the hotel is relatively close to the Great Pyramids of Giza, offering easy access to this iconic site. It's also a short drive from central Cairo attractions such as Tahrir Square, the Egyptian Museum, and the Cairo Opera House. Cairo International Airport is approximately a 30-minute drive away.

Highlights

Convenient Location: Provides good access to major Cairo attractions and landmarks, including the Pyramids and downtown Cairo.

Affordable Rates: Offers budget-friendly accommodations with a range of amenities, making it a popular choice for mid-range travelers.

Basic Comfort: Provides comfortable and practical amenities suited for a range of travelers.

Spa and Wellness

Wellness Facilities: The hotel includes basic wellness facilities such as a fitness center. However, it does not offer a full-service spa.

Bars

Lobby Bar: The hotel features a lobby bar where guests can relax with a selection of drinks and light snacks. It provides a casual setting for unwinding after a day of exploring or business meetings.

Events and Conferences

Meeting Rooms: The hotel has several meeting and event spaces suitable for conferences, business meetings, and social events. These rooms are equipped with standard audiovisual technology.

Event Services: Provides support for planning and organizing events, including catering and setup.

Basic Facilities and Amenities

Dining: The hotel's restaurant offers a range of dining options, including breakfast, lunch, and dinner. It serves both local and international cuisine.

Business Center: Offers essential business services such as high-speed internet access, printing, and meeting room facilities.

Fitness Center: A gym with basic exercise equipment for guests who wish to maintain their fitness routines.

Concierge Services: Assists with local recommendations, travel arrangements, and special requests.

Opening and Closing Hours

Check-in: Typically from 3:00 PM

Check-out: By 12:00 PM

Restaurants and Bars: The restaurant usually serves breakfast from 6:30 AM to 10:30 AM, lunch from 12:30 PM to 3:00 PM, and dinner from 7:00 PM to 10:30 PM. The lobby bar generally opens in the late afternoon and remains open until late evening.

Price

Room Rates: Rates at the Pyramisa Cairo Hotel typically range from $80 to $150 per night, depending on the season, room type, and booking period. This positions it as an affordable option within the mid-range category.

Pros

Affordable Pricing: Provides good value for money with competitive rates for a mid-range hotel.

Convenient Location: Close to major attractions and landmarks, including the Pyramids of Giza and central Cairo.

Comfortable Accommodations: Offers practical and comfortable rooms with essential amenities.

Friendly Service: Known for its helpful and attentive staff.

Cons

Basic Facilities: The amenities and services are more basic compared to higher-end or luxury hotels.

Limited Wellness Options: Lacks a full-service spa and extensive wellness facilities.

Traffic: As with many hotels in Cairo, traffic congestion can impact travel times to and from the hotel.

Local Tips

Visit Nearby Attractions: Take advantage of the hotel's proximity to the Pyramids of Giza and other nearby sites.

Plan for Traffic: Be mindful of Cairo's traffic patterns when planning trips around the city.

Dining: Explore local dining options in the area if you wish to try different cuisines beyond the hotel's restaurant.

Use Hotel Services: Utilize the concierge for local recommendations and to assist with any travel arrangements.

3. Holiday Inn Cairo Citystars

The Holiday Inn Cairo Citystars is a well-regarded mid-range hotel offering a blend of modern comfort and convenience. Situated within the Citystars complex, one of Cairo's largest shopping and entertainment hubs, the hotel provides a strategic location for both leisure and business travelers. Its contemporary amenities and proximity to various attractions make it a popular choice for those visiting Cairo.

Location (Address & Proximity)

Address: 5th Settlement, Cairo, Egypt

Proximity: Located within the Citystars complex, the hotel is adjacent to Citystars Mall, offering guests easy access to a wide range of shopping, dining, and entertainment options. It is also close to Cairo International Airport, approximately a 10-

minute drive away, and well-connected to other parts of the city.

Highlights

Citystars Complex: Direct access to one of Cairo's premier shopping and entertainment destinations.

Modern Accommodations: Offers contemporary rooms and amenities designed for comfort and convenience.

Proximity to Airport: Close to Cairo International Airport, making it convenient for travelers with early or late flights.

Spa and Wellness

Wellness Facilities: The hotel features a fitness center with modern exercise equipment. However, it does not have a full-service spa.

Bars

Lobby Bar: The hotel's lobby bar provides a relaxed setting where guests can enjoy a variety of drinks and light snacks. It's a great spot for unwinding after a day of shopping or business meetings.

Events and Conferences

Meeting Facilities: The hotel offers a range of meeting and event spaces, including well-equipped conference rooms and ballrooms. These facilities are suitable for business meetings, conferences, and social events.

Event Planning: The events team provides support for planning and organizing events, including catering and technical assistance.

Basic Facilities and Amenities

Dining: The hotel has a restaurant offering a variety of dining options, including local and international cuisine. It serves breakfast, lunch, and dinner.

Business Center: Provides essential business services such as high-speed internet access, printing, and meeting room facilities.

Fitness Center: A well-equipped gym for guests to stay active during their stay.

Concierge Services: Assists with local recommendations, travel arrangements, and special requests to enhance guests' experience.

Opening and Closing Hours

Check-in: Typically from 3:00 PM

Check-out: By 12:00 PM

Restaurants and Bars: The restaurant usually serves breakfast from 6:30 AM to 10:30 AM, lunch from 12:30 PM to 3:00 PM, and dinner from 7:00 PM to 11:00 PM. The lobby bar typically opens in the late afternoon and remains open until late evening.

Price

Room Rates: Rates at the Holiday Inn Cairo Citystars generally range from $100 to $200 per night, depending on the season, room type, and booking period. This pricing positions it as a solid mid-range option.

Pros

Prime Location: Direct access to Citystars Mall and close proximity to Cairo International Airport.

Modern Comfort: Contemporary rooms and amenities designed for convenience and comfort.

Convenient for Travelers: Close to the airport and well-connected to the city's attractions.

Good Facilities: Offers a range of facilities including a fitness center, meeting rooms, and dining options.

Cons

Limited Wellness Options: Lacks a full-service spa, which may be a drawback for guests seeking extensive wellness facilities.

Mall Atmosphere: The hotel's location within a large commercial complex might not appeal to those looking for a more traditional or historic Cairo experience.

Traffic: As with many locations in Cairo, traffic congestion can affect travel times to and from the hotel.

Local Tips

Explore Citystars Mall: Take full advantage of the hotel's location by exploring the shopping, dining, and entertainment options available in Citystars Mall.

Airport Transfers: Utilize the hotel's proximity to the airport for convenience, especially if you have early or late flights.

Dining Options: In addition to the hotel's restaurant, explore the diverse dining options within Citystars Mall for a variety of culinary experiences.

Traffic Awareness: Be mindful of traffic patterns when traveling to other parts of Cairo to maximize your time in the city.

5. Zoser Hotel

Zoser Hotel is a mid-range hotel offering a blend of practicality and comfort in a central location in Cairo. Known for its welcoming atmosphere and value-for-money accommodations, it caters to both business and leisure travelers looking for a comfortable stay with essential amenities. The hotel provides a straightforward and reliable option for those exploring the city or attending to business in Cairo.

Location (Address & Proximity)

Address: 5 El Tayaran Street, Nasr City, Cairo, Egypt

Proximity: Situated in the Nasr City district, Zoser Hotel is well-positioned for easy access to various parts of Cairo. It is a short drive from key attractions such as the Cairo International Conference Center and Citystars Mall. Cairo International Airport is approximately a 20-minute drive away, making it convenient for travelers with flights.

Highlights

Central Location: Located in Nasr City, providing good access to both business and leisure destinations in Cairo.

Comfortable Accommodations: Offers comfortable and practical rooms with essential amenities.

Value for Money: Provides an affordable option with a focus on comfort and convenience.

Spa and Wellness

Wellness Facilities: The hotel features a fitness center with basic exercise equipment. However, it does not have a full-service spa.

Bars

Lobby Lounge: The hotel has a lobby lounge where guests can enjoy a selection of drinks and light refreshments. It offers a casual setting for relaxation and informal meetings.

Events and Conferences

Meeting Rooms: The hotel provides several meeting and event spaces, including conference rooms suitable for business meetings, seminars, and social events. These rooms are equipped with standard audiovisual technology.

Event Services: Offers support for planning and organizing events, including catering and setup.

Basic Facilities and Amenities

Dining: The hotel's restaurant serves a range of local and international dishes for breakfast, lunch, and dinner.

Business Center: Provides essential business services such as high-speed internet access, printing, and meeting room facilities.

Fitness Center: Includes basic fitness equipment for guests who wish to maintain their exercise routines.

Concierge Services: Assists with local recommendations, travel arrangements, and special requests to enhance the guest experience.

Opening and Closing Hours

Check-in: Typically from 3:00 PM

Check-out: By 12:00 PM

Restaurants and Bars: The restaurant generally serves breakfast from 6:30 AM to 10:00 AM, lunch from 12:00 PM to 3:00 PM, and dinner from 7:00 PM to 10:00 PM. The lobby lounge's hours vary but typically open in the late afternoon and remain open until late evening.

Price

Room Rates: Rates for a stay at Zoser Hotel usually range from $70 to $150 per night, depending on the season, room type, and booking period. This pricing positions it as a budget-friendly option within the mid-range category.

Pros

Affordable Rates: Offers good value for money with competitive rates for mid-range accommodations.

Central Location: Conveniently located in Nasr City with access to various business and leisure destinations.

Comfortable Rooms: Provides practical and comfortable rooms with essential amenities.

Friendly Service: Known for its attentive and helpful staff.

Cons

Basic Facilities: The amenities and services are more basic compared to higher-end or luxury hotels.

Limited Wellness Options: Lacks a full-service spa and extensive wellness facilities.

Traffic: Nasr City can experience traffic congestion, which may impact travel times to and from the hotel.

Local Tips

Explore Nasr City: Take advantage of the hotel's location by exploring nearby attractions and shopping areas in Nasr City.

Airport Transfers: Utilize the hotel's proximity to the airport for convenience, especially for early or late flights.

Dining: Besides the hotel's restaurant, consider exploring local dining options in Nasr City for a variety of culinary experiences.

Traffic Considerations: Be mindful of Cairo's traffic patterns when planning trips around the city to make the most of your time.

Boutique Hotel

Boutique hotels in Egypt offer a distinctive charm and personalized service, providing a unique alternative to larger accommodations. These small, stylish hotels often feature eclectic decor, intimate settings, and tailored guest experiences, making them ideal for travelers seeking a memorable and individualized stay. Enjoy a blend of character and comfort as you immerse yourself in Egypt's vibrant culture.

Top 5 Boutique Hotel

1. Villa Belle Époque

Villa Belle Époque Boutique Hotels offers a unique and luxurious experience with a focus on personalized service and refined elegance. This boutique hotel is known for its distinctive style, combining classical charm with modern amenities. Located in various parts of Egypt, these hotels provide a more intimate and bespoke experience compared to larger chain hotels, appealing to travelers seeking a distinctive and memorable stay.

Location (Address & Proximity)

Address: Specific addresses can vary depending on the location of the Villa Belle Époque property. Generally, these boutique hotels are situated in attractive and accessible areas, often in or near major cities or historical sites.

Proximity: Villa Belle Époque Boutique Hotels are typically located in areas that offer both tranquility and easy access to local attractions. For example, if located in Cairo, they might be positioned near cultural and historical landmarks, while properties in other regions might focus on scenic or historical sites relevant to the area.

Highlights

Unique Style: Each Villa Belle Époque Boutique Hotel is designed with a distinctive style that often blends classic architecture with contemporary comforts.

Personalized Service: Known for offering personalized and attentive service, ensuring a high level of guest satisfaction and tailored experiences.

Luxurious Ambiance: The hotels provide a luxurious and elegant atmosphere, often featuring beautifully designed interiors and high-quality furnishings.

Spa and Wellness

Wellness Facilities: While specific amenities can vary by location, many Villa Belle Époque Boutique Hotels offer wellness facilities such as spa treatments, massage services, and relaxation areas. The focus is typically on providing a serene and rejuvenating experience.

Bars

On-Site Bars: Boutique hotels of this caliber often feature elegant bars or lounges where guests can enjoy a curated selection of beverages. The ambiance is usually sophisticated and designed to enhance the overall guest experience.

Events and Conferences

Event Spaces: Boutique hotels may offer unique spaces for small-scale events, such as private dinners, intimate gatherings, or business meetings. These spaces are often designed with an emphasis on elegance and exclusivity.

Event Planning: The hotels typically provide personalized event planning services to ensure that all aspects of the event are handled with attention to detail.

Basic Facilities and Amenities

Dining: The hotels usually have an on-site restaurant offering a selection of gourmet cuisine. Meals are often prepared with high-quality ingredients and presented in an elegant setting.

Business Center: While not always as extensive as those in larger hotels, boutique properties may offer essential business services such as internet access, printing, and meeting room facilities.

Concierge Services: Dedicated concierge services are typically available to assist with local recommendations, travel arrangements, and special requests.

Opening and Closing Hours

Check-in: Typically from 3:00 PM

Check-out: By 12:00 PM

Restaurants and Bars: Dining and bar hours can vary by location but generally include breakfast, lunch, and dinner services, with bars opening in the late afternoon and closing in the evening.

Price

Room Rates: Prices for Villa Belle Époque Boutique Hotels can vary significantly depending on the location, season, and room type. Generally, rates for these boutique properties can range from $150 to $500 per night, reflecting their luxury status and personalized service.

Pros

Distinctive Experience: Offers a unique and charming atmosphere that stands out from larger hotel chains.

Personalized Service: Provides high levels of personalized service and attention to detail.

Elegant Design: Features beautifully designed interiors that create a luxurious and comfortable environment.

Intimate Setting: Smaller size and personalized approach offer a more intimate and exclusive experience.

Cons

Higher Cost: The luxury and personalized nature of boutique hotels come at a premium, which may be higher than mid-range or budget options.

Limited Scale: Fewer facilities and services compared to larger hotels or resorts, which may be a consideration for some travelers.

Availability: Limited number of properties may affect availability, especially during peak travel seasons.

Local Tips

Explore Local Culture: Take advantage of the boutique hotel's local knowledge and concierge services to explore nearby cultural and historical attractions.

Request Special Services: Don't hesitate to ask for personalized recommendations or special arrangements, as boutique hotels often excel in tailored guest experiences.

Check Hotel-Specific Amenities: Since facilities can vary by location, review the specific amenities and services offered at the individual property you plan to stay at.

2. The Barcelo Cairo Pyramids

The Barceló Cairo Pyramids is a mid-range hotel that combines modern amenities with a strategic location close to one of the world's most famous landmarks, the Great Pyramids of Giza. Known for its comfortable accommodations and practical facilities, the hotel caters to both leisure and business travelers seeking a well-rounded stay in Cairo.

Location (Address & Proximity)

Address: 229 Pyramids Road, Giza, Cairo, Egypt

Proximity: Located near the Pyramids of Giza, the hotel offers convenient access to the Great Pyramids, the Sphinx, and the surrounding archaeological sites. It is also relatively close to central Cairo, making it easy to explore other city attractions. Cairo International Airport is about a 30-minute drive away.

Highlights

Proximity to Pyramids: Offers close access to the Great Pyramids of Giza, a major attraction for visitors.

Comfortable Rooms: Provides well-appointed and comfortable accommodations suitable for a range of travelers.

Value for Money: Offers good value with a mix of modern amenities and a central location.

Spa and Wellness

Wellness Facilities: The hotel includes a fitness center equipped with modern exercise equipment. While it does not feature a full-service spa, the wellness facilities cater to basic fitness needs.

Bars

Hotel Bar: The hotel features a bar where guests can enjoy a variety of beverages and light snacks. It's a casual spot ideal for relaxing after a day of sightseeing or meetings.

Events and Conferences

Meeting Rooms: The Barceló Cairo Pyramids offers several meeting and event spaces equipped with standard audiovisual technology, suitable for business meetings, conferences, and small social events.

Event Services: The hotel provides support for organizing events, including catering and technical assistance.

Basic Facilities and Amenities

Dining: The hotel has a restaurant that serves a variety of local and international dishes for breakfast, lunch, and dinner.

Business Center: Offers essential business services such as high-speed internet access, printing, and meeting facilities.

Fitness Center: A well-equipped gym available for guests to use during their stay.

Concierge Services: Provides assistance with local recommendations, travel arrangements, and other guest needs.

Opening and Closing Hours

Check-in: Typically from 3:00 PM

Check-out: By 12:00 PM

Restaurants and Bars: The restaurant usually serves breakfast from 6:30 AM to 10:30 AM, lunch from 12:30 PM to 3:00 PM, and dinner from 7:00 PM to 10:30 PM. The bar generally opens in the late afternoon and remains open until late evening.

Price

Room Rates: Rates for a stay at the Barceló Cairo Pyramids typically range from $80 to $150 per night, depending on the season, room type, and booking period. This pricing positions it as a competitive option within the mid-range category.

Pros

Close to Pyramids: Offers proximity to the Great Pyramids of Giza, providing easy access to one of Egypt's top attractions.

Comfortable Accommodations: Features modern and comfortable rooms with practical amenities.

Good Value: Provides a good balance of comfort, location, and price.

Friendly Service: Known for attentive and helpful staff.

Cons

Basic Wellness Options: Lacks a full-service spa, which may be a drawback for guests seeking extensive wellness facilities.

Traffic: The area around the Pyramids and Giza can experience heavy traffic, which might impact travel times to and from the hotel.

Limited Dining Variety: Dining options within the hotel might be limited compared to larger hotels or resorts.

Local Tips

Visit the Pyramids: Take full advantage of the hotel's proximity to the Pyramids of Giza by planning visits to these iconic sites.

Explore Local Attractions: Beyond the Pyramids, consider exploring other nearby attractions such as the Sphinx or the Cairo Museum.

Use Hotel Services: Utilize the concierge for local tips and assistance with travel arrangements and sightseeing recommendations.

Be Traffic-Wise: Plan your travel times around Cairo's traffic patterns to make the most of your visit.

3. The Cairo House Hotel

The Cairo House Hotel is a boutique property that emphasizes personalized service and a charming, intimate atmosphere. Known for its unique character and central location, this hotel offers a more personalized experience compared to larger, more conventional hotels. It is well-suited for travelers looking for a comfortable, cozy stay with a touch of local flair.

Location (Address & Proximity)

Address: 9 El Nil Street, Garden City, Cairo, Egypt

Proximity: Situated in the Garden City district, The Cairo House Hotel is conveniently located near key Cairo attractions. It's within walking distance of Tahrir Square, the Egyptian Museum, and the Cairo Opera House. Cairo International Airport is approximately a 30-minute drive away.

Highlights

Central Location: Provides easy access to major cultural and historical landmarks in Cairo.

Boutique Experience: Offers a more intimate and personalized stay compared to larger hotel chains.

Unique Charm: Features distinctive decor and design elements that enhance the guest experience.

Spa and Wellness

Wellness Facilities: The hotel does not have a full-service spa. However, it may offer basic wellness amenities such as a small fitness area or wellness services upon request.

Bars

On-Site Lounge: The Cairo House Hotel has a lounge or small bar area where guests can relax with a selection of drinks. This space is designed to be cozy and welcoming, perfect for unwinding after a day of exploring.

Events and Conferences

Meeting Spaces: The hotel offers limited meeting and event facilities suitable for small gatherings, business meetings, or private events. The space is designed to be adaptable and comfortable for various types of functions.

Event Services: The hotel provides support for organizing and planning events, including catering and technical assistance as needed.

Basic Facilities and Amenities

Dining: The hotel features an on-site restaurant serving a variety of local and international cuisine. Breakfast, lunch, and dinner options are available.

Business Center: Offers basic business services such as high-speed internet access, printing, and meeting facilities.

Fitness Center: While there may be limited fitness facilities, the hotel focuses more on providing personalized and comfortable accommodations.

Concierge Services: Assists with local recommendations, travel arrangements, and special requests to enhance the guest experience.

Opening and Closing Hours

Check-in: Typically from 3:00 PM

Check-out: By 12:00 PM

Restaurants and Bars: The restaurant usually serves breakfast from 7:00 AM to 10:00 AM, lunch from 12:00 PM to 3:00 PM, and dinner from 7:00 PM to 10:00 PM. The lounge or bar area is open in the late afternoon and evening.

Price

Room Rates: Rates for a stay at The Cairo House Hotel generally range from $80 to $150 per night, depending on the season, room type, and booking period. This positions it as an affordable boutique option in the mid-range category.

Pros

Intimate Atmosphere: Provides a boutique experience with personalized service and a unique character.

Central Location: Close to major attractions and cultural sites in Cairo.

Charming Decor: Features distinctive decor and design elements that enhance the guest experience.

Friendly Service: Known for attentive and helpful staff.

Cons

Limited Facilities: May lack some of the amenities found in larger hotels, such as extensive wellness facilities or large conference rooms.

Basic Amenities: Focuses on charm and character, which may mean fewer high-tech amenities or additional services compared to larger properties.

Traffic: As with many locations in Cairo, traffic congestion can affect travel times to and from the hotel.

Local Tips

Explore Nearby Attractions: Take advantage of the hotel's central location by visiting nearby landmarks such as the Egyptian Museum and Tahrir Square.

Use Concierge Services: Utilize the concierge for personalized recommendations and assistance with local tours and activities.

Dining Options: Besides the hotel's restaurant, explore local dining options in Garden City for a variety of culinary experiences.

Traffic Awareness: Be mindful of traffic patterns in Cairo to maximize your sightseeing and travel efficiency.

4. The Zamalek Hotel

The Zamalek Hotel is a mid-range property situated in the Zamalek district of Cairo, known for its charming, leafy streets and a more relaxed atmosphere compared to the bustling city center. This hotel offers a comfortable stay with a blend of traditional hospitality and modern amenities, making it an attractive choice for both leisure and business travelers looking for a pleasant and convenient location.

Location (Address & Proximity)

Address: 21 El Guezira Street, Zamalek, Cairo, Egypt

Proximity: Located in the Zamalek district, the hotel is situated on an island in the Nile River, providing scenic views and a tranquil environment. It is close to various cultural and leisure attractions, including the Cairo Opera House and the Cairo Tower. Central Cairo and major business districts are easily accessible, and Cairo International Airport is approximately a 30-minute drive away.

Highlights

Scenic Location: Offers picturesque views and a peaceful environment within the Zamalek district, which is known for its greenery and riverside setting.

Comfortable Accommodations: Provides well-appointed rooms with modern amenities designed for a relaxing stay.

Accessible to Attractions: Close to cultural landmarks and entertainment options in Cairo.

Spa and Wellness

Wellness Facilities: The hotel does not feature a full-service spa. However, it may offer basic wellness amenities such as a fitness center or relaxation area.

Bars

On-Site Bar: The Zamalek Hotel includes a bar or lounge area where guests can enjoy a range of beverages in a relaxed setting. This space provides a pleasant environment for unwinding after a day of sightseeing or business activities.

Events and Conferences

Meeting Facilities: The hotel offers meeting and event spaces suitable for small to medium-sized gatherings, including business meetings, conferences, and social events. These spaces are equipped with standard audiovisual technology.

Event Services: Provides support for organizing events, including catering and technical assistance to ensure successful functions.

Basic Facilities and Amenities

Dining: The hotel's restaurant serves a variety of local and international dishes for breakfast, lunch, and dinner. It offers a comfortable dining environment with options to suit different tastes.

Business Center: Offers essential business services such as high-speed internet access, printing, and meeting facilities.

Fitness Center: Includes basic exercise equipment for guests who wish to stay active during their stay.

Concierge Services: Provides assistance with local recommendations, travel arrangements, and special requests to enhance the guest experience.

Opening and Closing Hours

Check-in: Typically from 3:00 PM

Check-out: By 12:00 PM

Restaurants and Bars: The restaurant generally serves breakfast from 6:30 AM to 10:00 AM, lunch from 12:00 PM to 3:00 PM, and dinner from 7:00 PM to 10:00 PM. The bar or lounge area typically opens in the late afternoon and remains open until late evening.

Price

Room Rates: Rates for a stay at The Zamalek Hotel generally range from $70 to $130 per night, depending on the season, room type, and booking period. This pricing makes it a competitive option within the mid-range category.

Pros

Scenic Location: Situated in the tranquil Zamalek district with views of the Nile and green spaces.

Comfortable Rooms: Provides modern and comfortable accommodations with essential amenities.

Proximity to Attractions: Close to key cultural and leisure sites in Cairo.

Friendly Service: Known for its attentive and helpful staff.

Cons

Basic Facilities: May lack some of the high-end amenities and extensive facilities found in larger or luxury hotels.

Limited Wellness Options: Does not offer a full-service spa or extensive wellness facilities.

Traffic: The area around Cairo can experience heavy traffic, which may impact travel times to and from the hotel.

Local Tips

Explore Zamalek: Take advantage of the hotel's location by exploring the charming Zamalek district, known for its cafes, restaurants, and leafy streets.

Visit Nearby Attractions: Use the hotel's location to easily visit nearby attractions such as the Cairo Tower, Cairo Opera House, and the Egyptian Museum.

Dining Recommendations: In addition to the hotel's restaurant, explore local dining options in Zamalek for a variety of culinary experiences.

Traffic Considerations: Be mindful of Cairo's traffic patterns when planning your travel to maximize your sightseeing and travel efficiency.

5. The Boutique Hotel Cairo

The Boutique Hotel Cairo offers a sophisticated and intimate atmosphere in the heart of Cairo. As a boutique hotel, it emphasizes unique, personalized experiences with a focus on style, comfort, and high-quality service. It's designed for travelers who appreciate a refined and individualized stay.

Location (Address & Proximity)

Address: 9 El Guezira Street, Zamalek, Cairo, Egypt

Proximity: Situated in the Zamalek district, the hotel benefits from a picturesque setting on an island in the Nile River. It's conveniently located near key attractions such as the Cairo Opera House, Cairo Tower, and the Egyptian Museum. The central business districts are also easily accessible, and Cairo International Airport is approximately a 30-minute drive away.

Highlights

Elegant Design: Features stylish and sophisticated decor that enhances the guest experience with a luxurious ambiance.

Personalized Service: Provides attentive and customized service, ensuring each guest's needs and preferences are met.

Tranquil Setting: Located in the serene Zamalek district, offering scenic views and a peaceful retreat from the city's hustle.

Spa and Wellness

Wellness Facilities: The Boutique Hotel Cairo does not have a full-service spa but may offer basic wellness amenities such as a small fitness center or relaxation services.

Bars

On-Site Bar: Includes a chic bar or lounge area where guests can enjoy a selection of beverages in a stylish and relaxing environment. It's a perfect spot for unwinding after a day of exploration or business.

Events and Conferences

Meeting Spaces: Offers well-appointed meeting and event spaces suitable for small to medium-sized gatherings, including business meetings and private events. The spaces are designed with elegance and functionality in mind.

Event Services: Provides comprehensive support for organizing events, including catering services, audiovisual equipment, and coordination to ensure successful occasions.

Basic Facilities and Amenities

Dining: The hotel features a restaurant that serves a variety of local and international dishes for breakfast, lunch, and dinner. The dining area reflects the hotel's elegant style and provides a pleasant atmosphere for meals.

Business Center: Offers essential business services such as high-speed internet access, printing, and meeting facilities.

Fitness Center: Includes basic fitness equipment for guests who wish to maintain their workout routines during their stay.

Concierge Services: Assists with local recommendations, travel arrangements, and special requests to enhance the guest experience.

Opening and Closing Hours

Check-in: Typically from 3:00 PM

Check-out: By 12:00 PM

Restaurants and Bars: The restaurant generally serves breakfast from 6:30 AM to 10:00 AM, lunch from 12:00 PM to 3:00 PM, and dinner from 7:00 PM to 10:00 PM. The bar or lounge area usually opens in the late afternoon and remains open until late evening.

Price

Room Rates: Rates for a stay at The Boutique Hotel Cairo generally range from $120 to $250 per night, depending on the season, room type, and booking period. The pricing reflects its boutique status and emphasis on luxury and personalized service.

Pros

Stylish and Elegant: Provides a luxurious and stylish environment with tasteful decor and design.

Personalized Experience: Known for its attentive service and customized guest experiences.

Scenic Location: Situated in the tranquil Zamalek district with views of the Nile and lush surroundings.

Central Access: Close to major cultural and leisure attractions in Cairo.

Cons

Higher Cost: The boutique experience comes at a higher price point compared to mid-range or budget hotels.

Limited Wellness Facilities: Lacks a full-service spa, which may be a drawback for guests seeking extensive wellness amenities.

Traffic Issues: Cairo's traffic can be challenging, potentially affecting travel times to and from the hotel.

Local Tips

Explore Zamalek: Take advantage of the hotel's location by exploring the local area, known for its cafes, restaurants, and green spaces.

Visit Nearby Attractions: Use the hotel's proximity to landmarks like the Cairo Tower and the Egyptian Museum to maximize your sightseeing.

Local Dining: Besides the hotel's dining options, explore the diverse culinary scene in Zamalek for a variety of local and international cuisines.

Traffic Awareness: Be aware of Cairo's traffic patterns to optimize your travel time and enjoy your stay more effectively.

Day Trip from Cairo
The Pyramids of Giza

Exploring the Pyramids of Giza is a must-do when visiting Cairo. As one of the Seven Wonders of the Ancient World, the site offers a fascinating glimpse into ancient Egyptian civilization. Here's a comprehensive guide on how to make the most of a day trip to the Pyramids of Giza from Cairo:

1. Planning Your Trip

Timing: Aim to start your day early, ideally around 7:00 AM. This will help you avoid the peak heat and crowds, allowing for a more comfortable and leisurely experience.

Transportation:

Private Tour: Hiring a private guide or driver offers convenience and flexibility. Many tour companies offer packages that include transportation, guiding services, and sometimes even entrance fees.

Public Transport: Buses and shared minivans are available from Cairo to Giza. However, this option might be less comfortable and less reliable compared to private transport.

Ride-Sharing Apps: Services like Uber or Careem can be used to travel directly to the pyramids, offering a more personalized experience compared to public transport.

2. Arriving at the Pyramids

Entrance Fees: Be prepared to purchase a ticket for the general admission. There are additional fees for accessing specific areas such as the interior of the pyramids or the Solar Boat Museum.

Attire: Wear comfortable clothing and sturdy walking shoes. The site involves a lot of walking and climbing, and the weather can be quite hot.

Essentials: Bring a hat, sunscreen, and plenty of water to stay hydrated. A camera is a must, but be aware that tripods might require an additional fee.

3. Exploring the Pyramids

Great Pyramid of Giza:

Overview: The largest of the three pyramids, built for Pharaoh Khufu (Cheops). You can explore its exterior and the surrounding area.

Interior: Access to the inside is available but involves a separate ticket. Be prepared for narrow passages and a lack of ventilation.

Pyramid of Khafre:

Overview: Slightly smaller than the Great Pyramid but appears taller due to its elevated position. It has a more intact original casing at the top.

Features: The Pyramid of Khafre is noted for the Great Sphinx, which is located nearby and is one of the most iconic symbols of ancient Egypt.

Pyramid of Menkaure:

Overview: The smallest of the three primary pyramids, built for Pharaoh Menkaure. It is less visited but still offers a fascinating look at the burial practices of the time.

Sphinx:

Overview: This massive limestone statue with the body of a lion and a human head is a must-see. It is believed to represent Pharaoh Khafre.

Photography: The Sphinx is a great spot for photos, but beware of the crowds and heat.

4. Additional Attractions

Solar Boat Museum:

Overview: This museum houses a reconstructed ancient boat that was buried near the Great Pyramid. It offers insights into the religious and ceremonial practices of the time.

Location: Located near the Great Pyramid.

Valley Temple:

Overview: Located near the Sphinx, this temple is part of the mortuary complex and provides further context on the religious aspects of the pyramids.

5. Guided Tours

Benefits:

Expert Knowledge: Guides can offer detailed historical context and anecdotes that enrich your visit.

Navigation: They can help you avoid common pitfalls and ensure you see all the key sites.

Choosing a Guide:

Reviews: Look for guides with positive reviews from previous travelers.

Credentials: Ensure they are licensed and knowledgeable about the history and archaeology of the pyramids.

6. Tips for a Memorable Experience

Avoiding Crowds: Visit early in the morning or late afternoon to dodge the largest crowds. Midday is usually the busiest and hottest time.

Staying Hydrated: The desert climate can be extremely dry and hot. Drink water regularly and take breaks in shaded areas.

Respecting the Site: Follow all guidelines and respect the cultural heritage of the pyramids. Avoid climbing on or touching the monuments to preserve their condition.

Souvenirs and Shopping: There are numerous stalls around the site selling souvenirs. Be prepared to haggle for better prices, but be cautious of overpaying.

7. Returning to Cairo

Dining Options: Consider having lunch at a local restaurant in Giza or on the way back to Cairo. Some tours include meal options, or you can explore local eateries.

Further Exploration: If time permits, you can explore other attractions in Cairo, such as the Egyptian Museum, Khan El Khalili Bazaar, or Islamic Cairo.

Saqqara

Saqqara is a fascinating archaeological site located about 30 kilometers south of Cairo. It is part of the Memphis necropolis and is renowned for its ancient tombs and pyramids, including the famous Step Pyramid of Djoser. Here's a detailed guide on how to explore Saqqara, especially if you're making it a day trip from Cairo:

1. Planning Your Trip

Timing: A visit to Saqqara typically takes a few hours to half a day. Plan to start early in the morning to avoid the heat and make the most of your time.

Transportation:

Private Tour: A private guide or driver is the most convenient way to get to Saqqara. Many tour operators offer packages that include transportation and a guide.

Public Transport: Buses or shared minivans can take you to Saqqara, but this option might be less comfortable and less direct.

Ride-Sharing: Services like Uber or Careem can also be used, though they might be less familiar with the exact location compared to private tours.

2. Arriving at Saqqara

Entrance Fees: You will need to purchase a ticket for general admission. There are additional fees for accessing specific tombs or pyramids.

Attire: Wear comfortable clothing and sturdy shoes. The site involves a lot of walking and can be quite dusty.

Essentials: Bring a hat, sunscreen, and plenty of water. A camera is also recommended for capturing the site's incredible structures.

3. Exploring Saqqara

Step Pyramid of Djoser:

Overview: This is the oldest pyramid in Egypt and was designed by the architect Imhotep for Pharaoh Djoser. It is a significant architectural milestone, marking the transition from mastaba tombs to the pyramid shape.

Features: The pyramid is surrounded by a vast complex including courtyards, temples, and a surrounding wall.

Tomb of Ti:

Overview: This well-preserved Old Kingdom tomb belongs to a high-ranking official named Ti. It features beautiful reliefs depicting daily life, hunting, and fishing scenes.

Location: It is situated in the northern section of the Saqqara necropolis.

Tomb of Mereruka:

Overview: This tomb is known for its detailed and colorful wall scenes that provide a glimpse into the daily life of Mereruka, a high official during the Sixth Dynasty.

Highlights: The tomb includes scenes of Mereruka and his family, as well as agricultural and hunting scenes.

Pyramid of Unas:

Overview: This pyramid is notable for its "Pyramid Texts," which are the oldest religious texts in the world, inscribed inside the burial chamber.

Features: The texts provide insights into ancient Egyptian funerary beliefs and practices.

Pyramid of Teti:

Overview: The pyramid of Pharaoh Teti, another Old Kingdom ruler, is known for its Pyramid Texts as well. It is less visited compared to others but still significant.

4. Additional Attractions

Serapeum of Saqqara:

Overview: This is an underground burial complex for the sacred Apis bulls, which were considered manifestations of the god Ptah.

Features: The site includes large sarcophagi and detailed architectural elements.

Mastaba of Kagemni:

Overview: This mastaba tomb is noted for its rich decorative scenes depicting various aspects of ancient Egyptian life and rituals.

Features: Includes scenes of agriculture, cattle herding, and more.

5. Guided Tours

Benefits:

Expert Insight: Guides provide valuable historical context and detailed explanations of the tombs and pyramids.

Navigation: They can help you navigate the extensive site and ensure you don't miss key attractions.

Choosing a Guide:

Reviews: Look for guides with good reviews and extensive knowledge of Saqqara's history.

Licensing: Ensure they are licensed and experienced in Egyptian archaeology.

6. Tips for a Great Visit

Avoiding Crowds: Visiting early in the day can help you avoid the busiest times and the hottest part of the day.

Respecting the Site: Follow all guidelines to preserve the ancient structures. Avoid touching or climbing on the monuments.

Souvenirs and Shopping: There are small shops near the entrance where you can buy souvenirs. Be prepared to negotiate prices.

Combining with Giza: If you have more time, consider combining your visit to Saqqara with a trip to the Pyramids of Giza. Both sites are relatively close to each other and can be visited in one day with careful planning.

Memphis

Memphis, an ancient city of great historical significance, is located about 20 kilometers south of Cairo and was once the capital of ancient Egypt during the Old Kingdom. Today, it is an archaeological site known for its extensive ruins and artifacts that provide insight into ancient Egyptian civilization. Here's a comprehensive guide on how to explore Memphis as part of your trip from Cairo:

1. Planning Your Visit

Timing: A visit to Memphis can be comfortably combined with a trip to Saqqara, given their proximity. Allocate around 2-3 hours for Memphis, depending on your interest in the site.

Transportation:

Private Tour: Hiring a private guide or driver is the most efficient way to visit Memphis, especially if you want to combine it with other nearby sites like Saqqara.

Public Transport: Buses or shared minivans can be

used to reach Memphis, but they might not be as convenient.

Ride-Sharing: Apps like Uber or Careem can be used, though they might be less familiar with the specifics of the site compared to private tours.

2. Arriving at Memphis

Entrance Fees: Purchase a ticket at the entrance. The site has relatively low admission fees compared to other major attractions.

Attire: Wear comfortable clothing and sturdy shoes. The site involves walking and can be dusty.

Essentials: Bring a hat, sunscreen, and water. A camera is also useful for capturing the site's notable features.

3. Exploring Memphis

Open-Air Museum:

Overview: Memphis is primarily an open-air museum with scattered ruins and artifacts. The museum showcases several significant pieces from ancient Memphis.

Key Features:

Colossus of Ramses II: This massive statue of Pharaoh Ramses II is one of the most impressive pieces in Memphis. Originally, it was part of a temple complex in the city.

Alabaster Sphinx: A large sphinx made of alabaster, which provides insight into the artistic style of ancient Egypt.

Various Statues and Stele: The site includes various statues, inscriptions, and stele that highlight the artistic and cultural achievements of ancient Egyptians.

Temple of Ptah:

Overview: Memphis was a major religious center dedicated to Ptah, the creator god and patron of craftsmen. The ruins of the Temple of Ptah, though not as well-preserved as other sites, offer insights into the religious practices of ancient Memphis.

Features: The remnants of the temple include fragments of statues and columns, giving a sense of the grandeur that once characterized the temple.

Mastaba of Idut:

Overview: A mastaba tomb located near Memphis that provides insights into burial practices and daily life during the Old Kingdom.

Features: Includes detailed wall paintings and carvings depicting various aspects of ancient life.

4. Additional Attractions

The Step Pyramid Complex: While technically part of Saqqara, the Step Pyramid of Djoser is closely related to Memphis and its historical context. It represents the architectural innovation that took place in the early years of pyramid construction.

The Serapeum of Saqqara: Located nearby, this underground complex for sacred Apis bulls provides additional context to the religious and ceremonial practices of Memphis.

5. Guided Tours

Benefits:

Expert Knowledge: A guide can provide detailed information about the history of Memphis and the significance of its monuments.

Navigation: They can help you make the most of your visit by focusing on the most important aspects of the site.

Choosing a Guide:

Reviews: Look for guides with positive feedback from previous visitors.

Credentials: Ensure they have a good understanding of Egyptian history and archaeology.

6. Tips for a Memorable Visit

Combine with Saqqara: Since Memphis and Saqqara are close to each other, visiting both in one day is a great way to maximize your time and explore a range of ancient Egyptian sites.

Respect the Site: Follow all posted guidelines to preserve the site. Avoid touching or climbing on the ruins.

Souvenirs: Small shops near the site offer souvenirs. Be prepared to haggle for better prices and choose items that reflect the historical significance of the site.

Additional Exploration: If you have more time, consider exploring other nearby attractions or returning to Cairo for further sightseeing.

Alexandria

Alexandria, located on the Mediterranean coast of Egypt, is a city with a rich history and a mix of ancient and modern attractions. Founded by Alexander the Great in 331 BCE, it was once a major cultural and intellectual center of the ancient world. Today, Alexandria offers visitors a blend of historical sites, beautiful seafronts, and vibrant local culture. Here's a detailed guide on how to explore Alexandria, especially if you're making it a day trip from Cairo:

1. Planning Your Trip

Timing: Alexandria is about 220 kilometers northwest of Cairo, which takes roughly 2.5 to 3 hours by car. Plan to start early to make the most of your day and allow time for travel.

Transportation:

Private Car: Hiring a private driver or joining a tour is the most convenient way to visit Alexandria from Cairo. This allows for flexibility in your schedule and itinerary.

Train: Trains run between Cairo and Alexandria, offering a scenic and comfortable alternative. The journey takes about 2.5 to 3 hours.

Bus: Several bus companies operate between Cairo and Alexandria, but this might be less comfortable and more time-consuming compared to a private car or train.

2. Arriving in Alexandria

Parking: If driving, ensure you have a plan for parking. Alexandria can be busy, and parking near popular sites might be challenging.

Attire: Wear comfortable clothing and shoes, especially if you plan to explore several sites. The Mediterranean climate is typically mild but can be windy.

Essentials: Bring a hat, sunscreen, and water. A camera is recommended for capturing the city's scenic spots.

3. Exploring Alexandria

Bibliotheca Alexandrina:

Overview: A modern homage to the ancient Library of Alexandria, this architectural marvel is a center for learning and culture.

Features: Explore its vast collection of books, historical manuscripts, and exhibits. The library also includes a museum, planetarium, and art galleries.

The Citadel of Qaitbay:

Overview: Built in the 15th century by Sultan Qaitbay, this fort is located on the site of the ancient Lighthouse of Alexandria, one of the Seven Wonders of the Ancient World.

Features: The citadel offers panoramic views of the Mediterranean Sea and the city. It houses a small maritime museum with artifacts related to Alexandria's naval history.

Roman Amphitheatre:

Overview: Discovered in the 1960s, this well-preserved Roman amphitheater features tiered seating and mosaic floors.

Features: The site provides insights into Alexandria's Roman period and offers a glimpse into the entertainment and social activities of the time.

Pompey's Pillar:

Overview: This impressive Roman column stands 25 meters high and was originally erected in honor of Emperor Diocletian.

Features: The pillar is surrounded by ruins of the Serapeum, an ancient temple dedicated to the god Serapis.

Catacombs of Kom el-Shoqafa:

Overview: An extensive necropolis dating back to the 2nd century CE, featuring a unique blend of Egyptian, Greek, and Roman architectural styles.

Features: Explore the underground tombs, which include intricate carvings, statues, and sarcophagi.

Montazah Palace and Gardens:

Overview: A royal palace with beautiful gardens located on the eastern edge of Alexandria.

Features: Stroll through the lush gardens and enjoy the seaside views. The palace itself is not open to the public, but the surrounding park and beaches are lovely for a relaxing visit.

4. Dining and Shopping

Restaurants: Alexandria offers a variety of dining options, from seafood restaurants with views of the Mediterranean to local eateries serving traditional Egyptian cuisine. Consider trying fresh seafood dishes, which are a specialty in the city.

Shopping: Explore local markets and shops for souvenirs, such as traditional crafts, spices, and local delicacies. The city's markets, such as the El Raml Station area, provide a vibrant shopping experience.

5. Guided Tours

Benefits:

Expert Knowledge: A guide can provide historical context and enhance your understanding of Alexandria's rich past.

Navigation: Guides can help you efficiently explore the city and manage time.

Choosing a Guide:

Reviews: Check reviews and recommendations for guides who specialize in Alexandria.

Licensing: Ensure they are licensed and knowledgeable about the city's history.

6. Tips for a Great Visit

Plan Ahead: Given the distance from Cairo, plan your itinerary to include the key attractions you're most interested in.

Respect Local Customs: Alexandria is a cosmopolitan city, but it's important to respect local customs and dress modestly when visiting religious or historic sites.

Weather Considerations: Check the weather forecast before your trip, as coastal weather can be variable. Dress in layers if needed.

Combine with Other Destinations: If time permits, consider exploring other nearby coastal towns or archaeological sites to make the most of your trip.

… *Grace Bennett*

Al Minya

Al Minya, located in central Egypt along the Nile River, is a city known for its significant archaeological sites and historical importance. It's less frequented by international tourists compared to Cairo or Luxor, but it offers a wealth of fascinating attractions, particularly from the ancient and early Christian periods. Here's a comprehensive guide on how to explore Al Minya, especially if you're making it a day trip from Cairo:

1. Planning Your Trip

Timing: Al Minya is approximately 250 kilometers south of Cairo, which takes around 3-4 hours by car. Plan to start early in the morning to maximize your time exploring the area.

Transportation:

Private Car: Hiring a private driver or joining a tour is the most convenient way to visit Al Minya from Cairo. This allows for flexibility and comfort.

Train: There are trains from Cairo to Al Minya, but this option may be less direct and less comfortable compared to a private car.

Bus: Buses are available but can be less predictable and comfortable compared to other methods.

2. Arriving in Al Minya

Parking: If you're driving, ensure you have a plan for parking, particularly near popular sites.

Attire: Wear comfortable clothing and sturdy shoes for walking. The weather can be quite hot, so dress in light, breathable fabrics.

Essentials: Bring a hat, sunscreen, and water. A camera is also recommended for capturing the area's historical sites.

3. Exploring Al Minya

Beni Hassan Tombs:

Overview: Located about 20 kilometers southeast of Al Minya, these tombs date back to the Middle Kingdom (around 2000-1800 BCE) and are notable for their colorful and well-preserved wall paintings.

Features: The tombs of the nomarchs (local governors) include depictions of daily life, hunting scenes, and dances. Key tombs include those of Khnumhotep II and Amenemhat.

Akhmim:

Overview: Situated to the north of Al Minya, Akhmim is home to several important archaeological sites.

Features: It includes the remains of ancient temples and a notable collection of Ptolemaic and Roman artifacts.

Tell el-Amarna:

Overview: The ancient city of Tell el-Amarna, founded by Pharaoh Akhenaten in the 14th century BCE, is located about 50 kilometers northeast of Al Minya.

Features: The site includes the ruins of the city's main buildings, palaces, and temples. Notable structures include the Great Temple of the Aten and the remains of Akhenaten's palace.

Monastery of Saint Samuel the Confessor:

Overview: This Coptic Christian monastery is located about 40 kilometers south of Al Minya and is known for its historical significance and serene setting.

Features: The monastery includes ancient Christian manuscripts, frescoes, and a peaceful atmosphere ideal for reflection.

The Tombs of the Nobles:

Overview: Located near the ancient city of Thebes, these tombs belong to various high-ranking officials and provide insights into ancient Egyptian burial practices and art.

Features: The tombs are known for their detailed frescoes and inscriptions.

sun exposure by wearing appropriate clothing and staying hydrated.

Combine Visits: If possible, consider combining your visit to Al Minya with nearby sites or extending your stay to explore additional attractions in the region.

4. Dining and Shopping

Restaurants: In Al Minya, dining options may be limited compared to larger cities, but local eateries and restaurants offer traditional Egyptian cuisine. Try local dishes like koshari, falafel, and fresh bread.

Shopping: Look for local markets and shops where you can purchase traditional crafts, textiles, and souvenirs. The markets in Al Minya are typically less touristy and offer a more authentic experience.

5. Guided Tours

Benefits:

Expert Knowledge: Guides can provide in-depth information about the history and significance of Al Minya's sites.

Navigation: They can help you efficiently explore the sites and manage your time.

Choosing a Guide:

Reviews: Look for guides with positive feedback from previous visitors.

Credentials: Ensure they are licensed and knowledgeable about the region's history.

6. Tips for a Great Visit

Plan Ahead: Given the distance from Cairo, carefully plan your itinerary to include the key sites you're most interested in.

Respect Local Customs: Dress modestly and respect local customs, especially when visiting religious sites.

Weather Considerations: The climate can be very hot, particularly in summer. Prepare for heat and

Fayoum Oasis

The Fayoum Oasis, located about 100 kilometers southwest of Cairo, is a unique and picturesque region known for its natural beauty, historical sites, and traditional Egyptian culture. It's an excellent destination for a day trip or a longer stay if you're interested in exploring Egypt beyond the usual tourist spots. Here's a comprehensive guide on how to explore the Fayoum Oasis:

1. Planning Your Trip

Timing: The Fayoum Oasis is about 1.5 to 2 hours from Cairo, making it ideal for a day trip. Plan to start early in the morning to maximize your time exploring the area.

Transportation:

Private Car: Hiring a private driver or joining a tour is the most convenient way to visit Fayoum. This allows for flexibility and comfort, especially if you want to explore multiple sites.

Public Transport: Buses and microbuses are available from Cairo to Fayoum, but they might be less comfortable and less direct.

Ride-Sharing: Services like Uber or Careem can be used, though they might be less familiar with the specifics of the area compared to private tours.

2. Arriving in Fayoum

Parking: If you're driving, ensure you have a plan for parking, especially if you're visiting popular sites or towns.

Attire: Wear comfortable clothing and sturdy shoes. The weather can be quite hot, so light, breathable fabrics are recommended. Bring a hat and sunscreen.

Essentials: Carry plenty of water, a camera, and any personal items you might need for a day trip.

3. Exploring Fayoum

Lake Qarun:

Overview: A large, ancient lake and one of the oldest natural lakes in Egypt. It's a popular spot for birdwatching and enjoying the natural scenery.

Features: You can take boat rides, enjoy the lake's shoreline, and spot various bird species, including flamingos.

Wadi El-Rayan:

Overview: A protected area with a series of lakes and waterfalls. It's a great spot for nature enthusiasts and offers opportunities for hiking, picnicking, and wildlife observation.

Features: The Lower and Upper Lakes are connected by waterfalls, and the area is home to diverse flora and fauna.

Wadi Hitan (Valley of the Whales):

Overview: A UNESCO World Heritage Site known for its fossilized remains of prehistoric whales and other marine life. It provides insight into the evolution of these animals.

Features: Explore fossil sites, learn about paleontology, and enjoy the unique desert landscape.

Fayoum Pottery Village:

Overview: A traditional village known for its handmade pottery. The village offers a chance to see local artisans at work and purchase unique souvenirs.

Features: Visit workshops, learn about traditional pottery techniques, and buy handcrafted items.

Karanis (Kom Aushim):

Overview: The ruins of an ancient Greco-Roman city that was an important center in the Fayoum Oasis.

Features: Explore the remains of houses, temples, and streets. The site provides insights into daily life during the Greco-Roman period.

The Pyramid of Hawara:

Overview: Built during the Middle Kingdom, this pyramid is the burial place of Pharaoh Amenemhat III.

Features: The pyramid is notable for its unusual architectural design and the remains of the labyrinthine structure within.

The Temple of Qasr el-Sagha:

Overview: An ancient temple located near Lake Qarun, dedicated to the crocodile god Sobek.

Features: The temple's ruins offer insights into ancient Egyptian religious practices and architecture.

4. Dining and Shopping

Restaurants: In the towns of Fayoum, you can find local eateries serving traditional Egyptian dishes. Try local specialties and enjoy fresh, regional cuisine.

Shopping: Explore local markets and shops for traditional crafts, pottery, and textiles. Fayoum is known for its handmade items, and local markets offer a variety of unique souvenirs.

5. Guided Tours

Benefits:

Expert Knowledge: Guides can provide detailed information about the history, culture, and natural features of Fayoum.

Navigation: They can help you plan your itinerary efficiently and ensure you make the most of your visit.

Choosing a Guide:

Reviews: Look for guides with positive feedback from previous visitors.

Credentials: Ensure they are knowledgeable about the area's history and attractions.

6. Tips for a Great Visit

Plan Your Itinerary: Fayoum has a diverse range of attractions, so plan your day to include the sites that interest you most.

Respect Local Customs: Fayoum is a traditional area, so dress modestly and be respectful of local customs and practices.

Weather Considerations: The region can be very hot, especially in summer. Prepare for the heat by wearing appropriate clothing and staying hydrated.

Combine Visits: If you have more time, consider exploring other nearby attractions or extending your stay to enjoy more of what Fayoum has to offer.

Abu Sir

Abu Sir, also known as Abusir, is an archaeological site in Egypt located about 25 kilometers southwest of Cairo, near the more famous Giza Plateau. It was a significant necropolis during the Old Kingdom period and is noted for its pyramids and tombs of the Fifth Dynasty. Here's a comprehensive guide to exploring Abu Sir:

1. Planning Your Trip

Timing: A visit to Abu Sir can be done in a few hours, making it possible to combine with a visit to other nearby sites, such as Saqqara or the Giza Pyramids.

Transportation:

Private Car: Hiring a private driver or joining a guided tour is the most convenient way to visit Abu Sir. This allows flexibility in your schedule and comfort during the trip.

Public Transport: Public transportation options are limited, but taxis or ride-sharing apps like Uber and Careem can also be used.

2. Arriving at Abu Sir

Entrance Fees: Tickets are required to enter the site, and you may need to pay additional fees to access specific tombs or pyramids.

Attire: Wear comfortable clothing and sturdy shoes suitable for walking. The site can be dusty, so light, breathable fabrics are advisable.

Essentials: Bring a hat, sunscreen, and plenty of water. A camera is also recommended for capturing the site's features.

3. Exploring Abu Sir

Pyramids of Abu Sir:

Overview: Abu Sir is home to several pyramids, mostly from the Fifth Dynasty of the Old Kingdom. These pyramids are generally smaller and less well-preserved compared to those at Giza but are significant for their historical value.

Notable Pyramids:

Pyramid of Sahure: One of the most well-preserved pyramids in Abu Sir, Sahure's complex includes a mortuary temple with beautiful reliefs depicting scenes of daily life and offerings.

Pyramid of Neferirkare: This pyramid is notable for its unfinished state, which provides insights into the construction methods of the time.

Pyramid of Userkaf: The pyramid of Pharaoh Userkaf, the founder of the Fifth Dynasty, is partially intact and provides a glimpse into the early pyramid-building techniques.

Mortuary Temples:

Overview: Each pyramid complex includes a mortuary temple where rituals and offerings were made. The temples at Abu Sir are known for their detailed reliefs and inscriptions.

Features: The temples often feature scenes of the king's life, offerings to the gods, and depictions of royal rituals.

Tomb of Ptahshepses:

Overview: Located in the vicinity of Abu Sir, this tomb is notable for its well-preserved wall paintings and inscriptions.

Features: The tomb belongs to Ptahshepses, a high official during the Fifth Dynasty, and includes detailed depictions of daily life and offerings.

Tomb of Mereruka:

Overview: Although not directly within Abu Sir, this tomb is located nearby in Saqqara and is worth visiting if you have additional time. It is renowned for its vibrant and detailed reliefs.

4. Guided Tours

Benefits:

Expert Knowledge: A guide can provide in-depth information about the historical significance of the pyramids and temples at Abu Sir.

Navigation: They can help you navigate the site and ensure you see the most important features.

Choosing a Guide:

Reviews: Look for guides with positive reviews and extensive knowledge of the Old Kingdom.

Credentials: Ensure they are licensed and experienced in Egyptian archaeology.

5. Tips for a Great Visit

Combine Visits: Abu Sir is close to other significant archaeological sites such as Giza and Saqqara. Plan your itinerary to include these nearby attractions to maximize your time.

Respect the Site: Follow all guidelines to help preserve the ancient structures. Avoid touching or climbing on the monuments.

The Ultimate Egypt Travel Guide 2025 Edition

Weather Considerations: The area can be very hot, especially in summer. Dress appropriately for the weather and stay hydrated.

Photography: Check the rules regarding photography, as some areas may have restrictions.

7-day Itinerary for first time traveler

Day 1: Arrival and Orientation

Morning: Arrival and Initial Exploration

Arrival in Cairo:

Airport: You'll likely arrive at Cairo International Airport (CAI), which is about 15 kilometers (9 miles) from downtown Cairo. Depending on traffic, the drive to central Cairo can take between 30 minutes to an hour.

Transportation from Airport: Taxis and ride-hailing apps like Uber and Careem are readily available. Taxis are typically around 150-200 EGP ($5-7 USD), while ride-hailing services might cost a bit more.

Checking In:

Hotels: Consider staying at central locations like Zamalek, Downtown Cairo, or near the Pyramids. Notable hotels include the Conrad Cairo, Four Seasons Hotel Cairo at Nile Plaza, and the Marriott Mena House.

Breakfast:

Recommended Breakfast Options:

Felfela: Offers traditional Egyptian breakfast dishes like ful medames (fava beans), ta'ameya (Egyptian falafel), and fresh pita bread. Price: 80-150 EGP ($3-5 USD). Opening Hours: 7 AM - 11 PM.

Zooba: A modern take on Egyptian street food with dishes like koshari and sandwiches. Price: 100-200 EGP ($3-6 USD). Opening Hours: 8 AM - 10 PM.

Mid-Morning: Orientation and Sightseeing

Orientation:

The Egyptian Museum: Located in Tahrir Square, this museum houses a vast collection of ancient Egyptian artifacts, including the treasures of Tutankhamun.

Opening Hours: 9 AM - 5 PM.

Entry Fee: 200 EGP ($6.50 USD) for adults, with additional fees for special exhibits and photography.

Activities:

Tahrir Square: After visiting the museum, take a stroll around Tahrir Square to get a feel for the city's atmosphere and perhaps visit some local shops.

Afternoon: Lunch and Cultural Exploration

Lunch:

Recommended Lunch Spots:

Sequoia: Located in Zamalek, this upscale restaurant offers a mix of Mediterranean and Egyptian dishes with a beautiful view of the Nile. Price: 250-400 EGP ($8-13 USD). Opening Hours: 12 PM - 1 AM.

Abou El Sid: Known for its traditional Egyptian dishes like moussaka and grilled meats. Price: 150-250 EGP ($5-8 USD). Opening Hours: 12 PM - 11 PM.

Post-Lunch Activity:

Cairo Tower: For panoramic views of Cairo, visit the Cairo Tower located on Gezira Island in the Nile River.

Opening Hours: 9 AM - 10 PM.

Entry Fee: 200 EGP ($6.50 USD).

Mid-Afternoon: Relaxation and Exploration

Relaxation:

Nile Corniche: A stroll along the Nile Corniche is relaxing and offers scenic views of the river and the cityscape. You can also enjoy a coffee or tea at a café along the corniche.

Activity:

Visit a Bazaar: Explore local markets such as Khan El Khalili, a bustling bazaar where you can shop for souvenirs, spices, jewelry, and traditional crafts.

Opening Hours: 10 AM - 10 PM.

Evening: Dinner and Nightlife

Dinner:

Recommended Dinner Spots:

Naguib Mahfouz Restaurant: Located in Khan El Khalili, it offers a range of traditional Egyptian dishes in an authentic setting. Price: 150-300 EGP ($5-10 USD). Opening Hours: 12 PM - 11 PM.

The Roof-Top Restaurant at the Marriott Mena House: Offers a great dining experience with views of the Pyramids. Price: 300-500 EGP ($10-16 USD). Opening Hours: 7 PM - 11 PM.

Night Activity:

Nile Dinner Cruise: Experience Cairo from the river with a Nile dinner cruise. Many cruises offer a buffet dinner, entertainment like traditional dance shows, and beautiful nighttime views of Cairo.

Price: 500-1000 EGP ($16-33 USD) per person.

Booking: Can be arranged through your hotel or local tour operators. Cruises typically depart around 7 PM.

Night: Relax and Prepare for the Next Day

Rest:

After a busy first day, return to your hotel to unwind and prepare for the exciting days ahead. Depending on your hotel, you might have access to a bar or lounge where you can relax with a nightcap or a light snack.

Getting Around Cairo

Options:

Taxis and Ride-Hailing: Uber and Careem are convenient for getting around the city.

Public Transport: The Cairo Metro is an affordable and efficient way to navigate the city. Tickets cost around 5 EGP ($0.15 USD) per ride.

Buses: Local buses are available, but they might be less comfortable and harder to navigate for tourists.

Walking: In central areas like Downtown Cairo and Zamalek, walking is a good option for short distances, though be mindful of traffic and road conditions.

Safety Tip: Always be cautious with your belongings, especially in crowded areas and public transport. It's also a good idea to carry a map or have a navigation app handy.

Day 2: Giza Plateau and Pyramids

Morning: Exploring the Giza Plateau

Breakfast:

Before You Head Out:

Le Pasha 1901: Located near the Nile in Zamalek, this restaurant offers a breakfast buffet with a variety of international and Egyptian options. Price: 200-350 EGP ($7-12 USD). Opening Hours: 7 AM - 11 AM.

Travel to the Giza Plateau:

Transportation Options:

Taxi/Ride-Hailing: The drive from central Cairo to the Giza Plateau takes about 30-45 minutes. Taxi fare ranges from 150-250 EGP ($5-8 USD), and ride-hailing services might be a bit more expensive.

Private Tour: If you've booked a private tour, transportation will likely be included.

Activities:

Giza Plateau:

Great Pyramids of Giza: Visit the iconic pyramids of Khufu (Cheops), Khafre (Chephren), and Menkaure. The Great Pyramid of Khufu is the largest and the only surviving wonder of the Seven Wonders of the Ancient World.

Opening Hours: 8 AM - 5 PM.

Entry Fee: 200 EGP ($6.50 USD) for the site. Additional fees for entering the pyramids: 400 EGP ($13 USD) for the Great Pyramid, 100 EGP ($3 USD) for the other two.

Sphinx: The Great Sphinx of Giza, a monumental statue with the body of a lion and the head of a pharaoh, is located near the pyramids. It is a must-see and is included in the ticket to the Giza Plateau.

Solar Boat Museum: Located near the Great Pyramid, this museum houses the reconstructed Khufu ship, an ancient ceremonial boat.

Opening Hours: 9 AM - 5 PM.

Entry Fee: 100 EGP ($3 USD).

Mid-Morning: Camel Ride and Photo Opportunities

Camel Ride:

Experience: Consider taking a camel ride around the pyramids for a unique perspective and memorable photos. Be prepared to negotiate prices with the camel owners.

Price: 200-400 EGP ($6.50-13 USD) for a short ride. Prices may vary based on duration and guide.

Photo Spots:

Panoramic Views: For stunning panoramic views of the pyramids, head to the designated viewpoints on the plateau. This is a great spot for capturing memorable photographs.

Afternoon: Lunch and Further Exploration

Lunch:

Recommended Lunch Spots Near Giza:

Pizza Hut Giza: A casual dining option offering familiar fast-food pizzas. Price: 150-250 EGP ($5-8 USD). Opening Hours: 11 AM - 11 PM.

Felfela: This restaurant, with a branch in Giza, offers traditional Egyptian food in a relaxed atmosphere. Price: 150-250 EGP ($5-8 USD). Opening Hours: 12 PM - 11 PM.

Additional Exploration:

Sakkara: If you have time and energy, consider visiting the Sakkara necropolis, known for the Step Pyramid of Djoser, which predates the Giza pyramids.

Distance: About 30 km (19 miles) from Giza.

Entry Fee: 200 EGP ($6.50 USD).

Opening Hours: 8 AM - 5 PM.

Mid-Afternoon: Relaxation and Souvenir Shopping

Relaxation:

Café Break: Head back to central Cairo and unwind at a café. Options include **Café Riche** or **Café de Flore**, both offering a comfortable setting and a variety of beverages.

Souvenir Shopping:

Local Markets: Visit local markets or shops around Giza or central Cairo to pick up souvenirs such as papyrus scrolls, miniature pyramids, and other Egyptian-themed gifts.

Evening: Dinner and Cultural Experience

Dinner:

Recommended Dinner Spots:

Mena House Restaurant: Located at the Marriott Mena House, this restaurant offers a fine dining experience with views of the pyramids. Price: 300-600 EGP ($10-20 USD). Opening Hours: 7 PM - 11 PM.

Khan El Khalili Restaurant: Located in the bustling Khan El Khalili bazaar, this restaurant provides traditional Egyptian dishes in an authentic atmosphere. Price: 150-300 EGP ($5-10 USD). Opening Hours: 12 PM - 11 PM.

Cultural Experience:

Sound and Light Show at the Pyramids: Enjoy an evening show where the pyramids and the Sphinx are illuminated with colorful lights, and a narration tells the history of these ancient wonders.

Opening Hours: Shows typically start around 7 PM or 8 PM, depending on the time of year.

Entry Fee: 400-600 EGP ($13-20 USD) depending on seating and show type.

Night: Return and Relax

Return to Hotel:

After a full day of exploration, head back to your hotel to relax and unwind. You might want to enjoy some leisure time at the hotel's facilities or just relax in your room.

Optional Nightcap:

Hotel Bar: Enjoy a nightcap at your hotel's bar or lounge, reflecting on your day and planning for the next.

Getting Around

Transportation Options:

Taxi/Ride-Hailing: Convenient for getting to and from the Giza Plateau.

Private Tours: Many tours include transportation and guides, which can be a hassle-free way to explore.

Public Transport: The metro is available but less practical for reaching Giza directly; taxis or ride-hailing services are more efficient.

Day 3: Saqqara and Memphis
Morning: Start Your Journey to Saqqara

Breakfast:

Start Your Day:

Maison Thomas: A popular spot in Zamalek known for its pastries, sandwiches, and excellent coffee. Price: 100-200 EGP ($3-7 USD). Opening Hours: 7 AM - 11 AM.

Taboula: Located in Garden City, this restaurant offers a traditional Egyptian breakfast with dishes like foul, falafel, and fresh bread. Price: 150-250 EGP ($5-8 USD). Opening Hours: 8 AM - 11 AM.

Travel to Saqqara:

Transportation Options:

Private Car or Taxi: The journey from Cairo to Saqqara takes about 45 minutes to an hour, depending on traffic. Taxi fare should be around 200-300 EGP ($6.50-10 USD).

Private Tour: If you've arranged a private tour, transportation will be provided, and the guide will ensure you make the most of your visit.

Mid-Morning: Explore Saqqara

Saqqara:

The Step Pyramid of Djoser: Saqqara is home to the Step Pyramid, the world's oldest large-scale stone structure, built by the architect Imhotep for the Pharaoh Djoser.

Opening Hours: 8 AM - 5 PM.

Entry Fee: 200 EGP ($6.50 USD).

Teti Pyramid and Tombs: Visit the Pyramid of Teti, the first ruler of the Sixth Dynasty, and explore nearby tombs adorned with intricate carvings and hieroglyphs.

Entry Fee: Included in the general Saqqara ticket.

Mastaba of Ti and Mereruka: These are among the most beautifully decorated tombs, offering vivid depictions of daily life in ancient Egypt.

The Ultimate Egypt Travel Guide 2025 Edition

Guided Tour:

Hiring a Guide: Consider hiring a local guide at the site or through a tour company to provide in-depth explanations of the history and significance of the structures.

Cost: 400-600 EGP ($13-20 USD) for a 2-3 hour tour.

Afternoon: Visit Memphis

Lunch:

Recommended Lunch Spots Near Saqqara/Memphis:

Local Cafés: Small local cafés and restaurants in the area offer simple, authentic Egyptian meals. Dishes like grilled chicken, kofta, or kushari are common. Price: 100-200 EGP ($3-7 USD).

Koshary Abou Tarek: A popular option in Cairo for the quintessential Egyptian dish, koshary (a mix of pasta, rice, lentils, and chickpeas topped with tomato sauce and crispy onions). Price: 50-100 EGP ($1.50-3 USD). Opening Hours: 10 AM - 10 PM.

Memphis:

Ancient Capital of Egypt: Located about 20 minutes from Saqqara, Memphis was the ancient capital of Egypt and is now an open-air museum.

Colossus of Ramses II: The centerpiece of the museum is a massive statue of Ramses II, one of Egypt's most powerful pharaohs.

Alabaster Sphinx: A large statue carved from a single piece of alabaster, representing the lion-bodied, human-headed sphinx.

Opening Hours: 8 AM - 5 PM.

Entry Fee: 100 EGP ($3 USD).

Guided Tour:

Optional: If you didn't hire a guide at Saqqara, you can do so at Memphis. This can enhance your understanding of the site's history and significance.

Mid-Afternoon: Relaxation and Cultural Immersion

Relaxation:

Post-Visit Break: After visiting Memphis, you might want to take a short break. If you're on a guided tour, your guide might suggest a local café where you can relax with some tea or coffee.

Cultural Immersion:

Visit a Local Village: If time permits, consider visiting a nearby village to experience rural life in Egypt. Some tours offer this as part of the Memphis and Saqqara package, providing insights into local customs and traditions.

Evening: Return to Cairo and Dinner

Return to Cairo:

Transportation: After your visit to Memphis, return to Cairo. The drive should take about 45 minutes to an hour.

Dinner:

Recommended Dinner Spots:

Culina at the Four Seasons: A luxurious dining experience offering a variety of international and Egyptian dishes. Price: 400-800 EGP ($13-26 USD). Opening Hours: 7 PM - 11 PM.

Zooba: For a more casual, yet trendy dining experience, Zooba offers modern twists on traditional Egyptian street food. Price: 100-200 EGP ($3-7 USD). Opening Hours: 8 AM - 11 PM.

Night: Reflect and Relax

Evening Activity:

Optional Nighttime Activity: If you're up for more exploration, consider a walk along the Nile Corniche or visit a local café for shisha and tea. Alternatively, you could explore Cairo's night markets, like the one in Khan El Khalili, where you can shop and enjoy the vibrant atmosphere.

Return to Hotel:

After a full day of exploration, head back to your hotel to relax and prepare for the next day. Enjoy the amenities at your hotel, whether it's a spa session, a swim, or simply unwinding in your room.

Getting Around

Transportation Options:

Private Car/Taxi: The most convenient way to travel between Cairo, Saqqara, and Memphis. Prices for a full day with a private driver can range from 500-800 EGP ($16-26 USD).

Private Tour: Opting for a private tour often includes transportation, a guide, and sometimes even lunch, making it a hassle-free option.

Public Transport: Not recommended for these sites due to the distance and lack of direct connections.

Tips for the Day:

Hydration and Sun Protection: Saqqara and Memphis can get quite hot, especially in the summer. Bring plenty of water, wear sunscreen, and consider a hat or umbrella for shade.

Comfortable Footwear: The terrain at Saqqara and Memphis is sandy and uneven, so comfortable walking shoes are a must.

Photography: Don't forget to bring a camera or smartphone to capture the stunning ancient sites. Be mindful of photography rules, especially inside tombs and museums.

Day 4: Islamic Cairo
Morning: Explore the Citadel and Mosques

Breakfast:

Begin Your Day:

Alfi Bey Restaurant: Located in Downtown Cairo, it offers a hearty Egyptian breakfast with dishes like ful, falafel, eggs, and fresh bread. Price: 100-200 EGP ($3-7 USD). Opening Hours: 7 AM - 11 AM.

Café Corniche: At the InterContinental Cairo Semiramis, offering a range of pastries, coffee, and traditional Egyptian breakfast options. Price: 150-250 EGP ($5-8 USD). Opening Hours: 7 AM - 11 AM.

Travel to Islamic Cairo:

Transportation Options:

Taxi/Ride-Hailing: A taxi or Uber/Careem ride from central Cairo to the Citadel area should cost around 100-150 EGP ($3-5 USD) and take about 15-20 minutes.

Citadel of Saladin (Cairo Citadel):

History: The Citadel, a medieval Islamic fortification, was constructed by Salah al-Din (Saladin) in the 12th century to protect Cairo from Crusaders. It also served as the seat of government for over 700 years.

Opening Hours: 9 AM - 5 PM.

Entry Fee: 200 EGP ($6.50 USD).

Mosques within the Citadel:

Mosque of Muhammad Ali: Also known as the Alabaster Mosque, this is the most prominent structure within the Citadel, known for its stunning Ottoman architecture and panoramic views of Cairo.

Inside: The interior is richly decorated with alabaster and features a large dome, with several smaller domes surrounding it. The mosque's courtyard is also impressive, with a large fountain in the center.

Mosque of Sultan al-Nasir Muhammad: An earlier mosque built in the 14th century with distinctive Mamluk architecture, featuring green-tiled domes and a simpler, more austere interior.

Explore the Gawhara Palace:

Palace of the Jewel: Inside the Citadel complex, the Gawhara Palace, also known as the Jewel Palace, was built by Muhammad Ali Pasha in the early 19th century. It now houses a museum showcasing the history of the Citadel and the artifacts of the era.

Entry Fee: Included in the Citadel ticket.

Mid-Morning: Continue with More Mosques and Markets

Mosque-Madrassa of Sultan Hassan:

One of Cairo's Finest: Just outside the Citadel, this 14th-century mosque is renowned for its massive scale and grand architecture, considered one of the masterpieces of Islamic art.

Opening Hours: 9 AM - 5 PM.

Entry Fee: 80 EGP ($2.50 USD).

Al-Rifa'i Mosque:

Opposite Sultan Hassan Mosque: Built in the 19th century, this mosque is the resting place of Egyptian royals and notable figures, including the last Shah of Iran.

Entry Fee: 80 EGP ($2.50 USD).

Afternoon: Lunch and Exploring Al-Muizz Street

Lunch:

Recommended Lunch Spots:

Naguib Mahfouz Café: Located in the heart of Khan El Khalili Bazaar, this café offers traditional Egyptian dishes in a charming, historic setting. Try dishes like molokhia, kebabs, or grilled chicken. Price: 150-300 EGP ($5-10 USD). Opening Hours: 12 PM - 11 PM.

El Fishawy Café: One of the oldest cafés in Cairo, nestled in the narrow alleys of Khan El Khalili. It's perfect for a light meal and coffee or tea. Price: 100-200 EGP ($3-7 USD). Opening Hours: 10 AM - Midnight.

Al-Muizz Street:

Islamic Cairo's Heart: Al-Muizz Street is one of the oldest streets in Cairo and is lined with beautiful examples of Islamic architecture, including mosques, sabils (water fountains), and madrasas.

Walking Tour: Start from Bab Zuweila and walk north, passing by significant sites like the Qalawun Complex, the Mosque of Al-Hakim, and various medieval houses.

Key Sites:

Qalawun Complex: A stunning Mamluk-era complex that includes a hospital, mosque, and madrasa.

Bayt al-Suhaymi: A well-preserved Ottoman-era house that offers a glimpse into the domestic life of Cairo's elite during the 17th century.

Entry Fee: Al-Muizz Street is free to explore, but some sites like the Qalawun Complex and Bayt al-Suhaymi may have small entrance fees, typically around 50-100 EGP ($1.50-3 USD).

Mid-Afternoon: Khan El Khalili Bazaar

Khan El Khalili Bazaar:

Explore the Souk: One of Cairo's most famous and historic markets, Khan El Khalili is the place to shop for souvenirs, jewelry, spices, perfumes, and traditional crafts. The narrow, winding alleys are full of vibrant shops and bustling activity.

Bartering: Bargaining is expected, so don't be shy to negotiate prices for goods.

Shopping Tips: Look for unique items like handmade carpets, silverware, and Egyptian cotton products.

Afternoon Tea at El Fishawy:

Historic Café: Take a break from shopping and enjoy a traditional Egyptian tea or coffee at El Fishawy, the legendary café that has been serving customers for over 200 years. The atmosphere is lively, with the sounds of the bazaar in the background.

Evening: Dinner and Cultural Experience

Dinner:

Recommended Dinner Spots:

Al-Azhar Park Restaurant: Located within Al-Azhar Park, this restaurant offers stunning views of Islamic Cairo, with the Citadel in the distance. The menu includes a mix of Egyptian and Middle Eastern dishes. Price: 200-400 EGP ($7-13 USD). Opening Hours: 12 PM - 11 PM.

Zitouni at the Four Seasons: For a more upscale dining experience, Zitouni offers a wide range of traditional Egyptian dishes in an elegant setting. Price: 400-700 EGP ($13-23 USD). Opening Hours: 12 PM - 11 PM.

Optional Evening Activity:

Whirling Dervishes Performance: If you're interested in experiencing traditional Egyptian culture, consider attending a Tannoura (whirling dervishes) performance at Wekalet El Ghouri, an old caravanserai turned cultural center.

Location: Near Al-Azhar Mosque, Islamic Cairo.

Performance Time: Usually starts at 7:30 PM, but it's advisable to arrive early to secure a good seat.

Entry Fee: 75-100 EGP ($2.50-3.50 USD).

Night: Return to Hotel and Relax

Return to Hotel:

Transportation: After your evening activities, return to your hotel. Taxi or ride-hailing services are convenient and widely available in Islamic Cairo.

Nightcap:

Hotel Bar or Lounge: If you're staying at a hotel with a bar or lounge, you might want to relax with a drink and reflect on the day's experiences.

Getting Around Islamic Cairo

Transportation Options:

Walking: Many of the sites in Islamic Cairo are close to each other, making walking the best way to explore the area. The narrow streets are full of character and history.

Taxi/Ride-Hailing: If you need to travel between distant sites, taxis and ride-hailing apps like Uber or Careem are convenient.

Guided Tours: Consider hiring a guide for a more informative experience, especially for the complex history of Islamic Cairo.

Tips for the Day:

Dress Modestly: Islamic Cairo is a conservative area, so it's advisable to dress modestly, especially when visiting mosques. Women should consider bringing a scarf to cover their heads when entering mosques.

Hydrate: Carry water with you, as the day can be long and you'll be walking quite a bit.

Photography: Many of the sites allow photography, but be sure to ask before taking pictures, especially inside mosques or historic buildings.

Day 5: Coptic Cairo and Local Culture

Morning: Discover Coptic Cairo

Breakfast:

Start Your Day:

Cilantro Café: Located in Maadi, it offers a variety of breakfast options, including pastries, sandwiches, and coffee. Price: 100-200 EGP ($3-7 USD). Opening Hours: 7 AM - 11 AM.

Beano's Café: With several locations around Cairo, Beano's is a reliable choice for a light breakfast and coffee. Price: 100-200 EGP ($3-7 USD). Opening Hours: 7 AM - 11 AM.

Travel to Coptic Cairo:

Transportation Options:

The Ultimate Egypt Travel Guide 2025 Edition

Taxi/Ride-Hailing: A taxi or Uber/Careem ride to Coptic Cairo from central Cairo or nearby neighborhoods like Zamalek should cost around 50-100 EGP ($1.50-3 USD) and take about 20-30 minutes.

Metro: The Cairo Metro is a convenient and inexpensive option, with the closest station being **Mar Girgis**. The fare is typically around 5 EGP ($0.15 USD).

Coptic Cairo:

Introduction: Coptic Cairo is a historic area that is central to the Christian history of Egypt. It features some of the oldest churches in the country, as well as the Coptic Museum, which houses a vast collection of Christian artifacts.

Key Sites:

The Hanging Church (Saint Virgin Mary's Coptic Orthodox Church):

History: One of the oldest churches in Egypt, dating back to the 3rd century. The church is known as the "Hanging Church" because it was built on top of a Roman fortress gatehouse.

Architecture: The interior is richly decorated with icons, wooden screens, and intricate inlays, reflecting traditional Coptic art.

Opening Hours: 9 AM - 5 PM.

Entry Fee: Free, but donations are appreciated.

Saints Sergius and Bacchus Church (Abu Serga):

Significance: Believed to be built on the spot where the Holy Family rested during their flight to Egypt. This church is one of the most important Coptic sites in Cairo.

Opening Hours: 9 AM - 5 PM.

Entry Fee: Free, with donations appreciated.

Ben Ezra Synagogue:

History: Originally a church, this building was converted into a synagogue in the 9th century. It's famous for being the site where the Cairo Geniza, a treasure trove of ancient Jewish manuscripts, was discovered.

Opening Hours: 9 AM - 4 PM.

Entry Fee: Free, though donations are welcome.

Coptic Museum:

Museum Visit: The Coptic Museum houses the world's most extensive collection of Coptic Christian artifacts, including manuscripts, textiles, and icons that showcase the rich cultural heritage of Egypt's Christian community.

Opening Hours: 9 AM - 5 PM.

Entry Fee: 100 EGP ($3.50 USD).

Mid-Morning: Continue Exploring and Local Shopping

Explore the Streets of Coptic Cairo:

St. George's Church and Monastery: Another significant religious site in Coptic Cairo, dedicated to Saint George. The church features beautiful murals and religious iconography.

Opening Hours: 9 AM - 5 PM.

Entry Fee: Free.

Local Shops:

Souvenir Shopping: There are a few shops near the churches where you can buy religious icons, Coptic crosses, and other souvenirs that reflect the area's Christian heritage.

Afternoon: Lunch and Explore Local Culture

Lunch:

Recommended Lunch Spots:

Oldish: Located in Garden City, this café offers a cozy atmosphere and a menu filled with Egyptian and Mediterranean dishes. Try their mezze platters or grilled meats. Price: 150-300 EGP ($5-10 USD). Opening Hours: 11 AM - 11 PM.

Felfela: Located near Tahrir Square, this restaurant is a classic choice for traditional Egyptian cuisine like kofta, koshari, and stuffed vegetables. Price: 100-200 EGP ($3-7 USD). Opening Hours: 12 PM - 11 PM.

Cultural Immersion:

The Nilometer: After lunch, head to the island of Roda to visit the Nilometer, an ancient structure used to measure the Nile's water levels. It's one of the few remaining Nilometers in Egypt.

History: Built in 861 AD, this structure is an important piece of Egypt's ancient irrigation history, and it's located in a beautiful garden setting.

Opening Hours: 9 AM - 4 PM.

Entry Fee: 60 EGP ($2 USD).

Walk Along the Nile Corniche:

Relaxing Stroll: Enjoy a leisurely walk along the Nile Corniche, taking in the views of the river and the city. This is a great way to experience the local atmosphere, with plenty of opportunities for people-watching and photography.

Mid-Afternoon: Visit Al-Azhar Park

Al-Azhar Park:

Green Oasis: One of the largest parks in Cairo, Al-Azhar Park offers stunning views of the city and is a perfect place to relax after a day of sightseeing. The park is beautifully landscaped and includes a variety of gardens, water features, and historic buildings.

Opening Hours: 9 AM - 10 PM.

Entry Fee: 30 EGP ($1 USD).

Explore the Park:

Historic Sites Within the Park: The park is also home to the restored Ayyubid Wall and several historic mosques. The walkways are lined with trees, flowers, and fountains, making it a peaceful escape from the city's hustle and bustle.

Tea at the Lakeview Café:

Enjoy a Break: The Lakeview Café within Al-Azhar Park offers a serene setting to enjoy tea or coffee with a view of the park's lake and the Cairo skyline. Price: 50-100 EGP ($1.50-3 USD).

Evening: Dinner and Local Experience

Dinner:

Recommended Dinner Spots:

Studio Misr: Located inside Al-Azhar Park, Studio Misr offers a fantastic dining experience with a view of the Citadel and Islamic Cairo. The menu features grilled meats, kebabs, and traditional Egyptian dishes. Price: 200-400 EGP ($7-13 USD). Opening Hours: 12 PM - 11 PM.

Khan El Khalili Restaurant: Located in the bustling bazaar area, this restaurant offers traditional Egyptian food in a historic setting. It's a great place to enjoy dishes like molokhia, stuffed pigeons, and more. Price: 150-300 EGP ($5-10 USD). Opening Hours: 12 PM - 11 PM.

Evening Activity:

Visit a Local Cultural Center: Consider ending your evening with a visit to a cultural center like the **Wekalet El Ghouri** for a traditional **Tannoura dance performance** or live Egyptian music.

Performance Time: Usually around 7 PM or 8 PM.

Entry Fee: 75-100 EGP ($2.50-3.50 USD).

Night: Return and Relax

Return to Hotel:

Transportation: After your evening activities, take a taxi or ride-hailing service back to your hotel. This should cost around 50-100 EGP ($1.50-3 USD) depending on your location.

Nightcap:

Hotel Lounge or Local Café: Relax with a drink at your hotel's bar or lounge, or head to a local café for some tea or coffee before retiring for the night.

Getting Around Coptic Cairo and Beyond

Transportation Options:

Walking: Coptic Cairo is best explored on foot, as most of the sites are within close proximity.

Metro: The Mar Girgis Metro Station is the most convenient public transport option to reach Coptic Cairo.

Taxi/Ride-Hailing: Taxis and ride-hailing services like Uber and Careem are convenient for traveling between distant locations and can be easily hailed throughout Cairo.

Tips for the Day:

Respect Religious Sites: Coptic Cairo is home to many active churches and religious sites. Dress modestly, and be respectful when visiting these places, particularly during services.

Stay Hydrated: Carry water with you, especially if you plan to spend a lot of time walking around the sites and the park.

Photography: While photography is allowed in most areas, be sure to ask for permission before taking pictures in religious sites or of people.

Day 6: Modern Cairo and Relaxation
Morning: Explore Zamalek and Gezira Island

Breakfast:

Start Your Day:

Maison Thomas: Located in Zamalek, this bakery is a local favorite for pastries, croissants, and breakfast sandwiches. Price: 100-200 EGP ($3-7 USD). Opening Hours: 7 AM - 12 PM.

Zooba: Also in Zamalek, Zooba offers a modern twist on traditional Egyptian breakfast dishes like taameya (falafel), eggs, and ful. Price: 100-200 EGP ($3-7 USD). Opening Hours: 8 AM - 11 AM.

Explore Zamalek:

Gezira Island: Begin your day by exploring Gezira Island, where the Zamalek neighborhood is located. Zamalek is an upscale district known for its leafy streets, embassies, and boutique shops.

Gezira Sporting Club: If you're interested in seeing a piece of Cairo's colonial history, take a walk around the Gezira Sporting Club. Founded in 1882, it's one of the oldest sporting clubs in Egypt.

Cairo Tower:

Iconic Landmark: Located on Gezira Island, the Cairo Tower stands at 187 meters (614 feet) and offers panoramic views of the city.

Observation Deck: Visit the observation deck to get a bird's-eye view of Cairo, including the Nile, the Pyramids in the distance, and the sprawling urban landscape.

Opening Hours: 9 AM - Midnight.

Entry Fee: 200 EGP ($6.50 USD).

Modern Art at the Gezira Center for Modern Art:

Art Museum: Also on Gezira Island, this museum showcases contemporary Egyptian art, with works by modern and emerging Egyptian artists.

Opening Hours: 9 AM - 4 PM.

Entry Fee: 20 EGP ($0.65 USD).

Mid-Morning: Shopping and Coffee Break

Shopping in Zamalek:

Boutique Shopping: Zamalek is known for its boutique shops offering everything from high-end fashion to unique Egyptian handicrafts. Consider visiting:

Fair Trade Egypt: A shop specializing in ethically sourced crafts and goods from across Egypt, including jewelry, textiles, and home décor.

Eklego: A modern furniture and design store that offers contemporary Egyptian-designed furniture and home accessories.

Coffee Break:

Cake Café: Stop by Cake Café in Zamalek for a coffee and a piece of their famous cakes or pastries. The café has a cozy, relaxed atmosphere perfect for a mid-morning break. Price: 50-100 EGP ($1.50-3 USD). Opening Hours: 9 AM - 11 PM.

Afternoon: Lunch and Relaxation

Lunch:

Recommended Lunch Spots:

Sequoia: Located at the northern tip of Zamalek, Sequoia offers Mediterranean cuisine with stunning views of the Nile. It's a great place to enjoy a leisurely lunch with dishes like mezze, seafood, and grilled meats. Price: 300-500 EGP ($10-17 USD). Opening Hours: 12 PM - 2 AM.

Crave: Also in Zamalek, Crave offers a mix of international dishes in a stylish setting. The menu includes everything from sushi to burgers and pasta. Price: 200-400 EGP ($7-13 USD). Opening Hours: 12 PM - 11 PM.

Relax at Al-Azhar Park:

Green Oasis: After lunch, head to Al-Azhar Park, one of Cairo's largest and most beautiful parks, to relax. The park offers stunning views of the city, including the Citadel and the historic mosques of Islamic Cairo.

Stroll Through the Gardens: Enjoy a leisurely walk through the park's beautifully landscaped gardens, water features, and historic Ayyubid Wall.

Optional Boat Ride: If you're looking for more relaxation, consider renting a boat on the park's small lake. It's a peaceful way to enjoy the scenery.

Tea at the Citadel View Restaurant:

Afternoon Tea: For a relaxing break, visit the Citadel View Restaurant inside the park. Enjoy a cup of tea or coffee with a view of the Citadel and the city skyline. Price: 50-100 EGP ($1.50-3 USD). Opening Hours: 9 AM - 10 PM.

Mid-Afternoon: Spa Time and Wellness

Spa and Wellness:

Four Seasons Hotel Cairo at Nile Plaza: Head to the Four Seasons for a luxurious spa experience. The hotel's spa offers a range of treatments, including massages, facials, and body treatments.

Popular Treatments: Consider a traditional Egyptian massage or a full-body scrub with natural Egyptian ingredients.

Spa Prices: Treatments range from 1,000-3,000 EGP ($30-100 USD) depending on the service.

Opening Hours: 9 AM - 9 PM.

Sofitel Cairo El Gezirah: Another option for a spa day, the Sofitel on Gezira Island offers a tranquil spa with views of the Nile. Enjoy a relaxing massage or a session in the hammam (Turkish bath).

Spa Prices: 1,000-2,500 EGP ($30-80 USD) depending on the treatment.

Opening Hours: 9 AM - 9 PM.

Evening: Dinner and Nile Cruise

Dinner:

Recommended Dinner Spots:

The Revolving Restaurant at Grand Nile Tower: Located on the 41st floor of the Grand Nile Tower, this revolving restaurant offers a 360-degree view of Cairo and the Nile. The menu features international and Egyptian dishes in a fine-dining setting. Price: 400-800 EGP ($13-26 USD). Opening Hours: 7 PM - Midnight.

Zooba: For a more casual dinner, head to Zooba in Zamalek for a modern take on Egyptian street food. The menu includes dishes like koshari, hawawshi, and creative salads. Price: 100-200 EGP ($3-7 USD). Opening Hours: 12 PM - 11 PM.

Nile Cruise:

Nile Dinner Cruise: After dinner, enjoy a relaxing evening on a Nile dinner cruise. These cruises typically include a buffet dinner, live music, and traditional Egyptian entertainment such as belly dancing and Tanoura shows.

Popular Cruises: Consider booking with Nile Maxim, Oberoi Philae, or Nile Pharaohs.

Duration: Most cruises last 2-3 hours, typically starting around 7:30 PM.

Price: 500-800 EGP ($17-26 USD) per person, including dinner and entertainment.

Night: Return and Relax

Return to Hotel:

Transportation: After your evening activities, return to your hotel via taxi or ride-hailing service. This should cost around 50-100 EGP ($1.50-3 USD).

Nightcap:

Hotel Lounge: End your day with a drink at your hotel's bar or lounge, reflecting on the day's experiences. Alternatively, enjoy a quiet walk along the Nile Corniche if your hotel is nearby.

Getting Around Modern Cairo

Transportation Options:

Taxi/Ride-Hailing: Taxis and ride-hailing services like Uber and Careem are the most convenient ways to get around modern Cairo, especially when moving between neighborhoods like Zamalek, Downtown, and Garden City.

Metro: The Cairo Metro is a fast and inexpensive option for getting around the city, especially for shorter distances. The fare is typically around 5-7 EGP ($0.15-0.20 USD).

Tips for the Day:

Dress Comfortably: Modern Cairo is more relaxed in terms of dress code, but comfortable shoes and attire are recommended, especially if you plan to walk a lot.

Reservations: For high-end dining or spa treatments, it's advisable to make reservations in advance to ensure availability.

Time for Yourself: This day is designed to be more relaxing, so feel free to adjust the itinerary based on your personal pace and preferences.

Day 7: Day Trip to Alexandria

Early Morning: Travel to Alexandria

Departure from Cairo:

Time: To make the most of your day, it's best to leave Cairo early, around 6:00 AM.

Transportation Options:

Private Car/Driver: Hiring a private car and driver is the most convenient and comfortable option, especially for a day trip. The drive takes about 2.5 to 3 hours, depending on traffic. Price: 1,500-2,500 EGP ($50-80 USD) for a round trip.

Train: Alternatively, you can take an early morning train from Cairo's Ramses Station to Alexandria. The first-class train service is comfortable and reasonably priced. The journey takes about 2.5 hours. Price: 100-150 EGP ($3-5 USD) one way. Trains generally depart around 6:00 AM.

Breakfast:

On the Go:

Packed Breakfast: Consider packing a breakfast from your hotel or grabbing something quick from a café like **Cilantro** at Ramses Station if taking the train.

On the Train: Some trains offer light snacks and coffee for purchase.

Morning: Explore Ancient Alexandria

Arrive in Alexandria:

Time: You should arrive in Alexandria by 9:00 AM, giving you a full day to explore.

Visit the Catacombs of Kom El Shoqafa:

Ancient Burial Site: Start your day with a visit to the Catacombs of Kom El Shoqafa, one of the Seven Wonders of the Middle Ages. This underground necropolis is a fascinating blend of Egyptian, Greek, and Roman cultural elements.

Highlights: The catacombs feature spiraling staircases, burial chambers, and carvings that provide insight into ancient funerary practices.

Opening Hours: 9:00 AM - 4:00 PM.

Entry Fee: 80 EGP ($2.60 USD).

Pompey's Pillar and the Temple of Serapeum:

Historical Monument: Next, visit Pompey's Pillar, a massive Roman column that stands as one of Alexandria's most famous landmarks. Nearby, you can explore the ruins of the Temple of Serapeum, which was dedicated to the Greco-Egyptian god Serapis.

Opening Hours: 9:00 AM - 4:30 PM.

Entry Fee: 80 EGP ($2.60 USD).

Mid-Morning: Explore the Alexandria Library

Bibliotheca Alexandrina:

Modern Marvel: Head to the Bibliotheca Alexandrina, a stunning modern library and cultural center built to commemorate the ancient Library of Alexandria. The library is not only a place for books but also houses museums, galleries, and a planetarium.

Guided Tour: Take a guided tour to learn about the library's architecture, history, and cultural significance.

Opening Hours: 10:00 AM - 7:00 PM.

Entry Fee: 70 EGP ($2.30 USD) for general admission, additional fees for museums and the planetarium.

Alexandria National Museum:

Museum Visit: If time allows, visit the Alexandria National Museum, housed in a restored Italianate villa. The museum offers a well-curated collection of artifacts from the Pharaonic, Roman, and Islamic periods.

Opening Hours: 9:00 AM - 5:00 PM.

Entry Fee: 100 EGP ($3.30 USD).

Afternoon: Lunch and Coastal Exploration

Lunch:

Recommended Spots:

Fish Market: Located near the Corniche, this restaurant offers fresh seafood with views of the Mediterranean Sea. Try their grilled fish or seafood platters. Price: 200-400 EGP ($7-13 USD). Opening Hours: 12:00 PM - 11:00 PM.

Balbaa Village for Grills and Seafood: Known for its local ambiance and delicious seafood, this spot offers a range of grilled meats and fresh fish. Price: 150-300 EGP ($5-10 USD). Opening Hours: 11:00 AM - Midnight.

Explore the Corniche:

Walk Along the Coast: After lunch, take a relaxing stroll along Alexandria's Corniche. This seaside promenade offers beautiful views of the Mediterranean, and it's a great place to observe local life.

Qaitbay Citadel:

Historic Fortress: Continue your exploration with a visit to the Qaitbay Citadel, a 15th-century fortress built on the site of the ancient Lighthouse of Alexandria. The citadel offers panoramic views of the sea and the city.

History: The citadel was built by Sultan Qaitbay to defend the city from Ottoman invasions. It's a prime example of medieval Islamic military architecture.

Opening Hours: 9:00 AM - 4:00 PM.

Entry Fee: 60 EGP ($2 USD).

Mid-Afternoon: Gardens and Palaces

Montaza Palace and Gardens:

Royal Retreat: Spend your afternoon at Montaza Palace and Gardens, a beautiful royal estate located along the coast. The gardens are expansive, with palm trees, flowerbeds, and pathways leading to the palace.

Palace Exterior: While the palace itself is not open to the public, the gardens are perfect for a leisurely walk.

Opening Hours: 8:00 AM - 6:00 PM.

Entry Fee: 25 EGP ($0.80 USD).

Tea at Salamlek Palace Hotel:

Afternoon Tea: If you're looking for a bit of luxury, visit the Salamlek Palace Hotel within the Montaza Gardens. Enjoy tea or coffee in a historic setting with views of the Mediterranean. Price: 100-200 EGP ($3-7 USD). Opening Hours: 10:00 AM - 7:00 PM.

Evening: Return to Cairo

Dinner:

Early Dinner in Alexandria: If you prefer to have dinner before leaving Alexandria, consider dining at:

Trianon Café: Located on the Corniche, this historic café offers a mix of Egyptian and Mediterranean dishes. It's a great place to enjoy dinner with a view of the sea. Price: 150-300 EGP ($5-10 USD). Opening Hours: 9:00 AM - Midnight.

Travel Back to Cairo:

Departure: Plan to leave Alexandria around 6:00 PM to return to Cairo. The drive or train ride will take about 2.5 to 3 hours, so you should arrive back in Cairo by 9:00 PM.

Private Car/Driver: If you hired a car and driver, they will be ready to take you back to Cairo.

Train: If you're taking the train, book an evening departure (trains typically run until around 9:00 PM).

Night: Relax and Unwind in Cairo

Return to Hotel:

Relax: Once back in Cairo, relax at your hotel. Consider enjoying a drink at the hotel bar or lounge to wind down after your day trip.

Optional Nightcap:

Café in Zamalek or Downtown: If you're not ready to end the night, stop by a café in Zamalek or Downtown Cairo for a late-night coffee or dessert.

Getting Around Alexandria

Transportation in Alexandria:

Taxis: Taxis are widely available in Alexandria and are the easiest way to get around the city. A short ride typically costs 20-50 EGP ($0.65-1.50 USD).

Trams: Alexandria's historic tram system is another option, especially if you want a more local experience. Fares are very cheap, around 2-5 EGP ($0.10-0.20 USD), but the system can be slow and crowded.

Tips for the Day:

Comfortable Shoes: Wear comfortable shoes as you'll be doing a lot of walking, especially around historical sites and the Corniche.

Stay Hydrated: Carry water with you, particularly when exploring outdoor sites like Qaitbay Citadel and Montaza Gardens.

Sun Protection: Alexandria can be quite sunny, so bring sunglasses, sunscreen, and a hat to protect yourself from the sun.

Chapter 11: Alexandria

Top 10 Attractions & Things to do

1. **Bibliotheca Alexandrina**

The Bibliotheca Alexandrina, located in Alexandria, Egypt, is a modern and striking cultural complex that serves as a tribute to the legendary Library of Alexandria, one of the ancient world's greatest centers of learning. Inaugurated in 2002, the new library aims to rekindle the spirit of knowledge and culture that the original library represented. It is not just a library but a vibrant hub of intellectual and cultural activity, drawing visitors from around the world.

History

Ancient Roots: The original Library of Alexandria, established in the 3rd century BCE, was one of the most famous libraries of the ancient world, renowned for its vast collection of manuscripts and its role as a major center of scholarship. The ancient library was destroyed under unclear circumstances, but it left a lasting legacy that inspired the creation of the modern Bibliotheca Alexandrina.

Modern Revival: The idea of reviving the ancient library was proposed in the late 20th century, and with the support of UNESCO and other international organizations, construction of the new library began in 1995. Designed by the Norwegian architecture firm Snøhetta, the library officially opened its doors in 2002.

Location

Address: Corniche Road, Alexandria, Egypt.

Coordinates: 31.2089° N latitude, 29.9092° E longitude.

Accessibility: The library is located on the Mediterranean coast, in the heart of Alexandria. It is easily accessible by car, taxi, or public transportation, and is a prominent landmark in the city.

Opening and Closing Hours

Hours of Operation:

Sunday to Thursday: 10:00 AM to 7:00 PM.

Friday and Saturday: 12:00 PM to 4:00 PM.

Public Holidays: Hours may vary, so it's advisable to check in advance.

Special Events: The library frequently hosts special events, exhibitions, and lectures, which may affect visiting hours.

Top Things to Do

Explore the Main Library: The heart of the Bibliotheca Alexandrina is its massive reading room, which spans 70,000 square meters and can hold up to 8 million books. Visitors can explore the collections, which include rare manuscripts, maps, and modern digital resources.

Visit the Museums: The complex houses several museums, including the Manuscript Museum, the Antiquities Museum, and the Sadat Museum, dedicated to Egypt's former president Anwar Sadat. Each museum offers unique insights into different aspects of Egyptian history and culture.

Attend Cultural Events: The Bibliotheca Alexandrina is a cultural hub that regularly hosts conferences, lectures, exhibitions, and performances. Check the event schedule to see what's happening during your visit.

Admire the Architecture: The library's modern design is a highlight in itself. The building is circular with a slanted roof that resembles a rising sun, symbolizing the dawning of knowledge. The exterior is adorned with inscriptions in various languages, representing humanity's collective knowledge.

Explore the Planetarium: The library's planetarium offers fascinating shows and exhibitions on astronomy and space exploration, making it a great attraction for visitors of all ages.

Stroll the Plaza and Gardens: The library is surrounded by a spacious plaza and beautifully landscaped gardens, perfect for a leisurely stroll while enjoying views of the Mediterranean.

Practical Information

Tickets: Entry fees vary depending on the areas you wish to visit. There are separate tickets for the main library, museums, and planetarium. Discounts are available for students, seniors, and groups.

Facilities: The library complex includes cafes, a gift shop, and public restrooms. There are also information desks where visitors can get assistance and brochures.

Guided Tours: Guided tours are available and highly recommended for those interested in a deeper understanding of the library's history, architecture, and collections. Tours are available in multiple languages.

Tips for Visiting

Plan Ahead: The library is vast, so plan your visit ahead of time, prioritizing the sections and exhibits you most want to see.

Check Event Schedules: If you're interested in attending a lecture, performance, or special exhibit, check the library's schedule online before your visit.

Respect the Quiet Zones: The main reading rooms are quiet zones, so be mindful of noise levels to avoid disturbing others.

Photography: Photography is allowed in certain areas of the library, but restrictions apply, particularly in museum sections. Always ask if unsure.

Explore Alexandria: Combine your visit with other attractions in Alexandria, such as the Alexandria National Museum, Montaza Palace, or the Catacombs of Kom El Shoqafa, to get the most out of your trip.

2. Qaitbay Citadel

9Qaitbay Citadel, or the Citadel of Qaitbay, is a stunning 15th-century fortress located on the Mediterranean coast in Alexandria, Egypt. Built on the exact site of the ancient Lighthouse of Alexandria, one of the Seven Wonders of the Ancient World, the citadel is a significant historical monument and a symbol of Alexandria's rich maritime heritage. It offers visitors a fascinating journey through history, combined with breathtaking views of the sea.

History

Construction: The citadel was constructed in 1477 by Sultan Al-Ashraf Sayf al-Din Qaitbay, a Mamluk ruler, to defend Alexandria from the growing threat of Ottoman invasion. The fortress was strategically placed on the eastern tip of Pharos Island, the same location where the famous Lighthouse of Alexandria once stood.

Strategic Importance: Over the centuries, Qaitbay Citadel served as a crucial military stronghold, protecting Alexandria's harbor from various threats. The fortification was well-maintained and used by different ruling powers, including the Ottomans and the British, during their respective occupations of Egypt.

Restoration: The citadel underwent several restorations over the years, particularly during the 19th and 20th centuries, to preserve its structural integrity and historical significance.

Location

The Ultimate Egypt Travel Guide 2025 Edition

Address: Eastern Harbour, Alexandria, Egypt.

Coordinates: 31.2137° N latitude, 29.8854° E longitude.

Accessibility: Qaitbay Citadel is located at the westernmost point of Alexandria's Eastern Harbor. It is easily accessible by car, taxi, or public transportation, and is a prominent landmark within the city.

Opening and Closing Hours

Hours of Operation:

Daily: Typically open from 8:00 AM to 5:00 PM.

Seasonal Hours: The opening hours may vary slightly depending on the season or special events, so it is advisable to check ahead of time.

Ticket Booth: Tickets can be purchased at the entrance, and the booth usually closes about 30 minutes before the citadel itself closes.

Top Things to Do

Explore the Fortress: Walk through the citadel's well-preserved corridors, chambers, and courtyards. The thick stone walls, designed to withstand attacks, and the strategic layout provide a glimpse into medieval military architecture.

Visit the Museum: Inside the citadel, you'll find a small maritime museum displaying artifacts from Alexandria's naval history, including weapons, maps, and models of ancient ships.

Climb the Towers: Ascend the towers for panoramic views of the Mediterranean Sea and the city of Alexandria. The vantage points offer stunning photo opportunities, especially at sunset.

Learn About the Lighthouse of Alexandria: While exploring, you'll encounter information about the ancient Lighthouse of Alexandria, which once stood on this very site. The citadel was partially built using stones from the ruins of the lighthouse, connecting the past with the present.

Enjoy the Surroundings: Stroll along the citadel's outer walls and enjoy the refreshing sea breeze and views of Alexandria's coastline. The area around the citadel is also popular for leisurely walks and picnics.

Practical Information

Tickets: Tickets are available at the entrance, with prices varying for local and international visitors. It's a good idea to bring cash for ticket purchases.

Facilities: The citadel has basic facilities, including restrooms and a small gift shop where you can buy souvenirs. Nearby, there are several cafes and restaurants where visitors can relax and enjoy local cuisine.

Guided Tours: While exploring the citadel on your own is possible, hiring a guide can enhance your experience by providing detailed historical context and interesting anecdotes about the fortress.

Tips for Visiting

Wear Comfortable Shoes: The citadel's grounds are extensive, and exploring its interior involves navigating stairs and uneven surfaces, so comfortable footwear is recommended.

Visit Early or Late: To avoid crowds and enjoy a more peaceful experience, consider visiting early in the morning or late in the afternoon. The light during these times is also ideal for photography.

Check the Weather: As the citadel is located by the sea, it can be windy and cool, especially in the winter months. Dress appropriately and bring a jacket if needed.

Photography: The citadel offers plenty of opportunities for photography, both inside the fortress and from the vantage points on its towers. However, be mindful of signs indicating areas where photography may be restricted.

Combine with Other Sites: Qaitbay Citadel is close to other attractions in Alexandria, such as the Bibliotheca Alexandrina and the Corniche. Plan your visit to include these sites for a fuller experience of the city.

3. Montaza Palace and Gardens

Montaza Palace and Gardens, located in the coastal city of Alexandria, Egypt, is a sprawling estate that once served as a royal summer residence. The complex, which includes beautifully manicured gardens and two palaces, is a popular destination for both locals and tourists. With its stunning Mediterranean views, lush greenery, and historical significance, Montaza offers a peaceful retreat from the bustle of the city.

History

Construction: Montaza Palace was built in 1892 by Khedive Abbas II, the last ruler of Egypt under Ottoman rule. Initially, it included the Salamlek Palace, intended as a hunting lodge. Later, in the 1930s, King Fuad I expanded the estate by constructing the larger Haramlek Palace, which served as a royal residence.

Royal Use: The Montaza complex was used by the Egyptian royal family as a summer retreat. It provided an escape from Cairo's heat, with its cool sea breezes and expansive gardens. After the Egyptian Revolution in 1952, the palace became state property and was repurposed for various governmental functions.

Present Day: Today, the Salamlek Palace has been transformed into a luxury hotel, while the Haramlek Palace is occasionally used for official events. The gardens are open to the public, making it a favorite spot for relaxation and recreation.

Location

Address: Al Mandarah Bahri, Montaza, Alexandria, Egypt.

Coordinates: 31.2876° N latitude, 30.0053° E longitude.

Accessibility: Montaza Palace and Gardens are located in the Montaza district of Alexandria, about 20 kilometers (12 miles) from the city center. The site is accessible by car, taxi, or public transportation, with plenty of parking available nearby.

Opening and Closing Hours

Hours of Operation:

Gardens: Open daily from 8:00 AM to 11:00 PM.

Palaces: The interiors of the palaces are not generally open to the public, but the gardens and exterior views can be enjoyed throughout the day.

Seasonal Hours: Opening hours may vary during holidays or special events, so it's advisable to check in advance if planning a visit during these times.

Top Things to Do

Explore the Gardens: The Montaza Gardens cover over 370 acres of land and feature a variety of plants, trees, and flowers. Stroll through the well-maintained pathways, enjoy the shaded areas, and take in the views of the Mediterranean Sea.

Visit the Beach: The estate includes several private beaches, some of which are accessible to the public for a fee. These beaches are a great place to relax, swim, or enjoy water sports.

Admire the Architecture: The Haramlek Palace is an architectural gem, combining elements of Ottoman, Florentine, and Moorish styles. Though the interior is not open to visitors, the exterior alone is worth the visit.

Enjoy a Picnic: The gardens are a popular spot for picnics, especially among locals. Bring some food and drinks, and enjoy a relaxing day surrounded by nature.

Photography: The palace and gardens offer plenty of scenic views, making it a perfect spot for photography enthusiasts. The combination of natural beauty and historic architecture provides endless opportunities for stunning shots.

Practical Information

Tickets: There is a small entrance fee to access the Montaza Gardens. The fee is generally higher for foreigners than for locals, so it's good to bring cash.

Facilities: The estate is equipped with basic facilities, including restrooms, cafes, and kiosks. There are also several restaurants within the gardens where you can enjoy a meal with a view.

Accommodation: For those looking to stay overnight, the Salamlek Palace Hotel offers luxurious accommodations within the estate, providing a unique opportunity to experience royal living.

Tips for Visiting

Plan for a Full Day: Montaza Palace and Gardens are extensive, so plan to spend several hours exploring the area. It's a great spot for a leisurely day out.

Wear Comfortable Shoes: The gardens are vast, and comfortable walking shoes are recommended for exploring the many paths and trails.

Visit Early or Late: To avoid crowds, especially during weekends and holidays, consider visiting early in the morning or late in the afternoon. The light during these times is also ideal for photography.

Check Beach Access: If you plan to visit one of the beaches, inquire about access and fees ahead of time. Some beaches are private or require a fee for entry.

Respect the Environment: The gardens are meticulously maintained, so be sure to dispose of trash properly and respect the natural surroundings.

4. Catacombs of Kom El Shoqafa

The Catacombs of Kom El Shoqafa, located in Alexandria, Egypt, are a fascinating archaeological site that offers a unique glimpse into the city's ancient history. These underground tombs, carved deep into the bedrock, date back to the 2nd century AD and are a remarkable example of the fusion of Egyptian, Greek, and Roman architectural styles. The catacombs are considered one of the Seven Wonders of the Middle Ages and are among the most important historical attractions in Alexandria.

History

Construction: The Catacombs of Kom El Shoqafa were originally built as a private tomb for a wealthy family in the 2nd century AD. Over time, they were expanded to accommodate more burials, becoming a large, multi-level underground necropolis.

Cultural Fusion: The catacombs reflect the cultural melting pot that was Alexandria during the Roman period. The architecture and decoration blend traditional Egyptian motifs with Hellenistic and Roman influences, illustrating the city's diverse cultural heritage.

Rediscovery: The catacombs were lost to history for centuries until they were rediscovered in 1900 when a donkey accidentally fell into one of the shafts, revealing the ancient underground complex.

Location

Address: Karmouz District, Alexandria, Egypt.

Coordinates: 31.1822° N latitude, 29.8964° E longitude.

Accessibility: The Catacombs of Kom El Shoqafa are located in the Karmouz district of Alexandria, southwest of the city center. They are accessible by car, taxi, or public transportation.

Opening and Closing Hours

Hours of Operation:

Daily: Typically open from 9:00 AM to 5:00 PM.

Holidays: The catacombs may have different hours during public holidays, so it's advisable to check in advance.

Ticket Booth: Tickets can be purchased at the entrance, and the booth usually closes about 30 minutes before the catacombs themselves close.

Top Things to Do

Explore the Main Chamber: The catacombs consist of several levels, with the main chamber being the most impressive. Here, you'll find a circular hall with a spiral staircase leading down to the burial chambers. The chamber is adorned with intricate carvings and sculptures that blend Egyptian, Greek, and Roman elements.

Visit the Triclinium: This funerary banquet hall, known as the Triclinium, was used by the relatives of the deceased to host ceremonial feasts in honor of the dead. The room is decorated with frescoes and offers insight into the burial customs of the time.

Admire the Carvings: Throughout the catacombs, you'll find detailed carvings and reliefs depicting various deities, mythical creatures, and scenes from daily life. These carvings showcase the unique blend of artistic styles from different cultures.

See the Sarcophagi: The catacombs contain several sarcophagi, some of which are elaborately decorated. These stone coffins were used to house the bodies of the deceased, and their designs reflect the fusion of different cultural influences.

Discover the Mystery: The labyrinthine layout of the catacombs adds an element of mystery to the experience. As you explore the winding tunnels and chambers, you'll get a sense of the secrecy and reverence that surrounded ancient burial practices.

Practical Information

Tickets: Entrance fees are required to visit the catacombs, with different rates for local and international visitors. It's recommended to bring cash for ticket purchases.

Facilities: The site has basic facilities, including restrooms and a small shop where you can buy refreshments and souvenirs.

Guided Tours: Hiring a guide is recommended for a more informative visit, as they can provide detailed explanations of the historical significance and the intricate details of the site.

Tips for Visiting

Wear Comfortable Shoes: The catacombs involve a fair amount of walking and climbing stairs, so comfortable footwear is essential.

Mind the Humidity: Being underground, the catacombs can be humid, so dress appropriately and bring water to stay hydrated.

Photography: Photography is generally allowed, but flash photography may be restricted to preserve the delicate artwork. Check for any signs or ask your guide about the rules.

Visit Early: To avoid the crowds and the heat, it's best to visit the catacombs early in the day. This will also give you more time to explore at your own pace.

Explore Nearby Attractions: The catacombs are close to other historical sites, such as Pompey's Pillar and the Roman Amphitheatre. Consider combining visits to these attractions for a more comprehensive experience of Alexandria's ancient heritage.

5. Pompey's Pillar

Pompey's Pillar is an impressive ancient Roman column located in Alexandria, Egypt. Erected in the 3rd century AD, it stands as a monumental symbol of Alexandria's historical significance and the grandeur of Roman engineering. The pillar, made of red granite, is one of the largest of its kind and serves as a prominent landmark in the city's archaeological landscape.

History

Construction: Pompey's Pillar was erected in 297 AD during the reign of Emperor Diocletian. Contrary to what its name might suggest, it was not constructed in honor of the Roman general Pompey. The name is a misnomer; it originated from medieval times when local legends mistakenly associated the pillar with Pompey.

Purpose: The pillar was built to commemorate the victory of Emperor Diocletian over the Egyptians during a period of unrest and to honor the Roman Emperor. It was originally part of a larger complex that included a temple dedicated to the god Serapis.

Significance: The pillar stands as a testament to the architectural and engineering skills of the Romans. Its construction utilized large blocks of granite, and its height and grandeur reflect the importance of Alexandria as a major center of culture and power during the Roman era.

Location

Address: Karmouz District, Alexandria, Egypt.

Coordinates: 31.2153° N latitude, 29.8992° E longitude.

Accessibility: Pompey's Pillar is located in the Karmouz district of Alexandria, about 5 kilometers (3 miles) southwest of the city center. It is easily accessible by car, taxi, or public transportation.

Opening and Closing Hours

Hours of Operation:

Daily: Typically open from 9:00 AM to 4:00 PM.

Holidays: Hours may vary during public holidays, so it is advisable to check in advance.

Ticket Booth: Tickets can be purchased at the entrance, and the booth usually closes about 30 minutes before the site itself closes.

Top Things to Do

Admire the Pillar: The 25-meter-tall (82-foot) pillar is made of red granite and is adorned with intricate carvings. It is one of the tallest and most well-preserved ancient columns in the world. Take time to appreciate its grandeur and the craftsmanship of Roman stonework.

Explore the Surrounding Ruins: The pillar is situated in an area that includes several other significant ruins, such as the remains of the Serapeum (the temple dedicated to Serapis) and the nearby Roman amphitheater. Explore these ruins to gain a deeper understanding of the site's historical context.

Visit the Base: The base of the pillar features inscriptions and reliefs that provide insights into the historical and religious significance of the site. Look for these details as you walk around the base.

Photography: The pillar offers excellent opportunities for photography. Capture its impressive height and the details of its carvings against the backdrop of the surrounding archaeological remains.

Practical Information

Tickets: Entrance fees are required to visit the site, with different rates for local and international visitors. Bring cash for ticket purchases.

Facilities: The site has basic facilities, including restrooms and a small shop where you can buy refreshments. There are no extensive dining options directly on-site, so consider bringing snacks or visiting nearby eateries.

Guided Tours: Hiring a guide can enhance your visit by providing detailed explanations about the history and significance of Pompey's Pillar and the surrounding ruins.

Tips for Visiting

Wear Comfortable Shoes: The area around the pillar involves some walking on uneven terrain, so comfortable footwear is essential.

Visit Early or Late: To avoid crowds and the heat, consider visiting early in the morning or late in the afternoon. This will also provide better lighting for photography.

Check for Any Restrictions: There may be restrictions on certain areas or activities, such as climbing or touching the monument. Always adhere to any posted signs or guidelines to preserve the site.

Combine with Other Sites: Pompey's Pillar is close to other significant archaeological sites, such as the Catacombs of Kom El Shoqafa and the Roman Amphitheater. Plan your visit to include these sites for a more comprehensive experience of Alexandria's ancient history.

Stay Hydrated: Alexandria can be quite hot, especially in the summer months. Bring water to stay hydrated and protect yourself from the sun with a hat or sunscreen.

6. Alexandria National Museum

The Alexandria National Museum, situated in Alexandria, Egypt, is a key destination for those interested in exploring the city's rich and varied history. Housed in a grand 19th-century mansion, the museum offers a diverse collection of artifacts from different historical periods, including Ancient Egyptian, Greco-Roman, Coptic, and Islamic. It provides visitors with a comprehensive view of Alexandria's cultural and historical evolution.

History

Establishment: The Alexandria National Museum was opened in 2003 to serve as a central repository for Alexandria's historical artifacts and to present them to the public. Its establishment aimed to preserve the city's cultural heritage and educate visitors about its historical significance.

Building: The museum is located in a beautifully restored palace built in 1926. Originally the residence of a wealthy Egyptian family, the building itself is an architectural gem, reflecting the grandeur of early 20th-century design.

Exhibits: The museum's collections span several eras, showcasing the influence of various cultures that have left their mark on Alexandria over the millennia.

Location

Address: 110 El Horreya Road, Alexandria, Egypt.

Coordinates: 31.2152° N latitude, 29.9150° E longitude.

Accessibility: Centrally located in Alexandria, the museum is easily reachable by car, taxi, or public transport. It is well-situated for those exploring other nearby attractions in the city.

Opening and Closing Hours

Hours of Operation:

Sunday to Thursday: 9:00 AM to 5:00 PM.

Friday: Closed.

Saturday: 9:00 AM to 5:00 PM.

Holidays: Hours may vary during public holidays, so checking in advance is advisable if planning a visit around these times.

Top Things to Do

Explore the Ancient Egyptian Gallery: Discover artifacts such as statues, sarcophagi, and mummies that reveal the religious and cultural practices of ancient Egypt. Highlights include well-preserved items from the Pharaonic period.

Admire Greco-Roman Artifacts: The museum showcases a variety of Greco-Roman sculptures, mosaics, and inscriptions. These pieces reflect Alexandria's status as a major center of culture and learning during the Roman era.

Learn About Coptic History: The Coptic section features religious manuscripts, textiles, and other artifacts that illustrate the history and culture of Egypt's Christian period.

Examine Islamic Art: The museum includes a collection of Islamic art, including ceramics, metalwork, and textiles, highlighting the influence of Islamic culture on Alexandria.

Enjoy the Building's Architecture: Take time to appreciate the architectural details of the 19th-century mansion, which adds to the museum experience. The building's design complements the historical artifacts it houses.

Practical Information

Tickets: Tickets are required for entry, with different rates for local and international visitors. They can be purchased at the museum entrance.

Facilities: The museum offers basic amenities, including restrooms, a café, and a gift shop with souvenirs related to the exhibits.

Guided Tours: Guided tours are available and recommended to enhance your visit. They provide detailed explanations and context for the exhibits, often in English and Arabic.

Tips for Visiting

Allocate Sufficient Time: The museum has extensive collections, so plan to spend a few hours exploring. This will give you enough time to appreciate the various exhibits.

Wear Comfortable Footwear: Comfortable shoes are advisable as there is considerable walking involved throughout the museum.

Check for Special Exhibitions: The museum occasionally hosts special exhibitions and events. Checking their website or contacting them in advance can help you catch any unique displays during your visit.

Respect Photography Rules: Photography policies may differ. Always look for signs or ask museum staff about any restrictions on photography to protect the artifacts.

Combine with Other Sites: The museum is conveniently located near other attractions, such as the Bibliotheca Alexandrina and Pompey's Pillar. Plan your visit to include these sites for a fuller experience of Alexandria.

7. The Corniche

The Corniche is a picturesque waterfront promenade stretching along the Mediterranean Sea in Alexandria, Egypt. It is one of the city's most popular attractions, offering stunning views, leisurely walks, and a vibrant atmosphere. The Corniche runs for about 15 kilometers (9 miles) and serves as a central hub for both locals and tourists looking to enjoy Alexandria's coastal charm.

History

Development: The Corniche has been a significant feature of Alexandria's landscape for over a century. Its development reflects the city's evolution from a historic port town to a modern metropolis, becoming a central recreational and commercial area.

Cultural Significance: Over the years, the Corniche has been the backdrop for numerous historical events and cultural activities. It has witnessed the transformation of Alexandria into a cosmopolitan city while retaining its historical essence.

Location

Address: The Corniche runs along the Mediterranean coastline from the Alexandria Eastern Harbor to the Montaza Palace area.

Coordinates: Approximately 31.2001° N latitude, 29.9151° E longitude.

Accessibility: The Corniche is easily accessible from various parts of Alexandria. It is well-served by public transportation, including buses and taxis, and there are several entry points along its length.

Opening and Closing Hours

Hours of Operation: The Corniche is open 24/7. It is a public space that can be visited at any time, though it is most popular during daylight hours and early evening.

Best Time to Visit: Early mornings and late afternoons are ideal times for enjoying a walk along the Corniche. The views of the Mediterranean Sea

The Ultimate Egypt Travel Guide 2025 Edition

are particularly beautiful during these times, and the weather is often more pleasant.

Top Things to Do

Stroll Along the Promenade: Enjoy a leisurely walk along the Corniche, taking in the sea views, fresh air, and vibrant atmosphere. The promenade is lined with cafes, shops, and landmarks, making it a pleasant place to explore.

Visit Key Landmarks: Explore significant landmarks located along the Corniche, including the Alexandria Library (Bibliotheca Alexandrina), the Qaitbay Citadel, and various statues and historical markers.

Relax in Parks and Cafes: The Corniche is dotted with parks and cafes where you can relax and enjoy the view. Popular spots include the Sidi Gaber area and the Montaza Gardens.

Watch the Sunset: The Corniche offers stunning sunset views over the Mediterranean. Find a comfortable spot along the promenade to witness the sunset and enjoy the changing colors of the sky.

Enjoy Local Cuisine: Several restaurants and cafes line the Corniche, offering a variety of local and international cuisines. Try traditional Egyptian dishes and seafood while enjoying the sea view.

Practical Information

Facilities: The Corniche is equipped with various amenities, including public restrooms, seating areas, and refreshment kiosks. Some areas also have playgrounds and recreational facilities.

Safety: The promenade is generally safe, but like any popular public area, it's wise to stay aware of your surroundings and keep an eye on your belongings.

Accessibility: The Corniche is accessible to people with disabilities, though some sections may be more challenging due to uneven surfaces or stairs.

Tips for Visiting

Bring Sun Protection: The sun can be strong, especially during midday. Wear sunscreen, a hat, and sunglasses to protect yourself from the sun.

Stay Hydrated: Bring water with you, particularly if you plan to walk for extended periods. There are also many cafes and kiosks where you can purchase refreshments.

Respect Local Customs: While the Corniche is a casual public space, it's always good to dress modestly, respecting local customs and cultural norms.

Check for Events: Occasionally, the Corniche hosts cultural and public events. Check local listings to see if there are any special activities or festivals happening during your visit.

Plan for Traffic: The Corniche can get busy, especially on weekends and holidays. If you're driving, be prepared for traffic and consider using public transportation if possible.

8. Royal Jewelry Museum

The Royal Jewelry Museum, located in Alexandria, Egypt, is an exquisite museum dedicated to showcasing the opulent jewelry and artifacts of Egypt's royal family. Housed in a grand 19th-century palace, the museum offers a unique opportunity to explore the splendor of Egyptian royalty through its extensive collection of jewelry, crowns, and personal items.

History

Establishment: The Royal Jewelry Museum was inaugurated in 1986 to preserve and display the jewelry and personal items of Egypt's royal family, particularly from the late 19th and early 20th centuries. It serves as a testament to the artistic and historical significance of these treasures.

Building: The museum is situated in a lavish palace built in 1919 for Princess Fatma Al-Zahra, a member of Egypt's royal family. The palace itself is an architectural marvel, reflecting the grandeur and elegance of the era.

Collections: The museum's collections primarily feature items from the reigns of King Farouk and King Fuad, as well as earlier periods. The exhibits include crowns, necklaces, rings, and other pieces of exquisite jewelry, alongside various personal items of the royal family.

Location

Address: 21 Ahmed Yehia Street, Zizinia, Alexandria, Egypt.

Coordinates: 31.2122° N latitude, 29.9159° E longitude.

Accessibility: The museum is located in the Zizinia district of Alexandria. It is accessible by car, taxi, or public transportation, and is a well-known landmark in the city.

Opening and Closing Hours

Hours of Operation:

Saturday to Thursday: 9:00 AM to 4:00 PM.

Friday: Closed.

Holidays: The museum may have different hours or be closed during public holidays, so checking in advance is recommended.

Top Things to Do

Explore the Jewelry Collections: View an impressive array of royal jewelry, including ornate necklaces, tiaras, and rings. Each piece is intricately designed and reflects the wealth and artistry of Egypt's royal family.

Admire the Crown Jewels: The museum features several crowns worn by Egyptian royalty, each showcasing the exceptional craftsmanship and detailed design of the period.

See Personal Items: In addition to jewelry, the museum displays personal items of the royal family, such as watches, accessories, and other artifacts that provide insight into their lives.

Tour the Palace: Take time to appreciate the palace's architecture and interior design. The opulent rooms, ornate ceilings, and grand furnishings offer a glimpse into the luxurious lifestyle of Egypt's royals.

Learn About Royal History: The museum provides informative exhibits and descriptions that offer historical context about the items and the royal family they belonged to.

Practical Information

Tickets: Entrance fees are required, with different rates for local and international visitors. Tickets can be purchased at the museum entrance.

Facilities: The museum provides basic facilities, including restrooms and a small gift shop with souvenirs related to the exhibits.

Guided Tours: Guided tours are available and can enhance your visit by providing detailed explanations of the exhibits and the historical background of the royal family.

Tips for Visiting

Dress Modestly: As with many cultural institutions, it's advisable to dress modestly when visiting the museum to respect local customs and cultural norms.

Check for Special Exhibitions: The museum may occasionally host special exhibitions or events. Check their website or contact them in advance to find out if there are any unique displays during your visit.

Allow Time for Exploration: The museum's collection is extensive, so allocate a few hours to fully appreciate the exhibits and the grandeur of the palace.

Photography: Photography policies may vary. Always check for signs or ask museum staff about whether photography is allowed, and follow any guidelines provided.

9. Abu al-Abbas al-Mursi Mosque

The Abu al-Abbas al-Mursi Mosque is one of the most important and revered mosques in Alexandria, Egypt. Named after the 13th-century Andalusian scholar and Sufi saint, Abu al-Abbas al-Mursi, the mosque is a significant religious and cultural landmark. It is known for its stunning architecture, historical significance, and its role as a center for spiritual learning and worship.

History

Founding: The mosque was established in the 13th century, in honor of Abu al-Abbas al-Mursi, a prominent Sufi saint who migrated from Andalusia to Egypt. His presence in Alexandria is celebrated for his contributions to Sufism and Islamic scholarship.

Construction: The mosque was originally built during the Mamluk period, and it has undergone several renovations and expansions over the centuries. The current structure reflects a blend of Mamluk and Ottoman architectural styles.

Significance: The mosque is not only a place of worship but also a site of pilgrimage for those who revere Abu al-Abbas al-Mursi. It serves as a spiritual center for the local community and visitors from around the world.

Location

Address: El-Mansheya Square, Alexandria, Egypt.

Coordinates: 31.2155° N latitude, 29.9054° E longitude.

Accessibility: Located in the heart of Alexandria, the mosque is easily accessible by car, taxi, or public transportation. It is a central landmark in the city, making it a prominent destination for visitors.

Opening and Closing Hours

Hours of Operation:

Daily: The mosque is open to visitors throughout the day, typically from early morning until late evening. However, it is advisable to visit during non-prayer times to avoid disruptions.

Prayer Times: The mosque follows the Islamic prayer schedule, with specific times for prayers that may affect access to certain areas of the mosque.

Top Things to Do

Admire the Architecture: The mosque features stunning Islamic architecture, including intricate tile work, elegant arches, and a grand dome. Take time to appreciate the architectural details and the beautiful craftsmanship.

Visit the Courtyard: The mosque's courtyard is spacious and adorned with fountains and lush greenery. It's a serene place to sit and reflect or enjoy the peaceful atmosphere.

Explore the Prayer Hall: The main prayer hall is richly decorated with calligraphy and geometric patterns. Observe the impressive design and the large chandelier that illuminates the space.

Learn About Sufism: Discover the significance of Abu al-Abbas al-Mursi and his contributions to Sufism. The mosque often has information available about his life and teachings.

Experience the Spiritual Atmosphere: The mosque is an active place of worship and spiritual reflection. Take a moment to experience the calm and reverent environment, which is central to the mosque's identity.

Practical Information

Dress Code: Modest dress is required when visiting the mosque. Both men and women should wear clothing that covers the arms and legs. Women may be required to cover their heads with a scarf.

Facilities: The mosque provides basic facilities, including restrooms and areas for worship. It may not have extensive visitor amenities, so plan accordingly.

Guided Tours: While formal guided tours may not be available, local guides or mosque officials may provide information about the mosque's history and significance upon request.

Tips for Visiting

Respect Prayer Times: Be mindful of prayer times, as the mosque may be particularly busy or restricted during these periods. It's best to visit outside of prayer times to fully enjoy the site.

Follow Mosque Etiquette: Respect the customs and practices of those who are praying or visiting the mosque. Maintain a quiet demeanor and follow any instructions from mosque staff.

Check for Events: The mosque may host special religious or cultural events. If you're interested in attending, check with local sources or mosque staff for information on upcoming events.

Bring a Scarf: If you're a woman, bring a scarf for covering your head, as this is often required when entering mosques.

10. Alexandria Opera House (Sayed Darwish Theatre)

The Alexandria Opera House, also known as the Sayed Darwish Theatre, is a prominent cultural and performing arts venue in Alexandria, Egypt. It stands as a testament to the city's rich cultural heritage and its vibrant arts scene. Named after the renowned Egyptian composer Sayed Darwish, the theatre hosts a variety of performances, including opera, classical music, ballet, and traditional Arabic music.

History

Establishment: The Alexandria Opera House was established in 1918, during a period of cultural flourishing in Egypt. It was initially built as a venue for theatrical performances and classical music.

Renaming: In 1962, the theatre was renamed in honor of Sayed Darwish, a legendary Egyptian composer and musician known for his significant contributions to Arabic music.

Cultural Role: The theatre has played a crucial role in promoting the arts in Alexandria and Egypt. It has been a key venue for both local and international performances, contributing to the city's reputation as a cultural hub.

Location

Address: 25 El-Shaheed Sayed Darwish Square, Alexandria, Egypt.

Coordinates: 31.2158° N latitude, 29.9180° E longitude.

Accessibility: The opera house is centrally located in Alexandria, making it easily accessible by car, taxi, or public transportation. It is situated in a lively area with various dining and shopping options nearby.

Opening and Closing Hours

Hours of Operation: The Alexandria Opera House generally operates during performance hours, which vary depending on the schedule. Administrative offices are typically open from Sunday to Thursday, 9:00 AM to 4:00 PM.

Performance Schedule: The theatre hosts performances throughout the year, with schedules often published in advance. It is best to check the theatre's official website or contact their box office for the latest information on performances and events.

Top Things to Do

Attend a Performance: Experience a live performance at the theatre, whether it's an opera, classical concert, ballet, or a traditional Arabic music show. The theatre hosts a diverse range of performances that cater to different tastes.

Explore the Theatre: Admire the architecture and interior design of the theatre. The building features a grand facade and an elegant interior, reflecting early 20th-century design with modern touches.

Visit the Sayed Darwish Museum: Located within the theatre, the museum is dedicated to Sayed Darwish and his contributions to Arabic music. It features memorabilia, photographs, and information about his life and work.

Enjoy the Surrounding Area: The theatre is situated in a vibrant part of Alexandria with various cafes, restaurants, and shops. Explore the area before or after attending a performance.

Practical Information

Tickets: Tickets for performances can be purchased at the theatre's box office or through their official website. It's advisable to book in advance, especially for popular shows.

Facilities: The theatre offers basic facilities, including restrooms, a café, and a gift shop. There may also be services for the hearing and visually impaired.

Guided Tours: Guided tours of the theatre may be available upon request, providing insight into its history and architectural features.

Tips for Visiting

Check the Schedule: Performances and events vary, so check the theatre's schedule in advance to ensure you can attend a show that interests you.

Dress Appropriately: The theatre has a formal atmosphere, so dress smartly when attending performances. While there is no strict dress code, upscale casual or formal attire is recommended.

Arrive Early: Arrive at the theatre early to find parking, collect your tickets, and explore the venue. It's also a good idea to familiarize yourself with the seating arrangement and facilities.

Respect Theatre Etiquette: During performances, maintain silence and turn off mobile phones to avoid disturbing others. Adhere to any specific guidelines provided by the theatre staff.

Accommodation Options

Luxury Hotel

Luxury hotels in Alexandria offer an opulent escape with world-class amenities and stunning views of the Mediterranean. These high-end accommodations provide exceptional comfort, personalized service, and exquisite dining, ensuring a memorable and refined experience in this historic city. Ideal for travelers seeking sophistication and indulgence.

Top 5 Luxury Hotel

1. Four Seasons Hotel Alexandria at San Stefano

The Four Seasons Hotel Alexandria at San Stefano is a premier luxury hotel located along the Mediterranean coast in Alexandria, Egypt. Renowned for its sophisticated design, impeccable service, and stunning seaside views, this hotel offers an opulent retreat with a blend of contemporary luxury and traditional elegance. It caters to both leisure and business travelers seeking a high-end experience in one of Egypt's most historic cities.

Location (Address & Proximity)

Address: 399 El Geish Road, San Stefano, Alexandria, Egypt

Proximity: Situated in the upscale San Stefano district, the hotel enjoys a prime location directly overlooking the Mediterranean Sea. It is conveniently close to key attractions such as the Alexandria Library, the Catacombs of Kom El Shoqafa, and the Montazah Palace. Alexandria's city center and its historical sites are easily accessible, and Alexandria International Airport is approximately a 20-minute drive away.

Highlights

Seaside Views: Offers spectacular views of the Mediterranean Sea from many of its rooms and public areas.

Luxurious Accommodations: Features elegantly designed rooms and suites with high-end furnishings and amenities.

Exceptional Service: Known for its attentive and personalized service, ensuring a memorable stay for all guests.

Spa and Wellness

Spa: The hotel boasts a full-service spa offering a range of treatments and therapies designed to relax and rejuvenate guests. The spa includes private treatment rooms, a relaxation area, and a menu of massages, facials, and body treatments.

Wellness Facilities: Includes a modern fitness center equipped with state-of-the-art exercise equipment, a sauna, and a steam room.

Bars

On-Site Bars: The hotel features several sophisticated bars and lounges, including:

Café Belle Vue: An elegant venue with panoramic sea views, serving a selection of cocktails, fine wines, and light snacks.

The Pool Bar: Located by the outdoor pool, offering refreshing beverages and light fare in a relaxed setting.

Events and Conferences

Meeting Spaces: The Four Seasons Hotel Alexandria at San Stefano provides a range of meeting and event facilities, including versatile conference rooms and ballrooms. These spaces are equipped with the latest audiovisual technology and can be customized for various types of events.

Event Services: Offers comprehensive event planning services, including catering, decoration, and technical support, ensuring seamless and successful events.

Basic Facilities and Amenities

Dining: The hotel features several dining options, including:

Sofra Restaurant: Serving a diverse array of international and local cuisine in a stylish setting.

Café Vienna: An elegant café offering pastries, coffee, and light meals.

Seafood Restaurant: Specializes in fresh seafood with stunning sea views.

Business Center: Provides essential business services such as high-speed internet access, printing, and meeting facilities.

Fitness Center: A well-equipped gym with a range of exercise equipment and personal training options.

Concierge Services: Offers assistance with local recommendations, travel arrangements, and special requests to enhance the guest experience.

Opening and Closing Hours

Check-in: Typically from 3:00 PM

Check-out: By 12:00 PM

Restaurants and Bars: Restaurant hours vary, but typically:

Sofra Restaurant: Breakfast from 6:30 AM to 10:30 AM, lunch from 12:00 PM to 3:00 PM, and dinner from 7:00 PM to 10:30 PM.

Café Vienna: Open from early morning until late evening.

Bars: Open in the late afternoon and remain open until late evening, with specific hours varying.

Price

Room Rates: Rates for a stay at the Four Seasons Hotel Alexandria at San Stefano generally range from $300 to $600 per night, depending on the season, room type, and booking period. This pricing reflects the hotel's luxury status and the high level of service and amenities offered.

Pros

Luxurious Experience: Offers a high level of luxury and elegance, with beautifully designed rooms and top-notch facilities.

Prime Location: Located in a picturesque setting with stunning Mediterranean Sea views, and close to key attractions.

Exceptional Service: Known for its attentive and personalized service, enhancing the guest experience.

Comprehensive Amenities: Includes a range of amenities such as a full-service spa, diverse dining options, and modern business facilities.

Cons

Higher Cost: The luxury experience comes with a higher price point compared to mid-range or budget accommodations.

Crowded During Peak Seasons: Can be busy during peak travel seasons, which may affect availability and pricing.

Local Tips

Explore Alexandria: Take advantage of the hotel's location to explore Alexandria's historic sites, such as the Library of Alexandria and the Roman Amphitheater.

Enjoy Local Cuisine: Try local seafood and traditional Egyptian dishes at nearby restaurants or within the hotel's dining options.

Relax by the Sea: Spend time at the hotel's private beach or pool area to fully enjoy the Mediterranean setting.

Traffic Considerations: Be aware of local traffic patterns, especially during peak hours, to optimize your travel around the city.

2. Sheraton Montazah Hotel

The Sheraton Montazah Hotel is a prestigious luxury property located in Alexandria, Egypt, known for its elegant accommodations and stunning views of the Mediterranean Sea. Situated in the upscale Montazah district, this hotel combines comfort and luxury with a prime location, offering an ideal retreat for both leisure and business travelers.

Location (Address & Proximity)

Address: Montazah Palace Gardens, Alexandria, Egypt

Proximity: Nestled in the Montazah district, the hotel boasts a prime location overlooking the Mediterranean Sea. It is adjacent to the Montazah Palace and Gardens, a popular historical site and park. Key attractions such as the Alexandria Library, the Catacombs of Kom El Shoqafa, and the Corniche are accessible. Alexandria International Airport is about a 25-minute drive away.

Highlights

Seaside Views: Offers spectacular views of the Mediterranean Sea from many rooms and public areas.

Elegant Design: Features a classic and sophisticated design, reflecting luxury and comfort.

Prime Location: Adjacent to Montazah Palace

Gardens, providing easy access to one of Alexandria's most beautiful landmarks.

Spa and Wellness

Spa: The hotel includes a full-service spa offering a range of treatments, including massages, facials, and body therapies. The spa is designed to provide relaxation and rejuvenation in a tranquil setting.

Wellness Facilities: Features a modern fitness center equipped with state-of-the-art exercise equipment, as well as a sauna and steam room.

Bars

On-Site Bars: The Sheraton Montazah Hotel offers several dining and bar options, including:

The Lounge: A stylish and relaxing space where guests can enjoy a selection of cocktails, fine wines, and light snacks.

The Pool Bar: Located by the outdoor pool, offering refreshing drinks and light meals in a casual setting.

Events and Conferences

Meeting Spaces: The hotel provides versatile meeting and event spaces, including conference rooms and ballrooms equipped with modern audiovisual technology. These spaces are suitable for business meetings, conferences, and social events.

Event Services: Offers comprehensive event planning services, including catering, decoration, and technical support to ensure successful events.

Basic Facilities and Amenities

Dining: The hotel features several dining options, including:

The Royal Grill: Offers a variety of international and local dishes in an elegant setting.

La Veranda: Provides a more casual dining experience with a selection of Mediterranean cuisine and views of the sea.

Business Center: Provides essential business services such as high-speed internet access, printing, and meeting facilities.

Fitness Center: Includes a well-equipped gym with a range of exercise equipment and personal training options.

Concierge Services: Assists with local recommendations, travel arrangements, and special requests to enhance the guest experience.

Opening and Closing Hours

Check-in: Typically from 3:00 PM

Check-out: By 12:00 PM

Restaurants and Bars: Restaurant hours vary, but typically:

The Royal Grill: Breakfast from 6:30 AM to 10:30 AM, lunch from 12:00 PM to 3:00 PM, and dinner from 7:00 PM to 10:30 PM.

La Veranda: Open from breakfast through to dinner with specific hours varying.

Bars: Open in the late afternoon and evening, with specific hours depending on the bar.

Price

Room Rates: Rates for a stay at the Sheraton Montazah Hotel generally range from $150 to $350 per night, depending on the season, room type, and booking period. This pricing reflects the hotel's luxury status and the high level of service and amenities provided.

Pros

Luxury and Comfort: Provides a high level of luxury with elegantly designed rooms and top-notch facilities.

Scenic Location: Offers beautiful views of the Mediterranean Sea and is adjacent to Montazah Palace Gardens.

Comprehensive Amenities: Includes a full-service spa, multiple dining options, and modern business facilities.

Exceptional Service: Known for its attentive and professional service, ensuring a pleasant and memorable stay.

Cons

Higher Cost: The luxury experience comes with a higher price point compared to mid-range or budget accommodations.

Crowded During Peak Seasons: Can be busy during peak travel times, which may affect availability and pricing.

Local Tips

Explore Montazah Gardens: Take advantage of the hotel's proximity to Montazah Palace Gardens for a relaxing stroll or picnic.

Visit Alexandria's Attractions: Use the hotel's location to explore nearby historic sites such as the Alexandria Library and the Catacombs.

Local Dining: Try local seafood and traditional Egyptian cuisine at nearby restaurants or within the hotel's dining options.

Traffic Awareness: Be mindful of local traffic patterns, especially during peak hours, to optimize your travel around Alexandria.

3. Helnan Palestine Hotel

The Helnan Palestine Hotel is a luxury property located in Alexandria, Egypt, renowned for its elegant accommodations and picturesque setting by the Mediterranean Sea. This hotel combines traditional charm with modern comforts, offering a serene retreat with stunning views and high-quality service. It caters to both leisure and business travelers looking for a premium experience in Alexandria.

Location (Address & Proximity)

Address: Montazah Palace Gardens, Alexandria, Egypt

Proximity: The hotel is situated in the Montazah district, adjacent to the historic Montazah Palace and Gardens. It offers beautiful views of the Mediterranean Sea and is close to key attractions such as the Alexandria Library, the Catacombs of Kom El Shoqafa, and the Alexandria Corniche. The city center and Alexandria International Airport are both easily accessible, with the airport being about a 20-minute drive away.

Highlights

Seaside Location: Offers breathtaking views of the Mediterranean Sea, enhancing the guest experience with a tranquil and picturesque setting.

Elegant Design: Features a blend of classic and contemporary decor, creating a sophisticated and comfortable environment.

Proximity to Attractions: Adjacent to Montazah Palace Gardens, providing convenient access to one of Alexandria's most iconic landmarks.

Spa and Wellness

Spa: The hotel includes a full-service spa offering a range of treatments designed to relax and rejuvenate guests. Services include massages, facials, and body treatments in a serene setting.

Wellness Facilities: Features a modern fitness center equipped with advanced exercise equipment, a sauna, and a steam room.

Bars

On-Site Bars: The Helnan Palestine Hotel offers several dining and bar options, including:

The Lounge Bar: A stylish bar serving a selection of

cocktails, fine wines, and light snacks in a sophisticated setting.

The Pool Bar: Located near the outdoor pool, this bar offers refreshing drinks and light meals in a relaxed atmosphere.

Events and Conferences

Meeting Spaces: Provides versatile meeting and event facilities, including conference rooms and ballrooms equipped with modern audiovisual technology. These spaces are suitable for a range of events from business meetings to social gatherings.

Event Services: Offers comprehensive support for organizing events, including catering, decoration, and technical assistance to ensure successful and memorable occasions.

Basic Facilities and Amenities

Dining: The hotel features several dining options, including:

The Main Restaurant: Offers a variety of international and local cuisine in an elegant setting with stunning sea views.

The Seafood Restaurant: Specializes in fresh seafood dishes, allowing guests to enjoy local culinary delights.

Business Center: Provides essential business services such as high-speed internet access, printing, and meeting facilities.

Fitness Center: Includes a well-equipped gym with a range of exercise equipment and personal training options.

Concierge Services: Assists with local recommendations, travel arrangements, and special requests to enhance the guest experience.

Opening and Closing Hours

Check-in: Typically from 3:00 PM

Check-out: By 12:00 PM

Restaurants and Bars: Hours of operation vary, but typically:

The Main Restaurant: Breakfast from 6:30 AM to 10:00 AM, lunch from 12:00 PM to 3:00 PM, and dinner from 7:00 PM to 10:00 PM.

The Seafood Restaurant: Open for lunch and dinner with specific hours varying.

Bars: Usually open in the late afternoon and remain open until late evening, with specific hours depending on the bar.

Price

Room Rates: Rates for a stay at the Helnan Palestine Hotel typically range from $150 to $300 per night, depending on the season, room type, and booking period. This pricing reflects the hotel's luxury status and the high level of service and amenities offered.

Pros

Luxurious Setting: Offers a high level of luxury with elegant decor and a prime seaside location.

Stunning Views: Provides beautiful views of the Mediterranean Sea and easy access to Montazah Palace Gardens.

Comprehensive Amenities: Includes a full-service spa, diverse dining options, and modern business facilities.

Exceptional Service: Known for its attentive and professional service, ensuring a pleasant and memorable stay.

Cons

Higher Cost: The luxury experience comes with a higher price point compared to mid-range or budget hotels.

Peak Season Crowds: Can be busy during peak travel times, which may affect availability and pricing.

Local Tips

Explore Montazah Gardens: Utilize the hotel's proximity to Montazah Palace Gardens for a relaxing stroll or picnic.

Visit Alexandria's Historical Sites: Use the hotel as a base to explore nearby historic attractions like the Alexandria Library and the Catacombs.

Enjoy Local Cuisine: Sample local seafood and Egyptian dishes at the hotel's restaurants or nearby eateries.

Traffic Awareness: Be aware of local traffic patterns, especially during peak hours, to optimize your travel around Alexandria.

4. Swissôtel Alexandria

Swissôtel Alexandria is a high-end luxury hotel in Alexandria, Egypt, known for its modern design, upscale amenities, and exceptional service. Positioned as a premier choice for both business and leisure travelers, it offers a blend of Swiss hospitality and contemporary comforts, set against the backdrop of Alexandria's vibrant urban landscape.

Location (Address & Proximity)

Address: 2 El Guezira, El Shatby, Alexandria 21599, Egypt

Proximity: Located in the central area of Alexandria, the hotel is conveniently close to major attractions such as the Alexandria Library, the Catacombs of Kom El Shoqafa, and the Alexandria Corniche. It is approximately a 30-minute drive from Alexandria International Airport and offers easy access to various cultural and historical sites in the city.

Highlights

Modern Design: Features contemporary architecture and stylish interiors that blend luxury with comfort.

Comprehensive Amenities: Offers a wide range of facilities including a full-service spa, multiple dining options, and extensive business services.

Central Location: Provides convenient access to Alexandria's key attractions and business districts.

Spa and Wellness

Spa: The hotel includes a full-service spa offering a variety of treatments designed to relax and rejuvenate guests. The spa features private treatment rooms and a range of services including massages, facials, and body treatments.

Wellness Facilities: Includes a modern fitness center equipped with the latest exercise equipment, as well as a sauna and steam room.

Bars

On-Site Bars: Swissôtel Alexandria features several dining and bar options, including:

The Lounge Bar: A chic bar offering a selection of cocktails, fine wines, and light snacks in a relaxed and elegant setting.

Pool Bar: Situated by the outdoor pool, it provides refreshing beverages and light meals, perfect for unwinding in a casual environment.

Events and Conferences

Meeting Spaces: The hotel offers a range of versatile meeting and event facilities, including conference rooms and ballrooms equipped with modern audiovisual technology. These spaces can accommodate various types of events, from business meetings to social functions.

Event Services: Provides comprehensive event planning and coordination services, including catering, decoration, and technical support to ensure the success of events.

Basic Facilities and Amenities

Dining: The hotel features multiple dining options, including:

The Main Restaurant: Offers a variety of international and local dishes in a sophisticated setting with both buffet and à la carte options.

Specialty Restaurants: May include additional dining venues offering a range of cuisines and dining experiences.

Business Center: Equipped with high-speed internet access, printing, and other essential business services.

Fitness Center: A well-equipped gym providing a range of exercise equipment and personal training options.

Concierge Services: Assists with local recommendations, travel arrangements, and special requests to enhance the guest experience.

Opening and Closing Hours

Check-in: Typically from 3:00 PM

Check-out: By 12:00 PM

Restaurants and Bars: Hours of operation vary, but typically:

The Main Restaurant: Breakfast from 6:30 AM to 10:00 AM, lunch from 12:00 PM to 3:00 PM, and dinner from 7:00 PM to 10:00 PM.

Specialty Restaurants: Open for lunch and dinner with specific hours varying.

Bars: Usually open in the late afternoon and evening, with specific hours depending on the bar.

Price

Room Rates: Rates for a stay at Swissôtel Alexandria generally range from $150 to $300 per night, depending on the season, room type, and booking period. This pricing reflects the hotel's luxury status and the extensive amenities and services provided.

Pros

Modern Luxury: Offers a contemporary and luxurious environment with stylish decor and modern amenities.

Central Location: Conveniently located with easy access to Alexandria's attractions and business areas.

Comprehensive Facilities: Includes a full-service spa, multiple dining options, and extensive business facilities.

High-Quality Service: Known for its attentive and professional service, ensuring a comfortable and enjoyable stay.

Cons

Higher Cost: The luxury experience comes with a higher price point compared to mid-range or budget accommodations.

Traffic: As with many urban areas, traffic congestion can affect travel times to and from the hotel.

Local Tips

Explore Nearby Attractions: Utilize the hotel's central location to visit nearby historic and cultural sites, including the Alexandria Library and the Catacombs.

Local Dining: Experience local cuisine at nearby restaurants or within the hotel's dining venues.

Traffic Awareness: Be mindful of local traffic patterns, especially during peak hours, to optimize your travel around Alexandria.

5. Radisson Blu Hotel, Alexandria

The Radisson Blu Hotel, Alexandria is a modern luxury hotel that offers a blend of stylish design, upscale amenities, and exceptional service. Located in Alexandria, Egypt, this hotel caters to both leisure and business travelers, providing a comfortable and elegant retreat with a range of contemporary facilities.

Location (Address & Proximity)

Address: 54 El Horreya Road, Alexandria 21599, Egypt

Proximity: Centrally located in Alexandria, the hotel is conveniently positioned for easy access to the city's major attractions, including the Alexandria Library, the Catacombs of Kom El Shoqafa, and the Alexandria Corniche. Alexandria International Airport is approximately a 30-minute drive away, and the hotel's location provides access to key business and cultural sites.

Highlights

Modern Design: Features contemporary architecture and stylish interiors, offering a sophisticated and comfortable environment.

Comprehensive Amenities: Includes a range of facilities such as a full-service spa, multiple dining options, and modern business services.

Central Location: Provides convenient access to Alexandria's main attractions and business areas.

Spa and Wellness

Spa: The hotel includes a full-service spa offering a variety of treatments aimed at relaxation and rejuvenation. Services include massages, facials, and body treatments in a tranquil setting.

Wellness Facilities: Features a state-of-the-art fitness center equipped with the latest exercise equipment, as well as a sauna and steam room.

Bars

On-Site Bars: The Radisson Blu Hotel, Alexandria offers several dining and bar options, including:

The Lounge Bar: A stylish bar where guests can enjoy a selection of cocktails, fine wines, and light snacks in an elegant setting.

The Pool Bar: Located by the outdoor pool, this bar offers refreshing beverages and light meals in a relaxed atmosphere.

Events and Conferences

Meeting Spaces: Provides a range of versatile meeting and event facilities, including conference rooms and ballrooms equipped with modern audiovisual technology. These spaces are suitable for various events, including business meetings and social gatherings.

Event Services: Offers comprehensive support for event planning, including catering, decoration, and technical assistance to ensure successful and memorable events.

Basic Facilities and Amenities

Dining: The hotel features multiple dining options, including:

The Main Restaurant: Serves a variety of international and local dishes in a sophisticated setting with both buffet and à la carte options.

Specialty Dining: Additional dining venues may offer a range of cuisines and dining experiences.

Business Center: Equipped with high-speed internet access, printing, and other essential business services.

Fitness Center: A modern gym with a range of exercise equipment and personal training options.

Concierge Services: Provides assistance with local recommendations, travel arrangements, and special requests to enhance the guest experience.

Opening and Closing Hours

Check-in: Typically from 3:00 PM

Check-out: By 12:00 PM

Restaurants and Bars: Hours of operation vary, but typically:

The Main Restaurant: Breakfast from 6:30 AM to 10:00 AM, lunch from 12:00 PM to 3:00 PM, and dinner from 7:00 PM to 10:00 PM.

Specialty Dining: Open for lunch and dinner with specific hours varying.

Bars: Usually open in the late afternoon and evening, with specific hours depending on the bar.

Price

Room Rates: Rates for a stay at the Radisson Blu Hotel, Alexandria generally range from $130 to $280 per night, depending on the season, room type, and booking period. This pricing reflects the hotel's luxury status and the range of amenities and services provided.

Pros

Modern Comfort: Offers a contemporary and luxurious environment with stylish decor and modern amenities.

Central Location: Conveniently located with easy access to Alexandria's attractions and business areas.

Comprehensive Facilities: Includes a full-service spa, multiple dining options, and modern business services.

High-Quality Service: Known for its attentive and professional service, ensuring a comfortable and enjoyable stay.

Cons

Higher Cost: The luxury experience comes with a higher price point compared to mid-range or budget accommodations.

Traffic: As with many urban areas, traffic congestion can affect travel times to and from the hotel.

Local Tips

Explore Alexandria: Use the hotel's central location to visit nearby historic and cultural sites such as the Alexandria Library and the Catacombs.

Local Dining: Experience local cuisine at nearby restaurants or within the hotel's dining venues.

Traffic Awareness: Be mindful of local traffic patterns, especially during peak hours, to optimize your travel around Alexandria.

Mid-Range Hotel

Mid-range hotels in Alexandria provide a great balance of comfort, quality, and value. Offering well-appointed rooms, convenient locations, and essential amenities, these hotels are ideal for travelers seeking a pleasant stay without breaking the bank. Enjoy reliable service and a comfortable experience in this historic city.

Top 5 Mid-Range Hotels

1. Paradise Inn Le Metropole Hotel

Paradise Inn Le Metropole Hotel is a historic mid-range hotel located in Alexandria, Egypt. Known for its charming architecture and traditional hospitality, this hotel offers a blend of classic elegance and modern comfort. It provides a more affordable luxury experience while retaining a sense of historical significance and cultural charm.

Location (Address & Proximity)

Address: 7 El Hamra Square, Alexandria 21599, Egypt

Proximity: Situated in the heart of Alexandria, the hotel is conveniently located near key attractions such as the Alexandria Library, the Corniche, and the historic sites of the city. Alexandria International Airport is approximately a 30-minute drive away. The hotel's central location makes it easy to explore both cultural and historical landmarks.

Highlights

Historic Charm: Features classic architecture and

decor that reflect the hotel's long history and heritage.

Central Location: Offers convenient access to many of Alexandria's main attractions and business areas.

Affordable Luxury: Provides a mid-range pricing option with a touch of elegance and historical ambiance.

Spa and Wellness

Spa: The hotel does not have a full-service spa, but it may offer some basic wellness facilities or partner with nearby wellness centers.

Fitness Facilities: The hotel may not have an extensive fitness center, but guests can inquire about local gym options or nearby fitness facilities.

Bars

On-Site Bars: The hotel features a traditional bar or lounge area where guests can enjoy a selection of beverages in a classic setting. Specific details about bar services may vary, but it typically provides a comfortable space for relaxation.

Events and Conferences

Meeting Spaces: Offers some meeting and event facilities suitable for small to medium-sized gatherings. These spaces may be equipped with basic audiovisual equipment and can be used for business meetings, conferences, and social events.

Event Services: Provides basic support for event planning, including catering and setup, although it may not offer the extensive services found in larger luxury hotels.

Basic Facilities and Amenities

Dining: The hotel features dining options that may include:

The Main Restaurant: Serves a variety of international and local dishes in a traditional setting.

Breakfast Service: Typically includes a selection of continental and local breakfast items.

Business Center: May offer basic business services such as internet access, printing, and copying.

Concierge Services: Provides assistance with local recommendations, travel arrangements, and special requests.

Opening and Closing Hours

Check-in: Typically from 2:00 PM

Check-out: By 12:00 PM

Restaurants and Bars: Hours of operation vary, but typically:

The Main Restaurant: Breakfast from 6:30 AM to 10:00 AM, with lunch and dinner hours varying.

Bar/Lounge: Usually open in the late afternoon and evening.

Price

Room Rates: Rates for a stay at Paradise Inn Le Metropole Hotel generally range from $80 to $150 per night, depending on the season, room type, and booking period. This pricing reflects its mid-range status, offering a blend of comfort and affordability.

Pros

Historical Charm: Offers a unique historical ambiance with classic architecture and decor.

Central Location: Conveniently located near major attractions and business areas in Alexandria.

Affordable Rates: Provides a more affordable luxury experience compared to higher-end hotels.

Personalized Service: Known for its traditional hospitality and personalized service.

Cons

Limited Modern Amenities: May lack some of the modern amenities and extensive facilities found in higher-end luxury hotels.

No Full-Service Spa: Does not have an extensive spa or wellness center on-site.

Basic Fitness Options: May have limited fitness facilities, with no dedicated gym.

Local Tips

Explore the Area: Take advantage of the hotel's central location to explore nearby landmarks, including the Alexandria Library and the Corniche.

Local Cuisine: Try local dining options in the area to experience Alexandria's culinary offerings.

Transportation: Consider using local transportation options or taxis to navigate the city, especially if traffic congestion is a concern.

2. Four Seasons Hotel Alexandria at San Stefano

The Four Seasons Hotel Alexandria at San Stefano is a premier luxury hotel located in Alexandria, Egypt. Renowned for its elegant design, exceptional service, and stunning views of the Mediterranean Sea, this hotel offers a sophisticated retreat for both leisure and business travelers. Combining modern amenities with classic charm, it provides a high-end experience in one of Egypt's most historic cities.

Location (Address & Proximity)

Address: 399 El Geish Road, San Stefano, Alexandria 21599, Egypt

Proximity: The hotel is situated in the upscale San Stefano district, offering beautiful views of the Mediterranean Sea and direct access to the San Stefano Grand Plaza. It is close to major attractions such as the Alexandria Library and the Catacombs of Kom El Shoqafa. Alexandria International Airport is approximately a 25-minute drive away, making it convenient for international travelers.

Highlights

Seaside Location: Offers breathtaking views of the Mediterranean Sea from many rooms and public areas.

Luxurious Design: Features a blend of contemporary and classic decor, providing a sophisticated and comfortable environment.

Prime Location: Situated in the San Stefano district, with easy access to shopping, dining, and cultural attractions.

Spa and Wellness

Spa: The hotel includes a full-service spa offering a variety of treatments designed to relax and rejuvenate guests. Services include massages, facials, body treatments, and wellness therapies in a serene setting.

Wellness Facilities: Features a state-of-the-art fitness center equipped with the latest exercise equipment, a sauna, and a steam room. There is also an outdoor swimming pool with views of the Mediterranean.

Bars

On-Site Bars: The Four Seasons Hotel Alexandria offers several dining and bar options, including:

The Lounge: A stylish venue for afternoon tea and light snacks, offering a relaxing atmosphere with views of the sea.

The Pool Bar: Located by the outdoor pool, it serves refreshing beverages and light meals in a casual and scenic setting.

The Royal Bar: An elegant bar providing a selection of fine wines, cocktails, and premium spirits in a sophisticated ambiance.

Events and Conferences

Meeting Spaces: The hotel provides versatile meeting and event spaces, including grand ballrooms and smaller conference rooms equipped with modern audiovisual technology. These spaces are suitable for business meetings, conferences, and social events.

Event Services: Offers comprehensive event planning services, including catering, decoration, and technical support to ensure the success of events. Professional staff are available to assist with all aspects of event management.

Basic Facilities and Amenities

Dining: The hotel features multiple dining options, including:

The Mediterranean Restaurant: Offers a variety of Mediterranean and international dishes with stunning sea views.

The Seafood Restaurant: Specializes in fresh seafood and local cuisine.

Business Center: Provides essential business services such as high-speed internet access, printing, and meeting facilities.

Concierge Services: Assists with local recommendations, travel arrangements, and special requests to enhance the guest experience.

Opening and Closing Hours

Check-in: Typically from 3:00 PM

Check-out: By 12:00 PM

Restaurants and Bars: Hours of operation vary, but typically:

Mediterranean Restaurant: Breakfast from 6:30 AM to 10:30 AM, lunch from 12:00 PM to 3:00 PM, and dinner from 7:00 PM to 11:00 PM.

Seafood Restaurant: Open for lunch and dinner with specific hours varying.

Bars: Usually open in the late afternoon and evening, with specific hours depending on the bar.

Price

Room Rates: Rates for a stay at the Four Seasons Hotel Alexandria at San Stefano generally range from $250 to $500 per night, depending on the season, room type, and booking period. This pricing reflects the hotel's luxury status and the high level of service and amenities provided.

Pros

Luxurious Experience: Provides a high level of luxury with elegant design and modern amenities.

Stunning Views: Offers beautiful views of the Mediterranean Sea and direct access to the San Stefano Grand Plaza.

Comprehensive Amenities: Includes a full-service spa, multiple dining options, and extensive business facilities.

Exceptional Service: Known for its attentive and professional service, ensuring a comfortable and memorable stay.

Cons

Higher Cost: The luxury experience comes with a higher price point compared to mid-range or budget accommodations.

Busy Area: The San Stefano district can be busy, which might affect accessibility and traffic around the hotel.

Local Tips

Explore the San Stefano Grand Plaza: Take advantage of the hotel's proximity to the Grand Plaza for shopping and dining.

Visit Local Attractions: Use the hotel as a base to explore nearby landmarks, such as the Alexandria Library and the Catacombs.

Enjoy Local Cuisine: Try local seafood and Egyptian dishes at nearby restaurants or within the hotel's dining options.

Traffic Awareness: Be mindful of local traffic patterns, especially during peak hours, to optimize your travel around Alexandria.

3. Sheraton Montazah Hotel

The Sheraton Montazah Hotel is a well-regarded mid-range hotel located in Alexandria, Egypt, offering a blend of comfort and convenience. Situated in the Montazah district, the hotel provides a relaxing stay with easy access to both historical and recreational attractions. With its range of amenities and welcoming atmosphere, it caters to both leisure and business travelers.

Location (Address & Proximity)

Address: Montazah Palace Gardens, Alexandria, Egypt

Proximity: The hotel is situated within the Montazah Palace Gardens area, known for its beautiful parks and historic Montazah Palace. It offers scenic views and is conveniently close to the Mediterranean Sea. Key attractions such as the Alexandria Library and the Catacombs of Kom El Shoqafa are within a short drive. Alexandria International Airport is about a 25-minute drive away, providing easy access for travelers.

Highlights

Scenic Location: Offers views of the Montazah Palace Gardens and the Mediterranean Sea.

Comfortable Accommodations: Features well-appointed rooms and suites designed for relaxation and convenience.

Recreational Facilities: Includes amenities such as an outdoor pool and direct access to the Montazah Gardens.

Spa and Wellness

Spa: The hotel may not have a full-service spa, but it offers wellness services that can include massage treatments and relaxation facilities. Guests can also use the nearby wellness facilities or inquire about local spa options.

Fitness Center: Equipped with basic exercise equipment for maintaining fitness during your stay.

Bars

On-Site Bars: The Sheraton Montazah Hotel features several dining and bar options, including:

The Lobby Bar: A casual spot for enjoying a selection of cocktails, soft drinks, and light snacks in a relaxed setting.

The Pool Bar: Located by the outdoor pool, it serves a variety of refreshments and light meals in a casual environment.

Events and Conferences

Meeting Spaces: Provides versatile meeting and event facilities, including conference rooms and banquet halls. These spaces are equipped with essential audiovisual technology and can accommodate various types of events.

Event Services: Offers support for event planning, including catering, decoration, and technical assistance to ensure successful meetings and gatherings.

Basic Facilities and Amenities

Dining: The hotel features dining options, including:

The Main Restaurant: Offers a range of international and local dishes in a casual dining environment.

Breakfast Service: Includes a variety of continental and local breakfast options.

Business Center: Provides basic business services such as high-speed internet access, printing, and meeting facilities.

Concierge Services: Assists with local recommendations, travel arrangements, and special requests to enhance the guest experience.

Opening and Closing Hours

Check-in: Typically from 3:00 PM

Check-out: By 12:00 PM

Restaurants and Bars: Hours of operation vary, but typically:

The Main Restaurant: Breakfast from 6:30 AM to 10:00 AM, with lunch and dinner hours varying.

Bar/Lounge: Usually open in the late afternoon and evening.

Price

Room Rates: Rates for a stay at Sheraton Montazah Hotel generally range from $100 to $200 per night, depending on the season, room type, and booking period. This pricing reflects its mid-range status, offering a balance between comfort and affordability.

Pros

Scenic Setting: Offers beautiful views of the Montazah Palace Gardens and the Mediterranean Sea.

Comfortable Rooms: Features well-appointed accommodations with a focus on comfort and convenience.

Recreational Facilities: Includes an outdoor pool and easy access to the Montazah Gardens.

Convenient Location: Close to local attractions and provides easy access to transportation.

Cons

Limited Spa Services: May not have a full-service spa on-site, requiring guests to seek wellness options elsewhere.

Basic Fitness Center: The fitness center may be smaller and less equipped compared to luxury hotels.

Local Tips

Explore Montazah Gardens: Make use of the hotel's proximity to Montazah Palace Gardens for a leisurely stroll or picnic.

Visit Historical Sites: Use the hotel as a base to explore nearby historical and cultural attractions, such as the Alexandria Library.

Local Dining: Explore local dining options in the area to experience Alexandria's culinary offerings.

Traffic Considerations: Be aware of local traffic patterns, especially during peak hours, to optimize your travel around Alexandria.

4. Hotel Ibis Alexandria

Hotel Ibis Alexandria is a well-known budget-friendly hotel in Alexandria, Egypt, part of the global Ibis chain renowned for its reliable and consistent hospitality. Offering a comfortable stay at an affordable price, the hotel caters to both business and leisure travelers looking for a practical and well-maintained accommodation option.

Location (Address & Proximity)

Address: 304, El Geish Road, Alexandria, Egypt

Proximity: Located along El Geish Road, the hotel is conveniently situated near key city attractions and the Mediterranean Sea. It is relatively close to the Alexandria Corniche, the Alexandria Library, and the Catacombs of Kom El Shoqafa. Alexandria International Airport is about a 20-minute drive away, providing easy access for travelers.

Highlights

Affordable Rates: Provides a cost-effective accommodation option without compromising on basic comfort and quality.

Modern Design: Features contemporary decor and a straightforward design, emphasizing functionality and convenience.

Central Location: Offers easy access to local attractions and transportation links.

Spa and Wellness

Spa: The hotel does not have a full-service spa. However, guests can inquire about local wellness centers or nearby facilities offering spa treatments.

Fitness Center: The hotel may not have an extensive fitness center, but it typically provides basic exercise equipment or access to local gyms.

Bars

On-Site Bar:

The Bar: The hotel includes a simple bar area where guests can enjoy a selection of drinks and light snacks in a casual environment. It's a good spot for unwinding after a day of exploring or working.

Events and Conferences

Meeting Spaces: The hotel generally offers limited meeting and conference facilities. It may have a small business center or meeting room suitable for basic business needs. For larger events or more advanced facilities, guests might need to look for external venues.

Basic Facilities and Amenities

Dining:

The Main Restaurant: Serves a range of international and local dishes in a casual dining setting, including breakfast, lunch, and dinner options.

Breakfast Service: Offers a buffet-style breakfast with a selection of continental and local items.

Business Center: Provides essential services such as internet access, printing, and copying for business travelers.

Concierge Services: Assists with local recommendations, travel arrangements, and general inquiries to enhance the guest experience.

Opening and Closing Hours

Check-in: Typically from 2:00 PM

Check-out: By 12:00 PM

Restaurant and Bar Hours: Vary, but typically:

Restaurant: Breakfast from 6:30 AM to 10:00 AM, with lunch and dinner hours varying.

Bar: Usually open in the late afternoon and evening.

Price

Room Rates: Rates for a stay at Hotel Ibis Alexandria generally range from $50 to $90 per night, depending on the season, room type, and booking period. This pricing reflects the hotel's budget-friendly status and its focus on providing good value for money.

Pros

Cost-Effective: Provides affordable accommodation with essential amenities, making it a good choice for budget-conscious travelers.

Modern and Functional: Features contemporary design and practical facilities that meet basic comfort needs.

Central Location: Conveniently located with easy access to local attractions and transportation.

Cons

Limited Amenities: May lack some of the more luxurious amenities and services found in higher-end hotels.

No Full-Service Spa or Extensive Fitness Facilities: Limited wellness and fitness options compared to more upscale hotels.

Local Tips

Explore the Nearby Attractions: Use the hotel's central location to visit nearby landmarks such as the Alexandria Library and the Corniche.

Local Dining Options: Explore local eateries in the vicinity to experience Alexandria's cuisine.

Traffic Considerations: Be mindful of local traffic patterns, especially during peak hours, to make the most of your travel around the city.

5. Alexandria Mediterranean Suites

Alexandria Mediterranean Suites offers a mid-range accommodation option in Alexandria, providing guests with a comfortable and practical stay. Ideal for both short-term and extended stays, the property is designed to cater to travelers seeking a blend of home-like comfort and accessibility to local attractions.

Location (Address & Proximity)

Address: 43 El Khalifa El Maamoun Street, Alexandria 21599, Egypt

Proximity: Centrally located in Alexandria, the suites are close to the Mediterranean coast and offer easy access to major attractions such as the Alexandria Library, the Catacombs of Kom El Shoqafa, and the Corniche. Alexandria International Airport is approximately a 20-minute drive away, making it convenient for travelers.

Highlights

Spacious Suites: Offers larger accommodations compared to standard hotel rooms, ideal for longer stays or families.

Practical Amenities: Provides practical amenities such as kitchenettes or fully equipped kitchens, enhancing convenience for guests.

Central Location: Positioned in a central area with easy access to local landmarks and transportation options.

Spa and Wellness

Spa: The property does not have an on-site spa. Guests looking for spa treatments may need to explore nearby wellness centers or hotels with spa facilities.

Fitness Center: The hotel may not offer a dedicated fitness center, but there are often local gyms or fitness facilities nearby.

Bars

On-Site Bar: The property does not typically feature a bar. Guests can explore local dining and drinking options in the surrounding area.

Events and Conferences

Meeting Spaces: The Alexandria Mediterranean Suites does not have dedicated meeting or conference facilities. For business events or meetings, guests may need to find external venues or use facilities at nearby hotels.

Basic Facilities and Amenities

Dining:

In-Suite Dining: Suites are generally equipped with kitchenettes or full kitchens, allowing guests to prepare their own meals.

Local Dining: There are often dining options nearby, ranging from local eateries to more international restaurants.

Business Center: The property may not have a dedicated business center, but basic services like internet access are usually available.

Concierge Services: Offers assistance with local recommendations, travel arrangements, and general inquiries to enhance the guest experience.

Opening and Closing Hours

Check-in: Typically from 2:00 PM

Check-out: By 12:00 PM

Dining Services: Meals are usually prepared in the suite's kitchenette. For local dining, hours vary depending on the nearby restaurants.

Price

Room Rates: Rates for Alexandria Mediterranean Suites generally range from $60 to $120 per night, depending on the season, suite type, and booking period. This pricing reflects the mid-range status and the added comfort of suite-style accommodations.

Pros

Spacious Accommodations: Provides more space and self-catering options compared to standard hotel rooms.

Practical for Extended Stays: Ideal for guests staying for longer periods or those who prefer to cook their own meals.

Central Location: Convenient access to local attractions, dining, and transportation.

Cons

Limited On-Site Amenities: May lack some of the additional amenities found in higher-end hotels, such as a spa or extensive dining options.

No Dedicated Meeting Facilities: Does not offer dedicated conference or meeting rooms.

Local Tips

Explore Local Dining: Use the kitchenette to prepare meals or explore local restaurants for a variety of dining options.

Visit Nearby Attractions: Take advantage of the central location to visit nearby landmarks such as the Alexandria Library and the Corniche.

Transportation: Consider using local taxis or public transportation to navigate the city efficiently.

Boutique Hotel

Boutique hotels in Alexandria offer distinctive, stylish accommodations with a personal touch. These hotels feature unique decor, individualized service, and a cozy atmosphere, providing a memorable and intimate experience for travelers seeking charm and character during their stay.

Top 5 Boutique Hotel

1. The Grand Plaza Hotel

The Grand Plaza Hotel is a boutique hotel situated in Alexandria, Egypt, known for its distinctive charm and personalized service. It offers an intimate and stylish alternative to larger chain hotels, blending luxury with a unique, curated experience. The hotel is designed to provide guests with a refined and cozy atmosphere, emphasizing attention to detail and individualized hospitality.

Location (Address & Proximity)

Address: 23 El Ghaffar Street, Raml Station, Alexandria 21599, Egypt

Proximity: Centrally located in the Raml Station area, the hotel provides easy access to key attractions such as the Alexandria Library, the Corniche, and various cultural landmarks. Alexandria International Airport is approximately a 20-minute drive away, making it convenient for travelers.

Highlights

Boutique Charm: Features unique, stylish decor and personalized service, setting it apart from larger, more impersonal hotels.

Central Location: Offers convenient access to Alexandria's main attractions, shopping, and dining options.

Personalized Service: Emphasizes attentive and customized service to cater to individual guest needs.

Spa and Wellness

Spa: The Grand Plaza Hotel does not have a full-service spa on-site. Guests looking for wellness treatments may need to seek nearby wellness centers or spas.

Fitness Center: The hotel may have basic fitness facilities or offer access to nearby gyms. Specific details should be confirmed directly with the hotel.

Bars

On-Site Bar:

The Lounge Bar: The hotel typically features a stylish lounge bar where guests can enjoy a range of beverages, including cocktails, soft drinks, and light snacks. The atmosphere is often relaxed and sophisticated, making it a great spot to unwind.

Events and Conferences

Meeting Spaces: The Grand Plaza Hotel may offer small to medium-sized meeting and event spaces, ideal for intimate gatherings or business meetings. These spaces are generally equipped with basic audiovisual equipment.

Event Services: Provides support for event planning, including catering and setup, though it may not offer the extensive services available at larger conference hotels.

Basic Facilities and Amenities

Dining:

The Main Restaurant: Serves a variety of international and local dishes in a refined setting. The restaurant often emphasizes quality and presentation.

Breakfast Service: Offers a selection of continental and local breakfast options, typically served in a stylish dining area.

Business Center: May offer essential business services such as internet access, printing, and copying.

Concierge Services: Provides assistance with local recommendations, travel arrangements, and special requests to enhance the guest experience.

Opening and Closing Hours

Check-in: Typically from 2:00 PM

Check-out: By 12:00 PM

Restaurants and Bars: Hours of operation may vary, but generally:

Main Restaurant: Breakfast from 6:30 AM to 10:00 AM, with lunch and dinner hours varying.

Bar: Usually open in the late afternoon and evening.

Price

Room Rates: Rates at The Grand Plaza Hotel typically range from $80 to $150 per night, depending on the season, room type, and booking period. This pricing reflects its boutique status and the personalized service provided.

Pros

Unique Boutique Experience: Offers a distinctive and personalized experience with stylish decor and attentive service.

Central Location: Conveniently located near major attractions, shopping, and dining.

Personalized Service: Known for its focus on individual guest needs and high-quality service.

Cons

Limited Spa and Fitness Facilities: Does not have extensive spa or fitness amenities on-site, which may be a drawback for some guests.

Smaller Meeting Facilities: May not offer large-scale conference or event facilities compared to larger hotels.

Local Tips

Explore Local Attractions: Utilize the hotel's central location to visit nearby landmarks such as the Alexandria Library and the Corniche.

Local Dining: Discover local restaurants and cafes around the Raml Station area for a taste of Alexandria's cuisine.

Transportation: Use local taxis or public transportation to navigate the city easily, especially if planning to visit multiple attractions.

2. San Giovanni Hotel

San Giovanni Hotel is a historic and charming hotel located in Alexandria, Egypt. Known for its classic architecture and traditional hospitality, the hotel offers a blend of elegance and comfort. It caters to travelers seeking a refined, yet relaxed stay with a touch of nostalgia.

Location (Address & Proximity)

Address: 36 El-Gaish Road, Alexandria 21599, Egypt

Proximity: Situated along El-Gaish Road, the hotel offers beautiful views of the Mediterranean Sea and is conveniently located near the Alexandria Corniche. Key attractions such as the Alexandria Library and the Catacombs of Kom El Shoqafa are within a short drive. Alexandria International Airport is approximately a 25-minute drive away.

Highlights

Historic Charm: Features classic architecture and décor, providing a nostalgic and elegant atmosphere.

Seaside Views: Offers views of the Mediterranean Sea, adding a picturesque element to the stay.

Central Location: Provides easy access to local attractions, shopping, and dining options.

Spa and Wellness

Spa: San Giovanni Hotel does not have an on-site spa. Guests looking for wellness treatments will need to explore nearby spas or wellness centers.

Fitness Center: The hotel may have limited fitness facilities or offer access to local gyms. Details should be confirmed directly with the hotel.

Bars

On-Site Bar:

The Lounge Bar: The hotel features a lounge bar where guests can enjoy a selection of beverages, including cocktails, soft drinks, and light snacks. The ambiance is typically elegant and relaxing.

Events and Conferences

Meeting Spaces: The San Giovanni Hotel may offer small meeting rooms or event spaces suitable for intimate gatherings or business meetings. These spaces are usually equipped with basic audiovisual equipment.

Event Services: Provides support for event planning, including catering and setup, though it may not offer the extensive services available at larger conference venues.

Basic Facilities and Amenities

Dining:

The Main Restaurant: Serves a range of international and local dishes in a classic dining setting. The focus is on quality and presentation.

Breakfast Service: Typically offers a variety of continental and local breakfast options.

Business Center: May provide essential business services such as internet access, printing, and copying.

Concierge Services: Assists with local recommendations, travel arrangements, and general inquiries to enhance the guest experience.

Opening and Closing Hours

Check-in: Typically from 2:00 PM

Check-out: By 12:00 PM

Restaurants and Bars: Hours of operation may vary, but generally:

Main Restaurant: Breakfast from 6:30 AM to 10:00 AM, with lunch and dinner hours varying.

Bar: Usually open in the late afternoon and evening.

Price

Room Rates: Rates at San Giovanni Hotel generally range from $70 to $130 per night, depending on the season, room type, and booking period. This pricing reflects the hotel's classic charm and central location.

Pros

Historic Atmosphere: Offers a nostalgic and elegant stay with classic architecture and décor.

Seaside Views: Provides beautiful views of the Mediterranean Sea.

Central Location: Conveniently located near major attractions, shopping, and dining options.

Cons

Limited Modern Amenities: May lack some of the modern amenities and facilities found in more contemporary hotels.

No On-Site Spa or Extensive Fitness Facilities: Does not have extensive wellness or fitness options on-site.

Local Tips

Explore the Corniche: Take advantage of the hotel's location along the Corniche for leisurely walks and sea views.

Visit Local Attractions: Use the hotel as a base to explore nearby landmarks such as the Alexandria Library and the Catacombs.

Local Dining: Discover local restaurants and cafes in the surrounding area for a taste of Alexandria's culinary offerings.

Transportation: Utilize local taxis or public transportation to navigate the city and visit multiple attractions.

3. The Mediterranean Azur Hotel

The Mediterranean Azur Hotel is a contemporary hotel located in Alexandria, Egypt, offering a blend of modern amenities and traditional hospitality. Known for its comfortable accommodations and strategic location, the hotel caters to both business and leisure travelers, providing a relaxing and convenient stay in the heart of Alexandria.

Location (Address & Proximity)

Address: 54 El Geish Road, Alexandria 21599, Egypt

Proximity: Located on El Geish Road, the hotel is positioned close to the Mediterranean Sea and the Alexandria Corniche. It is conveniently near key attractions such as the Alexandria Library, the Catacombs of Kom El Shoqafa, and the Montazah Palace Gardens. Alexandria International Airport is approximately a 20-minute drive away.

Highlights

Modern Amenities: Offers contemporary accommodations with a focus on comfort and convenience.

Seaside Views: Features rooms and public areas with views of the Mediterranean Sea.

Central Location: Provides easy access to local attractions, shopping, and dining options.

Spa and Wellness

Spa: The hotel typically includes a spa or wellness center offering a range of treatments and therapies.

Services may include massages, facials, and relaxation therapies.

Fitness Center: Equipped with modern exercise equipment, the fitness center allows guests to maintain their workout routines during their stay.

Bars

On-Site Bars:

The Lounge Bar: A stylish bar offering a selection of beverages, including cocktails, soft drinks, and light snacks. It's a great place to unwind and enjoy a relaxed atmosphere.

The Pool Bar: Located near the outdoor pool, this bar provides refreshments and light meals in a casual setting.

Events and Conferences

Meeting Spaces: The Mediterranean Azur Hotel offers a range of meeting and conference facilities. These spaces are equipped with modern audiovisual technology and can accommodate various types of events.

Event Services: Provides comprehensive event planning services, including catering, decoration, and technical support to ensure successful meetings and gatherings.

Basic Facilities and Amenities

Dining:

The Main Restaurant: Serves a variety of international and local dishes in a contemporary setting. The restaurant typically offers breakfast, lunch, and dinner.

Breakfast Service: Features a buffet-style breakfast with a selection of continental and local options.

Business Center: Provides essential business services such as high-speed internet access, printing, and copying.

Concierge Services: Assists with local recommendations, travel arrangements, and general inquiries to enhance the guest experience.

Opening and Closing Hours

Check-in: Typically from 2:00 PM

Check-out: By 12:00 PM

Restaurants and Bars: Hours of operation may vary, but generally:

Main Restaurant: Breakfast from 6:30 AM to 10:00 AM, with lunch and dinner hours varying.

Bars: Usually open in the late afternoon and evening.

Price

Room Rates: Rates at The Mediterranean Azur Hotel typically range from $90 to $180 per night, depending on the season, room type, and booking period. This pricing reflects the hotel's modern amenities and prime location.

Pros

Modern Comfort: Offers contemporary accommodations with a focus on guest comfort and convenience.

Seaside Location: Provides beautiful views of the Mediterranean Sea and easy access to the Corniche.

Comprehensive Amenities: Includes a spa, fitness center, and multiple dining and bar options.

Cons

Higher Price Range: May be more expensive compared to budget or mid-range hotels in the area.

Busy Location: Being centrally located, the hotel may experience higher traffic and noise levels from the surrounding area.

Local Tips

Explore the Corniche: Take advantage of the hotel's proximity to the Corniche for leisurely walks and sea views.

Visit Nearby Attractions: Use the hotel as a base to explore local landmarks such as the Alexandria Library and the Catacombs of Kom El Shoqafa.

Local Dining: Discover local restaurants and cafes for a taste of Alexandria's diverse cuisine.

Transportation: Utilize local taxis or public transportation for easy access to various parts of the city and surrounding attractions.

4. Steigenberger Cecil Hotel

The Steigenberger Cecil Hotel is a historic and elegant property in Alexandria, Egypt, known for its classic charm and refined hospitality. As one of the city's prestigious hotels, it offers a blend of traditional luxury with modern comforts, catering to both leisure and business travelers.

Location (Address & Proximity)

Address: 15 El Andalus Street, Alexandria 21599, Egypt

Proximity: Situated in the heart of Alexandria, the hotel offers views of the Mediterranean Sea and is close to major attractions such as the Alexandria Corniche, the Alexandria Library, and the Catacombs of Kom El Shoqafa. Alexandria International Airport is about a 25-minute drive away, making it convenient for travelers.

Highlights

Historic Charm: Features classic architecture and décor, reflecting Alexandria's rich history and elegance.

Seaside Views: Provides rooms and common areas with views of the Mediterranean Sea.

Central Location: Offers easy access to local attractions, shopping, and dining.

Spa and Wellness

Spa: The Steigenberger Cecil Hotel may not have an extensive spa facility on-site. Guests seeking spa treatments will need to explore nearby wellness centers or other hotels with dedicated spa services.

Fitness Center: Typically includes a fitness center with modern exercise equipment for maintaining workout routines during the stay.

Bars

On-Site Bars:

The Lounge Bar: A sophisticated bar where guests can enjoy a selection of drinks, including cocktails, wines, and soft beverages. The ambiance is elegant and ideal for relaxing after a day of sightseeing or business meetings.

The Rooftop Bar: Offers panoramic views of Alexandria and the Mediterranean Sea, providing a stylish setting for enjoying drinks and light snacks.

Events and Conferences

Meeting Spaces: The hotel features several meeting and conference rooms equipped with modern audiovisual technology. These spaces can accommodate various types of events, from business meetings to social gatherings.

Event Services: Provides comprehensive event planning and catering services, including decoration and technical support, to ensure successful meetings and functions.

Basic Facilities and Amenities

Dining:

The Main Restaurant: Serves a variety of international and local dishes in a refined setting. Breakfast, lunch, and dinner are typically offered with an emphasis on quality and presentation.

Breakfast Service: Features a buffet-style breakfast with a selection of continental and local options.

Business Center: Provides essential business services such as high-speed internet access, printing, and copying.

Concierge Services: Assists with local recommendations, travel arrangements, and general inquiries to enhance the guest experience.

Opening and Closing Hours

Check-in: Typically from 3:00 PM

Check-out: By 12:00 PM

Restaurants and Bars: Hours of operation may vary, but generally:

Main Restaurant: Breakfast from 6:30 AM to 10:00 AM, with lunch and dinner hours varying.

Bars: Typically open in the late afternoon and evening.

Price

Room Rates: Rates at Steigenberger Cecil Hotel generally range from $120 to $250 per night, depending on the season, room type, and booking period. This pricing reflects its luxurious status and prime location.

Pros

Historic Elegance: Offers a blend of classic charm and modern comfort, with historic architecture and stylish interiors.

Seaside Location: Provides beautiful views of the Mediterranean Sea and proximity to the Alexandria Corniche.

Comprehensive Amenities: Includes a range of amenities such as dining options, meeting spaces, and a fitness center.

Cons

Higher Price Range: May be more expensive compared to other mid-range or budget hotels in the area.

Limited Spa Facilities: May not have extensive spa services on-site.

Local Tips

Explore Local Attractions: Take advantage of the hotel's central location to visit nearby landmarks such as the Alexandria Library and the Catacombs.

Enjoy the Corniche: Utilize the hotel's seaside location for leisurely walks along the Corniche and enjoy the Mediterranean views.

Local Dining: Discover local restaurants and cafes in the vicinity to experience Alexandria's diverse cuisine.

Transportation: Use local taxis or public transportation for easy access to various attractions and areas of the city.

5. Cherry Maryski Hotel

Cherry Maryski Hotel offers a practical and comfortable accommodation option in Alexandria, Egypt. Known for its affordability and convenient location, the hotel provides a welcoming environment for both leisure and business travelers. It combines essential amenities with a relaxed atmosphere, making it a suitable choice for a range of travelers.

Location (Address & Proximity)

Address: 16 Taha Hussein Street, Alexandria 21599, Egypt

Proximity: Situated in a central area of Alexandria, the hotel is close to major attractions such as the Alexandria Corniche, the Alexandria Library, and the Catacombs of Kom El Shoqafa. Alexandria International Airport is approximately a 25-minute drive away, making it relatively convenient for travelers.

Highlights

Affordability: Provides budget-friendly accommodation without sacrificing basic comfort and quality.

Central Location: Offers easy access to local attractions, shopping, and dining options.

Simple Comfort: Focuses on providing a comfortable stay with essential amenities.

Spa and Wellness

Spa: Cherry Maryski Hotel does not have a dedicated spa on-site. Guests seeking spa treatments will need to look for nearby wellness centers or spas.

Fitness Center: The hotel may not have an extensive fitness facility. Details on fitness options should be confirmed directly with the hotel.

Bars

On-Site Bar:

The Bar Lounge: Features a casual bar area where guests can enjoy a selection of drinks and light snacks. It provides a relaxed setting for unwinding after a day of sightseeing or work.

Events and Conferences

Meeting Spaces: The hotel typically offers small meeting rooms or event spaces suitable for business meetings or intimate gatherings. These rooms are equipped with basic audiovisual equipment.

Event Services: Provides some support for event planning, including catering and setup, though it may not offer the extensive services available at larger conference hotels.

Basic Facilities and Amenities

Dining:

The Main Restaurant: Serves a variety of international and local dishes in a straightforward dining environment. Breakfast, lunch, and dinner options are available.

Breakfast Service: Offers a buffet-style breakfast with a selection of continental and local items.

Business Center: May provide essential business services such as internet access, printing, and copying.

Concierge Services: Assists with local recommendations, travel arrangements, and general inquiries to enhance the guest experience.

Opening and Closing Hours

Check-in: Typically from 2:00 PM

Check-out: By 12:00 PM

Restaurants and Bars: Hours of operation may vary, but generally:

Main Restaurant: Breakfast from 6:30 AM to 10:00 AM, with lunch and dinner hours varying.

Bar Lounge: Usually open in the late afternoon and evening.

Price

Room Rates: Rates at Cherry Maryski Hotel generally range from $50 to $100 per night, depending on the season, room type, and booking period. This pricing reflects its budget-friendly status and focus on providing value.

Pros

Affordable: Provides a cost-effective option for travelers seeking basic comfort and convenience.

Central Location: Conveniently located near major attractions and amenities in Alexandria.

Simple Comfort: Focuses on offering essential amenities and a comfortable stay.

Cons

Limited Amenities: May lack some of the higher-end amenities and services found in more upscale hotels.

No Dedicated Spa or Extensive Fitness Facilities: Does not have an on-site spa or extensive fitness options.

Local Tips

Explore Nearby Attractions: Use the hotel's central location to visit local landmarks such as the Alexandria Library and the Corniche.

Local Dining: Check out nearby restaurants and cafes to experience Alexandria's culinary scene.

Transportation: Utilize local taxis or public transportation to navigate the city and visit various attractions.

Hostel

Hostels in Alexandria offer budget-friendly accommodations with a vibrant, social atmosphere. Ideal for travelers looking to save money and meet fellow explorers, these hostels provide basic amenities and a communal environment, perfect for a lively and economical stay in the city.

Top 5 Hostel

1. Alexandria Hostel

Alexandria Hostel offers a budget-friendly and social accommodation option for travelers in Alexandria, Egypt. Designed for backpackers, students, and budget-conscious travelers, the hostel provides a welcoming environment with basic amenities and a community-oriented atmosphere. It's an ideal choice for those looking to explore Alexandria on a budget while meeting fellow travelers.

Location (Address & Proximity)

Address: 45 Mohamed Farid Street, Alexandria 21599, Egypt

Proximity: Centrally located, the hostel is within walking distance of key attractions such as the Alexandria Corniche, the Alexandria Library, and local markets. Alexandria International Airport is about a 25-minute drive away, offering reasonable accessibility for travelers.

Highlights

Budget-Friendly: Offers affordable rates, making it an ideal choice for travelers on a tight budget.

Social Atmosphere: Provides a communal and social environment where guests can interact with fellow travelers.

Central Location: Conveniently situated near major attractions and local amenities.

Spa and Wellness

Spa: Alexandria Hostel does not have a spa facility on-site. Guests interested in spa treatments will need to explore local wellness centers or other hotels in the area.

Fitness Center: The hostel typically does not feature a fitness center. Guests may need to find local gyms or fitness facilities.

Bars

On-Site Bar:

Common Area: The hostel may have a common lounge or shared area where guests can socialize and enjoy drinks. However, it usually does not have a dedicated bar. The environment is often casual and conducive to meeting other travelers.

Events and Conferences

Meeting Spaces: Alexandria Hostel generally does not have dedicated meeting or conference rooms. It focuses on providing basic accommodations and common areas for socializing.

Event Services: The hostel may organize social events or tours for guests, but it does not offer extensive event planning services.

Basic Facilities and Amenities

Dining:

Self-Catering: Typically offers a shared kitchen where guests can prepare their own meals. This is a cost-effective option for long-term or budget travelers.

Local Dining: There are often local cafes and restaurants nearby where guests can experience Alexandria's cuisine.

Business Center: The hostel usually does not have a business center, but basic services like free Wi-Fi are commonly available.

Concierge Services: Staff may provide assistance with local recommendations and travel arrangements to enhance the guest experience.

Opening and Closing Hours

Check-in: Typically from 2:00 PM

Check-out: By 11:00 AM

Common Areas: Available 24/7 for guests to socialize and relax.

Price

Room Rates: Rates at Alexandria Hostel generally range from $15 to $30 per night for dormitory-style accommodation, depending on the season, room type, and availability. Private rooms, if available, may cost slightly more.

Pros

Affordable: Provides one of the most budget-friendly accommodation options in Alexandria.

Social Environment: Ideal for meeting other travelers and participating in communal activities.

Central Location: Convenient access to local attractions, dining, and transportation.

Cons

Basic Amenities: Offers minimal amenities compared to hotels or more upscale accommodations.

Limited Privacy: Dormitory-style rooms may not offer the level of privacy found in private rooms or hotel settings.

No On-Site Spa or Fitness Facilities: Lacks dedicated wellness and fitness amenities.

Local Tips

Explore Local Markets: Use the hostel's central location to visit local markets and experience Alexandria's vibrant street life.

Connect with Other Travelers: Take advantage of the social atmosphere to exchange travel tips and plan activities with fellow guests.

Local Dining: Discover nearby eateries and cafes to enjoy affordable and local cuisine.

Transportation: Utilize local public transportation or taxis for easy access to various parts of the city.

2. The Urban Hostel

The Urban Hostel provides a modern and sociable accommodation option for travelers in Alexandria, Egypt. Designed for budget-conscious travelers who seek a contemporary and vibrant atmosphere, The Urban Hostel combines affordability with a focus on social interaction and modern amenities.

Location (Address & Proximity)

Address: 21 Abdelkhalek Tharwat Street, Alexandria 21599, Egypt

Proximity: Centrally located in Alexandria, The Urban Hostel is close to key attractions such as the Alexandria Corniche, the Alexandria Library, and the local markets. Alexandria International Airport is approximately a 25-minute drive away, making it relatively convenient for travelers.

Highlights

Modern Design: Features contemporary décor and amenities that cater to modern travelers.

Social Atmosphere: Offers a vibrant and communal

environment for meeting fellow travelers and sharing experiences.

Central Location: Provides easy access to major attractions, dining, and shopping.

Spa and Wellness

Spa: The Urban Hostel does not have an on-site spa facility. Guests looking for spa treatments will need to seek local wellness centers or other hotels with dedicated spa services.

Fitness Center: Typically, the hostel does not have a fitness center. Guests may need to find nearby gyms or fitness facilities.

Bars

On-Site Bar:

Common Lounge: The hostel features a common lounge area where guests can socialize and enjoy beverages. While it may not have a dedicated bar, the lounge provides a casual space for relaxation and interaction.

Events and Conferences

Meeting Spaces: The Urban Hostel generally does not offer dedicated meeting or conference rooms. It focuses on providing communal spaces for socializing and relaxation.

Event Services: The hostel may organize social events or group activities, but it does not provide extensive event planning services.

Basic Facilities and Amenities

Dining:

Self-Catering: Includes a shared kitchen where guests can prepare their own meals. This option is convenient for those traveling on a budget.

Local Dining: Nearby cafes and restaurants offer opportunities to experience Alexandria's local cuisine.

Business Center: Typically does not have a business center, but free Wi-Fi is usually available for guests.

Concierge Services: Staff can provide assistance with local recommendations, travel arrangements, and general inquiries.

Opening and Closing Hours

Check-in: Typically from 2:00 PM

Check-out: By 11:00 AM

Common Areas: Available 24/7 for guests to socialize and relax.

Price

Room Rates: Rates at The Urban Hostel generally range from $15 to $35 per night, depending on the season, room type, and availability. Private rooms, if offered, may be priced higher.

Pros

Affordable: Provides a budget-friendly option for travelers without compromising on modern comfort.

Social Environment: Encourages interaction among guests with its communal areas and social activities.

Modern Amenities: Offers contemporary amenities and design that appeal to modern travelers.

Cons

Basic Amenities: May lack some of the additional services and luxury amenities found in higher-end accommodations.

Limited Privacy: Dormitory-style accommodations may not provide the same level of privacy as private rooms or hotel settings.

No On-Site Spa or Fitness Facilities: Does not feature dedicated wellness or fitness amenities.

Local Tips

Explore Nearby Attractions: Utilize the hostel's

central location to visit local landmarks such as the Alexandria Library and the Corniche.

Engage with Fellow Travelers: Take advantage of the social atmosphere to connect with other travelers and share tips and experiences.

Sample Local Cuisine: Discover local dining options and cafes near the hostel to experience Alexandria's food scene.

Use Public Transportation: Local public transportation and taxis are convenient for exploring the city and reaching various attractions.

3. Backpackers Alexandria

Backpackers Alexandria is a budget-friendly hostel catering primarily to travelers seeking a social and economical accommodation option in Alexandria, Egypt. Designed for backpackers and budget travelers, the hostel offers a comfortable and communal environment with essential amenities for a pleasant stay.

Location (Address & Proximity)

Address: 3 Moharram Bek Street, Alexandria 21599, Egypt

Proximity: Centrally located, Backpackers Alexandria is close to major attractions such as the Alexandria Corniche, the Alexandria Library, and local markets. The hostel is also a short drive from Alexandria International Airport, making it relatively accessible for travelers.

Highlights

Affordable Rates: Provides budget-friendly accommodation options that cater to cost-conscious travelers.

Social Atmosphere: Focuses on creating a communal and friendly environment where guests can interact with each other and share travel experiences.

Central Location: Conveniently situated near local attractions, dining options, and transportation links.

Spa and Wellness

Spa: Backpackers Alexandria does not have an on-site spa. Guests looking for spa treatments will need to find local wellness centers or other hotels offering such services.

Fitness Center: The hostel does not typically feature a fitness center. Guests interested in fitness may need to explore nearby gyms or other fitness facilities.

Bars

On-Site Bar:

Common Area: The hostel includes a common lounge or shared area where guests can relax and enjoy beverages. While it may not have a dedicated bar, this space encourages social interaction among guests.

Events and Conferences

Meeting Spaces: The hostel generally does not provide dedicated meeting or conference rooms. It focuses on offering communal spaces for socializing rather than formal event facilities.

Event Services: May organize occasional social events or group activities to enhance the guest experience, but does not offer extensive event planning services.

Basic Facilities and Amenities

Dining:

Self-Catering: Features a shared kitchen where guests can prepare their own meals. This option is particularly useful for travelers on a budget.

Local Dining: Nearby cafes and restaurants provide opportunities to enjoy Alexandria's local cuisine.

Business Center: Typically does not have a business center, but free Wi-Fi is usually available for guests.

Concierge Services: Staff can offer assistance with local recommendations, travel arrangements, and general inquiries to help guests make the most of their stay.

Opening and Closing Hours

Check-in: Typically from 2:00 PM

Check-out: By 11:00 AM

Common Areas: Open 24/7, providing a space for guests to socialize and relax.

Price

Room Rates: Rates at Backpackers Alexandria generally range from $10 to $25 per night for dormitory-style accommodations, depending on the season, room type, and availability. Private rooms, if available, may be priced higher.

Pros

Budget-Friendly: Offers one of the most affordable accommodation options in Alexandria.

Social Environment: Provides a communal and interactive atmosphere ideal for meeting other travelers.

Central Location: Conveniently located near attractions, dining, and transportation.

Cons

Basic Facilities: Offers minimal amenities compared to hotels or more upscale accommodations.

Limited Privacy: Dormitory-style rooms may not provide the level of privacy found in private rooms or hotel settings.

No Dedicated Spa or Fitness Facilities: Lacks on-site wellness and fitness amenities.

Local Tips

Explore Nearby Attractions: Take advantage of the hostel's location to visit local landmarks such as the Alexandria Library and the Corniche.

Connect with Fellow Travelers: Utilize the social environment to exchange travel tips and plan activities with other guests.

Try Local Cuisine: Discover nearby eateries and cafes to experience Alexandria's diverse food scene.

Public Transportation: Use local public transportation or taxis for convenient travel around the city and to visit various attractions.

4. Hostel City Centre

Hostel City Centre provides a budget-friendly and practical accommodation option for travelers in Alexandria, Egypt. It is designed to offer essential comforts and a sociable environment for backpackers and budget-conscious travelers, making it an ideal base for exploring the city.

Location (Address & Proximity)

Address: 45 El Horreya Road, Alexandria 21599, Egypt

Proximity: Centrally located in Alexandria, Hostel City Centre is close to key attractions such as the Alexandria Corniche, the Alexandria Library, and local shopping areas. Alexandria International Airport is approximately a 25-minute drive away, making it reasonably accessible for travelers.

Highlights

Affordable Rates: Offers budget-friendly accommodation options that cater to travelers looking for economical stays.

Central Location: Conveniently situated for easy access to major city attractions and amenities.

Social Environment: Focuses on creating a communal and friendly atmosphere for guests.

Spa and Wellness

Spa: Hostel City Centre does not feature an on-site spa. Guests seeking spa treatments will need to visit nearby wellness centers or other hotels with spa facilities.

Fitness Center: The hostel does not have a fitness center. Travelers interested in fitness routines may need to find local gyms or fitness centers.

Bars

On-Site Bar:

Common Lounge: The hostel features a common lounge area where guests can relax and socialize. While it may not have a dedicated bar, the lounge offers a casual environment for guests to unwind and meet others.

Events and Conferences

Meeting Spaces: Hostel City Centre generally does not have dedicated meeting or conference rooms. It emphasizes offering basic accommodation and communal spaces for relaxation and interaction.

Event Services: The hostel may occasionally organize social events or group activities but does not provide extensive event planning or conference services.

Basic Facilities and Amenities

Dining:

Self-Catering: Includes a shared kitchen where guests can prepare their own meals, which is a cost-effective option for budget travelers.

Local Dining: Nearby restaurants and cafes offer opportunities to experience local cuisine.

Business Center: The hostel typically does not have a business center. Free Wi-Fi is commonly available for guests to stay connected.

Concierge Services: Staff can assist with local recommendations, travel arrangements, and general inquiries to help enhance the guest experience.

Opening and Closing Hours

Check-in: Typically from 2:00 PM

Check-out: By 11:00 AM

Common Areas: Open 24/7 for guests to relax and socialize.

Price

Room Rates: Rates at Hostel City Centre generally range from $10 to $30 per night for dormitory-style accommodations. Private rooms, if available, may cost more depending on the season and availability.

Pros

Budget-Friendly: Offers affordable rates, making it an excellent choice for cost-conscious travelers.

Central Location: Provides convenient access to local attractions, shopping, and dining options.

Social Atmosphere: Encourages interaction among guests with its communal areas and shared spaces.

Cons

Basic Amenities: Limited amenities compared to higher-end accommodations.

Limited Privacy: Dormitory-style rooms may not offer the privacy found in private hotel rooms or more upscale lodgings.

No On-Site Spa or Fitness Facilities: Lacks dedicated wellness and fitness amenities.

Local Tips

Explore Nearby Attractions: Utilize the hostel's central location to visit attractions such as the Alexandria Library and the Corniche.

Connect with Other Guests: Take advantage of the social atmosphere to share travel experiences and tips with other travelers.

Experience Local Cuisine: Discover nearby cafes and restaurants to enjoy Alexandria's local food scene.

Use Public Transportation: Local public transportation and taxis can be convenient for getting around the city and visiting various sites.

5. Cairo Lodge Alexandria

Cairo Lodge Alexandria provides a comfortable and affordable lodging option for travelers visiting Alexandria, Egypt. It caters to those looking for a budget-friendly stay with essential amenities and a welcoming atmosphere. The lodge offers a mix of simplicity and convenience, making it suitable for various types of travelers.

Location (Address & Proximity)

Address: 11 Abdel Aziz Street, Alexandria 21599, Egypt

Proximity: Centrally located, Cairo Lodge Alexandria is close to significant attractions such as the Alexandria Corniche, the Alexandria Library, and the local markets. It is approximately a 25-minute drive from Alexandria International Airport, offering reasonable accessibility for travelers.

Highlights

Budget-Friendly: Provides an affordable accommodation option with essential comforts.

Convenient Location: Situated in a central area, offering easy access to major city attractions and amenities.

Simple Comfort: Focuses on providing a straightforward and comfortable stay.

Spa and Wellness

Spa: Cairo Lodge Alexandria does not have an on-site spa facility. Guests interested in spa treatments will need to seek local wellness centers or other hotels with dedicated spa services.

Fitness Center: The lodge does not feature a fitness center. Travelers interested in maintaining their fitness routine will need to find local gyms or fitness facilities.

Bars

On-Site Bar:

Common Lounge: The lodge may have a common lounge area where guests can relax and socialize. It typically does not have a dedicated bar but offers a casual environment for guests to unwind.

Events and Conferences

Meeting Spaces: Cairo Lodge Alexandria generally does not have dedicated meeting or conference rooms. It focuses on providing basic accommodations and communal areas for relaxation.

Event Services: The lodge may assist with local recommendations and general inquiries but does not offer extensive event planning or conference services.

Basic Facilities and Amenities

Dining:

On-Site Restaurant: May offer a simple dining option with breakfast and possibly other meals. The exact dining services should be confirmed directly with the lodge.

Self-Catering: Some lodges provide a shared kitchen for guests to prepare their own meals, though this should be verified with the specific property.

Business Center: Typically does not have a business center. Free Wi-Fi is commonly available for guests to stay connected.

Concierge Services: Staff can offer assistance with local recommendations, travel arrangements, and general inquiries.

Opening and Closing Hours

Check-in: Typically from 2:00 PM

Check-out: By 11:00 AM

Common Areas: Open 24/7, providing a space for guests to relax and socialize.

Price

Room Rates: Rates at Cairo Lodge Alexandria generally range from $20 to $50 per night, depending on the season, room type, and availability. Pricing reflects its budget-friendly approach.

Pros

Affordable: Offers economical rates suitable for budget-conscious travelers.

Central Location: Provides convenient access to local attractions, dining, and shopping.

Comfortable: Focuses on delivering a straightforward and comfortable stay.

Cons

Basic Amenities: May lack some of the amenities and services found in more upscale accommodations.

Limited Privacy: Depending on the room type, privacy may be limited compared to more upscale lodgings.

No Dedicated Spa or Fitness Facilities: Lacks on-site wellness and fitness amenities.

Local Tips

Explore Local Attractions: Use the lodge's central location to visit nearby landmarks such as the Alexandria Library and the Corniche.

Experience Local Cuisine: Discover nearby eateries and cafes to enjoy Alexandria's local food scene.

Connect with Other Travelers: Utilize common areas to interact with other guests and share travel experiences.

Public Transportation: Local public transportation and taxis can be convenient for exploring the city and visiting various attractions.

Day Trip from Alexandria
Cairo

Taking a day trip from Cairo to Alexandria can be a fantastic way to experience a different facet of Egyptian culture and history. Here's a quick rundown of what you can expect and plan for:

Travel Time and Options

Distance: Alexandria is about 220 kilometers (137 miles) northwest of Cairo.

By Car: The drive usually takes around 2.5 to 3 hours, depending on traffic.

By Train: Trains run regularly between Cairo and Alexandria, with travel times around 2.5 hours. Opt for the express trains for a faster journey.

By Bus: Buses are also available and can be a bit cheaper, with similar travel times to the train.

Highlights in Alexandria

The Bibliotheca Alexandrina: This modern library is a tribute to the ancient Library of Alexandria. It's a stunning piece of architecture with a vast collection of books and cultural exhibits.

The Citadel of Qaitbay: A historic fortress located on the Mediterranean coast, offering great views and insight into Alexandria's military history.

The Roman Amphitheatre: An ancient Roman theater that provides a glimpse into the city's Greco-Roman past.

The Catacombs of Kom el Shoqafa: An impressive necropolis with a mix of Egyptian, Greek, and Roman influences.

Montaza Palace and Gardens: A beautiful palace with expansive gardens and views of the Mediterranean.

Tips for Your Trip

Start Early: To make the most of your day, leave Cairo early in the morning.

Dress Comfortably: Alexandria's coastal climate can be breezy and cooler than Cairo, so dress in layers and wear comfortable shoes.

Plan Your Itinerary: Given the limited time, prioritize the sights you're most interested in.

Local Cuisine: Try some seafood at a local restaurant; Alexandria is known for its fresh fish and seafood dishes.

Practical Considerations

Traffic and Timing: Consider potential traffic delays, especially if traveling by car or bus.

Entry Fees: Some attractions may have entry fees, so it's good to have cash on hand.

Local Guides: Hiring a local guide might enhance your experience, providing deeper insights into the history and culture of Alexandria.

Overall, Alexandria offers a rich historical and cultural experience that's distinct from Cairo, making it a worthwhile day trip.

Siwa Oasis

Siwa Oasis is one of Egypt's most unique and enchanting destinations, located in the Western Desert. It's renowned for its stunning landscapes, rich history, and distinct cultural heritage. Here's an overview of what makes Siwa Oasis special and what to consider if you're planning a visit:

Highlights of Siwa Oasis

Siwa's Unique Landscape: The oasis is surrounded by dramatic desert scenery, with salt lakes, sand dunes, and lush palm groves. The contrast between the desert and the greenery is striking.

The Ancient Oracle Temple: The Temple of the Oracle of Amun, located near the town of Siwa, was famously visited by Alexander the Great. The temple ruins and inscriptions are a major historical attraction.

Shali Fortress: The remains of this ancient mud-brick fortress offer a glimpse into the traditional architecture of the region and provide panoramic views of the oasis.

Cleopatra's Bath: A natural spring with crystal-clear water, believed to be one of Cleopatra's favorite bathing spots.

Siwan Culture: The local Siwan people have a unique cultural identity with distinct traditions, crafts, and a language that's different from Arabic. Visiting local markets and interacting with the community can provide a deep cultural experience.

Sand Dunes and Salt Lakes: The surrounding desert features stunning sand dunes, perfect for activities like dune bashing and sandboarding. The salt lakes, like Lake Siwa and Lake Garaboulli, offer striking natural beauty and photo opportunities.

Getting There

By Car: The journey from Cairo to Siwa is about 750 kilometers (466 miles) and can take around 9-10 hours. It's a good idea to rent a 4x4 vehicle for the trip, as the roads can be challenging.

By Bus: There are long-distance buses from Cairo to Siwa, which can be more convenient but still requires a long travel time.

Tips for Visiting Siwa Oasis

Travel in the Cooler Months: The best time to visit is from October to March when temperatures are more moderate. Summers can be extremely hot.

Accommodation: There are several eco-lodges and boutique hotels in Siwa that offer unique experiences and views of the surrounding landscape.

Guided Tours: Consider hiring a local guide to help navigate the area and provide insights into the cultural and historical significance of the sights.

Cultural Sensitivity: Respect local customs and traditions. The Siwan people have their own unique ways of life and appreciate visitors who are mindful of their culture.

Stay Hydrated and Prepare for the Heat: Even in cooler months, the desert climate can be dry and hot during the day. Carry plenty of water and sun protection.

Siwa Oasis is a remote gem with a blend of history, culture, and natural beauty, making it a memorable destination for those who venture there.

Rosetta (Rashid)

Rosetta, known locally as Rashid, is a historic town located on the Mediterranean coast of Egypt, approximately 65 kilometers (40 miles) east of Alexandria. It's renowned for its rich history, particularly in connection with the Rosetta Stone, and its well-preserved Ottoman and Mamluk architecture. Here's a detailed look at what makes Rosetta an interesting destination:

Historical Significance

Rosetta Stone: The town is famous for the Rosetta Stone, a granodiorite stele inscribed with a decree issued in 196 BC during the Ptolemaic dynasty. The stone features the same text written in three scripts: Greek, Demotic, and Egyptian hieroglyphs. The discovery of the stone in 1799 by French soldiers was crucial in deciphering Egyptian hieroglyphs and understanding ancient Egyptian civilization. The original stone is now housed in the British Museum.

Key Attractions

Historic Architecture: Rosetta is renowned for its well-preserved Ottoman and Mamluk-era buildings. Walking through the town, you can see beautiful examples of traditional architecture, including:

The Mansions of Rosetta: Elegant Ottoman-era houses with distinctive architectural features such as intricate woodwork and elaborate facades.

Al-Muayyad Mosque: An important mosque

showcasing the architectural style of the Mamluk period.

The Old Lighthouse: Though not as famous as the Lighthouse of Alexandria, it's an interesting historical site that provides context for Rosetta's maritime history.

Rosetta Museum: Located in the town, the museum showcases local artifacts, including items related to the Rosetta Stone and the history of the town itself.

The Citadel of Qaitbay: An Ottoman-era fortress located on the Mediterranean coast, offering great views of the sea and historical insight into the region's military past.

Cultural Experience

Local Markets: Rosetta has traditional markets where you can experience local life and shop for regional crafts, textiles, and spices. The markets offer a taste of daily life in a smaller Egyptian town.

Cuisine: Enjoy traditional Egyptian dishes at local restaurants. Rosetta, being a coastal town, has some great seafood options.

Practical Information

Traveling to Rosetta:

By Car: It's about a 1 to 1.5-hour drive from Alexandria and around 3 hours from Cairo. The drive is relatively straightforward, though traffic conditions should be checked.

By Bus: There are bus services from Alexandria and Cairo to Rosetta, but they might be less frequent.

Best Time to Visit: The best time to visit is during the cooler months from October to April, when the weather is pleasant. Summer can be quite hot and humid, especially along the coast.

Tips for Visitors

Respect Local Customs: As with any historical site, it's important to respect local customs and traditions, especially when visiting religious sites.

Plan Your Visit: Given Rosetta's relatively small size, you can explore most of the key attractions in a day. However, if you have more time, spending an extra day can allow for a more relaxed exploration.

Guided Tours: Consider hiring a local guide to get more in-depth information about the history and significance of the sites, particularly the Rosetta Stone and the town's architecture.

Rosetta offers a unique blend of historical significance and charming local culture, making it a worthwhile destination for those interested in Egypt's rich heritage and architecture.

Marsa Matrouh

Marsa Matrouh, often just called Matrouh, is a beautiful coastal city located on Egypt's Mediterranean Sea, about 240 kilometers (150 miles) west of Alexandria. It's renowned for its stunning beaches, clear turquoise waters, and laid-back atmosphere. Here's an overview of what makes Marsa Matrouh a popular destination:

Attractions

Beaches: Marsa Matrouh is famous for its pristine, sandy beaches and crystal-clear waters. Some of the most notable ones include:

Agiba Beach: Known for its stunning scenery and clear waters. It's a great spot for swimming and sunbathing.

Om El Donia Beach: Popular for its picturesque setting and calm waters.

Cleopatra Beach: Named after the legendary queen, it's a beautiful beach with calm, shallow waters ideal for families.

Cleopatra's Bath: This natural pool is located near Cleopatra Beach and is believed to have been a favorite bathing spot of Cleopatra. It's a great place for a refreshing swim in a natural setting.

Alamein War Museum: Situated about 30 kilometers (19 miles) from Marsa Matrouh, this museum provides insights into the battles fought during World War II in the area. It's a good complement to a visit to the nearby El Alamein battlefield sites.

Roman Ruins: There are several ancient Roman ruins scattered around the area, including remnants of old temples and city walls. These sites offer a glimpse into the region's historical past.

Activities

Water Sports: Marsa Matrouh is ideal for water sports such as snorkeling, diving, and windsurfing due to its clear waters and vibrant marine life.

Relaxation: The city's serene beaches and relaxed atmosphere make it an excellent place to unwind. Many resorts offer amenities like private beaches and pools.

Practical Information

Traveling to Marsa Matrouh:

By Car: It's about a 3 to 4-hour drive from Alexandria and around 6 to 7 hours from Cairo. The road is generally in good condition, but check traffic conditions before setting out.

By Bus: There are regular buses from Cairo and Alexandria to Marsa Matrouh, which can be a convenient and cost-effective option.

Accommodation: There are various hotels and resorts ranging from budget to luxury options. Many offer direct beach access and a range of amenities, making them perfect for a relaxing stay.

Best Time to Visit: The best time to visit is from April to October when the weather is warm and suitable for beach activities. Summer months can be quite hot, but the coastal breeze helps to moderate the temperature.

Tips for Visitors

Sun Protection: The Mediterranean sun can be quite strong, so make sure to bring sunscreen, a hat, and sunglasses to protect yourself.

Local Cuisine: Enjoy fresh seafood and traditional Egyptian dishes at local restaurants. Marsa Matrouh's coastal location means you'll find a variety of delicious fish and seafood options.

Respect Local Customs: As with other parts of Egypt, it's important to be respectful of local customs and traditions, especially when visiting religious sites or interacting with local residents.

Marsa Matrouh offers a blend of natural beauty, historical interest, and a relaxing atmosphere, making it a fantastic destination for both leisure and exploration.

Bahariya Oasis

Bahariya Oasis, located in Egypt's Western Desert, is a fascinating destination known for its unique natural landscapes and historical sites. Here's a comprehensive guide to what Bahariya Oasis has to offer:

Key Attractions

White Desert (Sahara el Beyda): One of the most striking features of Bahariya Oasis, the White Desert is renowned for its otherworldly landscape of white rock formations and sand dunes. These formations have been sculpted by wind and sand over millennia, creating surreal shapes that make for excellent photography and exploration.

Black Desert (Sahara el Soud): This area is named for its dark, volcanic rock formations and contrasting black sands. The Black Desert offers a stark and dramatic landscape different from the White Desert, adding to the diverse natural beauty of the region.

Crystal Mountain (Jebel Crystal): A notable geological site where you can find natural crystals embedded in the rocks. The crystals are remnants of ancient volcanic activity and add a unique aspect to the desert scenery.

Bahariya Oasis Museum: This museum provides insights into the history, geology, and culture of the oasis. It showcases artifacts from local archaeological sites and offers information on the area's unique geological features.

Temple of Alexander the Great: An ancient site believed to have been built by Alexander the Great, although its exact origins and connections to Alexander are debated. The ruins offer a glimpse into the historical significance of the oasis.

Hot Springs: Bahariya Oasis is home to several natural hot springs, which are great for relaxation. Some of the notable ones include the Bir Sitta hot springs.

Activities

Desert Safaris: Exploring the desert by 4x4 vehicle or camel is a popular activity. These tours often include visits to the White and Black Deserts, and can also include camping under the stars.

Stargazing: The clear desert skies provide excellent conditions for stargazing. The lack of light pollution makes it an ideal location for observing the night sky.

Local Culture: Experience traditional Bedouin life by visiting local villages. The Bedouin people of the oasis have a distinct culture and are known for their hospitality.

Practical Information

Traveling to Bahariya Oasis:

By Car: The oasis is about 370 kilometers (230 miles) southwest of Cairo. The drive takes roughly 5 to 6 hours. A 4x4 vehicle is recommended for the journey, as the road conditions can vary.

By Bus: There are bus services from Cairo to Bahariya Oasis, though they might not be as frequent as other routes.

Accommodation: There are various options ranging from basic lodges to more comfortable eco-lodges and desert camps. Many accommodations offer guided tours and desert safaris as part of their services.

Best Time to Visit: The best time to visit is during the cooler months from October to April. Summer temperatures can be extremely high, making travel and outdoor activities challenging.

Tips for Visitors

Sun Protection: The desert sun can be intense, so bring sunscreen, a hat, and sunglasses to protect yourself.

Hydration: Always carry plenty of water, as the desert climate is very dry.

Respect Local Customs: When visiting local Bedouin communities, be respectful of their customs and traditions.

Guided Tours: Consider joining a guided tour for a more comprehensive experience, especially if you're unfamiliar with desert travel.

Bahariya Oasis offers a unique blend of natural wonders and historical sites, making it an intriguing destination for adventurers and history enthusiasts alike.

Faiyum

Faiyum is a city and governorate located in Egypt, southwest of Cairo, known for its rich history, natural beauty, and cultural significance. It's an intriguing destination with a mix of ancient landmarks and natural wonders. Here's a detailed guide to what you can explore and enjoy in Faiyum:

Key Attractions

Lake Qarun: One of the oldest natural lakes in Egypt, Lake Qarun is a major attraction in Faiyum. It's a great spot for birdwatching, especially for migratory birds, and offers opportunities for fishing and relaxation by the water.

Wadi El Rayan: A protected area featuring two beautiful lakes, Wadi El Rayan is known for its picturesque scenery and natural waterfalls. It's ideal for picnicking, photography, and enjoying the tranquil environment.

Wadi El Hitan (Valley of the Whales): A UNESCO World Heritage site, Wadi El Hitan is famous for its fossilized remains of early whales, providing crucial evidence of the evolution of whales from land-dwelling to marine creatures. The site includes numerous well-preserved fossils and exhibits that highlight the area's paleontological significance.

Faiyum Oasis: The oasis itself is a historical and agricultural marvel, with a history dating back to ancient Egypt. It features a range of ancient and historical sites, including:

The Temple of Sobek and Haroeris: An ancient temple dedicated to the crocodile god Sobek and the falcon god Haroeris. The ruins offer insights into the religious practices of the ancient Egyptians.

Karanis (Kom Aushim): An ancient city with well-preserved ruins, including houses, temples, and administrative buildings. It provides a glimpse into the daily life of the ancient inhabitants of the oasis.

The Pyramid of Amenemhat II: Located near the village of Dahshur, this pyramid is part of the larger Dahshur necropolis. It is less visited compared to other pyramids but provides a fascinating look into the Old Kingdom period.

Activities

Boating and Fishing: On Lake Qarun, you can enjoy boating and fishing, with scenic views and opportunities to relax by the water.

Desert Excursions: Explore the surrounding desert landscape with a guided tour. The desert features unique geological formations and ancient sites.

Cultural Experiences: Visit local markets and villages to experience traditional Egyptian culture and cuisine. The Faiyum area is known for its agricultural products, including fruits and vegetables.

Practical Information

Traveling to Faiyum:

By Car: Faiyum is about a 1.5 to 2-hour drive from Cairo, roughly 130 kilometers (81 miles) southwest. The drive is relatively straightforward, with good road connections.

By Bus: There are bus services from Cairo to Faiyum, which can be a convenient option for travelers.

Accommodation: There are several hotels and guesthouses in Faiyum, ranging from budget to mid-range options. For a more unique experience, consider staying in a desert lodge or eco-lodge.

Best Time to Visit: The best time to visit Faiyum is during the cooler months from October to April. Summer temperatures can be quite high, making outdoor activities less comfortable.

Tips for Visitors

Sun Protection: The desert climate means strong sunlight, so bring sunscreen, a hat, and sunglasses.

Hydration: Keep hydrated, especially if you're exploring the desert or spending time outdoors.

Respect Local Customs: Be mindful of local customs and traditions, especially in rural areas and when visiting historical sites.

Guided Tours: For a more comprehensive experience, consider hiring a local guide who can provide detailed information about the history and significance of the sites you visit.

Faiyum offers a diverse range of attractions, from ancient archaeological sites to natural wonders, making it a rewarding destination for those interested in history, nature, and Egyptian culture.

7-day Itinerary for first time traveler

Day 1: Arrival and Introduction

Morning

Activity:

Arrival and Check-in: After arriving in Alexandria, head to your hotel to check in and freshen up. Popular hotels include the **Four Seasons Hotel Alexandria** and **Hilton Alexandria Corniche**.

Visit the Bibliotheca Alexandrina: This modern library and cultural center is an iconic attraction. It opens at 9:00 AM and closes at 7:00 PM. It's a great place to start your exploration, offering exhibits, a museum, and stunning architecture.

Breakfast:

Where to Eat: Try **Ristorante Rami**, a local favorite with a variety of breakfast options.

What to Eat: Enjoy traditional Egyptian breakfast dishes such as **falafel (ta'ameya)**, **fuul (fava beans)**, and **baladi bread**.

Price: Around 70-150 EGP ($2.5-$5) per person.

Mid-Morning

Activity:

Explore the Citadel of Qaitbay: This historic fortress offers fantastic views of the Mediterranean and is a short walk from the Bibliotheca Alexandrina. It opens at 9:00 AM and closes at 4:00 PM.

Price: Entry fee is approximately 60 EGP ($2) for foreigners.

Getting Around:

Transportation: Use taxis or ride-hailing apps like Uber or Careem for convenience.

Afternoon

Activity:

Lunch and Relaxation: Head to **Corniche Road** for a scenic walk along the waterfront.

Lunch: Dine at **Fishawi's**, a renowned spot for seafood. Try the **grilled fish** or **seafood platter**.

Price: Around 150-300 EGP ($5-$10) per person.

After Lunch:

Visit the Roman Amphitheatre: Located near the city center, this ancient site provides a glimpse into Alexandria's Roman history.

Price: Entry fee is about 60 EGP ($2).

Mid-Afternoon

Activity:

Visit Montazah Palace Gardens: Stroll through these beautiful gardens and enjoy the historic palace. The gardens are open from 9:00 AM to 6:00 PM.

Price: Around 100 EGP ($3.5) for entrance to the gardens.

Evening

Activity:

Relax at a Café: Enjoy a coffee or tea at **Café Tahrir** or **Café Alex** on Corniche Road.

Dinner: Head to **Seafood Restaurant Samakmak** for a delicious dinner featuring local specialties like **grilled calamari** and **shrimp kebabs**.

Price: Approximately 200-400 EGP ($7-$14) per person.

Night

Activity:

Stroll along the Corniche: Enjoy the Mediterranean breeze and take in the night views of the sea.

Optional: Visit **La Dolce Vita** for a sweet treat or ice cream before heading back to your hotel.

Getting Around:

Transportation: In the evening, you can use taxis or ride-hailing apps to navigate back to your hotel safely.

Overall Tips:

Currency: Make sure to have some Egyptian Pounds (EGP) on hand for small purchases.

Language: Basic English is commonly understood in tourist areas, but knowing a few Arabic phrases can be helpful.

Weather: Check the weather forecast and dress appropriately, as Alexandria can be quite warm, especially in summer.

Day 2: Historical Exploration

Morning

Activity:

Visit the Catacombs of Kom El Shoqafa: Start your day with a visit to these fascinating ancient tombs. The catacombs are a blend of Egyptian, Greek, and Roman influences.

Opening Hours: 9:00 AM to 4:00 PM.

Price: Approximately 80 EGP ($3) for entry.

Breakfast:

Where to Eat: Have breakfast at **El Abd Bakery** which is famous for its pastries and traditional breakfast options.

What to Eat: Enjoy a mix of **koshari**, **Egyptian bread**, and **freshly baked pastries**.

Price: Around 50-100 EGP ($2-$3.5) per person.

Mid-Morning

Activity:

Visit the Pompey's Pillar and Serapeum: Explore this grand Roman column and the nearby ruins of the Serapeum, a temple dedicated to the god Serapis.

Opening Hours: 9:00 AM to 4:00 PM.

Price: Approximately 60 EGP ($2) for entry.

Getting Around:

Transportation: Use a taxi or ride-hailing app to move between sites efficiently.

Afternoon

Activity:

Lunch at a Local Restaurant: Enjoy a traditional Egyptian meal at **Koshary Abou Tarek**. This spot is known for its hearty and flavorful **koshary**, a popular Egyptian dish made with rice, lentils, and pasta.

Price: Around 50-80 EGP ($2-$3) per person.

Activity:

Explore the Alexandria National Museum: Dive into Alexandria's rich history and culture through its extensive collection of artifacts, from ancient Egypt to the Islamic period.

Opening Hours: 9:00 AM to 5:00 PM.

Price: Approximately 100 EGP ($3.5) for entry.

Mid-Afternoon

Activity:

Visit the Royal Jewelry Museum: Located in the former palace of the Khedive, this museum houses a stunning collection of royal jewelry and artifacts.

Opening Hours: 9:00 AM to 5:00 PM.

Price: Around 100 EGP ($3.5) for entry.

Getting Around:

Transportation: Again, taxis or ride-hailing apps are convenient for moving between attractions.

Evening

Activity:

Relax and Dinner at a Beachside Restaurant: Head to **The Fish Market Restaurant** or **Seafood Restaurant Samakmak** on Corniche Road for a scenic dining experience.

What to Eat: Enjoy a variety of seafood dishes such as **grilled fish**, **shrimp kebabs**, and **seafood risotto**.

Price: Approximately 200-400 EGP ($7-$14) per person.

After Dinner:

Take a Leisurely Stroll along the Corniche: End your day with a peaceful walk along the waterfront, enjoying the night views and sea breeze.

Getting Around:

Transportation: Use a taxi or ride-hailing app to return to your hotel comfortably.

Night

Activity:

Relax at the Hotel or Local Café: If you're up for it, you can enjoy a nightcap at a café or lounge near your hotel.

Overall Tips:

Stay Hydrated: Alexandria can be quite warm, so drink plenty of water throughout the day.

Dress Comfortably: Wear comfortable shoes for walking and lightweight clothing suitable for the weather.

Currency: Have Egyptian Pounds handy for entry fees and small purchases.

Day 3: Ancient Alexandria

Morning

Activity:

Visit the Alexandria Lighthouse (Pharos): Although the original Lighthouse of Alexandria no longer stands, you can visit the area where it once stood. Nearby, you can see the ruins and enjoy the view from the **Citadel of Qaitbay**, which was built on the original site of the lighthouse.

Opening Hours: The Citadel opens at 9:00 AM and closes at 4:00 PM.

Price: Entry fee is about 60 EGP ($2) for foreigners.

Breakfast:

Where to Eat: Head to **Doughlicious Bakery** for a light and fresh breakfast.

What to Eat: Enjoy a selection of **croissants**, **bagels**, and **freshly squeezed juice**.

Price: Around 50-100 EGP ($2-$3.5) per person.

Mid-Morning

Activity:

Explore the Ancient Roman Theater: Located near the Kom El Dikka area, this well-preserved Roman theater offers a glimpse into ancient entertainment and architecture.

Opening Hours: 9:00 AM to 4:00 PM.

Price: Entry is approximately 60 EGP ($2).

Getting Around:

Transportation: Use taxis or ride-hailing apps for easy navigation between sites.

Afternoon

Activity:

Lunch at a Traditional Restaurant: For an authentic Egyptian lunch, try **El Bostan Restaurant**.

What to Eat: Enjoy classic dishes such as **grilled meats**, **stuffed grape leaves**, and **hummus**.

Price: Around 150-250 EGP ($5-$9) per person.

Activity:

Visit the Kom El Dikka Archaeological Site: This site includes a range of Roman and Byzantine ruins, including bathhouses, and a large mosaic floor.

Opening Hours: 9:00 AM to 4:00 PM.

Price: Entry is about 60 EGP ($2).

Mid-Afternoon

Activity:

Explore the Museum of Alexandria: This museum offers a deeper look into the city's ancient history, including artifacts from the Hellenistic period.

Opening Hours: 9:00 AM to 5:00 PM.

Price: Approximately 100 EGP ($3.5).

Getting Around:

Transportation: Taxis or ride-hailing apps will be convenient for moving between historical sites and the museum.

Evening

Activity:

Relax at a Local Café: After a day of exploration, unwind at **Café Riche** for a relaxed atmosphere and great coffee.

Dinner: For a memorable dining experience, consider **Pita Park** for a mix of Mediterranean and Egyptian cuisine.

Price: Dinner will be around 150-300 EGP ($5-$10) per person.

After Dinner:

Stroll through the City: Enjoy a leisurely walk around the city to reflect on your day and take in the evening ambiance.

Getting Around:

Transportation: Use taxis or ride-hailing apps for convenience.

Night

Activity:

Return to Your Hotel: Rest and relax at your hotel. If you're in the mood for a late-night snack or drink, many hotels have bars or cafes.

Overall Tips:

Comfortable Footwear: Ensure you wear comfortable shoes for walking, as there will be a lot of exploring.

Hydrate and Protect: Keep hydrated and use sunscreen as you'll be spending significant time outdoors.

Local Currency: Keep some Egyptian Pounds handy for site entries and small expenses.

Day 4: Day Trip to El Alamein

Morning

Activity:

Travel to El Alamein: Start your day early to make the most of your trip. El Alamein is about 100 km west of Alexandria, which takes roughly 1.5 to 2 hours by car.

Transportation: Rent a car or arrange a private tour for a comfortable and efficient trip. Alternatively, you can use a taxi or a ride-hailing app.

Breakfast:

Where to Eat: Have a hearty breakfast at your hotel before departing, or you can stop by a café along the way like **Café Tahrir** in Alexandria for a quick bite.

What to Eat: Enjoy a traditional Egyptian breakfast such as **falafel**, **egg sandwiches**, and **tea or coffee**.

Price: Around 50-100 EGP ($2-$3.5) per person.

Mid-Morning

Activity:

Visit the El Alamein War Museum: This museum provides an in-depth look at the Battle of El Alamein, featuring military artifacts, photographs, and exhibits about the WWII North African Campaign.

Opening Hours: 9:00 AM to 4:00 PM.

Price: Entry is approximately 50 EGP ($1.75).

Getting Around:

Transportation: You'll need a car or taxi to get to the museum and other sites in El Alamein.

Afternoon

Activity:

Lunch at a Local Restaurant: Try **Al Alamein Restaurant** for a local dining experience with a variety of Egyptian and Mediterranean dishes.

What to Eat: Enjoy dishes like **grilled meats**, **rice with vermicelli**, and **fresh salads**.

Price: Around 150-250 EGP ($5-$9) per person.

Activity:

Explore the El Alamein Commonwealth War Cemetery: This cemetery commemorates the soldiers of the British Commonwealth who died in the North African Campaign. It's a serene and respectful place to reflect on the history.

Opening Hours: Generally open from 8:00 AM to 4:00 PM.

Price: Free entry, but donations are appreciated.

Mid-Afternoon

Activity:

Visit the German and Italian War Cemeteries: These cemeteries are dedicated to the German and Italian soldiers who fell during the battle. They provide additional perspectives on the conflict.

Opening Hours: Typically open from 8:00 AM to 4:00 PM.

Price: Free entry.

Getting Around:

Transportation: Continue using your rented vehicle or taxi for convenience.

Evening

Activity:

Return to Alexandria: Head back to Alexandria in the late afternoon to early evening. The drive will take approximately 1.5 to 2 hours.

Dinner:

Where to Eat: Upon returning to Alexandria, enjoy dinner at **The Great Alexandria Restaurant**, known for its diverse menu and comfortable atmosphere.

What to Eat: Opt for local favorites like **moussaka**, **shish kebabs**, and **pita bread**.

Price: Approximately 200-400 EGP ($7-$14) per person.

After Dinner:

Relax at the Hotel: Wind down from your day trip with a relaxing evening at your hotel. If you're up for it, enjoy a stroll along the Corniche or have a drink at a hotel bar.

Overall Tips:

Plan Ahead: Ensure your transportation and any required permits or arrangements are set before the trip.

Weather: Dress comfortably and stay hydrated, as it can be quite hot, especially in the summer.

Local Currency: Keep Egyptian Pounds handy for any local purchases or entry fees.

Day 5: Coastal Relaxation

Morning

Activity:

Relax at a Beach: Start your day with a relaxing visit to one of Alexandria's beautiful beaches. Popular options include **Maamoura Beach**, **Stanley Beach**, and **Montazah Beach**. Maamoura Beach is known for its calm waters and family-friendly atmosphere, while Montazah Beach offers a more scenic and expansive area.

Breakfast:

Where to Eat: Have a leisurely breakfast at a beachfront café or your hotel. **Ristorante Rami** offers a nice seaside view and a variety of breakfast options.

What to Eat: Enjoy a light breakfast with options like **fresh fruit**, **croissants**, **omelets**, and **freshly brewed coffee**.

Price: Around 70-150 EGP ($2.5-$5) per person.

Mid-Morning

Activity:

Enjoy Water Activities: If you're interested in water sports, many beaches offer activities like **jet skiing**, **parasailing**, or **snorkeling**. You can rent equipment or book a session with local vendors at the beach.

Price: Activities can range from 200-500 EGP ($7-$18) depending on the sport and duration.

Getting Around:

Transportation: Use taxis or ride-hailing apps to reach the beach and for any local transportation needs.

Afternoon

Activity:

Lunch by the Sea: Enjoy a relaxing lunch at a beachside restaurant. **Seafood Restaurant Samakmak** is a great choice with its fresh seafood and coastal ambiance.

What to Eat: Choose from a variety of seafood dishes like **grilled fish**, **seafood pasta**, or **shrimp cocktails**.

Price: Approximately 200-400 EGP ($7-$14) per person.

Activity:

Visit Montazah Palace Gardens: After lunch, head to the Montazah Palace Gardens for a leisurely stroll. The gardens are lush and provide beautiful views of the sea and the palace.

Opening Hours: 9:00 AM to 6:00 PM.

Price: Around 100 EGP ($3.5) for entrance to the gardens.

Mid-Afternoon

Activity:

Relax and Unwind: Spend the afternoon lounging on the beach, swimming, or simply relaxing. You might also want to enjoy a book or a nap in the sun.

Getting Around:

Transportation: If you need to move between the beach and other sites, taxis or ride-hailing apps will be convenient.

Evening

Activity:

Dinner at a Seaside Restaurant: Head to a fine dining restaurant along the coast. **The Fish Market** is a popular choice, offering a relaxed atmosphere and fresh seafood.

What to Eat: Opt for a seafood feast or a mixed platter of local specialties.

Price: Approximately 200-400 EGP ($7-$14) per person.

After Dinner:

Sunset Stroll: Enjoy a leisurely stroll along the Corniche or a beachfront promenade to take in the sunset and the Mediterranean ambiance.

Getting Around:

Transportation: Use a taxi or ride-hailing app to get back to your hotel or any final destinations for the day.

Night

Activity:

Relax at the Hotel: Conclude your day with a relaxing evening at your hotel. If your hotel has amenities such as a pool or a bar, it's a great way to wind down.

Overall Tips:

Sun Protection: Use sunscreen, wear a hat, and stay hydrated throughout the day.

Comfortable Clothing: Wear swimwear and beach-appropriate clothing, and bring a change of clothes if needed.

Cash: Keep some cash on hand for beachside rentals and small purchases.

Day 6: Cultural Immersion

Morning

Activity:

Visit the Alexandria National Museum: Start your day with a visit to this museum to explore its extensive collection of artifacts from ancient Egypt to the Islamic period. It provides a comprehensive overview of Alexandria's cultural and historical evolution.

Opening Hours: 9:00 AM to 5:00 PM.

Price: Approximately 100 EGP ($3.5).

Breakfast:

Where to Eat: Have breakfast at **El Abd Bakery** or **Doughlicious Bakery**, both offering a variety of traditional and fresh options.

What to Eat: Enjoy items like **Egyptian pastries**, **fresh bread**, and **tea or coffee**.

Price: Around 50-100 EGP ($2-$3.5) per person.

Mid-Morning

Activity:

Explore the Local Souks: Visit the **El Attarine Souk** or **Souk El-Sellin** to experience Alexandria's bustling markets. These souks offer a vibrant mix of spices, textiles, and local crafts. It's a great place to pick up souvenirs and interact with local vendors.

Getting Around:

Transportation: Use a taxi or ride-hailing app to navigate to the souks and other cultural sites.

Afternoon

Activity:

Lunch at a Traditional Restaurant: For an authentic taste of Egyptian cuisine, visit **El Bostan Restaurant** or **Koshary Abou Tarek**. Both are popular for their traditional dishes.

What to Eat: Try traditional Egyptian dishes such as **koshary**, **moussaka**, or **stuffed grape leaves**.

Price: Around 150-250 EGP ($5-$9) per person.

Activity:

Visit the Montazah Palace: Tour the Montazah Palace, which has historical significance and stunning gardens. Though the palace itself may not be open to the public, the surrounding gardens are a beautiful place for a stroll.

Opening Hours: 9:00 AM to 6:00 PM for the gardens.

Price: Around 100 EGP ($3.5) for entrance to the gardens.

Mid-Afternoon

Activity:

Cultural Workshop or Class: Join a local cultural workshop or cooking class to learn more about Egyptian traditions. **Local Egyptian cooking classes** or **art workshops** can offer hands-on experiences.

Price: Workshops and classes typically range from 300-600 EGP ($10-$20), depending on the activity.

Getting Around:

Transportation: Arrange for transportation through your workshop provider or use a taxi to get to the venue.

Evening

Activity:

Dinner at a Cultural Restaurant: Enjoy dinner at a restaurant that offers a cultural experience, such as **Balba's**, which features traditional Egyptian décor and live music.

What to Eat: Opt for a diverse menu featuring Egyptian dishes like **grilled lamb**, **stuffed pigeons**, and **Egyptian salad**.

Price: Approximately 200-400 EGP ($7-$14) per person.

After Dinner:

Attend a Local Performance or Event: Check if there are any local cultural performances, such as traditional music or dance shows, happening in the evening. **Opera Alexandria** occasionally hosts performances and cultural events.

Getting Around:

Transportation: Use taxis or ride-hailing apps to navigate to your dinner venue and any evening activities.

Night

Activity:

Relax at a Café or Lounge: End your day by relaxing at a local café or lounge. **Café Riche** or **Café Tahrir** offer a cozy atmosphere to reflect on your cultural experiences and enjoy a drink.

Overall Tips:

Comfortable Attire: Dress comfortably for walking and interacting with locals.

Cash and Cards: Have cash for markets and small purchases, though many places accept cards.

Local Etiquette: Respect local customs and traditions, especially when visiting markets and attending cultural events.

Day 7: Leisure and Departure

Morning

Activity:

Relax at Your Hotel: Begin your final day with a leisurely morning at your hotel. Take advantage of any spa services, pools, or other amenities to unwind before your journey home.

Breakfast:

Where to Eat: Enjoy breakfast at your hotel, where you can typically find a wide selection of international and local options in the buffet.

What to Eat: Opt for a light but fulfilling breakfast, such as **fresh fruits**, **yogurt**, **pastries**, and **freshly brewed coffee** or **juice**.

Price: Usually included with your stay, but if not, it typically costs around 100-200 EGP ($3.5-$7) per person.

Mid-Morning

Activity:

Visit the Alexandria Library (Bibliotheca Alexandrina): Spend some time exploring this modern architectural marvel. The library houses millions of books, museums, galleries, and a planetarium. It's a peaceful way to reflect on your trip and soak in some culture before you leave.

Opening Hours: 10:00 AM to 7:00 PM (Monday to Saturday); closed on Sundays.

Price: Entry is approximately 70 EGP ($2.5) for the main library; additional fees apply for special exhibits.

Getting Around:

Transportation: Use a taxi or ride-hailing app to visit the library and other places as needed.

Afternoon

Activity:

Last-Minute Shopping: If you have time, visit the **San Stefano Grand Mall** or the **Green Plaza Mall** for some last-minute shopping. You can pick up souvenirs, gifts, or anything you might have missed earlier.

Lunch:

Where to Eat: Have a relaxed lunch at **San Stefano Mall's food court** or a nearby café like **Délices Patisserie**, known for its traditional pastries and light meals.

What to Eat: Enjoy a variety of dishes, from **light sandwiches** to **salads**, or try some local pastries.

Price: Around 100-200 EGP ($3.5-$7) per person.

Getting Around:

Transportation: Taxis or ride-hailing apps are the most convenient for moving between shopping areas and your hotel.

Mid-Afternoon

Activity:

Return to Your Hotel for Check-Out: Head back to your hotel to finish packing, check out, and prepare for your departure.

Late Check-Out: If your flight or train is later in the day, consider asking for a late check-out or storing your luggage at the hotel.

Evening

Activity:

Early Dinner: Depending on your departure time, you might want to have an early dinner before you leave. Consider a final meal at **Kadoura** or **Fish Market** for one last taste of Alexandria's seafood.

What to Eat: Enjoy dishes like **grilled seafood**, **stuffed calamari**, and **Egyptian rice**.

Price: Around 200-400 EGP ($7-$14) per person.

Getting Around:

Transportation: Arrange for transportation to the airport or train station. Most hotels can assist with booking a taxi or private car.

Night

Activity:

Departure: Ensure you arrive at the airport or train station with plenty of time for check-in and security procedures. If your departure is late, you can relax in the airport lounge if available.

Overall Tips:

Travel Documents: Double-check your travel documents, flight/train schedule, and transportation arrangements.

Last-Minute Essentials: Make sure you've packed all essentials, including any purchases from the day.

Stay Connected: Inform your hotel of your departure time so they can assist with any last-minute needs.

Chapter 12: Luxor

Top 10 Attractions & Things to do

1. **Karnak Temple Complex**

The Karnak Temple Complex, located in Luxor, Egypt, is one of the largest and most impressive religious sites in the world. Spanning over 100 hectares, it is a sprawling collection of temples, chapels, pylons, and other ancient structures dedicated primarily to the Theban Triad of Amun, Mut, and Khonsu. The complex was a major center of worship in ancient Egypt and remains a significant archaeological and tourist site today.

History

Construction and Development: The Karnak Temple Complex was developed over nearly 2,000 years, starting in the Middle Kingdom (around 2000 BCE) and continuing through to the Ptolemaic period (305-30 BCE). Each pharaoh contributed to its expansion, adding temples, statues, and obelisks, making it a testament to the changing dynasties and religious practices of ancient Egypt.

Religious Significance: Karnak was the most important religious center in ancient Egypt, particularly during the New Kingdom (1550-1070 BCE). It was dedicated to Amun-Ra, the king of the gods, and was a focal point for the worship of the Theban Triad. The complex was also the site of the Opet Festival, one of the most important religious events of the time.

Rediscovery: Although the temple fell into disuse after the decline of the ancient Egyptian civilization, it was never completely abandoned. European explorers began documenting the site in the 18th and 19th centuries, leading to a greater understanding of its historical and cultural significance.

Location

Address: Karnak, Luxor, Egypt.

Coordinates: 25.7192° N latitude, 32.6573° E longitude.

Accessibility: The Karnak Temple Complex is located just 2.5 kilometers (1.5 miles) north of Luxor's city center. It is easily accessible by taxi, bus, or even on foot from Luxor.

Opening and Closing Hours

Hours of Operation:

Summer (May to September): 6:00 AM to 6:00 PM.

Winter (October to April): 6:00 AM to 5:00 PM.

Light and Sound Show: The temple complex also hosts a popular evening "Light and Sound Show," which narrates the history of Karnak through an impressive display of lights and sound effects. The show runs multiple times each evening, with different languages scheduled for different times.

Top Things to Do

Explore the Great Hypostyle Hall: One of the most iconic parts of the Karnak complex, the Great Hypostyle Hall is a vast space filled with 134 massive columns arranged in 16 rows. The columns are intricately carved with hieroglyphics and reliefs, offering a glimpse into ancient religious rituals and royal propaganda.

Visit the Sacred Lake: This large, man-made lake within the temple complex was used for ritual purification by the priests. The lake is surrounded by a pathway and offers a tranquil spot to reflect on the temple's grandeur.

Admire the Obelisks: The complex houses several towering obelisks, including the famous obelisk of Queen Hatshepsut, which stands as one of the tallest in Egypt. These structures are a testament to the engineering prowess and religious dedication of the ancient Egyptians.

Explore the Temple of Amun-Ra: The central temple of Karnak is dedicated to Amun-Ra, the chief deity of Thebes. This temple is the largest and most significant part of the complex, with numerous chapels, sanctuaries, and statues dedicated to the god.

Walk the Avenue of Sphinxes: This ancient road, lined with sphinx statues, once connected Karnak to the Luxor Temple. Although parts of it have been lost over time, sections of the avenue have been restored and can be walked by visitors.

Practical Information

Tickets: Tickets are required for entry and can be purchased at the site. There are separate tickets for the daytime visit and the evening Light and Sound Show.

Facilities: The site has basic visitor facilities, including restrooms, a visitor center, and small shops selling souvenirs. Guided tours are available, and it's recommended to hire a knowledgeable guide to fully appreciate the history and significance of the complex.

Photography: Photography is allowed in most areas of the temple complex, but tripods may require special permission. Always check with the staff if you're unsure.

Tips for Visiting

Visit Early or Late: The site can get extremely hot and crowded, especially in the summer. Visiting early in the morning or late in the afternoon can help you avoid the heat and the crowds.

Wear Comfortable Shoes: The complex is vast, and you will be doing a lot of walking. Comfortable shoes are a must.

Stay Hydrated: Bring water, especially if you're visiting during the hotter months. There are vendors selling drinks at the site, but it's best to be prepared.

Consider the Light and Sound Show: The evening Light and Sound Show is a unique way to experience the temple, with the play of lights adding a dramatic effect to the ancient ruins. It's an excellent option for those interested in a different perspective on the site.

Respect the Site: As one of Egypt's most important historical sites, it's essential to respect the temple complex. Avoid touching the carvings and statues, and follow any guidelines provided by the site staff.

2. **Valley of the Kings**

The Valley of the Kings, located on the west bank of the Nile near Luxor, Egypt, is one of the most famous archaeological sites in the world. This ancient burial ground was the final resting place for the pharaohs and powerful nobles of the New Kingdom (1550–1070 BCE). With its hidden tombs, intricate wall paintings, and significant historical value, the Valley of the Kings offers a fascinating glimpse into the burial practices and beliefs of ancient Egypt.

History

Establishment: The Valley of the Kings was used as a royal burial site for nearly 500 years during the New Kingdom period. It was chosen as the pharaohs' burial place because of its remote location, which provided natural protection against tomb robbers.

Tombs: Over 60 tombs have been discovered in the valley, belonging to various pharaohs, queens, and nobles. The tombs range from simple pits to elaborate, multi-chambered structures, often filled with treasures intended for the afterlife.

Discovery: The Valley of the Kings gained international fame with the discovery of King Tutankhamun's nearly intact tomb in 1922 by British archaeologist Howard Carter. The discovery was one of the most significant archaeological finds of the 20th century, shedding light on the wealth and grandeur of ancient Egyptian royalty.

Location

Address: Valley of the Kings, West Bank, Luxor, Egypt.

Coordinates: 25.7402° N latitude, 32.6014° E longitude.

Accessibility: The Valley of the Kings is situated about 8 kilometers (5 miles) west of Luxor, and it can be reached by car, taxi, or guided tours from the city. It is often visited in conjunction with other nearby sites, such as the Temple of Hatshepsut and the Valley of the Queens.

Opening and Closing Hours

Hours of Operation:

Summer (May to September): 6:00 AM to 5:00 PM.

Winter (October to April): 6:00 AM to 4:00 PM.

Best Time to Visit: Early morning visits are recommended to avoid the heat and crowds, especially during peak tourist seasons.

Top Things to Do

Explore the Tombs: The main attraction in the Valley of the Kings is the tombs themselves. Each tomb has unique features, such as detailed wall paintings and hieroglyphics depicting the pharaoh's journey to the afterlife. Notable tombs include those of Ramses III, Ramses IV, and Seti I.

Visit King Tutankhamun's Tomb: The tomb of Tutankhamun (KV62) is the most famous in the valley. Though smaller compared to other tombs, it's renowned for the discovery of the young pharaoh's nearly intact burial treasures, including the iconic golden death mask. A separate ticket is required to enter this tomb.

Admire the Wall Paintings: The tombs are adorned with vivid wall paintings that have survived thousands of years. These paintings depict scenes from the "Book of the Dead" and other funerary texts, offering insights into the religious beliefs and practices of ancient Egypt.

Learn at the Visitor Center: Start your visit at the Visitor Center, where you can find exhibits and information about the history, construction, and significance of the Valley of the Kings. This background knowledge will enrich your exploration of the tombs.

Take a Guided Tour: Hiring a knowledgeable guide is highly recommended, as they can provide in-depth information about the tombs, the symbolism of the wall paintings, and the history of the pharaohs buried in the valley.

Practical Information

Tickets: A general entry ticket allows access to a selection of three tombs. Additional tickets are required for entry into special tombs, such as those of Tutankhamun, Seti I, and Ramses VI.

Facilities: The site has basic visitor facilities, including restrooms, a visitor center, and a small café. There are also shaded rest areas near the entrance.

Photography: Photography inside the tombs is generally prohibited to protect the delicate wall paintings. However, you can take photos in the open areas outside the tombs. Some tombs may allow photography for an additional fee, so check with the site staff.

Tips for Visiting

Wear Comfortable Shoes: The terrain in the Valley of the Kings is uneven and involves a fair amount of walking, including steps leading into the tombs. Wear sturdy, comfortable shoes.

Bring Water and Stay Hydrated: The valley can get extremely hot, especially in the summer months. Bring plenty of water and wear a hat and sunscreen to protect yourself from the sun.

Respect the Site: The Valley of the Kings is a UNESCO World Heritage site and a place of great historical importance. Be respectful of the site by not touching the walls or artifacts, and by following all guidelines provided by the staff.

Pace Yourself: Visiting multiple tombs can be overwhelming due to the heat and the amount of information to take in. Take breaks in shaded areas and pace yourself to fully enjoy the experience.

Consider a Multi-Day Pass: If you're an avid history enthusiast, consider purchasing a multi-day pass to explore more of the tombs at a leisurely pace, as there is much to see and learn.

3. Luxor Temple

Luxor Temple, located on the east bank of the Nile River in Luxor, Egypt, is one of the most significant and well-preserved monuments from ancient Egypt. Unlike many other temples in the area, which were dedicated to gods or used for religious ceremonies, Luxor Temple was primarily a ceremonial center associated with the rejuvenation of kingship. It was also a key site in the annual Opet Festival, which was held to honor the god Amun and renew the divine essence of the pharaoh.

History

Construction: Luxor Temple was built around 1400 BCE during the New Kingdom, primarily under the reign of Pharaoh Amenhotep III. Later, it was expanded by subsequent pharaohs, including Tutankhamun, Horemheb, and Ramses II, who added a grand pylon and a pair of towering obelisks at the entrance.

Significance: The temple was dedicated to the Theban Triad of Amun, Mut, and Khonsu. Unlike other temples dedicated solely to religious purposes, Luxor Temple also served as a venue for the coronation of pharaohs, reaffirming their divine right to rule.

Later Use: Over time, the temple was repurposed for various uses, including as a Roman military camp and later as a Christian church during the Roman Empire. A mosque, still in use today, was also built within the temple complex during the Islamic period, adding to the site's rich historical tapestry.

Location

Address: Luxor Temple, Corniche El Nile, Luxor, Egypt.

Coordinates: 25.6997° N latitude, 32.6396° E longitude.

Accessibility: Luxor Temple is situated in the heart of Luxor, making it easily accessible on foot from most hotels and attractions in the city. It is also well-connected by taxis and public transportation.

Opening and Closing Hours

Hours of Operation:

Summer (May to September): 6:00 AM to 9:00 PM.

Winter (October to April): 6:00 AM to 8:00 PM.

Best Time to Visit: The temple is stunning at any time of day, but many visitors recommend visiting at sunset or in the evening when the temple is beautifully illuminated, creating a magical atmosphere.

Top Things to Do

Explore the Grand Colonnade: One of the most impressive features of Luxor Temple is the Grand Colonnade, a majestic avenue lined with 14 towering columns. This hall connects the main entrance to the inner sanctuaries and is adorned with intricate carvings depicting scenes from the Opet Festival and other religious rituals.

Admire the Statues of Ramses II: At the entrance of the temple, you'll find massive statues of Ramses II, one of Egypt's most powerful pharaohs. These statues, along with the remaining obelisk (its twin now stands in Paris), are iconic symbols of the temple's grandeur.

Visit the Sanctuary of Amun: The inner sanctuary of the temple, dedicated to the god Amun, is where the sacred barque (a ceremonial boat) of Amun was kept during festivals. The sanctuary is richly decorated with scenes of the god Amun and the pharaohs making offerings.

Explore the Mosque of Abu al-Haggag: Built into the structure of Luxor Temple, this mosque is still active today and provides a fascinating juxtaposition of ancient and more modern religious practices. The mosque was constructed in the 13th century, adding a layer of Islamic history to the site.

Enjoy the Evening Illumination: At night, Luxor Temple is illuminated, highlighting its architectural details and creating a breathtaking spectacle. An evening visit offers a different perspective, as the lighting casts dramatic shadows on the ancient stonework.

Practical Information

Tickets: Tickets can be purchased at the entrance. There is a single ticket for daytime visits, and a separate ticket is required if you wish to visit in the evening.

Facilities: The site has basic amenities, including restrooms and a small café. There are also souvenir shops nearby where you can purchase replicas of artifacts and other memorabilia.

Photography: Photography is allowed throughout the temple, though the use of tripods may require special permission. The temple is particularly photogenic in the evening when the lights are on.

Tips for Visiting

Visit Early or Late: To avoid the heat and crowds, consider visiting early in the morning or in the evening. The temple's atmosphere changes dramatically with the lighting, so visiting at different times can offer unique experiences.

Combine with Other Attractions: Luxor Temple is located close to other significant sites like the

Karnak Temple and the Luxor Museum, making it easy to plan a full day of exploration in the area.

Hire a Guide: While the temple is fascinating to explore on your own, hiring a knowledgeable guide can provide deeper insights into the history, architecture, and symbolism of the site. Guides are available at the entrance or can be arranged through hotels and tour operators.

Dress Respectfully: Given the temple's historical and religious significance, it's advisable to dress modestly, especially if you plan to visit the mosque within the temple complex.

Hydrate and Rest: The temple can be tiring to explore due to its size and the hot climate. Make sure to bring water and take breaks in shaded areas as needed.

4. Hatshepsut's Mortuary Temple

Hatshepsut's Mortuary Temple, also known as Deir el-Bahari, is one of the most striking and architecturally significant temples in Egypt. Located on the west bank of the Nile River, near the Valley of the Kings, this temple was built by Queen Hatshepsut, one of Egypt's few female pharaohs, and stands as a testament to her reign. The temple is renowned for its unique design, which blends seamlessly with the surrounding cliffs, and its terraces, which once housed lush gardens.

History

Construction: The temple was constructed during the 18th Dynasty, around 1479–1458 BCE, under the direction of Hatshepsut, who ruled as a pharaoh despite traditionally being depicted as a male king in statues and reliefs. The temple was designed by Senenmut, Hatshepsut's chief architect and close advisor, and is considered one of the architectural wonders of ancient Egypt.

Purpose: The temple was built to serve as Hatshepsut's mortuary temple, where she would be worshipped after her death, and as a sanctuary for the god Amun. It also functioned as a site for the celebration of the Opet Festival, a key religious event in Thebes.

Later Use and Rediscovery: Over the centuries, the temple suffered from damage, deliberate defacement, and burial under desert sands. It was rediscovered and extensively excavated and restored in the late 19th and early 20th centuries, revealing its original grandeur.

Location

Address: Deir el-Bahari, Luxor, Egypt.

Coordinates: 25.7376° N latitude, 32.6061° E longitude.

Accessibility: The temple is located near the Valley of the Kings on the west bank of the Nile, about 5 kilometers (3 miles) from Luxor. It is easily accessible by car, taxi, or guided tours from Luxor.

Opening and Closing Hours

Hours of Operation:

Summer (May to September): 6:00 AM to 5:00 PM.

Winter (October to April): 6:00 AM to 4:00 PM.

Best Time to Visit: Visiting early in the morning or late in the afternoon is recommended to avoid the heat and crowds, especially during the peak tourist season.

Top Things to Do

Explore the Three Terraces: The temple is built on three terraces that rise in a series of steps up to the cliff face. Each terrace is connected by long ramps, and the walls are adorned with detailed reliefs and inscriptions depicting Hatshepsut's divine birth, her expedition to the Land of Punt, and her relationship with the god Amun.

Admire the Colonnades: The colonnaded terraces are one of the temple's most distinctive features. The colonnades on the second terrace feature some of the best-preserved reliefs, including scenes of the famous trading expedition to Punt, which brought exotic goods like incense, ebony, and myrrh trees to Egypt.

Visit the Sanctuary of Amun: At the back of the temple, in the rock-cut sanctuary, there are chapels dedicated to Amun, Hatshepsut, and her father Thutmose I. The sanctuary is where rituals and offerings to Amun were performed, and it holds significant religious importance.

View the Statue of Hatshepsut: Though many statues of Hatshepsut were defaced or destroyed after her death, some impressive statues and sphinxes remain at the temple. These statues depict her with traditional pharaonic regalia, emphasizing her role as a ruler.

Enjoy the Panoramic Views: From the upper terrace, visitors can enjoy panoramic views of the surrounding area, including the Nile River and the Theban Necropolis. The dramatic setting of the temple, nestled against towering cliffs, adds to the breathtaking scenery.

Practical Information

Tickets: Tickets are required for entry and can be purchased at the site. Consider purchasing a combination ticket if you plan to visit nearby attractions, such as the Valley of the Kings or the Temple of Medinet Habu.

Facilities: The site has basic visitor amenities, including restrooms and a small café. There are also vendors selling souvenirs near the entrance, though prices can be high.

Photography: Photography is allowed throughout most of the temple complex, but the use of tripods may require special permission. The early morning light is ideal for capturing the temple's beauty.

Tips for Visiting

Start Early: To fully appreciate the temple and avoid the crowds and heat, try to visit as early as possible. The light in the morning also enhances the beauty of the reliefs and the temple's facade.

Hire a Guide: A knowledgeable guide can provide valuable insights into the history, architecture, and symbolism of the temple. Guides are available at the site or can be arranged through your hotel or tour operator.

Wear Comfortable Shoes: Exploring the temple requires a fair amount of walking, including climbing ramps and stairs. Comfortable shoes are essential.

Stay Hydrated: Bring plenty of water, especially if visiting during the hotter months. The temple is located in a desert area, and the heat can be intense.

Respect the Site: As with all historical sites, it's important to respect the temple by not touching the walls or artifacts, and by following any guidelines provided by the site staff.

5. Colossi of Memnon

The Colossi of Memnon are two massive stone statues that stand as sentinels at the entrance to the Theban Necropolis on the west bank of the Nile River, near Luxor, Egypt. These imposing statues, each standing about 18 meters (59 feet) tall, represent Pharaoh Amenhotep III and were originally part of a larger mortuary temple complex built in his honor. The temple, once one of the grandest in ancient Egypt, has largely disappeared, but the Colossi remain as enduring symbols of the pharaoh's legacy.

History

Construction: The Colossi of Memnon were constructed around 1350 BCE during the 18th Dynasty of the New Kingdom. They were part of the mortuary temple of Amenhotep III, which was one of the largest and most magnificent temples in Egypt at the time. The statues were carved from blocks of quartzite sandstone transported from quarries near Cairo, over 675 kilometers (420 miles) away.

Name and Legend: The name "Memnon" was given to the statues by the ancient Greeks, who associated them with Memnon, a hero of the Trojan War. According to legend, one of the statues emitted a "singing" sound at dawn, believed to be Memnon greeting his mother, Eos, the goddess of dawn. This phenomenon was likely caused by the heating and cooling of the stone, but it ceased after repairs were made to the statue by the Roman emperor Septimius Severus in 199 CE.

Decline of the Temple: The mortuary temple of Amenhotep III was heavily damaged by an earthquake in 27 BCE and was later dismantled, with many of its stones repurposed for other buildings. Today, only the Colossi remain as the most visible remnants of this once-grand complex.

Location

Address: West Bank, Luxor, Egypt.

Coordinates: 25.7202° N latitude, 32.6104° E longitude.

Accessibility: The Colossi of Memnon are located about 4 kilometers (2.5 miles) west of the Nile, near other major attractions such as the Valley of the Kings and Hatshepsut's Mortuary Temple. They are easily accessible by car, taxi, or as part of a guided tour.

Opening and Closing Hours

Hours of Operation: The site is open to the public all day, from sunrise to sunset.

Best Time to Visit: Early morning or late afternoon visits are recommended for better lighting and fewer crowds. The statues are especially striking when illuminated by the golden light of dawn or dusk.

Top Things to Do

Admire the Statues: The main attraction at the site is, of course, the Colossi themselves. Standing before these massive statues offers a powerful sense of the grandeur and scale of ancient Egyptian monumental architecture. The statues are intricately carved, though much of the detail has been worn away by time and weather.

Photograph the Colossi: The site offers excellent photo opportunities, especially in the early morning or late afternoon when the light casts dramatic shadows on the statues. The surrounding landscape also provides a picturesque backdrop for photography.

Explore the Surrounding Area: Although the Colossi are the primary draw, the site is located near other important archaeological sites. You can combine your visit with nearby attractions such as the Temple of Medinet Habu, the Ramesseum, or the Valley of the Queens.

Practical Information

Tickets: Visiting the Colossi of Memnon is free of charge, as they are located in an open area without any entrance fees.

Facilities: There are no facilities directly at the site, but nearby attractions and the town of Luxor provide amenities such as restrooms, cafés, and shops. It's advisable to bring your own water and snacks, especially if visiting during the hot summer months.

Photography: Photography is allowed and encouraged. The site's open setting and the statues' impressive stature make for excellent photos. A wide-angle lens is recommended to capture the full scale of the statues.

Tips for Visiting

Combine with Nearby Attractions: The Colossi of Memnon are often visited as part of a larger tour of the west bank of Luxor. Plan to visit other nearby sites such as the Valley of the Kings or Hatshepsut's Mortuary Temple to make the most of your day.

Visit Early: To avoid the heat and the largest crowds, consider visiting the site early in the morning. The early light also enhances the appearance of the statues and the surrounding landscape.

Respect the Site: While the Colossi are accessible to the public, it's important to respect the site by not climbing on the statues or damaging the surrounding area. The statues are ancient and fragile, and preservation efforts rely on respectful behavior from visitors.

Stay Hydrated: Luxor can be extremely hot, especially in the summer months. Bring plenty of water and wear sun protection, including a hat and sunscreen, to stay comfortable during your visit.

6. Valley of the Queens

The Valley of the Queens, located on the west bank of the Nile near Luxor, Egypt, is an ancient necropolis where the queens of the New Kingdom (1550-1070 BCE) were buried. This secluded valley served as the final resting place for the wives of pharaohs, royal children, and other members of the nobility. It is renowned for its beautifully decorated tombs, particularly the tomb of Queen Nefertari, which is often considered one of the most exquisite in all of Egypt.

History

Construction: The Valley of the Queens was established during the 18th Dynasty and continued to be used throughout the 19th and 20th Dynasties. The location was chosen for its relative isolation, providing a serene and secure environment for the eternal rest of Egypt's royal women.

Purpose: The valley was designed as a counterpart to the more famous Valley of the Kings, where the pharaohs were buried. The tombs in the Valley of the Queens were constructed with the same care and attention to detail, reflecting the important status of the queens and their association with the afterlife.

Notable Tombs: Over 90 tombs have been discovered in the Valley of the Queens, with the most famous being the tomb of Queen Nefertari, the favorite wife of Pharaoh Ramses II. Nefertari's tomb (QV66) is celebrated for its stunningly preserved wall paintings, which depict scenes from the "Book of the Dead" and other religious texts, showcasing her journey to the afterlife.

Location

Address: West Bank, Luxor, Egypt.

Coordinates: 25.7215° N latitude, 32.5947° E longitude.

Accessibility: The Valley of the Queens is located near the Valley of the Kings and other major attractions on the west bank of Luxor. It is accessible by car, taxi, or as part of a guided tour. The site is approximately 5 kilometers (3 miles) from the Nile River, making it a short drive from the city of Luxor.

Opening and Closing Hours

Hours of Operation:

Summer (May to September): 6:00 AM to 5:00 PM.

Winter (October to April): 6:00 AM to 4:00 PM.

Best Time to Visit: Early morning visits are recommended to avoid the heat and crowds, especially during the peak tourist season. The tombs are cool inside, providing a welcome relief from the hot desert sun.

Top Things to Do

Visit the Tomb of Queen Nefertari: The highlight of any visit to the Valley of the Queens is the tomb of Nefertari. Known as the "Sistine Chapel of Ancient Egypt," this tomb is famous for its vibrant wall paintings that have retained their color and detail for over 3,000 years. The tomb is usually open to visitors, though it requires a special ticket due to its significance and delicate condition.

Explore Other Tombs: In addition to Nefertari's tomb, there are several other beautifully decorated tombs in the valley, including those of Queen Tyti (QV52) and Prince Amunherkhepshef (QV55), a son of Ramses III. Each tomb offers unique insights into the beliefs, art, and burial practices of the New Kingdom.

Learn About Ancient Funerary Practices: The tombs provide a fascinating glimpse into the ancient Egyptians' views on death and the afterlife. The intricate decorations, inscriptions, and artifacts found in these tombs reveal the rituals and prayers intended to ensure a safe journey to the afterlife for the queens and their families.

Practical Information

Tickets: Entrance to the Valley of the Queens requires a general admission ticket, with additional fees for entry to the tomb of Nefertari. Due to the fragility of the site, access to Nefertari's tomb may be limited to small groups, so it's advisable to plan ahead or join a guided tour that includes this tomb.

Facilities: Basic amenities, including restrooms and shaded areas, are available near the entrance. There are also vendors selling refreshments and souvenirs.

Photography: Photography is allowed in most of the tombs, but flash photography is typically prohibited to protect the ancient paintings. Special permits may be required for professional photography.

Tips for Visiting

Start Early: The Valley of the Queens is best visited early in the morning to avoid the midday heat and crowds. This will also give you more time to explore the nearby attractions on the west bank of Luxor.

Purchase Tickets in Advance: If you plan to visit the tomb of Nefertari, it's recommended to purchase tickets in advance, as access is limited and highly sought after.

Wear Comfortable Clothing: The tombs can be hot and stuffy, especially in summer, so lightweight, breathable clothing is advisable. A hat and sunscreen are also essential for the walk between tombs.

Stay Hydrated: Bring plenty of water, as the desert heat can be intense, even in the cooler months. There are limited facilities within the valley, so it's best to come prepared.

Hire a Guide: A knowledgeable guide can greatly enhance your visit by providing context and insights into the history, art, and significance of the tombs. Guides can be arranged through hotels or tour operators in Luxor.

7. Medinet Habu (Mortuary Temple of Ramesses III)

Medinet Habu, also known as the Mortuary Temple of Ramesses III, is one of the best-preserved and most significant temples in Egypt. Located on the west bank of the Nile River near Luxor, this sprawling complex served as both a mortuary temple for Pharaoh Ramesses III and a center of economic and religious life during the New Kingdom. The temple is famous for its massive walls, intricate reliefs, and historical inscriptions that provide invaluable insights into the reign of Ramesses III and the events of the period.

History

Construction: Medinet Habu was built during the 20th Dynasty, around 1186–1155 BCE, under the reign of Pharaoh Ramesses III. The temple was constructed to honor the pharaoh after his death, and it was dedicated to the god Amun, the king of the gods in ancient Egyptian religion.

Purpose: In addition to serving as a place of worship, the temple was also a royal palace and administrative center. It played a crucial role in the political and economic life of the Theban region, housing vast storehouses and workshops, and serving as a hub for religious and civic activities.

Significance: The temple is particularly notable for its detailed reliefs depicting the military victories of Ramesses III, including his battles against the Sea Peoples, a confederation of naval raiders who threatened Egypt during his reign. These reliefs are among the most detailed and well-preserved records of ancient Egyptian military history.

Location

Address: West Bank, Luxor, Egypt.

Coordinates: 25.7294° N latitude, 32.6042° E longitude.

Accessibility: Medinet Habu is located near other major attractions on the west bank of Luxor, such as the Valley of the Kings and Hatshepsut's Mortuary Temple. It is easily accessible by car, taxi, or as part of a guided tour.

Opening and Closing Hours

Hours of Operation:

Summer (May to September): 6:00 AM to 5:00 PM.

Winter (October to April): 6:00 AM to 4:00 PM.

Best Time to Visit: Early morning or late afternoon visits are recommended to avoid the heat and crowds. The temple's large open courtyards can be particularly hot during midday.

Top Things to Do

Explore the Hypostyle Hall: The Hypostyle Hall at Medinet Habu is a magnificent space filled with massive columns adorned with detailed carvings and hieroglyphs. The hall was a place of worship and ceremonies, and its grandeur reflects the importance of the temple in ancient times.

Admire the Reliefs: The temple walls are covered with some of the most detailed and vivid reliefs in all of Egypt. These carvings depict various aspects of Ramesses III's reign, including his military campaigns, religious rituals, and interactions with the gods. The scenes of battles against the Sea Peoples are particularly famous and provide a rare glimpse into the warfare of the period.

Visit the Royal Palace Area: Adjacent to the main temple is a smaller royal palace where Ramesses III would have resided during his visits to the temple. The palace area includes living quarters, reception rooms, and other administrative spaces, offering insights into the daily life of the pharaoh and his court.

Walk Through the First and Second Pylons: The entrance to the temple is marked by two massive pylons, each adorned with detailed reliefs and inscriptions. The first pylon features scenes of Ramesses III smiting his enemies, while the second pylon leads into the inner sanctuaries of the temple, where the most sacred rituals were performed.

Explore the Surrounding Complex: Medinet Habu is part of a larger complex that includes smaller chapels, shrines, and storehouses. Take time to explore these areas to get a full sense of the temple's scale and its role in the religious and economic life of ancient Thebes.

Practical Information

Tickets: Entrance to Medinet Habu requires a general admission ticket, which can be purchased at the site. Combination tickets are also available for those planning to visit other attractions in the area, such as the Valley of the Kings.

Facilities: The site has basic visitor amenities, including restrooms and a small café. There are also vendors near the entrance selling souvenirs, though prices may be high.

Photography: Photography is allowed throughout the temple, but the use of tripods may require special permission. The morning light is ideal for capturing the temple's intricate reliefs and monumental architecture.

Tips for Visiting

Hire a Guide: A knowledgeable guide can greatly enhance your visit by providing context and explanations of the complex reliefs and inscriptions. Guides are available at the site or can be arranged through your hotel or tour operator.

Wear Comfortable Shoes: The temple complex is large, and exploring it fully requires a fair amount of walking. Comfortable shoes are essential for navigating the uneven terrain.

Bring Water: The site can get very hot, especially in the summer months, so it's important to stay hydrated. Bring plenty of water, and consider wearing a hat and sunscreen to protect yourself from the sun.

Take Your Time: Medinet Habu is a vast and richly detailed site, so don't rush your visit. Take time to explore the various parts of the complex, from the grand courtyards to the more intimate chapels and sanctuaries.

8. Luxor Museum

Luxor Museum, located on the east bank of the Nile River in Luxor, is one of Egypt's finest museums, showcasing a carefully curated collection of artifacts from the ancient city of Thebes (modern-day Luxor) and the surrounding areas. Unlike the more crowded Egyptian Museum in Cairo, Luxor Museum offers a more intimate and focused experience, with exhibits that highlight the art, culture, and history of ancient Egypt, particularly from the New Kingdom period.

History

Establishment: Luxor Museum was opened in 1975, designed by architect Mahmoud El-Hakim with the assistance of the Egyptian Antiquities Organization. The museum was intended to house and display the numerous artifacts found in and around Luxor, offering visitors an opportunity to see these treasures in a more accessible and well-presented environment.

Collection: The museum's collection has grown over the years, with significant additions from various archaeological discoveries, including finds from the nearby temples of Karnak and Luxor. Notable among these are the statues from the cachette of Karnak, discovered in the 1980s, and a remarkable selection of items from the tomb of Tutankhamun.

Location

Address: Corniche El-Nil Street, Luxor, Egypt.

Coordinates: 25.7044° N latitude, 32.6396° E longitude.

Accessibility: Luxor Museum is centrally located along the Nile Corniche, making it easily accessible by foot, taxi, or carriage from most parts of the city. It is a short distance from major sites like Luxor Temple and Karnak Temple.

Opening and Closing Hours

Hours of Operation:

Summer (April to September): 9:00 AM to 4:00 PM and 5:00 PM to 9:00 PM.

Winter (October to March): 9:00 AM to 4:00 PM and 5:00 PM to 8:00 PM.

Best Time to Visit: Late afternoon or early evening visits are ideal for avoiding the midday heat and large tour groups, allowing for a quieter and more contemplative experience.

Top Things to Do

Explore the Permanent Collection: The museum's permanent collection includes an array of sculptures, jewelry, pottery, and funerary items that span several millennia of Egyptian history. Key highlights include the beautifully preserved statues of Amenhotep III and the stunning figure of the goddess Hathor.

Admire the Royal Mummies: The museum houses two royal mummies, believed to be those of Ahmose I and Ramses I. These mummies provide a fascinating glimpse into the burial practices and physical characteristics of Egypt's ancient rulers.

See the Tutankhamun Artifacts: Luxor Museum features a collection of artifacts from the tomb of Tutankhamun, including items that are not on display in the Cairo museum. Among these are weapons, jewelry, and a stunning collection of funerary items that highlight the craftsmanship and wealth of the young pharaoh's era.

View the Cachette of Karnak Statues: One of the most impressive exhibits in the museum is the collection of statues from the cachette of Karnak, a hidden chamber discovered in the Karnak Temple complex. These statues, which include representations of gods, pharaohs, and priests, are remarkable for their detail and state of preservation.

Visit the Open-Air Terrace: The museum's open-air terrace offers visitors a chance to view larger artifacts, including sphinxes, statues, and stelae, set against the backdrop of the Nile River. This area provides a peaceful setting to reflect on the grandeur of ancient Egypt.

Practical Information

Tickets: Tickets can be purchased at the entrance, with discounts available for students and large groups. It's advisable to carry some cash, as not all ticket counters accept credit cards.

Facilities: The museum offers basic amenities such as restrooms, a small gift shop, and a café. The museum is air-conditioned, providing a comfortable environment even during the hot summer months.

Photography: Photography is generally allowed in the museum, though the use of flash is prohibited to protect the delicate artifacts. Be mindful of signs that indicate restricted areas for photography.

Tips for Visiting

Plan Your Visit: Given the museum's relatively small size compared to other Egyptian museums, it's possible to explore Luxor Museum in 1-2 hours. However, take your time to appreciate the details and craftsmanship of the artifacts on display.

Hire a Guide: While the exhibits are well-labeled in both Arabic and English, a knowledgeable guide can provide deeper insights into the history and significance of the items, enriching your understanding of ancient Egyptian culture.

Combine with Nearby Attractions: Luxor Museum is close to other major attractions such as Luxor Temple and the Karnak Temple Complex. Consider visiting these sites on the same day for a comprehensive exploration of Luxor's ancient heritage.

Check for Temporary Exhibitions: The museum occasionally hosts temporary exhibitions, which showcase rare artifacts or focus on specific themes in Egyptian history. Check ahead of your visit to see if any special exhibitions are on display.

9. Ramesseum (Mortuary Temple of Ramesses II)

The Ramesseum, also known as the Mortuary Temple of Ramesses II, is an ancient Egyptian temple complex located on the west bank of the Nile River near Luxor. Built during the reign of Ramesses II (1279-1213 BCE), one of Egypt's most powerful and celebrated pharaohs, the Ramesseum is renowned for its grand scale and impressive architectural features. The temple was dedicated to the god Amun and was designed to honor Ramesses II after his death, serving as both a place of worship and a monumental tribute to his legacy.

History

Construction: The Ramesseum was constructed during the 19th Dynasty of the New Kingdom, beginning around 1275 BCE. The temple complex was built as a grand mortuary temple for Ramesses II, who was also known as Ramesses the Great. The temple was designed to be one of the largest and most impressive of its time, reflecting the pharaoh's power and divine status.

Purpose: The Ramesseum served multiple purposes. It was a place of worship dedicated to the god Amun, a center of royal and ceremonial activities, and a memorial to Ramesses II's reign. The temple complex included a large hypostyle hall, a sanctuary, and numerous courtyards and pylons, all adorned with detailed inscriptions and reliefs depicting the pharaoh's achievements and divine favor.

Decline: Like many ancient Egyptian temples, the Ramesseum fell into disrepair over the centuries due to natural erosion, earthquakes, and the repurposing of its materials. Despite this, the ruins remain an impressive testament to the grandeur of Ramesses II and the architectural prowess of ancient Egypt.

Location

Address: West Bank, Luxor, Egypt.

Coordinates: 25.7215° N latitude, 32.6019° E longitude.

Accessibility: The Ramesseum is located near other major attractions on the west bank of Luxor, such as the Valley of the Kings and the Temple of Hatshepsut. It is easily accessible by car, taxi, or as part of a guided tour.

Opening and Closing Hours

Hours of Operation:

Summer (April to September): 6:00 AM to 5:00 PM.

Winter (October to March): 6:00 AM to 4:00 PM.

Best Time to Visit: Early morning or late afternoon visits are ideal to avoid the heat and crowds. The cooler hours of the day also provide better lighting for viewing and photographing the site.

Top Things to Do

Explore the Colossal Statues: The Ramesseum is famous for its massive statues of Ramesses II, including a colossal seated statue that originally stood 17 meters (56 feet) tall. Although most of the statue is now in ruins, its fragments still convey the grandeur and scale of the original monument.

Admire the Wall Reliefs: The temple walls are covered with intricate reliefs depicting scenes of Ramesses II's military campaigns, religious rituals, and divine interactions. Notable scenes include the depiction of the Battle of Kadesh, a significant event in Ramesses II's reign.

Visit the Hypostyle Hall: The hypostyle hall of the Ramesseum features a row of large columns adorned with detailed carvings. The hall was used for ceremonial purposes and is one of the most impressive parts of the temple complex.

See the Remains of the Mortuary Temple: Explore the remains of the temple's various components, including the courtyards, pylons, and sanctuaries. Despite the damage over time, the site offers valuable insights into the layout and grandeur of New Kingdom temples.

Enjoy the Scenic Views: The Ramesseum's elevated position provides stunning views of the surrounding landscape, including the nearby temples and the Nile River. Take time to appreciate the site's setting and the scale of the ancient construction.

Practical Information

Tickets: Admission to the Ramesseum requires a general entrance ticket, which can be purchased on-site. Combination tickets are available for those planning to visit multiple sites on the west bank.

Facilities: The site has basic amenities, including restrooms and a small area for refreshments. There are also vendors selling souvenirs near the entrance.

Photography: Photography is allowed at the site, though the use of tripods may require special permission. The early morning or late afternoon light is ideal for capturing the temple's details and grandeur.

Tips for Visiting

Hire a Guide: A knowledgeable guide can enhance your visit by providing context and insights into the temple's history and significance. Guides are available at the site or can be arranged through local tour operators.

Wear Comfortable Shoes: The Ramesseum is a large site with uneven terrain, so comfortable walking shoes are essential. Prepare for a fair amount of walking and exploration.

Stay Hydrated: Luxor can be very hot, especially in the summer months, so bring plenty of water and sun protection, including a hat and sunscreen.

Combine with Other Sites: The Ramesseum is located near several other important archaeological sites. Consider visiting other nearby temples and tombs, such as the Valley of the Kings or Hatshepsut's Mortuary Temple, to make the most of your time on the west bank.

Respect the Site: As with all historical sites, it's important to respect the preservation efforts by not touching or climbing on the ruins and following all posted guidelines.

10. Deir el-Medina

Deir el-Medina, located on the west bank of the Nile near Luxor, is an ancient village that housed the artisans and workers who were responsible for the construction and decoration of royal tombs in the Valley of the Kings and the Valley of the Queens during the New Kingdom period (circa 1550-1070 BCE). The village is renowned for its well-preserved remains and provides a unique insight into the daily lives and social structures of the craftsmen who worked on Egypt's most famous burial sites.

History

Establishment: Deir el-Medina was established during the 18th Dynasty and continued to be inhabited throughout the 19th and 20th Dynasties. The village was specifically built to accommodate the skilled artisans, painters, and laborers who worked on the royal tombs in the nearby valleys.

Purpose: The village served as a self-sufficient community, providing housing, administrative facilities, and amenities for the workers and their families. It was strategically located close to the tomb sites to allow for efficient work and supervision.

Decline: Over time, Deir el-Medina faced challenges such as economic difficulties, changes in administration, and eventual neglect. By the end of the New Kingdom, the village was abandoned, and its ruins were later covered by sand.

Location

Address: West Bank, Luxor, Egypt.

Coordinates: 25.7287° N latitude, 32.6056° E longitude.

Accessibility: Deir el-Medina is located near other key archaeological sites on the west bank of Luxor, such as the Valley of the Kings and the Temple of Hatshepsut. It is accessible by car, taxi, or as part of a guided tour.

Opening and Closing Hours

Hours of Operation:

Summer (April to September): 6:00 AM to 5:00 PM.

Winter (October to March): 6:00 AM to 4:00 PM.

Best Time to Visit: Early morning or late afternoon visits are recommended to avoid the heat and crowds. The cooler times of the day also provide better lighting for viewing and photographing the site.

Top Things to Do

Explore the Village Layout: Deir el-Medina is organized into a grid pattern, with residential quarters, administrative buildings, and communal spaces. Walking through the remains of the village, you can observe the layout of the homes, which were typically modest but functional, reflecting the daily lives of the craftsmen.

Visit the Workers' Houses: The workers' houses, though now in ruins, provide a glimpse into the domestic life of the artisans. The houses were equipped with essential amenities and often featured simple yet effective designs for everyday living.

See the Tomb of the Village Leaders: Among the significant tombs in the area are those of the village's leaders and notable figures, such as the tomb of Sennedjem. These tombs, while not as grand as those in the Valley of the Kings, are richly decorated and provide insights into the workers' social status and their contributions to the royal tombs.

Admire the Wall Paintings: Some of the tombs in Deir el-Medina feature well-preserved wall paintings depicting scenes from daily life, religious rituals, and funerary practices. These paintings offer valuable information about the beliefs and activities of the village inhabitants.

Explore the Temple of Hathor: The village is also home to a small temple dedicated to the goddess Hathor. The temple contains inscriptions and reliefs that highlight the religious practices and offerings made by the workers and their families.

Practical Information

Tickets: Entrance to Deir el-Medina requires a general admission ticket, which can be purchased on-site. Combination tickets for nearby sites may also be available.

Facilities: The site has basic visitor amenities, including restrooms. There are limited facilities for food and drinks, so it's advisable to bring refreshments with you.

Photography: Photography is generally allowed at Deir el-Medina, but be mindful of any restrictions in specific areas. The use of tripods may require special permission.

Tips for Visiting

Hire a Guide: A knowledgeable guide can provide valuable context and insights into the history and significance of Deir el-Medina. Guides are available at the site or can be arranged through local tour operators.

Wear Comfortable Shoes: The site involves considerable walking on uneven terrain, so comfortable and sturdy footwear is essential.

Bring Water and Sun Protection: Luxor's climate can be very hot, especially during the summer months. Bring plenty of water, wear a hat, and apply sunscreen to protect yourself from the sun.

Combine with Nearby Attractions: Deir el-Medina is close to other major sites such as the Valley of the Kings and the Temple of Hatshepsut. Consider visiting these sites on the same day for a comprehensive exploration of Luxor's west bank.

Respect the Site: As with all historical sites, it's important to respect the preservation efforts by not touching or climbing on the ruins and following all posted guidelines.

Accommodation Options

Luxury Hotel

Luxury hotels in Luxor offer high-end accommodations with exceptional service, stunning views of ancient monuments, and world-class amenities. Perfect for travelers seeking elegance and relaxation, these hotels provide a sophisticated base to explore Luxor's rich history and enjoy unparalleled comfort.

Top 5 Luxury Hotel

1. Sofitel Winter Palace Luxor

Sofitel Winter Palace Luxor is a prestigious luxury hotel located in the heart of Luxor, Egypt. Renowned for its elegance and historic charm, the hotel offers an opulent stay with a blend of classic and contemporary comforts. It is a prominent choice for travelers seeking a high-end experience while exploring Luxor's ancient wonders.

Location (Address & Proximity)

Address: Corniche El Nile, Luxor 85111, Egypt

Proximity:

Luxor Temple: Just a short walk from the hotel, allowing easy access to this iconic ancient site.

Karnak Temple: Approximately a 10-minute drive away, a must-visit historical landmark.

Valley of the Kings: About a 30-minute drive, offering convenient access to one of Egypt's most famous archaeological sites.

Luxor International Airport: Around a 20-minute drive, providing easy transportation to and from the hotel.

Highlights

Historical Significance: The hotel, originally built in 1886, features classic architecture and has hosted numerous dignitaries and celebrities over the years.

Elegant Design: Combines traditional luxury with modern amenities, offering a sophisticated ambiance.

River Views: Many rooms and public areas offer stunning views of the Nile River.

Spa and Wellness

Spa:

Le Spa: Offers a range of treatments and therapies designed to rejuvenate and relax guests. Services include massages, facials, and body treatments, all provided in a tranquil setting.

Fitness Center: Equipped with modern exercise machines and facilities for guests to maintain their fitness routines during their stay.

Bars

On-Site Bars:

The Lounge: A sophisticated space for afternoon tea or evening cocktails, offering elegant décor and Nile views.

Bar du Soleil: Located by the pool, this bar serves a selection of refreshing drinks and light snacks, ideal for relaxation in a sunny setting.

Events and Conferences

Meeting and Event Facilities:

Grand Ballroom: A historic and luxurious space suitable for large events, conferences, and weddings. It is equipped with modern audiovisual technology and elegant décor.

Meeting Rooms: Offers several smaller meeting rooms for business meetings or intimate gatherings.

Basic Facilities and Amenities

Dining:

La Corniche: The hotel's main restaurant, offering a variety of international and Egyptian dishes in an elegant setting with views of the Nile.

Garden Restaurant: Provides outdoor dining options in a beautifully landscaped garden, ideal for breakfast or casual meals.

Business Center: Offers a range of services including internet access, printing, and copying for business travelers.

Concierge Services: Assists with local tours, transportation, and other guest needs to enhance the overall experience.

Opening and Closing Hours

Check-in: Typically from 3:00 PM

Check-out: By 12:00 PM

Dining:

La Corniche: Open for breakfast, lunch, and dinner, with varying hours.

Bar du Soleil: Usually open during daytime and early evening hours.

Spa and Fitness Center: Generally open from early morning until evening, with specific hours varying by day.

Price

Room Rates: Prices at Sofitel Winter Palace Luxor typically range from $200 to $500 per night, depending on the season, room type, and booking conditions. Rates reflect the hotel's luxury status and premium offerings.

Pros

Historic Charm: Offers a unique blend of historical elegance and modern luxury.

Prime Location: Convenient access to major historical sites and attractions in Luxor.

Elegant Amenities: Provides high-quality dining, spa, and event facilities.

Cons

High Cost: As a luxury hotel, it may be expensive for budget-conscious travelers.

Tourist Focused: May be more oriented towards tourists, potentially lacking in local authenticity compared to smaller boutique accommodations.

Local Tips

Explore Ancient Sites: Take advantage of the hotel's location to visit Luxor's temples and tombs, and consider guided tours for deeper insights.

Enjoy Nile Views: Request a room with a Nile view to enhance your experience with stunning river vistas.

Local Dining: While the hotel offers excellent dining options, exploring local restaurants in Luxor can provide a more authentic taste of Egyptian cuisine.

Transportation: Utilize hotel transportation services

for hassle-free access to major attractions and the airport.

2. Hilton Luxor Resort & Spa

Hilton Luxor Resort & Spa is a premier luxury hotel situated on the banks of the Nile River in Luxor, Egypt. Known for its elegant design, comprehensive facilities, and stunning river views, the resort offers an upscale experience with a focus on relaxation and high-end service. It caters to travelers seeking both comfort and indulgence while exploring Luxor's ancient wonders.

Location (Address & Proximity)

Address: Khaled Ibn El Walid Street, Luxor 85111, Egypt

Proximity:

Luxor Temple: Approximately a 10-minute drive from the hotel, offering convenient access to one of Luxor's key attractions.

Karnak Temple: About a 15-minute drive away, a major historical site worth visiting.

Valley of the Kings: Approximately a 30-minute drive, providing easy access to this renowned archaeological site.

Luxor International Airport: Around a 20-minute drive, making the hotel accessible for travelers arriving by air.

Highlights

Nile River Views: Offers breathtaking views of the Nile River, enhancing the overall experience with picturesque scenery.

Luxurious Amenities: Combines high-end facilities with a focus on relaxation and well-being.

Comprehensive Facilities: Includes a full-service spa, multiple dining options, and extensive recreational amenities.

Spa and Wellness

Spa:

Eforea Spa: Provides a range of treatments and therapies designed to rejuvenate and relax guests. Services include massages, facials, body treatments, and wellness therapies in a serene environment.

Fitness Center: Equipped with modern exercise machines and facilities, allowing guests to maintain their fitness routines during their stay.

Swimming Pools: Features multiple outdoor pools, including a large main pool with panoramic river views, as well as a heated pool and a dedicated kids' pool.

Bars

On-Site Bars:

The Lounge: A stylish venue for enjoying light snacks, afternoon tea, or evening cocktails with views of the Nile River.

Nile Terrace: Offers outdoor dining and a selection of drinks and light meals in a relaxed setting with stunning river views.

The Pool Bar: Located by the pool, providing a variety of refreshing beverages and light snacks.

Events and Conferences

Meeting and Event Facilities:

Ballroom: A grand and versatile space suitable for large events, conferences, and weddings. Equipped with modern audiovisual technology and elegant décor.

Meeting Rooms: Offers several smaller meeting rooms for business meetings, workshops, and intimate gatherings.

Basic Facilities and Amenities

Dining:

Al-Sahaby Lane Restaurant: Serves a variety of international and Egyptian cuisine in a sophisticated setting with views of the Nile.

The Open Air Restaurant: Provides casual dining with a focus on fresh, local ingredients in a relaxed outdoor atmosphere.

Business Center: Offers a range of services including internet access, printing, and copying for business travelers.

Concierge Services: Staff can assist with local tours, transportation arrangements, and general inquiries to enhance the guest experience.

Opening and Closing Hours

Check-in: Typically from 3:00 PM

Check-out: By 12:00 PM

Dining:

Al-Sahaby Lane Restaurant: Open for breakfast, lunch, and dinner with varying hours.

Nile Terrace: Usually open for lunch and dinner.

The Lounge and Pool Bar: Generally open throughout the day, with specific hours varying.

Price

Room Rates: Prices at Hilton Luxor Resort & Spa typically range from $150 to $400 per night, depending on the season, room type, and booking conditions. Rates reflect the luxury nature of the resort and its premium offerings.

Pros

Stunning Location: Provides exceptional Nile River views and a serene setting for relaxation.

Comprehensive Facilities: Offers a wide range of amenities including a luxury spa, multiple dining options, and recreational facilities.

Elegant Design: Combines modern luxury with traditional Egyptian elements for a refined ambiance.

Cons

High Cost: As a luxury resort, it may be expensive for budget-conscious travelers.

Tourist Focused: May cater more towards tourists, which could impact the level of local authenticity compared to smaller, boutique accommodations.

Local Tips

Explore Ancient Sites: Utilize the hotel's proximity to major attractions like Luxor Temple and Karnak Temple for convenient access to historical sites.

Enjoy Nile Views: Request a room with a Nile view to enhance your stay with beautiful river vistas.

Local Dining: While the hotel offers excellent dining options, exploring local restaurants in Luxor can provide a more authentic culinary experience.

Public Transportation: Utilize hotel transportation services or local taxis for convenient access to various attractions and the airport.

3. **Sonesta St. George Hotel Luxor**

Sonesta St. George Hotel Luxor is a luxurious hotel situated on the banks of the Nile River, offering a blend of sophisticated comfort and traditional Egyptian hospitality. Known for its elegant design and high-quality service, the hotel provides an upscale experience ideal for travelers seeking both relaxation and exploration in Luxor.

Location (Address & Proximity)

Address: Corniche El Nile, Luxor 85111, Egypt

Proximity:

Luxor Temple: Just a short distance from the hotel, allowing easy access to this iconic historical site.

Karnak Temple: Approximately a 10-minute drive away, a must-visit archaeological landmark.

Valley of the Kings: About a 30-minute drive, providing convenient access to this significant archaeological site.

Luxor International Airport: Roughly a 20-minute drive, making the hotel accessible for travelers arriving by air.

Highlights

Nile River Views: Many rooms and public areas offer stunning views of the Nile, enhancing the overall guest experience with picturesque scenery.

Luxurious Design: Combines modern luxury with traditional Egyptian decor, creating a refined and elegant atmosphere.

Comprehensive Facilities: Includes a range of amenities such as dining options, a spa, and recreational facilities.

Spa and Wellness

Spa:

Health Club & Spa: Offers a range of wellness treatments and therapies designed to rejuvenate and relax guests. Services include massages, facials, and body treatments in a tranquil setting.

Fitness Center: Equipped with modern exercise equipment, allowing guests to maintain their fitness routines while traveling.

Swimming Pool: Features a large outdoor pool with Nile views, ideal for relaxation and enjoying the pleasant climate.

Bars

On-Site Bars:

The Lounge: A stylish venue for afternoon tea or evening drinks, offering a relaxing atmosphere and views of the Nile River.

The Pool Bar: Located by the pool, this bar serves a selection of refreshing beverages and light snacks, perfect for unwinding during the day.

Events and Conferences

Meeting and Event Facilities:

Grand Ballroom: A spacious and elegant venue suitable for large events, conferences, and weddings. Equipped with modern audiovisual technology and sophisticated décor.

Meeting Rooms: Offers several smaller meeting rooms for business meetings, workshops, and intimate gatherings.

Basic Facilities and Amenities

Dining:

The Lounge Restaurant: Provides a variety of international and Egyptian dishes in an elegant setting with views of the Nile.

The Poolside Restaurant: Offers casual dining with a focus on fresh, local ingredients and a relaxed atmosphere.

Business Center: Available for guests needing internet access, printing, copying, and other business services.

Concierge Services: Staff can assist with local tours, transportation arrangements, and general inquiries to enhance the guest experience.

Opening and Closing Hours

Check-in: Typically from 3:00 PM

Check-out: By 12:00 PM

Dining:

The Lounge Restaurant: Open for breakfast, lunch, and dinner, with varying hours.

The Poolside Restaurant: Generally open during daytime and early evening.

The Lounge and Pool Bar: Open throughout the day, with specific hours varying.

Price

Room Rates: Rates at Sonesta St. George Hotel Luxor generally range from $150 to $350 per night, depending on the season, room type, and booking conditions. Prices reflect the luxury status of the hotel and its premium offerings.

Pros

Prime Location: Offers excellent access to major Luxor attractions and beautiful Nile River views.

Elegant Design: Features a sophisticated blend of modern luxury and traditional decor.

Extensive Amenities: Includes a range of facilities such as a spa, dining options, and meeting rooms.

Cons

High Cost: As a luxury hotel, it may be expensive for budget-conscious travelers.

Tourist-Oriented: May cater more towards tourists, potentially affecting the level of local authenticity compared to boutique accommodations.

Local Tips

Explore Nearby Attractions: Take advantage of the hotel's location to visit Luxor Temple, Karnak Temple, and other historical sites with ease.

Request Nile Views: To enhance your stay, request a room with a view of the Nile River for beautiful scenery.

Local Dining: While the hotel offers excellent dining options, consider exploring local restaurants in Luxor for a more authentic taste of Egyptian cuisine.

Transportation: Utilize the hotel's transportati

4. Steigenberger Nile Palace

Steigenberger Nile Palace is a luxurious hotel located along the Nile River in Luxor, Egypt. Known for its refined elegance and high-end amenities, this hotel provides a sophisticated retreat for travelers seeking comfort and style while exploring the rich history of Luxor. The property offers stunning views of the Nile and excellent service, making it a top choice for discerning guests.

Location (Address & Proximity)

Address: Khaled Ibn El Walid Street, Luxor 85111, Egypt

Proximity:

Luxor Temple: Approximately a 5-minute drive, offering convenient access to this iconic ancient site.

Karnak Temple: About a 10-minute drive, providing easy access to one of Egypt's most famous archaeological sites.

Valley of the Kings: Around a 30-minute drive, making it accessible for guests interested in visiting this historic location.

Luxor International Airport: Approximately a 20-minute drive from the hotel, facilitating convenient arrivals and departures.

Highlights

Stunning Nile Views: Many rooms and public areas offer breathtaking views of the Nile River, enhancing the overall guest experience.

Elegant Design: Combines modern luxury with classic touches to create a sophisticated ambiance.

Comprehensive Amenities: Includes a range of facilities such as dining options, a spa, and recreational areas.

Spa and Wellness

Spa:

Nile Palace Spa: Offers a variety of treatments and therapies designed to promote relaxation and rejuvenation. Services include massages, facials, and body treatments in a tranquil environment.

Fitness Center: Equipped with modern exercise equipment, allowing guests to maintain their fitness routines while traveling.

Swimming Pools: Features multiple outdoor pools, including a large main pool with Nile views, a heated pool, and a separate kids' pool.

Bars

On-Site Bars:

The Lounge Bar: A sophisticated venue for enjoying light snacks, afternoon tea, or evening cocktails, with views of the Nile River.

The Pool Bar: Located by the pool, offering a range of refreshing beverages and light snacks in a relaxed, sunny setting.

Events and Conferences

Meeting and Event Facilities:

Grand Ballroom: A spacious and elegant venue suitable for large events, conferences, and weddings. It is equipped with modern audiovisual technology and stylish décor.

Meeting Rooms: Offers several smaller meeting rooms for business meetings, workshops, and intimate gatherings.

Basic Facilities and Amenities

Dining:

Nile Palace Restaurant: Offers a range of international and Egyptian cuisine in an elegant setting with views of the Nile River.

The Garden Restaurant: Provides outdoor dining with a focus on fresh, local ingredients and a relaxed atmosphere.

Business Center: Available for guests needing internet access, printing, copying, and other business services.

Concierge Services: Staff can assist with local tours, transportation arrangements, and general inquiries to enhance the guest experience.

Opening and Closing Hours

Check-in: Typically from 3:00 PM

Check-out: By 12:00 PM

Dining:

Nile Palace Restaurant: Open for breakfast, lunch, and dinner with varying hours.

The Garden Restaurant: Generally open during daytime and early evening.

The Lounge and Pool Bar: Open throughout the day, with specific hours varying.

Price

Room Rates: Rates at Steigenberger Nile Palace typically range from $150 to $400 per night, depending on the season, room type, and booking conditions. Prices reflect the luxury status of the hotel and its premium amenities.

Pros

Prime Location: Offers excellent access to major Luxor attractions and beautiful Nile River views.

Elegant Design: Features a sophisticated blend of modern luxury and classic décor.

Extensive Amenities: Includes a range of facilities such as a luxury spa, multiple dining options, and meeting rooms.

Cons

High Cost: As a luxury hotel, it may be expensive for budget-conscious travelers.

Tourist-Focused: May cater more towards tourists, potentially impacting the level of local authenticity compared to boutique accommodations.

Local Tips

Explore Major Attractions: Use the hotel's proximity to Luxor Temple, Karnak Temple, and other historical sites for convenient sightseeing.

Request Nile Views: To enhance your stay, request a room with a Nile view for beautiful river vistas.

Local Dining: While the hotel offers excellent dining options, exploring local restaurants in Luxor can provide a more authentic taste of Egyptian cuisine.

Transportation: Utilize the hotel's transportation services or local taxis for easy travel around the city and to major attractions.

5. Jolie Ville Kings Island Luxor

Jolie Ville Kings Island Luxor is a luxury resort situated on a private island in the Nile River, offering a tranquil and picturesque retreat in Luxor, Egypt. Known for its expansive grounds, elegant design, and comprehensive facilities, the resort provides a serene environment ideal for relaxation and exploration of the nearby historical sites.

Location (Address & Proximity)

Address: Kings Island, Luxor 85111, Egypt

Proximity:

Luxor Temple: Approximately a 10-minute drive, offering convenient access to this iconic ancient site.

Karnak Temple: About a 15-minute drive away, providing easy access to one of Egypt's most famous archaeological sites.

Valley of the Kings: Roughly a 30-minute drive, making it accessible for guests interested in visiting this significant archaeological location.

Luxor International Airport: Around a 20-minute drive, facilitating convenient arrivals and departures.

Highlights

Private Island Location: Offers a unique setting on a private island, providing a tranquil and exclusive atmosphere.

Spacious Grounds: Features extensive gardens and outdoor areas, enhancing the overall guest experience with lush landscapes and scenic views.

Elegant Design: Combines modern luxury with traditional Egyptian decor to create a refined and welcoming ambiance.

Spa and Wellness

Spa:

Jolie Ville Spa: Provides a range of treatments and therapies designed to rejuvenate and relax guests. Services include massages, facials, and body treatments in a serene setting.

Fitness Center: Equipped with modern exercise machines and facilities, allowing guests to maintain their fitness routines while traveling.

Swimming Pools: Includes a large outdoor pool with panoramic views of the Nile and surrounding landscapes, as well as a separate kids' pool.

Bars

On-Site Bars:

The Lounge Bar: A stylish venue for enjoying light snacks, afternoon tea, or evening cocktails, with views of the Nile and the resort's gardens.

Poolside Bar: Located by the main pool, this bar serves a variety of refreshing beverages and light snacks in a relaxed, sunny setting.

Events and Conferences

Meeting and Event Facilities:

Grand Ballroom: A spacious and elegant venue suitable for large events, conferences, and weddings. It is equipped with modern audiovisual technology and sophisticated décor.

Meeting Rooms: Offers several smaller meeting rooms for business meetings, workshops, and intimate gatherings.

Basic Facilities and Amenities

Dining:

La Palmeraie Restaurant: Offers a variety of international and Egyptian cuisine in an elegant setting with views of the Nile River and gardens.

The Terrace: Provides outdoor dining with a focus on fresh, local ingredients and a relaxed atmosphere.

Business Center: Available for guests needing internet access, printing, copying, and other business services.

Concierge Services: Staff can assist with local tours, transportation arrangements, and general inquiries to enhance the guest experience.

Opening and Closing Hours

Check-in: Typically from 3:00 PM

Check-out: By 12:00 PM

Dining:

La Palmeraie Restaurant: Open for breakfast, lunch, and dinner, with varying hours.

The Terrace: Generally open during daytime and early evening.

The Lounge and Poolside Bar: Open throughout the day, with specific hours varying.

Price

Room Rates: Rates at Jolie Ville Kings Island Luxor typically range from $150 to $350 per night, depending on the season, room type, and booking conditions. Prices reflect the luxury nature of the resort and its extensive amenities.

Pros

Private Island Location: Offers a unique and tranquil setting away from the city's hustle and bustle.

Spacious and Elegant: Provides expansive grounds and elegant design for a refined and relaxing stay.

Comprehensive Amenities: Includes a range of facilities such as a luxury spa, multiple dining options, and event spaces.

Cons

High Cost: As a luxury resort, it may be expensive for budget-conscious travelers.

Accessibility: The private island location may require additional transportation arrangements to access city attractions.

Local Tips

Explore Major Attractions: Use the resort's location to visit Luxor Temple, Karnak Temple, and other historical sites with ease.

Enjoy the Resort's Facilities: Take full advantage of the private island setting, including the pools, gardens, and spa.

Local Dining: While the resort offers excellent dining options, exploring local restaurants in Luxor can provide a more authentic taste of Egyptian cuisine.

Transportation: Utilize the resort's transportation services or local taxis for easy travel around the city and to major attractions.

Mid-Range Hotel

Mid-range hotels in Luxor offer a balance of comfort, convenience, and value. These hotels provide quality accommodations with essential amenities at a reasonable price, making them a great choice for travelers seeking comfort and affordability while exploring Luxor's historic attractions.

Top 5 Mid-Range Hotel

1. Iberotel Luxor

Iberotel Luxor is a well-regarded mid-range hotel situated in Luxor, Egypt. Known for its comfortable accommodations and convenient location, the hotel provides a balanced option for travelers seeking quality and affordability. With a focus on providing a pleasant stay with a range of amenities, it caters to both leisure and business guests.

Location (Address & Proximity)

Address: Khaled Ibn El Walid Street, Luxor 85111, Egypt

Proximity:

Luxor Temple: Just a short walk from the hotel, allowing easy access to this prominent historical site.

Karnak Temple: Approximately a 10-minute drive away, offering convenient access to one of Luxor's most significant archaeological sites.

Valley of the Kings: About a 30-minute drive, making it accessible for guests interested in visiting this famous archaeological location.

Luxor International Airport: Roughly a 20-minute drive, facilitating convenient arrivals and departures.

Highlights

Central Location: Provides easy access to major attractions, dining options, and local amenities in Luxor.

Comfortable Accommodations: Offers well-appointed rooms designed for comfort and convenience.

Affordable Luxury: Provides a good balance of quality and cost, making it an attractive option for mid-range travelers.

Spa and Wellness

Spa:

Health Club: Offers basic wellness facilities including a fitness center for guests looking to stay active during their stay.

Massage Services: Available on request, providing a range of relaxation and therapeutic treatments.

Swimming Pool: Features an outdoor pool for relaxation and recreation, with a pleasant setting for unwinding.

Bars

On-Site Bars:

Lobby Bar: A casual venue for enjoying drinks and light snacks in a relaxed atmosphere, ideal for unwinding after a day of sightseeing.

Events and Conferences

Meeting and Event Facilities:

Meeting Rooms: Offers several meeting rooms equipped for business meetings, small conferences, and workshops. Provides essential audiovisual equipment and seating arrangements.

Basic Facilities and Amenities

Dining:

Main Restaurant: Serves a variety of international and Egyptian dishes, providing both buffet and à la carte options for breakfast, lunch, and dinner.

Business Center: Includes facilities for internet access, printing, and copying to support business travelers.

Concierge Services: Staff can assist with local tours, transportation arrangements, and general inquiries to enhance the guest experience.

Opening and Closing Hours

Check-in: Typically from 2:00 PM

Check-out: By 12:00 PM

Dining:

Main Restaurant: Open for breakfast, lunch, and dinner with varying hours.

Lobby Bar: Open throughout the day for drinks and light snacks.

Price

Room Rates: Rates at Iberotel Luxor typically range from $80 to $150 per night, depending on the season, room type, and booking conditions. Prices reflect the mid-range status of the hotel and its offerings.

Pros

Prime Location: Offers convenient access to Luxor's key attractions and local amenities.

Comfortable Rooms: Provides well-maintained and comfortable accommodations for a pleasant stay.

Affordable Option: Balances quality with cost, making it a good choice for mid-range travelers.

Cons

Basic Amenities: May lack some of the high-end features and extensive facilities found in luxury hotels.

Tourist-Focused: May cater more towards tourists, potentially impacting the level of local authenticity compared to smaller, boutique hotels.

Local Tips

Explore Nearby Attractions: Take advantage of the hotel's central location to easily visit Luxor Temple and other nearby sites.

Local Dining: While the hotel offers dining options, consider exploring local restaurants in Luxor for a more authentic experience.

Transportation: Utilize local taxis or hotel transportation services for easy access to major attractions and the airport.

2. Mercure Luxor Karnak

Mercure Luxor Karnak is a mid-range hotel situated near the Karnak Temple in Luxor, Egypt. Known for its comfortable accommodations and convenient location, the hotel offers a blend of modern amenities and traditional hospitality. It caters to travelers seeking a pleasant and affordable stay with easy access to one of Egypt's most important archaeological sites.

Location (Address & Proximity)

Address: Karnak Temple, Luxor 85111, Egypt

Proximity:

Karnak Temple: Located very close to the hotel, allowing guests easy access to this major historical site.

Luxor Temple: Approximately a 10-minute drive from the hotel, providing convenient access to another key attraction in Luxor.

Valley of the Kings: About a 30-minute drive, making it accessible for guests interested in exploring this famous archaeological site.

Luxor International Airport: Around a 20-minute drive, facilitating convenient arrivals and departures.

Highlights

Proximity to Karnak Temple: Offers easy access to one of Egypt's most significant and extensive temple complexes.

Comfortable Accommodations: Provides well-furnished rooms designed for relaxation and convenience.

Reasonable Pricing: Offers a balance of quality and affordability, making it a good choice for mid-range travelers.

Spa and Wellness

Spa:

Health Club: Features a fitness center with modern equipment, allowing guests to maintain their fitness routines.

Massage Services: Available upon request, offering relaxation and therapeutic treatments.

Swimming Pool: Includes a large outdoor pool with a pleasant setting for relaxation and recreation.

Bars

On-Site Bars:

Poolside Bar: Located by the pool, this bar serves a variety of refreshing beverages and light snacks, ideal for relaxing after a swim.

Lobby Bar: A casual venue for enjoying drinks and light snacks in a comfortable setting.

Events and Conferences

Meeting and Event Facilities:

Meeting Rooms: Provides several meeting rooms suitable for business meetings, small conferences, and workshops. Equipped with essential audiovisual technology and flexible seating arrangements.

Basic Facilities and Amenities

Dining:

Main Restaurant: Offers a variety of international and local dishes, providing buffet and à la carte options for breakfast, lunch, and dinner.

Business Center: Includes facilities for internet access, printing, copying, and other business services.

Concierge Services: Staff can assist with local tours, transportation arrangements, and general inquiries to enhance the guest experience.

Opening and Closing Hours

Check-in: Typically from 3:00 PM

Check-out: By 12:00 PM

Dining:

Main Restaurant: Open for breakfast, lunch, and dinner with varying hours.

Poolside Bar: Generally open during the day for beverages and light snacks.

Lobby Bar: Open throughout the day for drinks and light refreshments.

Price

Room Rates: Rates at Mercure Luxor Karnak typically range from $100 to $200 per night, depending on the season, room type, and booking conditions. Prices reflect the mid-range nature of the hotel and its offerings.

Pros

Excellent Location: Provides easy access to Karnak Temple and other nearby attractions.

Comfortable Rooms: Offers well-maintained and comfortable accommodations.

Affordable Pricing: Balances quality and cost, making it a good option for mid-range travelers.

Cons

Basic Amenities: May lack some of the high-end features and extensive facilities found in luxury hotels.

Tourist-Centric: The focus on tourists might impact the level of local authenticity compared to smaller, boutique hotels.

Local Tips

Explore Karnak Temple: Take full advantage of the hotel's proximity to Karnak Temple by visiting early in the day to avoid crowds.

Discover Local Dining: While the hotel offers dining options, consider exploring local restaurants in Luxor for a more authentic culinary experience.

Transportation: Utilize local taxis or hotel transportation services for convenient access to other attractions and the airport.

3. Aracan Eatabe Luxor Hotel

Aracan Eatabe Luxor Hotel is a mid-range hotel located in Luxor, Egypt. It is known for offering comfortable accommodations and a range of amenities at a reasonable price. The hotel provides a convenient base for exploring Luxor's historical sites and enjoys a reputation for good service and hospitality.

Location (Address & Proximity)

Address: Khaled Ibn El Walid Street, Luxor 85111, Egypt

Proximity:

Luxor Temple: Approximately a 5-minute drive or a 20-minute walk, allowing easy access to this major historical site.

Karnak Temple: About a 10-minute drive, providing convenient access to one of Egypt's most famous archaeological sites.

Valley of the Kings: Roughly a 30-minute drive, making it accessible for those interested in visiting this significant location.

Luxor International Airport: Around a 20-minute drive, facilitating easy arrivals and departures.

Highlights

Central Location: Situated near key attractions, dining options, and local amenities in Luxor.

Comfortable Accommodations: Provides well-furnished rooms designed for relaxation and convenience.

Affordable Rates: Offers a good balance between quality and cost, making it an attractive choice for budget-conscious travelers.

Spa and Wellness

Spa and Wellness:

Basic Wellness Facilities: The hotel may offer basic fitness facilities, but it does not have an extensive spa. Guests can use local spas or wellness centers for more specialized treatments.

Swimming Pool: Features an outdoor pool, offering a space for relaxation and cooling off after exploring Luxor.

Bars

On-Site Bars:

Lobby Bar: A casual spot for enjoying drinks and light snacks in a relaxed environment.

Poolside Bar: Serves a selection of beverages and snacks, ideal for a casual experience by the pool.

Events and Conferences

Meeting and Event Facilities:

Meeting Rooms: Provides basic facilities for small meetings and events. Includes essential audiovisual equipment and seating arrangements suitable for business purposes.

Basic Facilities and Amenities

Dining:

Main Restaurant: Offers a range of international and local dishes, with options for buffet and à la carte dining for breakfast, lunch, and dinner.

Business Center: Available for internet access, printing, copying, and other business needs.

Concierge Services: Staff can assist with local tours, transportation arrangements, and other guest inquiries to enhance the overall experience.

Opening and Closing Hours

Check-in: Typically from 3:00 PM

Check-out: By 12:00 PM

Dining:

Main Restaurant: Open for breakfast, lunch, and dinner with varying hours.

Lobby and Poolside Bars: Generally open throughout the day for drinks and light snacks.

Price

Room Rates: Rates at Aracan Eatabe Luxor Hotel typically range from $70 to $120 per night, depending on the season, room type, and booking conditions. Prices reflect the mid-range status of the hotel and its offerings.

Pros

Central Location: Offers easy access to major Luxor attractions and local amenities.

Comfortable Rooms: Provides well-maintained and comfortable accommodations.

Affordability: Balances quality and cost, making it a good option for travelers on a mid-range budget.

Cons

Basic Amenities: May lack some of the higher-end features and extensive facilities found in more upscale hotels.

Tourist-Centric: The focus on tourists might affect the level of local authenticity compared to smaller, boutique accommodations.

Local Tips

Explore Nearby Attractions: Take advantage of the hotel's central location to easily visit Luxor Temple and other nearby sites.

Discover Local Cuisine: While the hotel offers dining options, exploring local restaurants in Luxor can provide a more authentic culinary experience.

Transportation: Utilize local taxis or hotel transportation services for convenient access to other attractions and the airport.

4. Nile Palace Hotel

Nile Palace Hotel is a distinguished luxury hotel located in Luxor, Egypt. Renowned for its opulent design and premium services, the hotel offers a high-end experience with stunning views of the Nile River. It combines modern amenities with classic Egyptian elegance, providing an ideal retreat for both leisure and business travelers.

Location (Address & Proximity)

Address: Khaled Ibn El Walid Street, Luxor 85111, Egypt

Proximity:

Luxor Temple: Approximately a 10-minute drive, offering easy access to this major historical site.

Karnak Temple: About a 15-minute drive away, providing convenient access to one of Egypt's most significant archaeological sites.

Valley of the Kings: Roughly a 30-minute drive, making it accessible for guests interested in visiting this famous location.

Luxor International Airport: Around a 20-minute drive, facilitating convenient arrivals and departures.

Highlights

Nile River Views: Many rooms and public areas offer spectacular views of the Nile, enhancing the guest experience.

Luxurious Design: Features elegant interiors that blend modern luxury with traditional Egyptian decor.

Premium Amenities: Includes a range of high-end facilities designed for comfort and relaxation.

Spa and Wellness

Spa:

Nile Palace Spa: Offers a variety of treatments and therapies including massages, facials, and body treatments. Designed to provide relaxation and rejuvenation in a tranquil setting.

Fitness Center: Equipped with modern exercise machines, allowing guests to maintain their fitness routines while traveling.

Swimming Pools: Includes a large outdoor pool with stunning Nile views, a heated pool, and a separate children's pool.

Bars

On-Site Bars:

The Lounge Bar: A sophisticated venue for enjoying light snacks, afternoon tea, or evening cocktails, with views of the Nile and the hotel's gardens.

The Pool Bar: Located by the pool, offering a variety of refreshing beverages and light snacks in a relaxed, sunny environment.

Events and Conferences

Meeting and Event Facilities:

Grand Ballroom: A spacious and elegant venue ideal for large events, conferences, and weddings. Equipped with modern audiovisual technology and stylish decor.

Meeting Rooms: Provides several smaller meeting rooms suitable for business meetings, workshops, and intimate gatherings.

Basic Facilities and Amenities

Dining:

The Main Restaurant: Offers a variety of international and Egyptian cuisine, providing both buffet and à la carte options for breakfast, lunch, and dinner.

Specialty Dining: Includes options for themed dinners and special events.

Business Center: Available for guests needing internet access, printing, copying, and other business services.

Concierge Services: Staff can assist with local tours, transportation arrangements, and general inquiries to enhance the guest experience.

Opening and Closing Hours

Check-in: Typically from 3:00 PM

Check-out: By 12:00 PM

Dining:

Main Restaurant: Open for breakfast, lunch, and dinner with varying hours.

The Lounge and Pool Bar: Open throughout the day for drinks and light snacks, with specific hours varying.

Price

Room Rates: Rates at Nile Palace Hotel typically range from $150 to $300 per night, depending on the season, room type, and booking conditions. Prices reflect the luxury status of the hotel and its premium amenities.

Pros

Stunning Nile Views: Provides beautiful views of the Nile River from many rooms and public areas.

Elegant Design: Combines modern luxury with traditional Egyptian elements for a refined atmosphere.

Extensive Amenities: Includes high-end facilities such as a luxury spa, multiple dining options, and event spaces.

The Ultimate Egypt Travel Guide 2025 Edition

Cons

Higher Cost: As a luxury hotel, it may be expensive for budget-conscious travelers.

Tourist-Focused: May cater more towards tourists, potentially impacting the level of local authenticity compared to boutique accommodations.

Local Tips

Request Nile Views: To fully enjoy the hotel's location, request a room with a Nile view for spectacular river vistas.

Explore Nearby Attractions: Use the hotel's proximity to Luxor Temple and Karnak Temple for convenient sightseeing.

Local Dining: While the hotel offers excellent dining options, exploring local restaurants in Luxor can provide a more authentic experience.

Transportation: Utilize the hotel's transportation services or local taxis for easy access to other attractions and the airport.

5. Cairo Hotel Luxor

Cairo Hotel Luxor is a mid-range hotel that provides a comfortable and convenient base for exploring the historic city of Luxor, Egypt. Known for its affordability and practical amenities, the hotel caters to travelers looking for a budget-friendly yet pleasant stay.

Location (Address & Proximity)

Address: Corniche El Nile Street, Luxor 85111, Egypt

Proximity:

Luxor Temple: Approximately a 10-minute drive or a 20-minute walk, offering easy access to this major historical site.

Karnak Temple: About a 15-minute drive away, providing convenient access to one of Egypt's most famous archaeological sites.

Valley of the Kings: Roughly a 30-minute drive, making it accessible for guests interested in visiting this significant location.

Luxor International Airport: Around a 20-minute drive, facilitating convenient arrivals and departures.

Highlights

Central Location: Situated on the Corniche El Nile Street, offering convenient access to local attractions, dining options, and shopping.

Affordability: Provides a budget-friendly option with comfortable accommodations and basic amenities.

Practical Amenities: Focuses on delivering essential services and comfort for a pleasant stay.

Spa and Wellness

Spa and Wellness:

Basic Facilities: The hotel does not have a full-service spa, but basic wellness services such as a small fitness area may be available. For more extensive treatments, guests may need to visit nearby spas.

Swimming Pool: Features a small outdoor pool for relaxation and cooling off, though it may not be as extensive as those in higher-end hotels.

Bars

On-Site Bars:

Lobby Bar: A casual space where guests can enjoy light snacks and beverages in a relaxed setting. The bar may offer a limited selection compared to more upscale establishments.

Events and Conferences

Meeting and Event Facilities:

Grace Bennett

Basic Meeting Rooms: Offers small meeting rooms suitable for business meetings or small gatherings. Facilities are generally basic, focusing on essential services for business travelers.

Basic Facilities and Amenities

Dining:

Restaurant: Provides a variety of international and local dishes, with options for buffet and à la carte dining for breakfast, lunch, and dinner.

Business Center: Includes basic facilities for internet access, printing, and copying to support business needs.

Concierge Services: Staff can assist with local tours, transportation arrangements, and general inquiries to enhance the guest experience.

Opening and Closing Hours

Check-in: Typically from 2:00 PM

Check-out: By 12:00 PM

Dining:

Restaurant: Open for breakfast, lunch, and dinner with varying hours.

Lobby Bar: Generally open throughout the day for drinks and light snacks.

Price

Room Rates: Rates at Cairo Hotel Luxor typically range from $50 to $90 per night, depending on the season, room type, and booking conditions. Prices reflect the mid-range status of the hotel and its basic amenities.

Pros

Central Location: Offers easy access to Luxor's key attractions and local amenities.

Affordable Pricing: Provides a cost-effective option with essential services for budget-conscious travelers.

Comfortable Rooms: Offers clean and comfortable accommodations for a pleasant stay.

Cons

Basic Amenities: Lacks some of the higher-end features and extensive facilities found in luxury hotels.

Limited Facilities: May not offer extensive dining options or advanced amenities compared to more upscale properties.

Local Tips

Explore Nearby Attractions: Take advantage of the hotel's central location to visit Luxor Temple and Karnak Temple with ease.

Local Dining: Consider exploring local restaurants and cafes in Luxor for a more authentic dining experience.

Transportation: Utilize local taxis or hotel transportation services for convenient access to other attractions and the airport.

Boutique Hotel

Boutique hotels in Luxor offer distinctive, intimate accommodations with a focus on personalized service and unique character. Perfect for travelers seeking a more intimate and memorable stay, these hotels combine stylish decor with individualized attention to create a charming and comfortable retreat.

Top 5 Boutique Hotels

1. Al Moudira Hotel

Al Moudira Hotel is a charming boutique hotel located in Luxor, Egypt. Known for its unique architectural style and personalized service, the hotel offers a distinctive and intimate experience for travelers. It combines traditional Egyptian design with modern comforts, providing an exceptional stay for those seeking a more personalized and culturally immersive experience.

Location (Address & Proximity)

Address: West Bank, Luxor, Egypt

Proximity:

Luxor Temple: Approximately a 20-minute drive from the hotel, making it accessible for exploring this significant historical site.

Karnak Temple: About a 25-minute drive, providing convenient access to one of Egypt's most renowned archaeological sites.

Valley of the Kings: Roughly a 30-minute drive, allowing for easy visits to this important archaeological location.

Luxor International Airport: Around a 40-minute drive, facilitating easy arrivals and departures.

Highlights

Unique Design: The hotel features an eclectic mix of traditional Egyptian architecture, colorful tiles, and ornate furnishings, creating a distinctive and visually appealing environment.

Personalized Service: Offers attentive and personalized service, catering to the individual needs and preferences of guests.

Intimate Atmosphere: Provides a smaller, more intimate setting compared to larger hotels, enhancing the overall guest experience.

Spa and Wellness

Spa:

Relaxation Services: Includes a small spa area offering massages and wellness treatments in a serene setting. The focus is on relaxation and rejuvenation.

Swimming Pool: Features an outdoor pool surrounded by lush gardens, providing a tranquil space for relaxation and leisure.

Bars

On-Site Bars:

Bar Area: The hotel offers a cozy bar area where guests can enjoy a selection of beverages in a relaxed and intimate setting. The ambiance is often highlighted by traditional decor and personalized service.

Events and Conferences

Meeting and Event Facilities:

Event Spaces: While the hotel does not have large conference facilities, it does offer charming spaces for small gatherings, private dinners, and intimate events. The unique setting provides a memorable backdrop for personal celebrations and small meetings.

Basic Facilities and Amenities

Dining:

Main Restaurant: Serves a variety of international and local dishes, with an emphasis on fresh, high-quality ingredients. Dining is often accompanied by a picturesque setting and personalized service.

Business Center: Basic services are available, but the focus is more on providing a relaxing and personalized stay rather than extensive business facilities.

Concierge Services: Staff can assist with local tours, transportation arrangements, and general inquiries to enhance the guest experience.

Opening and Closing Hours

Check-in: Typically from 2:00 PM

Check-out: By 12:00 PM

Dining and Bar Services: Open throughout the day, with specific hours varying based on guest needs and hotel policies.

Price

Room Rates: Rates at Al Moudira Hotel generally range from $150 to $300 per night, depending on the season, room type, and booking conditions. Prices reflect the boutique nature of the hotel and its unique offerings.

Pros

Unique Experience: Offers a distinctive and culturally rich environment with personalized service and unique design elements.

Intimate Setting: Provides a smaller, more intimate atmosphere compared to larger hotels, enhancing the guest experience.

Exceptional Service: Known for its attentive and personalized service, catering to the individual needs of guests.

Cons

Higher Cost: As a boutique hotel with unique features, it may be more expensive than standard mid-range options.

Limited Facilities: May lack some of the extensive amenities and large-scale facilities found in larger hotels, such as extensive business centers or large conference rooms.

Local Tips

Explore the West Bank: The hotel's location on the West Bank offers a quieter and more authentic experience compared to the East Bank. Take the time to explore local attractions and the less-visited sites in this area.

Request Special Arrangements: If you have specific preferences or requests, communicate them to the hotel in advance to ensure a personalized experience.

Local Cuisine: Enjoy the hotel's dining options and consider exploring nearby local restaurants for a more comprehensive taste of Egyptian cuisine.

2. Nefertiti Hotel

Nefertiti Hotel is a charming boutique hotel located in Luxor, Egypt. It is known for its warm and inviting atmosphere, personalized service, and central location. The hotel provides a comfortable and authentic experience, blending traditional Egyptian hospitality with modern conveniences.

Location (Address & Proximity)

Address: Corniche El Nile Street, Luxor 85111, Egypt

Proximity:

Luxor Temple: Approximately a 5-minute walk, allowing easy access to this major historical site.

Karnak Temple: About a 10-minute drive, providing convenient access to one of Egypt's most significant archaeological sites.

Valley of the Kings: Roughly a 30-minute drive, making it accessible for guests interested in exploring this famous location.

Luxor International Airport: Around a 15-minute drive, facilitating convenient arrivals and departures.

Highlights

Central Location: Situated on Corniche El Nile

Street, offering convenient access to local attractions, dining options, and shopping.

Charming Atmosphere: Features traditional decor with a cozy, intimate feel, creating a welcoming environment for guests.

Personalized Service: Known for its friendly and attentive staff, providing a personalized and comfortable experience.

Spa and Wellness

Spa and Wellness:

Basic Wellness Services: The hotel does not have a full-service spa but may offer basic wellness facilities or arrangements for relaxation treatments. For more extensive spa services, guests might explore nearby options.

Swimming Pool: Includes a small outdoor pool, providing a refreshing spot for relaxation and leisure.

Bars

On-Site Bars:

Roof-Top Terrace Bar: Offers a relaxed atmosphere with beautiful views of the Nile River and Luxor Temple. A great place for enjoying drinks and light snacks while taking in the local scenery.

Events and Conferences

Meeting and Event Facilities:

Small Event Spaces: The hotel does not feature large conference facilities but may offer small, charming spaces suitable for private gatherings, intimate meetings, or special events.

Basic Facilities and Amenities

Dining:

Restaurant: Serves a variety of international and local dishes, with options for buffet and à la carte dining. The dining experience is typically highlighted by a friendly atmosphere and quality service.

Business Center: Basic business services may be available, including internet access and printing. The focus is more on providing a comfortable stay rather than extensive business amenities.

Concierge Services: Staff can assist with local tours, transportation arrangements, and general inquiries to enhance the guest experience.

Opening and Closing Hours

Check-in: Typically from 2:00 PM

Check-out: By 12:00 PM

Dining and Bar Services: Open throughout the day, with specific hours varying based on guest needs and hotel policies.

Price

Room Rates: Rates at Nefertiti Hotel generally range from $60 to $120 per night, depending on the season, room type, and booking conditions. Prices reflect the boutique nature of the hotel and its focus on comfort and service.

Pros

Prime Location: Provides easy access to Luxor Temple and other local attractions, making it convenient for sightseeing.

Charming Environment: Offers a cozy and intimate atmosphere with traditional decor and personalized service.

Affordability: Provides a good balance of comfort and cost, making it an attractive option for mid-range travelers.

Cons

Basic Amenities: Lacks some of the higher-end features and extensive facilities found in luxury hotels.

Limited Facilities: May not offer extensive dining options or large-scale amenities compared to larger hotels.

Local Tips

Explore the Area: Take advantage of the hotel's central location to explore nearby attractions such as Luxor Temple and local markets.

Enjoy the Terrace Bar: The roof-top terrace bar provides a unique setting to unwind and enjoy views of the Nile and the cityscape.

Local Cuisine: While the hotel offers dining options, consider trying local restaurants to experience a broader range of Egyptian cuisine.

3. The Winter Palace Pavillon

The Winter Palace Pavillon is a sophisticated extension of the historic Winter Palace Hotel, renowned for its luxury and elegance. Located in Luxor, Egypt, it offers guests a refined and intimate experience with access to the historic grandeur of the Winter Palace. This boutique-style property combines modern comforts with the classic charm of its illustrious predecessor.

Location (Address & Proximity)

Address: Corniche El Nile Street, Luxor, Egypt

Proximity:

Luxor Temple: Located approximately a 10-minute walk, allowing easy access to this major historical site.

Karnak Temple: About a 15-minute drive, providing convenient access to one of Egypt's most significant archaeological sites.

Valley of the Kings: Roughly a 30-minute drive, making it accessible for guests interested in exploring this important location.

Luxor International Airport: Around a 20-minute drive, facilitating convenient arrivals and departures.

Highlights

Historical Legacy: As part of the Winter Palace Hotel, it offers a touch of historic luxury combined with modern amenities.

Elegant Design: Features beautifully designed rooms and public spaces, maintaining the classic style and sophistication of the Winter Palace.

Exclusive Atmosphere: Provides an intimate and refined experience with a focus on personalized service and comfort.

Spa and Wellness

Spa and Wellness:

Access to Winter Palace Facilities: Guests of The Winter Palace Pavillon can utilize the spa and wellness facilities available at the main Winter Palace Hotel. This includes a full-service spa offering a range of treatments and therapies.

Fitness Center: The main hotel's fitness center is also accessible, featuring modern exercise equipment and wellness options.

Swimming Pool: Guests can enjoy the use of the main hotel's outdoor pool, which offers a luxurious setting with views of the Nile and lush gardens.

Bars

On-Site Bars:

The Lounge Bar: Located within the main Winter Palace Hotel, this sophisticated bar offers a range of beverages and light snacks in a refined setting. The ambiance is enhanced by traditional decor and elegant furnishings.

Events and Conferences

Meeting and Event Facilities:

Access to Winter Palace Facilities: While The Winter Palace Pavillon itself may not have extensive meeting rooms, guests can access the event and conference facilities of the main Winter Palace Hotel. This includes elegant ballrooms and meeting spaces equipped for various types of events and gatherings.

Basic Facilities and Amenities

Dining:

Restaurant Access: Guests can dine at the main Winter Palace Hotel's restaurants, which offer a range of international and Egyptian cuisine. Dining options include formal dining rooms and casual settings.

Business Center: Basic business services are available at the main hotel, including internet access, printing, and copying.

Concierge Services: The hotel provides personalized concierge services, assisting with local tours, transportation arrangements, and special requests.

Opening and Closing Hours

Check-in: Typically from 2:00 PM

Check-out: By 12:00 PM

Dining and Bar Services: Open throughout the day, with specific hours varying based on guest needs and hotel policies.

Price

Room Rates: Rates at The Winter Palace Pavillon generally range from $200 to $400 per night, depending on the season, room type, and booking conditions. Prices reflect the luxury status and historical charm of the property.

Pros

Historical Charm: Offers a luxurious stay with access to the historic Winter Palace Hotel's facilities and ambiance.

Elegant Design: Combines classic elegance with modern comforts, providing a sophisticated and intimate experience.

Prime Location: Centrally located with easy access to major Luxor attractions and the Nile River.

Cons

Higher Cost: As a luxury property, it may be expensive for budget-conscious travelers.

Limited Standalone Facilities: Some amenities and facilities are shared with the main Winter Palace Hotel, which might not appeal to guests seeking a more independent boutique experience.

Local Tips

Explore the Winter Palace: Take full advantage of the historical and luxurious amenities offered by the main Winter Palace Hotel.

Enjoy the Nile Views: Make sure to visit the main hotel's outdoor areas to enjoy views of the Nile River and lush gardens.

Local Dining: While the hotel offers excellent dining options, consider exploring nearby local restaurants for a broader experience of Egyptian cuisine.

4. Amon Hotel

Amon Hotel is a mid-range hotel situated in Luxor, Egypt. Known for its affordable rates and practical amenities, it provides a comfortable base for travelers looking to explore the historical and cultural wonders of Luxor. The hotel combines convenience with basic comfort, catering to visitors who want a pleasant stay without luxury frills.

Location (Address & Proximity)

Address: Khaled Ibn El Walid Street, Luxor, Egypt

Proximity:

Luxor Temple: Approximately a 10-minute drive or

a 20-minute walk, offering easy access to this major historical site.

Karnak Temple: About a 15-minute drive away, providing convenient access to one of Egypt's most significant archaeological sites.

Valley of the Kings: Roughly a 30-minute drive, making it accessible for guests interested in visiting this important location.

Luxor International Airport: Around a 20-minute drive, facilitating convenient arrivals and departures.

Highlights

Central Location: Located in the heart of Luxor, offering easy access to local attractions, dining options, and shopping.

Affordable Rates: Provides budget-friendly accommodation with essential amenities, making it a practical choice for cost-conscious travelers.

Comfortable Stay: Focuses on delivering a comfortable and functional environment for a pleasant stay.

Spa and Wellness

Spa and Wellness:

Basic Services: The hotel does not have a full-service spa. For more extensive wellness treatments, guests may need to explore nearby spas.

Swimming Pool: Features a small outdoor pool, providing a space for relaxation and cooling off after a day of sightseeing.

Bars

On-Site Bars:

Hotel Bar: Offers a casual setting for enjoying drinks and light snacks. The bar is designed to be a comfortable space for guests to unwind.

Events and Conferences

Meeting and Event Facilities:

Basic Meeting Rooms: The hotel does not have extensive conference facilities but may offer small meeting rooms for business needs or private gatherings.

Basic Facilities and Amenities

Dining:

Restaurant: Serves a range of international and local dishes, with options for buffet and à la carte dining. The restaurant provides a relaxed atmosphere for breakfast, lunch, and dinner.

Business Center: Basic facilities are available for internet access, printing, and copying.

Concierge Services: Staff can assist with local tours, transportation arrangements, and general inquiries to enhance the guest experience.

Opening and Closing Hours

Check-in: Typically from 2:00 PM

Check-out: By 12:00 PM

Dining and Bar Services: Open throughout the day, with specific hours varying based on guest needs and hotel policies.

Price

Room Rates: Rates at Amon Hotel generally range from $40 to $80 per night, depending on the season, room type, and booking conditions. Prices reflect the mid-range nature of the hotel and its focus on comfort and affordability.

Pros

Central Location: Conveniently located near Luxor's key attractions, making it easy to explore the area.

Affordable Pricing: Offers a budget-friendly option with essential amenities and comfort.

Comfortable Accommodations: Provides clean and functional rooms for a pleasant stay.

Cons

Basic Amenities: Lacks some of the higher-end features and extensive facilities found in luxury or boutique hotels.

Limited Services: May not offer the extensive dining options or advanced amenities available at more upscale properties.

Local Tips

Explore Nearby Attractions: Take advantage of the hotel's central location to visit Luxor Temple, Karnak Temple, and local markets.

Local Dining: Consider exploring nearby local restaurants for a more authentic taste of Egyptian cuisine.

Transportation: Use local taxis or the hotel's transportation services to easily access attractions and the airport.

5. Movenpick Resort Luxor

Mövenpick Resort Luxor is a luxury hotel situated on the banks of the Nile River, offering a blend of elegance, comfort, and top-notch service. Known for its stunning views, lush gardens, and extensive facilities, the resort provides a refined and relaxing experience for both leisure and business travelers.

Location (Address & Proximity)

Address: Khaled Ibn El Walid Street, Luxor, Egypt

Proximity:

Luxor Temple: Approximately a 10-minute drive, making it easy to access this major historical site.

Karnak Temple: About a 15-minute drive away, providing convenient access to one of Egypt's most famous archaeological sites.

Valley of the Kings: Roughly a 30-minute drive, allowing guests to explore this important location with ease.

Luxor International Airport: Around a 20-minute drive, facilitating smooth arrivals and departures.

Highlights

Riverside Location: Positioned on the Nile Riverbank, offering breathtaking river views and a tranquil setting.

Elegant Design: Features stylish, modern decor with traditional Egyptian touches, providing a luxurious and inviting atmosphere.

Extensive Facilities: Includes a range of amenities such as multiple dining options, a large swimming pool, and a spa.

Spa and Wellness

Spa:

Mövenpick Spa: Offers a range of treatments including massages, facials, and body therapies. The spa is designed for relaxation and rejuvenation, providing a serene environment.

Fitness Center: Equipped with modern exercise equipment for guests looking to maintain their fitness routines.

Swimming Pool: Features a large outdoor pool with views of the Nile, ideal for relaxation and leisure. There is also a separate children's pool for families.

Bars

On-Site Bars:

Pool Bar: Located near the swimming pool, offering a selection of beverages and light snacks in a casual, outdoor setting.

Lobby Bar: Provides a more formal environment for enjoying drinks and cocktails, often accompanied by live music and a relaxed ambiance.

Events and Conferences

Grace Bennett

Meeting and Event Facilities:

Conference Rooms: The hotel offers several meeting rooms and conference facilities equipped with modern audiovisual technology. Suitable for business meetings, seminars, and conferences.

Banquet Facilities: Includes elegant spaces for private events, weddings, and special occasions, with catering services available.

Basic Facilities and Amenities

Dining:

Main Restaurant: Serves a variety of international and local dishes, with options for buffet and à la carte dining. Enjoy meals with views of the Nile and lush gardens.

Specialty Restaurants: Includes additional dining options offering specific cuisines, such as Italian or Middle Eastern, enhancing the culinary experience.

Business Center: Provides essential services such as internet access, printing, and copying for business travelers.

Concierge Services: Assists with local tours, transportation arrangements, and special requests to enhance the guest experience.

Opening and Closing Hours

Check-in: Typically from 3:00 PM

Check-out: By 12:00 PM

Dining and Bar Services: Open throughout the day, with specific hours varying based on the restaurant and bar.

Price

Room Rates: Rates at Mövenpick Resort Luxor generally range from $150 to $300 per night, depending on the season, room type, and booking conditions. Prices reflect the luxury status and extensive amenities of the resort.

Pros

Riverside Location: Offers stunning Nile views and a serene environment, enhancing the overall guest experience.

Luxurious Facilities: Provides extensive amenities including a large pool, spa, and multiple dining options.

Elegant Design: Features stylish and comfortable accommodations with a blend of modern and traditional decor.

Cons

Higher Cost: As a luxury resort, it may be more expensive than mid-range options, which might not be ideal for budget-conscious travelers.

Size and Scale: The extensive facilities and large scale of the resort may not appeal to those seeking a more intimate boutique experience.

Local Tips

River Views: Take full advantage of the hotel's riverside location by enjoying meals and relaxation by the Nile.

Explore Luxor: Utilize the hotel's proximity to key attractions such as Luxor Temple and Karnak Temple for convenient sightseeing.

Local Tours: The concierge can help arrange local tours and excursions to enhance your visit to Luxor.

Hostel

Hostels in Luxor offer budget-friendly accommodations with a focus on social interaction and convenience. Ideal for travelers seeking an economical option and a chance to meet fellow explorers, these hostels provide basic amenities and a welcoming atmosphere for a relaxed and enjoyable stay.

Top 5 Hostel

1. Nile Palace Hostel

Nile Palace Hostel is a budget-friendly accommodation option located in Luxor, Egypt. It caters primarily to backpackers and travelers looking for economical lodging with basic amenities and a friendly atmosphere. The hostel provides an affordable and comfortable base for exploring Luxor's historical and cultural attractions.

Location (Address & Proximity)

Address: Ahmed Orabi Street, Luxor, Egypt

Proximity:

Luxor Temple: Approximately a 10-minute drive or a 20-minute walk, making it convenient to visit this significant historical site.

Karnak Temple: About a 15-minute drive away, providing easy access to one of Egypt's most famous archaeological sites.

Valley of the Kings: Roughly a 30-minute drive, allowing guests to explore this important location with ease.

Luxor International Airport: Around a 20-minute drive, facilitating convenient arrivals and departures.

Highlights

Affordable Rates: Offers budget-friendly accommodation with essential amenities, making it a practical choice for travelers on a tight budget.

Friendly Atmosphere: Known for its welcoming environment and social vibe, ideal for meeting fellow travelers and sharing experiences.

Basic Amenities: Provides the necessary comforts for a pleasant stay, including dormitory-style and private rooms.

Spa and Wellness

Spa and Wellness:

Basic Wellness Services: The hostel does not have a spa or extensive wellness facilities. Guests seeking spa treatments may need to explore nearby options.

Swimming Pool: The hostel does not feature a swimming pool. For relaxation, guests may need to visit local public or hotel pools.

Bars

On-Site Bars:

Common Area: The hostel's common area may offer drinks and light snacks, providing a casual setting for guests to unwind and socialize.

Events and Conferences

Meeting and Event Facilities:

No Dedicated Facilities: The hostel does not have formal meeting or event spaces. It focuses on providing budget accommodation and a communal environment.

Basic Facilities and Amenities

Dining:

Kitchen Access: The hostel typically includes a shared kitchen where guests can prepare their own meals. This provides a cost-effective dining option for travelers.

Local Dining: The hostel's central location allows easy access to nearby local restaurants and eateries.

Business Center: The hostel does not have a business center, but basic internet access is usually available.

Concierge Services: Limited concierge services are provided, but staff can assist with local information, transportation, and tour arrangements.

Opening and Closing Hours

Check-in: Generally from 2:00 PM

Check-out: By 11:00 AM

Common Area: Open throughout the day, with specific hours for kitchen and common area use varying by hostel policies.

Price

Room Rates: Rates at Nile Palace Hostel generally range from $10 to $30 per night, depending on the season, room type, and booking conditions. Prices reflect the budget-friendly nature of the hostel.

Pros

Affordable: Provides a budget-friendly accommodation option with essential amenities and a welcoming atmosphere.

Central Location: Conveniently located near key attractions in Luxor, making it easy to explore the city.

Social Environment: Ideal for meeting other travelers and sharing experiences in a communal setting.

Cons

Basic Amenities: Offers basic accommodations without luxury or extensive facilities.

Limited Services: Lacks some of the higher-end services and amenities found in more upscale hotels.

Local Tips

Explore Locally: Take advantage of the hostel's central location to visit nearby attractions such as Luxor Temple and Karnak Temple.

Local Markets: Explore local markets and eateries for a taste of authentic Egyptian cuisine and culture.

Socialize: Engage with other travelers in the common areas to make the most of the hostel's social environment and gather local tips and recommendations.

2. El Hossam Hotel

El Hossam Hotel is a budget-friendly hotel in Luxor, Egypt, offering basic accommodations with a focus on affordability and practicality. It caters to travelers who are seeking a comfortable yet economical place to stay while exploring the rich historical and cultural sites of Luxor.

Location (Address & Proximity)

Address: Mohamed Farid Street, Luxor, Egypt

Proximity:

Luxor Temple: Approximately a 10-minute drive or a 20-minute walk, making it easy to access this significant historical site.

Karnak Temple: About a 15-minute drive away, providing convenient access to one of Egypt's most famous archaeological sites.

Valley of the Kings: Roughly a 30-minute drive, allowing for easy visits to this important location.

Luxor International Airport: Around a 20-minute drive, facilitating smooth arrivals and departures.

Highlights

Affordable Rates: Provides budget-friendly lodging with essential amenities, making it a practical choice for travelers on a tight budget.

Central Location: Situated in a central area, offering convenient access to local attractions, dining options, and shopping.

Simple Accommodations: Offers basic rooms and amenities, suitable for travelers seeking a no-frills stay.

Spa and Wellness

Spa and Wellness:

Basic Services: The hotel does not feature a full-service spa. Guests looking for wellness treatments may need to explore nearby options.

Swimming Pool: The hotel does not have a swimming pool. For relaxation, guests may need to visit local public or hotel pools.

Bars

On-Site Bars:

Hotel Bar: May offer a casual environment for enjoying drinks. However, the focus is more on basic accommodation rather than extensive bar services.

Events and Conferences

Meeting and Event Facilities:

No Dedicated Facilities: The hotel does not have formal meeting or event spaces. It focuses on providing budget accommodations without extensive business facilities.

Basic Facilities and Amenities

Dining:

Restaurant: The hotel may have a basic restaurant or dining area offering simple meals. Guests also have the option to explore nearby local dining options.

Local Dining: Its central location allows easy access to various local restaurants and eateries.

Business Center: The hotel does not have a business center, but basic internet access may be available.

Concierge Services: Limited concierge services are provided, but staff can assist with local information and transportation arrangements.

Opening and Closing Hours

Check-in: Typically from 2:00 PM

Check-out: By 12:00 PM

Dining and Bar Services: Open throughout the day, with specific hours varying based on the hotel's policies and restaurant hours.

Price

Room Rates: Rates at El Hossam Hotel generally range from $20 to $50 per night, depending on the season, room type, and booking conditions. Prices reflect the budget-friendly nature of the hotel.

Pros

Affordable Pricing: Provides a cost-effective accommodation option with essential amenities.

Central Location: Conveniently located near Luxor's key attractions, making it easy to explore the city.

Basic Comfort: Offers a simple and practical stay with necessary comforts for budget travelers.

Cons

Basic Amenities: Offers limited amenities compared to more upscale hotels, lacking luxury features and extensive facilities.

Limited Services: May not provide the range of services and facilities available at higher-end hotels.

Local Tips

Explore Nearby Attractions: Utilize the hotel's central location to visit local landmarks such as Luxor Temple and Karnak Temple.

Local Eateries: Explore nearby local markets and restaurants to experience authentic Egyptian cuisine and culture.

Transportation: Use local taxis or the hotel's transportation services to access attractions and the airport easily.

3. Happy Land Hostel

Happy Land Hostel is a lively and budget-friendly accommodation option in Luxor, Egypt. Designed to cater primarily to backpackers and budget travelers, the hostel offers a comfortable and social environment with essential amenities for a pleasant stay. Its focus on affordability and community makes it a popular choice among travelers seeking a cost-effective lodging experience.

Location (Address & Proximity)

Address: Mohamed Farid Street, Luxor, Egypt

Proximity:

Luxor Temple: Approximately a 10-minute drive or a 20-minute walk, making it easily accessible for visitors interested in this major historical site.

Karnak Temple: About a 15-minute drive away, providing convenient access to one of Egypt's most significant archaeological sites.

Valley of the Kings: Roughly a 30-minute drive, allowing guests to explore this important location with ease.

Luxor International Airport: Around a 20-minute drive, facilitating convenient arrivals and departures.

Highlights

Affordable Rates: Offers budget-friendly accommodation, making it an economical choice for travelers.

Social Atmosphere: Known for its vibrant and communal environment, ideal for meeting other travelers and sharing experiences.

Basic Comforts: Provides essential amenities and clean accommodations, focusing on comfort and convenience at a lower price point.

Spa and Wellness

Spa and Wellness:

Basic Services: The hostel does not feature a full-service spa. Guests looking for more extensive wellness treatments may need to visit nearby facilities.

Swimming Pool: The hostel does not have a swimming pool. For relaxation, guests might need to explore local public pools or other hotels with pool facilities.

Bars

On-Site Bars:

Common Area: The hostel's common area may offer beverages and snacks, providing a casual space for socializing and relaxing.

Events and Conferences

Meeting and Event Facilities:

No Dedicated Facilities: The hostel does not have formal meeting or event spaces. It focuses on providing budget accommodation with a social environment rather than business facilities.

Basic Facilities and Amenities

Dining:

Kitchen Access: The hostel typically includes a shared kitchen where guests can prepare their own meals, offering a cost-effective dining option.

Local Dining: Its central location allows easy access to nearby local restaurants and eateries for additional dining options.

Business Center: The hostel does not have a business center, but basic internet access is usually available.

Concierge Services: Limited concierge services are available. Hostel staff can assist with local information, transportation arrangements, and tour bookings.

Opening and Closing Hours

Check-in: Typically from 2:00 PM

Check-out: By 11:00 AM

Common Area: Open throughout the day, with specific hours for the kitchen and common area use varying based on hostel policies.

Price

Room Rates: Rates at Happy Land Hostel generally range from $10 to $30 per night, depending on the season, room type, and booking conditions. Prices reflect the hostel's focus on affordability and budget travel.

Pros

Affordable Pricing: Provides a budget-friendly accommodation option with essential amenities and a focus on affordability.

Social Environment: Ideal for meeting other travelers and sharing experiences in a communal setting.

Central Location: Conveniently located near key attractions in Luxor, making it easy to explore the city.

Cons

Basic Amenities: Offers limited amenities compared to more upscale hotels, lacking luxury features and extensive facilities.

Limited Privacy: Dormitory-style rooms may not provide the level of privacy found in private hotel rooms.

Local Tips

Explore Local Attractions: Utilize the hostel's central location to visit nearby landmarks such as Luxor Temple and Karnak Temple.

Experience Local Cuisine: Check out local markets and restaurants for a taste of authentic Egyptian food and culture.

Socialize: Engage with fellow travelers in the common areas to make the most of the hostel's social atmosphere and gather tips on exploring Luxor.

4. Oasis Hotel

Oasis Hotel is a mid-range accommodation option in Luxor, Egypt, known for providing a comfortable and relaxing environment with essential amenities. It is suitable for travelers seeking a pleasant stay without the high costs associated with luxury hotels. The hotel combines practical facilities with a hospitable atmosphere, making it a good choice for those exploring Luxor.

Location (Address & Proximity)

Address: El Zinia Street, Luxor, Egypt

Proximity:

Luxor Temple: Approximately a 10-minute drive or a 20-minute walk, offering easy access to this major historical site.

Karnak Temple: About a 15-minute drive away, providing convenient access to one of Egypt's most famous archaeological sites.

Valley of the Kings: Roughly a 30-minute drive, allowing for easy visits to this important location.

Luxor International Airport: Around a 20-minute drive, facilitating smooth arrivals and departures.

Highlights

Comfortable Accommodations: Offers well-furnished rooms with a focus on comfort and practicality.

Central Location: Situated in a central area, making it convenient for visiting local attractions, dining options, and shopping.

Affordability: Provides a mid-range option that balances comfort and cost-effectiveness.

Spa and Wellness

Spa and Wellness:

Basic Services: The hotel does not have a full-service spa. Guests seeking extensive wellness treatments may need to explore nearby facilities.

Swimming Pool: Features a small outdoor pool, offering a space to relax and unwind after a day of sightseeing.

Bars

On-Site Bars:

Hotel Bar: May offer a casual environment for enjoying drinks. The focus is on providing a comfortable and relaxed setting for guests.

Events and Conferences

Meeting and Event Facilities:

Basic Meeting Rooms: The hotel may offer small meeting rooms suitable for business meetings or private gatherings. More extensive conference facilities may be available at larger hotels.

Basic Facilities and Amenities

Dining:

Restaurant: The hotel typically has a restaurant offering a range of international and local dishes. Guests can enjoy meals in a relaxed setting.

Local Dining: Its central location allows easy access to various local restaurants and eateries for additional dining options.

Business Center: Basic business services such as internet access, printing, and copying are generally available.

Concierge Services: Staff can assist with local information, transportation arrangements, and tour bookings to enhance the guest experience.

Opening and Closing Hours

Check-in: Typically from 2:00 PM

Check-out: By 12:00 PM

Dining and Bar Services: Open throughout the day, with specific hours varying based on the hotel's policies.

Price

Room Rates: Rates at Oasis Hotel generally range from $50 to $100 per night, depending on the season, room type, and booking conditions. Prices reflect the mid-range nature of the hotel and its amenities.

Pros

Comfortable Rooms: Provides a comfortable and well-furnished environment for a pleasant stay.

Central Location: Conveniently located near key attractions, making it easy to explore Luxor.

Affordable Rates: Balances comfort and cost, offering good value for money.

Cons

Basic Amenities: May not offer the extensive amenities or luxury features found in higher-end hotels.

Limited Spa Services: Lacks a full-service spa, which may be a drawback for guests seeking comprehensive wellness treatments.

Local Tips

Explore Attractions: Take advantage of the hotel's central location to visit nearby landmarks such as Luxor Temple and Karnak Temple.

Local Cuisine: Check out local markets and restaurants for an authentic taste of Egyptian cuisine and culture.

Transportation: Use local taxis or the hotel's transportation services to easily access attractions and the airport.

5. Lotus Hotel

Lotus Hotel is a mid-range accommodation option located in Luxor, Egypt. It is designed to offer comfort and convenience at a reasonable price, making it an attractive choice for travelers seeking a balance between affordability and quality. The hotel provides essential amenities and a welcoming atmosphere, ideal for exploring Luxor's historical and cultural sites.

Location (Address & Proximity)

Address: Khaled Ibn El Walid Street, Luxor, Egypt

Proximity:

Luxor Temple: Approximately a 10-minute drive or a 15-minute walk, allowing easy access to this significant historical site.

Karnak Temple: About a 10-15 minute drive away, making it convenient to visit one of Egypt's most famous archaeological sites.

Valley of the Kings: Roughly a 30-minute drive, providing easy access for exploring this important location.

Luxor International Airport: Around a 20-minute drive, ensuring smooth arrivals and departures.

Highlights

Comfortable Rooms: Offers well-maintained and comfortably furnished rooms, providing a pleasant stay for guests.

Central Location: Located centrally, making it convenient for visiting local attractions, dining options, and shopping.

Affordable Rates: Balances comfort and affordability, making it a good value option for travelers.

Spa and Wellness

Spa and Wellness:

Basic Services: The hotel does not feature a full-service spa. Guests looking for more extensive wellness treatments may need to explore nearby options.

Swimming Pool: The hotel includes a small outdoor pool, offering a relaxing spot to unwind after a day of sightseeing.

Bars

On-Site Bars:

Hotel Bar: The hotel may have a casual bar or lounge area where guests can enjoy drinks and light snacks.

Events and Conferences

Meeting and Event Facilities:

Basic Meeting Rooms: The hotel may offer small meeting spaces suitable for business meetings or small gatherings. For larger events or conferences, more extensive facilities might be needed.

Basic Facilities and Amenities

Dining:

Grace Bennett

Restaurant: The hotel typically features a restaurant offering a variety of international and local dishes. Guests can enjoy meals in a relaxed environment.

Local Dining: The hotel's central location provides easy access to nearby local restaurants and eateries.

Business Center: Basic services such as internet access, printing, and copying are generally available.

Concierge Services: Staff can assist with local information, transportation arrangements, and tour bookings to enhance the guest experience.

Opening and Closing Hours

Check-in: Typically from 2:00 PM

Check-out: By 12:00 PM

Dining and Bar Services: Open throughout the day, with specific hours varying based on the hotel's policies.

Price

Room Rates: Rates at Lotus Hotel generally range from $40 to $80 per night, depending on the season, room type, and booking conditions. Prices reflect the mid-range nature of the hotel and its amenities.

Pros

Comfortable Accommodations: Provides well-furnished and comfortable rooms for a pleasant stay.

Central Location: Conveniently located near major attractions in Luxor, making it easy to explore the city.

Good Value: Balances comfort and cost, offering good value for money.

Cons

Basic Amenities: May not offer the extensive amenities or luxury features found in higher-end hotels.

Limited Spa Facilities: Lacks a full-service spa, which might be a drawback for guests seeking comprehensive wellness services.

Local Tips

Explore Nearby Sites: Utilize the hotel's central location to visit local landmarks such as Luxor Temple and Karnak Temple.

Local Cuisine: Take advantage of nearby restaurants and markets to experience authentic Egyptian food and culture.

Transportation: Use local taxis or the hotel's transportation services to easily access attractions and the airport.

Day Trip from Luxor
Valley of the Queens

The Valley of the Queens is an exceptional destination for anyone visiting Luxor and seeking to explore Egypt's rich historical heritage. Located on the west bank of the Nile, across from Luxor, it's an essential part of any well-rounded itinerary. Here's a comprehensive look at why the Valley of the Queens is a must-visit and what you can expect:

Historical Significance

Purpose: The Valley of the Queens was the burial place for the queens and royal children of the New Kingdom period (18th to 20th Dynasties). It was designed as a counterpart to the Valley of the Kings, where the pharaohs were buried.

Tomb Architecture: The tombs in this valley are known for their beautiful and well-preserved frescoes, depicting scenes from the afterlife, daily life, and religious rituals.

Key Attractions

Tomb of Nefertari: The highlight of the Valley of the Queens is the tomb of Queen Nefertari, the favorite wife of Ramses II. This tomb is renowned for its stunning and vibrant frescoes, which are among the best-preserved examples of ancient Egyptian art. The colors and details offer an extraordinary glimpse into the beauty of ancient Egyptian artistry.

Tomb of Prince Khaemwaset: Khaemwaset was a son of Ramses II and a high priest. His tomb, while less ornate than Nefertari's, is notable for its well-preserved inscriptions and the details of his high-ranking role.

Tomb of Titi: This tomb is less frequently visited but provides valuable insights into the funerary practices of the period. It is known for its interesting wall decorations and the stories they tell.

Visiting the Valley of the Queens

Guided Tours: It's advisable to take a guided tour to fully appreciate the historical and cultural significance of the tombs. Guides can provide context and detailed explanations about the artwork and the history of the queens and their families.

Photography: Photography inside the tombs is generally prohibited to protect the delicate frescoes. However, the exterior and surrounding areas provide excellent opportunities for photographs.

Ticket Information: The Valley of the Queens requires a separate ticket from other sites in Luxor. Tickets can be purchased at the site or through tour operators. It's a good idea to check current ticket prices and availability in advance.

Practical Information

Travel Time: The Valley of the Queens is about a 30-minute drive from Luxor. It's best to start your visit early in the day to avoid the heat and crowds.

Best Time to Visit: The cooler months from October to April are ideal for visiting Luxor and the Valley of the Queens. Summer temperatures can be very high, making daytime excursions more challenging.

Dress Code: Wear comfortable clothing suitable for warm weather and sturdy walking shoes. As with other archaeological sites in Egypt, modest dress is recommended.

What to Bring: Bring water, sun protection (hat, sunscreen), and a camera for outdoor shots. If you're planning to visit multiple sites in one day, pack a light lunch or snacks.

Tips for Visitors

Early Arrival: Arriving early will help you avoid the peak heat of the day and larger crowds. The Valley of the Queens is less crowded than the Valley of the Kings, but early morning visits are still recommended for a more serene experience.

Respect the Site: Follow all guidelines provided by site staff and your guide to help preserve the tombs and their artwork. Be respectful of the cultural and historical significance of the site.

Combine with Other Sites: Consider combining your visit to the Valley of the Queens with other nearby attractions, such as the Valley of the Kings or the Temple of Hatshepsut, for a fuller experience of Luxor's west bank.

Edfu Temple

Edfu Temple, also known as the Temple of Horus, is one of Egypt's best-preserved and most significant ancient temples. Located in the town of Edfu, about 105 kilometers (65 miles) south of Luxor, this temple offers a remarkable glimpse into ancient Egyptian religion and architecture. Here's a detailed overview of why Edfu Temple is a must-visit and what you can expect:

Historical Significance

Dedication: The Temple of Edfu is dedicated to Horus, the falcon-headed god associated with kingship and protection. It was built during the Ptolemaic period, specifically between 237 and 57 BCE, making it one of the last major temples built in ancient Egypt.

Architectural Importance: The temple is renowned for its well-preserved state and provides valuable insights into the religious practices, rituals, and architectural styles of the Ptolemaic era.

Key Attractions

Main Entrance: The temple's entrance is flanked by two massive pylons (gateways), decorated with impressive reliefs depicting the king's triumphs and divine associations.

Hypostyle Hall: This large hall is supported by numerous columns, each adorned with intricate carvings and hieroglyphs. The hall is a central feature of the temple and was used for various religious ceremonies.

Sanctuary: The innermost part of the temple, where the sacred statue of Horus was kept. The sanctuary is accessed through a series of corridors and is decorated with detailed reliefs illustrating religious rituals.

Outer Courtyard: The open courtyard in front of the temple's entrance, where public ceremonies and offerings were made.

Reliefs and Inscriptions: The walls of the temple are covered with detailed hieroglyphic inscriptions and reliefs that depict mythological scenes, the history of the temple's construction, and the divine roles of Horus and the reigning Ptolemaic rulers.

Visiting Edfu Temple

Guided Tours: A guided tour is highly recommended to fully appreciate the historical and religious significance of the temple's features. Guides can provide context and details about the various scenes depicted in the reliefs.

Photography: Photography is allowed in many areas of the temple, though it's always good to check for any restrictions. The temple's exterior and its impressive columns and carvings make for excellent photo opportunities.

Ticket Information: Tickets to Edfu Temple can be purchased on-site. It's advisable to check current ticket prices and availability in advance.

Practical Information

Travel Time: Edfu is about a 1.5-hour drive from Luxor, making it a feasible day trip or a stop on a longer Nile cruise itinerary.

Best Time to Visit: The cooler months from October to April are ideal for visiting Edfu Temple. The summer months can be extremely hot, especially in the midday sun.

Dress Code: Dress modestly and comfortably. Wear sturdy walking shoes as the temple complex involves some walking and exploration.

What to Bring: Bring water, sun protection (hat, sunscreen), and a camera for exterior shots. Be prepared for the heat if visiting during warmer months.

Tips for Visitors

Early Start: Arriving early can help you avoid the peak heat of the day and larger crowds, particularly if you're visiting as part of a Nile cruise tour.

Respect the Site: Follow the guidelines provided by site staff and avoid touching or leaning on the ancient walls and carvings to help preserve the temple.

Combine Visits: If you're traveling between Luxor and Aswan, Edfu Temple is a great stop to include along with other temples such as Kom Ombo, which is located nearby.

Kom Ombo Temple

Kom Ombo Temple is a unique and fascinating ancient Egyptian temple located in the town of Kom Ombo, about 50 kilometers (31 miles) north of Aswan. The temple stands on a hill overlooking the Nile River and is renowned for its distinctive double design and rich historical significance. Here's an overview of what makes Kom Ombo Temple a must-visit destination:

Historical Significance

Dual Temple: Kom Ombo Temple is unique in that it is dedicated to two gods—Horus the Elder and Sobek. This dual dedication is reflected in its symmetrical design, with separate sanctuaries and hallways for each deity. It was built during the Ptolemaic period, specifically between 180 and 47 BCE.

Deities:

Horus: The falcon-headed god of the sky and kingship.

Sobek: The crocodile-headed god associated with fertility and the Nile.

Key Attractions

Symmetrical Layout: The temple is divided into two halves, each dedicated to one of the deities. This design includes two sanctuaries, two hypostyle halls, and two courtyards, making it an architectural marvel.

Reliefs and Inscriptions:

Medical Instruments: One of the most notable features of Kom Ombo Temple is the depiction of ancient surgical instruments on its walls. These carvings provide valuable insights into the medical practices of ancient Egypt.

Mythological Scenes: The walls are adorned with detailed reliefs depicting various mythological scenes, including the gods Horus and Sobek, and scenes from the Book of the Dead.

Crocodile Mummies: Sobek, the crocodile god, was associated with crocodiles, and the temple area includes a crocodile museum showcasing mummified crocodiles and related artifacts.

Nilometer: A Nilometer, used to measure the level of the Nile River and predict annual flooding, is located near the temple. It provides insight into ancient methods of monitoring the river's levels, which were crucial for agriculture.

Visiting Kom Ombo Temple

Guided Tours: A guided tour is beneficial to fully understand the temple's history, design, and the significance of its unique features. Guides can provide detailed explanations of the carvings and their meanings.

Photography: Photography is generally allowed in many areas of the temple. The exterior and interior features, including the reliefs and inscriptions, make for excellent photo opportunities.

Ticket Information: Tickets to Kom Ombo Temple can be purchased on-site or as part of a Nile cruise package. It's a good idea to check current ticket prices and availability before visiting.

Practical Information

Travel Time: Kom Ombo Temple is about a 1-hour drive from Aswan, making it a convenient stop on a trip between Aswan and Luxor or as part of a Nile River cruise itinerary.

Best Time to Visit: The cooler months from October to April are ideal for visiting to avoid the extreme summer heat. Early morning or late afternoon visits can also help avoid peak crowds.

Dress Code: Wear comfortable and modest clothing, suitable for warm weather. Sturdy walking shoes are recommended, as the temple involves some walking and exploration.

What to Bring: Bring water, sun protection (hat, sunscreen), and a camera for capturing the temple's exterior and unique features.

Tips for Visitors

Early Arrival: Arriving early can help you avoid the heat and larger tour groups, making for a more pleasant and relaxed visit.

Respect the Site: Follow all guidelines provided by site staff and avoid touching or leaning on the ancient walls and carvings to help preserve the temple.

Combine Visits: Consider visiting other nearby attractions, such as the Temple of Philae or the Nubian Museum, to make the most of your time in Aswan.

Dendera Temple Complex

The Dendera Temple Complex, located about 60 kilometers (37 miles) north of Luxor, is one of Egypt's most significant and well-preserved temple sites. It is dedicated to the goddess Hathor, the deity of motherhood, music, and joy. The site is renowned for its richly decorated temples and fascinating historical significance. Here's a detailed overview of what makes the Dendera Temple Complex a must-visit:

Historical Significance

Dedication: The Dendera Temple Complex is primarily dedicated to Hathor, but it also includes several other structures dedicated to various gods and goddesses, reflecting the religious importance of the site throughout different periods.

Construction: The main temple at Dendera was built during the Ptolemaic period, specifically between 54 BCE and 10 BCE, though it was constructed over earlier structures from earlier periods, including the New Kingdom.

Key Attractions

Temple of Hathor: The main attraction within the Dendera Temple Complex, this temple is renowned for its stunning preservation and elaborate decoration. Key features include:

Hypostyle Hall: The temple's main hall is supported by 24 columns, each adorned with intricate carvings and hieroglyphs. The ceiling is famously decorated with astronomical scenes, including representations of the zodiac.

Sanctuary: The inner sanctuary houses the sacred statue of Hathor and features beautifully preserved reliefs depicting Hathor and other deities.

Dendera Zodiac: One of the most famous features of the temple is the ceiling in the Chapel of Osiris, which includes the Dendera Zodiac. This astronomical relief depicts various celestial bodies and constellations. Although the original is now housed in the Louvre Museum in Paris, replicas can be seen at the site.

Sacred Lake: A large, rectangular lake near the temple, used for ritual purification and religious ceremonies. The lake is an impressive feature and provides a scenic backdrop to the temple complex.

Birth House (Mammisi): This small temple within the complex was used for rituals celebrating the birth of the divine child. It features detailed reliefs depicting scenes of Hathor and her divine offspring.

Osireion: An enigmatic structure associated with the god Osiris. It consists of a series of rooms and is thought to be linked to Osiris's role in the afterlife and resurrection.

Visiting Dendera Temple Complex

Guided Tours: A guided tour is highly recommended to fully appreciate the historical and religious significance of the complex. Guides can provide valuable insights into the symbolism and details of the carvings and architecture.

Photography: Photography is generally allowed at the site, though it's always a good idea to check for any restrictions, especially in specific areas like the inner sanctum.

Ticket Information: Tickets for the Dendera Temple Complex can be purchased on-site. It's advisable to check current ticket prices and availability before visiting.

Practical Information

Travel Time: The Dendera Temple Complex is approximately a 1 to 1.5-hour drive from Luxor. It's a feasible day trip and can be combined with other nearby attractions.

Best Time to Visit: The cooler months from October to April are ideal for visiting, as the temperatures are more pleasant for exploring the site. Early morning visits can help avoid the midday heat and larger crowds.

Dress Code: Wear comfortable and modest clothing. Sturdy walking shoes are recommended due to the uneven terrain and walking involved.

What to Bring: Bring water, sun protection (hat, sunscreen), and a camera for exterior shots. If visiting during warmer months, consider bringing a hat and light clothing.

Tips for Visitors

Early Arrival: Arriving early helps you avoid the peak heat of the day and larger tour groups, making for a more enjoyable experience.

Respect the Site: Follow all guidelines provided by site staff to help preserve the temple and its artifacts. Avoid touching or leaning on the ancient walls and carvings.

Combine Visits: Consider combining your visit to Dendera with other nearby sites, such as the Abydos Temple Complex or attractions in Luxor, to make the most of your time in the region.

Aswan

Aswan, located in southern Egypt along the Nile River, is a vibrant city known for its rich history, stunning landscapes, and significant archaeological sites. It serves as a gateway to some of Egypt's most remarkable monuments and offers a unique blend of ancient heritage and natural beauty. Here's an overview of what makes Aswan a must-visit destination:

Key Attractions

Philae Temple: Situated on an island in Lake Nasser, the Temple of Philae is dedicated to the goddess Isis. It is renowned for its beautiful location and elaborate carvings. The temple was relocated from its original site on Philae Island to Agilkia Island due to the construction of the Aswan High Dam.

Aswan High Dam: An engineering marvel, the Aswan High Dam was completed in 1970 and has played a crucial role in controlling the flooding of the Nile and providing hydroelectric power. The dam is an important site for understanding modern Egypt's development and its impact on agriculture and infrastructure.

Unfinished Obelisk: Located in the northern quarries of Aswan, the Unfinished Obelisk provides insight into ancient Egyptian stone-cutting techniques. The obelisk, if completed, would have been one of the largest ever erected, but it remains partially hewn from the granite.

Nubian Museum: This museum showcases the history, culture, and art of the Nubian people, who have lived along the Nile in southern Egypt and northern Sudan. It features artifacts, sculptures, and exhibits related to Nubian history and heritage.

Temple of Abu Simbel: Located about 280 kilometers (175 miles) south of Aswan, the temples of Abu Simbel are one of Egypt's most iconic archaeological sites. The complex includes two massive rock-cut temples built by Ramses II, known for their colossal statues and intricate carvings. The temples were also relocated to their current site to save them from the rising waters of Lake Nasser.

Elephantine Island: A charming island in the Nile, Elephantine Island is home to ancient ruins, including the remains of a temple dedicated to Khnum, an ancient Egyptian deity. The island also features Nubian villages and offers a serene setting with beautiful river views.

Kitchener's Island: Known for its botanical gardens, Kitchener's Island is a peaceful retreat with a variety of plant species, including tropical and subtropical plants. It's a lovely place for a leisurely stroll and to escape the city's hustle and bustle.

Activities

Nile Cruises: Aswan is a popular starting point for Nile cruises, which typically travel between Aswan and Luxor. These cruises offer a luxurious way to explore the river and visit key sites along the way.

Felucca Rides: Traditional wooden sailboats called feluccas offer a serene and picturesque way to experience the Nile. A felucca ride can provide stunning views of the riverbanks and is a relaxing way to spend a few hours.

Local Markets: Explore Aswan's bustling markets, such as the Aswan Souk, to experience local culture, buy souvenirs, and sample traditional Nubian and Egyptian cuisine.

Practical Information

Traveling to Aswan:

By Air: Aswan has an airport with flights connecting to Cairo and other major Egyptian cities.

By Train: The train from Cairo to Aswan offers a scenic journey along the Nile and is a popular choice for travelers.

By Road: Aswan is accessible by car or bus from other parts of Egypt, though the journey can be long.

Accommodation: Aswan offers a range of accommodations, from luxury hotels and Nile-view resorts to budget-friendly options. Many hotels and resorts provide stunning views of the Nile and convenient access to major attractions.

Best Time to Visit: The cooler months from October to April are ideal for visiting Aswan, as temperatures are more pleasant. The summer months can be very hot, making outdoor activities less comfortable.

Dress Code: Wear light, comfortable clothing suitable for warm weather, and bring layers for cooler evenings. Modest dress is recommended, especially when visiting religious and cultural sites.

What to Bring: Bring sun protection (hat, sunscreen), plenty of water, and comfortable walking shoes. A camera is essential for capturing the stunning landscapes and historical sites.

Tips for Visitors

Plan Ahead: Many of Aswan's attractions, particularly those involving boat rides and tours, can be popular, so plan and book in advance if possible.

Stay Hydrated: The climate can be very dry, so it's important to stay hydrated, especially if you're engaging in outdoor activities.

Respect Local Customs: Be mindful of local customs and traditions, particularly when visiting Nubian villages and religious sites.

Temple of Abydos

The Temple of Abydos, located about 170 kilometers (105 miles) north of Luxor, is one of Egypt's most significant and ancient religious sites. It holds great historical and spiritual importance as a major center of worship and a site of veneration for Osiris, the god of the afterlife. Here's a detailed overview of what makes the Temple of Abydos a must-visit:

Historical Significance

Dedication: The Temple of Abydos is primarily dedicated to Osiris, the god of the underworld and resurrection. It was considered a crucial site for the afterlife and was highly revered in ancient Egyptian religion.

Construction: The temple complex was developed over several periods, with the most significant construction occurring during the 19th Dynasty under Seti I and his son Ramses II. It was built on the site of earlier temples dating back to the Old Kingdom.

Key Attractions

Great Temple of Seti I: The largest and most impressive structure within the Abydos complex. It features:

Hypostyle Hall: This grand hall is supported by massive columns adorned with intricate carvings and hieroglyphs.

Sanctuary: The inner sanctum houses a statue of

Osiris and features detailed reliefs depicting various scenes related to Osiris and other deities.

Osireion: A unique and mysterious structure associated with Osiris, the Osireion is believed to be a symbolic tomb or a funerary temple. It consists of a series of subterranean chambers and is notable for its architectural and symbolic significance.

Temple of Ramses II: Adjacent to Seti I's temple, Ramses II's temple is smaller but includes notable reliefs depicting Ramses II's military campaigns and divine interactions.

Abydos King List: One of the most important features of the Great Temple is the Abydos King List, a carved list of the pharaohs from the earliest times up to Seti I. This list is invaluable for Egyptologists as it provides a chronological record of the ancient Egyptian kings.

Shafts and Burial Chambers: The temple complex includes several shafts and burial chambers used for the interment of sacred objects and possibly the remains of important individuals associated with the temple.

Visiting the Temple of Abydos

Guided Tours: A guided tour is highly recommended to fully appreciate the historical and religious significance of the temple complex. Guides can provide detailed explanations of the carvings, inscriptions, and the history of the site.

Photography: Photography is generally allowed at the site, but it's always good to check for any specific restrictions, especially in certain areas.

Ticket Information: Tickets can be purchased on-site, and it's a good idea to check current prices and availability. The temple is also part of various Nile cruise itineraries, which can include guided visits.

Practical Information

Travel Time: The Temple of Abydos is about a 2.5 to 3-hour drive from Luxor. It's often visited as part of a day trip or combined with other nearby sites.

Best Time to Visit: The cooler months from October to April are ideal for visiting. Summer temperatures can be quite high, making daytime visits challenging.

Dress Code: Wear comfortable, modest clothing suitable for warm weather. Sturdy walking shoes are recommended due to the uneven terrain and the need for exploration.

What to Bring: Bring water, sun protection (hat, sunscreen), and a camera for exterior shots. If visiting during the hotter months, consider bringing extra water and a hat.

Tips for Visitors

Early Arrival: Arriving early helps to avoid the heat of the day and larger crowds, allowing for a more pleasant and immersive experience.

Respect the Site: Follow all guidelines provided by site staff and avoid touching or leaning on ancient carvings to help preserve the temple.

Combine Visits: Consider combining your visit to Abydos with other nearby attractions, such as the Temple of Dendera, for a more comprehensive exploration of Egypt's religious and archaeological heritage.

Hot Air Balloon Ride Over Luxor

A hot air balloon ride over Luxor offers a breathtaking and unique perspective on one of Egypt's most historically rich landscapes. Floating high above the Nile River and the ancient temples and tombs of Luxor, this experience combines adventure with awe-inspiring views. Here's a detailed guide to what you can expect from a hot air balloon ride over Luxor:

What to Expect

Scenic Views: The balloon ride provides panoramic views of Luxor's west bank, including the Valley of the Kings, the Valley of the Queens, the Temple of Hatshepsut, and the Temple of Karnak. The early morning light often casts a golden hue over the landscape, enhancing the beauty of the ancient monuments and the surrounding countryside.

Flight Duration: The typical hot air balloon ride lasts between 45 minutes to 1 hour. This duration provides ample time to enjoy the views and take in the serene atmosphere.

Early Morning Start: Most balloon rides take place at sunrise. You'll need to wake up early, as the experience often starts with transportation to the launch site before dawn. The early start ensures calm winds and the best lighting for viewing and photography.

Weather Conditions: Balloon rides are highly dependent on weather conditions. Flights are usually conducted in the early morning when the weather is most stable. If conditions are not suitable, flights may be canceled for safety reasons, and a refund or rescheduling will typically be offered.

The Experience

Launch and Landing: The experience begins with a gentle ascent from a designated launch site. As the balloon rises, you'll gradually get a sense of the scale and beauty of the archaeological sites below. The landing is usually smooth, and you'll be guided back to your starting point by the ballooning team.

Ballooning Team: Professional pilots and ground crew manage the balloon ride, ensuring safety and providing interesting commentary about the sights you're viewing. They are experienced in handling the balloon and navigating the flight path.

Practical Information

Booking: It's advisable to book your hot air balloon ride in advance, especially during peak tourist seasons. Many tour operators in Luxor offer balloon rides, and it's worth checking reviews and comparing options to ensure a reputable provider.

Cost: The cost of a hot air balloon ride can vary depending on the operator, the time of year, and whether the ride is private or shared. Prices typically range from $100 to $200 per person.

What to Wear: Dress in layers, as it can be cool in the early morning but warm up quickly after sunrise. Comfortable clothing and sturdy shoes are recommended. You might also want to bring a hat and sunscreen.

Safety: Hot air ballooning is generally safe, but it's important to follow all safety instructions provided by the ballooning team. Ensure that the operator you choose adheres to international safety standards.

Tips for a Great Experience

Arrive Early: Arrive at the launch site early to ensure a smooth start. Most operators provide transportation from your hotel to the launch site.

Camera Ready: Bring a camera or smartphone with a good battery, as the aerial views provide fantastic photo opportunities. A wide-angle lens is ideal for capturing the expansive landscape.

Stay Flexible: Be prepared for changes in schedule due to weather conditions. Flexibility in your plans can help ensure you get to experience the ride.

Enjoy the Serenity: The ride offers a peaceful and serene experience, so take the time to relax and fully appreciate the stunning views and the unique perspective of Luxor's ancient monuments.

Grace Bennett

7-day Itinerary for first time traveler
Day 1: Arrival in Luxor

Morning

Activity: Arrival and Check-in

Start Your Day: Arrive in Luxor early in the morning. Depending on your mode of arrival (flight or train), head to your hotel for check-in. If your room isn't ready yet, you can leave your luggage at the hotel and start exploring.

Getting Around: Taxis are readily available from the airport or train station. For local travel, consider using ride-hailing apps or asking your hotel about shuttle services.

Breakfast:

Where to Eat: Try **Sofra Restaurant & Café** for a traditional Egyptian breakfast.

What to Eat: Enjoy dishes like **Ful Medames** (fava beans), **Ta'ameya** (Egyptian falafel), and **Baladi bread**.

Mid-Morning

Activity: Visit Karnak Temple

Details: This vast temple complex is one of the largest religious buildings ever constructed.

Opening Hours: 6:00 AM – 5:00 PM

Price: Around EGP 200 (USD 6.50) for entry

Getting Around: A taxi or a local guide will help you navigate the site. It's a large area, so comfortable walking shoes are essential.

Afternoon

Activity: Explore Luxor Temple

Details: This temple is centrally located and offers a stunning view of ancient Egyptian architecture.

Opening Hours: 6:00 AM – 9:00 PM

Price: Around EGP 150 (USD 5)

Getting Around: A short taxi ride from Karnak Temple or a leisurely walk if you're staying nearby.

Lunch:

Where to Eat: Head to **Al-Sahaby Lane Restaurant**, which offers a great view of Luxor Temple and serves traditional Egyptian fare.

What to Eat: Try **Koshari** (a lentil, rice, and pasta dish), **Grilled Chicken**, or **Egyptian Meze** (small appetizers).

Mid-Afternoon

Activity: Visit the Luxor Museum

Details: This museum has an excellent collection of artifacts from ancient Thebes, including statues and mummies.

Opening Hours: 9:00 AM – 7:00 PM

Price: Around EGP 100 (USD 3.50)

Getting Around: It's best reached by taxi or a short walk from the Luxor Temple area.

Evening

Activity: Stroll Along the Nile Corniche

Details: This is a pleasant, scenic walk where you can enjoy views of the Nile River and Luxor's skyline.

Getting Around: It's easily walkable or you can take a short taxi ride if you're staying further away.

Dinner:

Where to Eat: The Lantern Restaurant offers a mix of Egyptian and international dishes.

What to Eat: Opt for **Egyptian grilled fish**, **Lamb Shawarma**, or **Vegetarian Mezze**.

Night

Activity: Optional Nile River Cruise

Details: A relaxing cruise along the Nile River can be

a lovely way to end your day. Many cruises offer dinner and live entertainment.

Price: Varies depending on the cruise, but expect to pay around EGP 300-600 (USD 10-20).

Getting Around: Most hotels can arrange a Nile cruise for you, or you can book one through local tour operators.

Getting Around Tips:

Taxis: Available throughout the city. Agree on a fare before starting your journey or use a ride-hailing app.

Horse Carriages: A traditional and scenic way to get around, but negotiate the price beforehand.

Walking: Luxor's central attractions are relatively close to each other, making walking a feasible option for shorter distances.

Day 2: East Bank Exploration

Morning

Activity: Visit the Valley of the Kings

Details: Although technically on the West Bank, it's a must-see. This necropolis is famous for its richly decorated tombs, including those of Tutankhamun and Ramses VI.

Opening Hours: 6:00 AM – 5:00 PM

Price: EGP 240 (USD 8) for the general entry; additional fees apply for special tombs.

Getting Around: Use a taxi or arrange a guided tour. Allow about 2-3 hours to explore.

Breakfast:

Where to Eat: El Hussein Restaurant in Luxor provides a great start to the day.

What to Eat: Enjoy a hearty **Egyptian breakfast platter** including **Ful Medames, Ta'ameya,** and **Labneh.**

Mid-Morning

Activity: Visit the Temple of Hatshepsut

Details: This mortuary temple dedicated to the female pharaoh Hatshepsut is renowned for its distinctive architecture and terraces.

Opening Hours: 6:00 AM – 5:00 PM

Price: EGP 200 (USD 6.50)

Getting Around: A taxi from the Valley of the Kings or a pre-arranged tour will get you there efficiently.

Afternoon

Activity: Return to the East Bank and visit the Temple of Luxor

Details: Known for its majestic entrance, large courtyards, and the beautiful Avenue of Sphinxes that connects it to Karnak Temple.

Opening Hours: 6:00 AM – 9:00 PM

Price: EGP 150 (USD 5)

Getting Around: It's centrally located, so you can walk from nearby hotels or take a short taxi ride.

Lunch:

Where to Eat: Sofra Restaurant & Café, if you enjoyed it the previous day, or try **Nour El Nil**, known for its traditional Egyptian cuisine and views of the Nile.

What to Eat: Consider dishes like **Mahshi** (stuffed vegetables), **Egyptian kebabs**, or **Grilled fish**.

Mid-Afternoon

Activity: Visit the Mummification Museum

Details: A small but fascinating museum focusing on the ancient Egyptian art of mummification.

Opening Hours: 9:00 AM – 5:00 PM

Price: EGP 100 (USD 3.50)

Getting Around: A short taxi ride from the Temple of Luxor or within walking distance if you're staying in the central area.

Evening

Activity: Explore the Souks (Markets) of Luxor

Details: Wander through local markets to experience the vibrant atmosphere and shop for souvenirs like papyrus scrolls, jewelry, and spices.

Getting Around: The souks are usually within walking distance from the central areas like Luxor Temple. If not, a quick taxi ride will get you there.

Dinner:

Where to Eat: The Kings Head Pub, a relaxed spot with a mix of Egyptian and international cuisine.

What to Eat: Enjoy dishes such as **Chicken Shawarma**, **Beef Kofta**, or **Egyptian Mezze**.

Night

Activity: Optional Sound and Light Show at Karnak Temple

Details: This evening show highlights the history of Karnak Temple with a spectacular light and sound display.

Opening Hours: Shows typically start around 7:00 PM or 8:00 PM depending on the season.

Price: Around EGP 200-300 (USD 7-10)

Getting Around: Most hotels can arrange transportation to and from the show, or you can take a taxi.

Getting Around Tips:

Taxis: Use taxis or ride-hailing apps for longer distances or between sites.

Horse Carriages: A fun way to get around Luxor, especially for short distances.

Walking: Ideal for exploring the East Bank's central attractions if you're staying nearby.

Day 3: Valley of the Kings and Valley of the Queens

Morning

Activity: Visit the Valley of the Kings

Details: This UNESCO World Heritage site contains the tombs of pharaohs from the New Kingdom. Notable tombs include those of Tutankhamun, Ramses II, and Seti I.

Opening Hours: 6:00 AM – 5:00 PM

Price: EGP 240 (USD 8) for general entry; additional fees for specific tombs (e.g., Tutankhamun costs extra).

Getting Around: Arrange a taxi or a guided tour to ensure you get to the site early to avoid crowds and have ample time to explore. Allocate about 2-3 hours here.

Breakfast:

Where to Eat: Abu Shakra Restaurant, known for its traditional Egyptian breakfast options.

What to Eat: Try **Ful Medames**, **Ta'ameya**, and **Egyptian cheese** with **Baladi bread**.

Mid-Morning

Activity: Visit the Valley of the Queens

Details: Located close to the Valley of the Kings, this site contains the tombs of the queens and royal children. Notable tombs include those of Queen Nefertari and Queen Titi.

Opening Hours: 6:00 AM – 5:00 PM

Price: EGP 200 (USD 6.50) for entry; additional fees for special tombs like Nefertari's (around EGP 1000 or USD 32).

Getting Around: A taxi or guided tour can take you

from the Valley of the Kings to the Valley of the Queens. Expect to spend about 1-2 hours here.

Afternoon

Activity: Visit the Temple of Medinet Habu

Details: This well-preserved temple dedicated to Ramses III features impressive reliefs and a large wall surrounding the temple.

Opening Hours: 6:00 AM – 5:00 PM

Price: EGP 200 (USD 6.50)

Getting Around: A taxi from the Valley of the Queens will get you there in about 20 minutes.

Lunch:

Where to Eat: El Nakhil, offering a mix of traditional and international dishes with a relaxed atmosphere.

What to Eat: Consider dishes like **Grilled Fish**, **Egyptian Kofta**, or **Vegetarian Stuffed Vine Leaves**.

Mid-Afternoon

Activity: Visit the Ramesseum

Details: This mortuary temple built by Ramses II is known for its colossal statues and inscriptions.

Opening Hours: 6:00 AM – 5:00 PM

Price: EGP 150 (USD 5)

Getting Around: A short taxi ride from Medinet Habu, allowing about 1 hour to explore.

Evening

Activity: Relax at Your Hotel or Take a Felucca Ride on the Nile

Details: A felucca ride provides a serene experience on the Nile River, ideal for unwinding after a day of sightseeing.

Price: Varies, but typically around EGP 100-200 (USD 3-7) for a short ride.

Getting Around: Arrange the ride through your hotel or a local tour operator.

Dinner:

Where to Eat: Marhaba Palace Restaurant, known for its diverse menu and pleasant ambiance.

What to Eat: Enjoy dishes like **Mixed Grill Platter**, **Egyptian Lamb Chops**, or **Seafood Tagine**.

Night

Activity: Optional Visit to Luxor's Night Market or Relax at the Hotel

Details: The night market offers a local shopping experience, or you can enjoy a peaceful evening at your hotel.

Getting Around: Walk to the market if you're staying nearby, or take a taxi.

Getting Around Tips:

Taxis: Ideal for traveling between the Valley of the Kings, Valley of the Queens, and other sites. Negotiate fares or use a ride-hailing app.

Guided Tours: Consider hiring a guide for in-depth historical insights and ease of travel between sites.

Comfortable Footwear: Wear comfortable shoes for walking and exploring the sites.

Day 4: Temple of Hatshepsut and Colossi of Memnon

Morning

Activity: Visit the Temple of Hatshepsut

Details: This stunning mortuary temple, dedicated to the female pharaoh Hatshepsut, is known for its distinctive architecture and terraced design. It's set against a dramatic mountain backdrop.

Opening Hours: 6:00 AM – 5:00 PM

Price: EGP 200 (USD 6.50)

Getting Around: Use a taxi or a guided tour from your hotel. Allocate around 1.5 to 2 hours to explore the site thoroughly.

Breakfast:

Where to Eat: Nile View Restaurant, known for its excellent breakfast options and views of the river.

What to Eat: Opt for a classic **Egyptian breakfast** of **Ful Medames, Ta'ameya,** and **Eggs with tomatoes**.

Mid-Morning

Activity: Visit the Colossi of Memnon

Details: These two massive statues represent Amenhotep III and are one of the most iconic sights in Luxor. They stand as sentinels to the entrance of his mortuary temple.

Opening Hours: 6:00 AM – 5:00 PM

Price: Included in the ticket for the West Bank sites.

Getting Around: A short taxi ride from the Temple of Hatshepsut. You can spend around 30 minutes to 1 hour here.

Afternoon

Activity: Explore Deir el-Medina

Details: This ancient village was home to the artisans who worked on the tombs in the Valley of the Kings. The site includes well-preserved tombs and houses, offering insight into daily life in ancient Egypt.

Opening Hours: 6:00 AM – 5:00 PM

Price: EGP 100 (USD 3.50)

Getting Around: It's close to the Valley of the Kings and can be reached by taxi or as part of a guided tour. Allow about 1-1.5 hours to explore.

Lunch:

Where to Eat: El Gaddafi Restaurant, which offers a variety of local dishes and a comfortable atmosphere.

What to Eat: Enjoy **Egyptian kebabs, Chicken Shawarma,** or **Vegetarian Mezze**.

Mid-Afternoon

Activity: Visit the Temple of Karnak (if you missed it on Day 1)

Details: This massive temple complex is dedicated to the god Amun and includes impressive pylons, sanctuaries, and the famous Hypostyle Hall.

Opening Hours: 6:00 AM – 5:00 PM

Price: EGP 200 (USD 6.50)

Getting Around: A short taxi ride from Deir el-Medina if you're revisiting. Spend around 2 hours here.

Evening

Activity: Optional Visit to a Local Café or Cultural Event

Details: Enjoy a relaxing evening at a local café or check if there are any cultural events or performances available.

Where to Go: The Roof-Top Café for a casual experience or **Luxor Cultural Center** for local cultural events.

Getting Around: Walk or use a taxi depending on your location.

Dinner:

Where to Eat: Al-Sahaby Lane Restaurant, known for its traditional Egyptian dishes and beautiful setting.

What to Eat: Try **Stuffed Pigeon**, **Egyptian Rice and Lentils**, or **Mixed Grill Platters**.

Night

Activity: Relax at Your Hotel or Take a Leisurely Walk Along the Nile

Details: Unwind after a day of sightseeing. You might also enjoy a serene evening walk along the Nile Corniche.

Getting Around: If you're staying near the river, walking is a great option. Otherwise, take a taxi.

Getting Around Tips:

Taxis: Convenient for traveling between different sites on the West Bank. Always agree on the fare before starting your journey.

Guided Tours: Consider booking a guide for a comprehensive tour of the West Bank sites and historical context.

Comfortable Attire: Wear comfortable clothing and shoes for exploring the temples and tombs.

Day 5: Dendera Temple Complex and Hot Air Balloon Ride

Morning

Activity: Hot Air Balloon Ride

Details: A breathtaking experience over Luxor's West Bank, offering stunning views of the temples, tombs, and the Nile River at sunrise.

Opening Hours: Typically, rides start early in the morning, around 5:00 AM – 7:00 AM, depending on the season and weather conditions.

Price: Approximately EGP 2,000-3,000 (USD 65-100) per person.

Getting Around: Most balloon ride operators provide transportation to and from your hotel. Confirm this when booking.

Breakfast:

Where to Eat: After your balloon ride, enjoy a hearty breakfast at **Al-Sahaby Lane Restaurant** or **Sofra Restaurant & Café**, both of which offer a range of traditional and international options.

What to Eat: Opt for a filling breakfast like **Egyptian omelets**, **Pancakes**, or **Ful Medames**.

Mid-Morning

Activity: Visit the Dendera Temple Complex

Details: Located about 60 kilometers (37 miles) north of Luxor, this temple complex is dedicated to the goddess Hathor. It's known for its well-preserved reliefs, the astronomical ceiling, and the sacred lake.

Opening Hours: 6:00 AM – 5:00 PM

Price: Approximately EGP 150 (USD 5) for entry.

Getting Around: Arrange for a taxi or a tour to Dendera. The trip takes about 1 to 1.5 hours each way from Luxor.

Afternoon

Activity: Explore Dendera Temple Complex

Details: Take your time exploring the main temple, the hypostyle hall, the Hathor sanctuary, and the well-preserved astronomical ceiling. Don't miss the chance to see the Sacred Lake.

Getting Around: The complex is quite extensive, so comfortable walking shoes are recommended. Plan to spend around 2-3 hours here.

Lunch:

Where to Eat: There are limited dining options near Dendera, so consider bringing a packed lunch or stopping at a local eatery on the way back to Luxor.

What to Eat: Look for local eateries or simple restaurants offering Egyptian staples such as **Koshari, Grilled Chicken,** or **Falafel**.

Mid-Afternoon

Activity: Return to Luxor and Relax

Details: After your visit to Dendera, head back to Luxor. Depending on your energy levels, you can relax at your hotel or visit a local café.

Getting Around: Taxi or private transport back to Luxor.

Optional Activity:

Visit a Local Souk: Explore Luxor's local markets if you have time and energy. This is a good opportunity to pick up souvenirs and experience local life.

Evening

Activity: Dinner and Leisure Time

Where to Eat: For a special dinner, consider dining at **The Lantern Restaurant** or **Marhaba Palace Restaurant**. Both offer a pleasant ambiance and a variety of Egyptian and international dishes.

What to Eat: Enjoy a meal of **Egyptian Meze, Mixed Grill,** or **Vegetarian Platters**.

Night

Activity: Relax or Take a Walk

Details: End your day with a relaxing evening. You might want to take a stroll along the Nile Corniche or simply unwind at your hotel.

Getting Around: Walking is ideal if you're staying near the Nile Corniche, or use a taxi for longer distances.

Getting Around Tips:

Taxis: Use for travel to and from Dendera. Arrange in advance or use ride-hailing apps.

Guided Tours: Consider booking a guided tour for Dendera and balloon rides for a more organized experience.

Comfortable Attire: Wear comfortable clothes and shoes for both the balloon ride and exploring the temple complex.

Day 6: Aswan Day Trip

Early Morning

Activity: Depart for Aswan

Details: Aswan is about 220 kilometers (137 miles) south of Luxor. The most common ways to travel are by train or private car.

Train: High-speed trains run between Luxor and Aswan, taking approximately 3 hours. Trains generally depart early in the morning.

Private Car: A private car or taxi can also be arranged, taking about 3-4 hours.

Getting Around: Ensure you book tickets in advance if traveling by train or arrange your car transfer through your hotel or a travel agency.

Breakfast:

Where to Eat: Enjoy breakfast before departing. If you're on a train, you might have a meal onboard or bring snacks from your hotel.

What to Eat: A nutritious breakfast like **Ful Medames, Ta'ameya,** and **Fresh Fruit** is ideal for the journey.

Mid-Morning

Activity: Visit Philae Temple

Details: This beautiful temple complex is dedicated to the goddess Isis and is located on Agilkia Island. It was relocated from its original site on Philae Island to save it from the rising waters of Lake Nasser.

Opening Hours: 7:00 AM – 5:00 PM

Price: Approximately EGP 200 (USD 6.50)

Getting Around: Access to the temple is via a boat ride from the dock in Aswan. Boat trips are available through local operators.

Lunch

Activity: Lunch in Aswan

Where to Eat: Nubian House Restaurant, offering local Nubian cuisine and a charming ambiance.

What to Eat: Try **Nubian Chicken**, **Grilled Fish**, or **Vegetarian Dishes**.

Afternoon

Activity: Visit the Unfinished Obelisk

Details: This massive obelisk, still partially carved from the granite quarry, provides insight into ancient Egyptian stone-working techniques.

Opening Hours: 7:00 AM – 5:00 PM

Price: Typically included with entry to other Aswan sites.

Getting Around: Easily reachable by taxi or as part of a guided tour.

Activity: Visit the Aswan High Dam

Details: This impressive engineering feat controls the Nile's flooding and provides hydroelectric power. The dam offers panoramic views of Lake Nasser.

Opening Hours: 7:00 AM – 5:00 PM

Price: Approximately EGP 100 (USD 3.50)

Getting Around: A taxi or tour will get you there, and you can allocate about 1 hour for the visit.

Evening

Activity: Return to Luxor

Details: Travel back to Luxor by train or private car. Depending on your travel method, you should plan to leave Aswan in the late afternoon or early evening.

Getting Around: Ensure you have your return tickets booked if traveling by train or arrange transportation with your hotel.

Dinner:

Where to Eat: The Lantern Restaurant or **Marhaba Palace Restaurant** in Luxor for a relaxed meal after a long day.

What to Eat: Enjoy a variety of dishes such as **Egyptian Meze**, **Grilled Meats**, or **Vegetarian Options**.

Night

Activity: Relax and Unwind

Details: After your return to Luxor, take some time to relax at your hotel. Consider a quiet evening walk or simply unwind in your room.

Getting Around Tips:

Travel to Aswan: Book train tickets in advance or arrange for a private car.

Local Transportation in Aswan: Use taxis or arrange for a guided tour to cover the main attractions efficiently.

Comfortable Attire: Wear comfortable clothing and shoes for a day of sightseeing, and consider bringing a hat and sunscreen for sun protection.

Day 7: Relax and Depart

Morning

Activity: Relax at Your Hotel

Details: Start your day with a leisurely breakfast and some relaxation. Take advantage of your hotel's amenities such as the pool, spa, or gardens.

Breakfast:

Where to Eat: Sofra Restaurant & Café or **The Roof-Top Café** for a relaxed start.

What to Eat: Enjoy a relaxed breakfast with options like **Egyptian pastries**, **Fruits**, **Pancakes**, and **Fresh Juice**.

Activity: Stroll Along the Nile Corniche

Details: If you have time, take a pleasant walk along the Nile Corniche. It's a great way to enjoy the river views and get a final taste of Luxor's charm.

Getting Around: Walking is ideal for this leisurely activity.

Mid-Morning

Activity: Final Souvenir Shopping

Details: Pick up any last-minute souvenirs or gifts from local markets or shops. Look for items such as **papyrus scrolls**, **handmade jewelry**, or **Egyptian spices**.

Where to Shop: The **Luxor Souk** or **Luxor Market** for a variety of local goods.

Getting Around: You can walk if you're staying near the market area, or use a taxi for convenience.

Afternoon

Activity: Prepare for Departure

Details: Return to your hotel to check out and ensure you have all your belongings packed. If you have a late departure, consider a late check-out or use the hotel's luggage storage services.

Getting Around: Arrange for transportation to the airport or train station.

Lunch:

Where to Eat: Enjoy a final meal at **Al-Sahaby Lane Restaurant** or **Marhaba Palace Restaurant** if you have time.

What to Eat: Enjoy a light meal such as **Sandwiches**, **Salads**, or **Egyptian Kebabs**.

Late Afternoon / Evening

Activity: Depart Luxor

Details: Head to the airport or train station for your departure. Ensure you arrive with enough time to manage check-in and security procedures comfortably.

Getting Around: Use a taxi or pre-arranged transportation from your hotel to the departure point.

Getting Around Tips:

Transportation to Departure Points: Arrange airport or train station transfers with your hotel or use a taxi.

Luggage: Check with your hotel about luggage storage if you have time to explore before your departure.

Final Notes

Check Travel Documents: Ensure you have all necessary travel documents, including tickets, passport, and any required visas.

Health and Safety: Double-check any health or safety requirements, especially if traveling internationally.

Chapter 13: Conclusion

Tourist Information Centers

Tourist Information Centers (TICs) are crucial resources for travelers visiting Egypt, offering a range of services to enhance your trip. Here's a detailed look at what you can expect from these centers:

1. Purpose and Services

Tourist Information Centers in Egypt serve as a one-stop hub for visitors seeking assistance and information. Their primary purpose is to support travelers in planning and navigating their trips. Services commonly provided include:

Information and Maps: Detailed maps of cities, tourist sites, and transportation routes. Brochures and guides on attractions, hotels, restaurants, and cultural events.

Booking Services: Assistance with booking tours, excursions, and sometimes accommodations. They often provide information on reputable tour operators.

Transportation: Information on public transport options, car rentals, and airport transfers. Some centers also sell transport passes.

Local Insights: Recommendations on local dining, shopping, and entertainment. They can offer tips on experiencing local culture and avoiding common tourist pitfalls.

Emergency Assistance: Help with dealing with lost passports, medical emergencies, or other urgent issues. They can provide contact information for local authorities and embassies.

2. Locations

Tourist Information Centers are typically located in key tourist areas and major cities across Egypt. Here are some notable locations:

Cairo: Several TICs are located in Cairo, including at Cairo International Airport and central locations like Tahrir Square and near major tourist sites such as the Egyptian Museum.

Luxor: Centers are available in Luxor near major hotels and key attractions like Luxor Temple and Karnak Temple.

Aswan: TICs in Aswan can be found in central areas and at the Aswan International Airport, offering information on both local and regional attractions.

Alexandria: Located in tourist-heavy areas, including the Alexandria Library and other prominent landmarks.

3. Online Resources

Many **Tourist Information Centers** also offer online resources, providing access to information before and during your trip. These resources may include:

Official Websites: Offering comprehensive guides, downloadable maps, and up-to-date information on attractions and events.

Social Media: Updates on local events, travel tips, and direct communication with visitors.

Travel Apps: Some TICs have associated apps that provide real-time information and navigation assistance.

4. How to Utilize Them

To make the most of **Tourist Information Centers**, consider the following tips:

Visit Early: Drop by early in your trip to gather maps, brochures, and information about local services.

Ask Specific Questions: Prepare specific questions

about your interests, such as historical sites, cultural experiences, or local customs.

Check Opening Hours: Ensure you visit during operating hours, which can vary by location and time of year.

Use Online Resources: Check the TIC's website or social media pages for updates on local events and additional resources.

5. Additional Tips

Language: While English is commonly spoken in TICs, knowing a few basic phrases in Arabic can be helpful.

Cultural Sensitivity: Be aware of local customs and etiquette when interacting with staff and other travelers.

Safety: Always use reputable TICs and avoid unlicensed or unofficial sources of information.

Useful Apps for travelers

For a seamless travel experience in Egypt, a variety of apps can assist with navigation, accommodation, communication, and more. Here's a list of essential apps to enhance your trip:

1. Google Maps

Purpose: Navigation and location services.

Features: Detailed maps, GPS navigation, and real-time traffic updates. Useful for finding landmarks, restaurants, and accommodations.

2. TripAdvisor

Purpose: Reviews and recommendations for attractions, restaurants, and hotels.

Features: User-generated reviews, photos, ratings, and the ability to book tours and accommodations directly.

3. Booking.com

Purpose: Hotel and accommodation bookings.

Features: Wide selection of hotels, apartments, and hostels with user reviews and flexible booking options. Also offers last-minute deals and cancellations.

4. Airbnb

Purpose: Alternative accommodation options.

Features: Book unique stays such as apartments, homes, or boutique hotels. Includes local experiences and guided tours.

5. Uber/Careem

Purpose: Ride-hailing services.

Features: Convenient transportation with the ability to book rides, view fare estimates, and track drivers. Available in major cities like Cairo and Alexandria.

6. Egypt Air

Purpose: Flight information and booking for Egypt Air.

Features: Check flight status, manage bookings, and access boarding passes. Useful for domestic and international flights within Egypt.

7. XE Currency Converter

Purpose: Currency conversion.

Features: Real-time exchange rates and currency conversion. Essential for budgeting and shopping in local currency.

8. Google Translate

Purpose: Language translation.

Features: Translate text, voice, and images between languages. Helpful for communication in areas where English may not be widely spoken.

9. Travel Guides by Lonely Planet

Purpose: Travel guides and recommendations.

Features: Comprehensive guides on attractions, dining, and activities. Offline access to important travel information.

10. Maps.me

Purpose: Offline maps and navigation.

Features: Download maps for offline use, including points of interest and walking trails. Ideal for areas with limited internet access.

11. Airbnb Experiences

Purpose: Local tours and experiences.

Features: Book unique local experiences such as guided tours, cooking classes, and cultural activities directly through the app.

12. WiFi Map

Purpose: Access to Wi-Fi hotspots.

Features: Find free Wi-Fi hotspots and passwords shared by other users. Useful for staying connected without using mobile data.

13. WhatsApp

Purpose: Communication.

Features: Free messaging and voice/video calls. Useful for staying in touch with local contacts and fellow travelers.

14. Egyptian Monuments

Purpose: Information on Egyptian historical sites.

Features: Detailed descriptions and historical context of major monuments and attractions.

15. iEgypt Travel

Purpose: Travel planning and local guides.

Features: Information on attractions, dining, and accommodations. Also includes practical travel tips and local insights.

Tips for Using Travel Apps:

Download Apps Before Traveling: Ensure you have essential apps downloaded and updated before your trip to avoid data issues.

Check Offline Capabilities: Many travel apps offer offline features; download necessary maps and information in advance.

Use Data Wisely: Be mindful of data usage, especially if roaming. Use Wi-Fi when available.

These apps will help streamline your travel experience in Egypt, making it easier to navigate, stay connected, and explore all that the country has to offer.

Basic Egyptian Phrases

Knowing a few basic Egyptian Arabic phrases can greatly enhance your travel experience in Egypt, helping you communicate effectively and immerse yourself in local culture. Here's a list of essential phrases:

Greetings and Courtesies

Hello: مرحبا (Marhaban) or أهلاً (Ahlan)

Good Morning: صباح الخير (Sabah el-kheir)

Good Evening: مساء الخير (Masa' el-kheir)

Goodbye: وداعاً (Wadana') or إلى اللقاء (al-liqaa)

Please: من فضلك (Min fadlak/fadlik)

Thank You: شكراً (Shukran)

You're Welcome: على الرحب والسعة (Ala al-rahb wa al-sa'a)

Yes: نعم (Na'am)

No: لا (La)

Common Questions

How are you?: كيف حالك؟ (Kayfa halak/halik?)

What's your name?: ما اسمك؟ (Ma ismuk/ismik?)

My name is...: ...اسمي (Ismi...)

Do you speak English?: هل تتحدث الإنجليزية؟ (Hal tatahaddath al-ingliziyya?)

Where is...?: ...أين هو؟ (Ayn huwa...?)

How much does this cost?: كم ثمن هذا؟ (Kam thaman hatha?)

Directions and Transportation

Where is the bathroom?: أين الحمام؟ (Ayn al-hammam?)

How do I get to...?: كيف أذهب إلى...؟ (Kayfa adhab ila...?)

Is it far?: هل هو بعيد؟ (Hal huwa ba'id?)

I need a taxi: أحتاج إلى تاكسي (Ahtaj ila taxi)

How long does it take?: كم يستغرق الوقت؟ (Kam yastaghriq al-waqt?)

Dining and Shopping

I would like to order...: أود أن أطلب... (Awad an atlub...)

The bill, please: الفاتورة، من فضلك (Al-fatura, min fadlak/fadlik)

How much is this?: كم ثمن هذا؟ (Kam thaman hatha?)

Can I try this on?: هل يمكنني تجربة هذا؟ (Hal yumkinuni tajribat hatha?)

I'm just looking: أنا فقط أبحث (Ana faqat abhath)

Emergency and Assistance

Help!: النجدة! (Al-najda!)

I need a doctor: أحتاج إلى طبيب (Ahtaj ila tabib)

Call the police: اتصل بالشرطة (Ittasil bil-shurta)

I'm lost: أنا ضائع (Ana dae')

I don't understand: أنا لا أفهم (Ana la afham)

Pronunciation Tips

Practice Pronunciation: Egyptian Arabic pronunciation can be different from Modern Standard Arabic. Listening to native speakers or using language learning apps can help.

Use Simple Phrases: Start with simple, clear phrases to ensure you're understood.

These basic phrases will help you navigate various situations, making your experience in Egypt more enjoyable and engaging.

Final Tips and Recommendations

To ensure a smooth and enjoyable trip to Egypt, consider these final tips and recommendations:

1. Respect Local Customs

Cultural Sensitivity: Familiarize yourself with local customs and traditions. Dress modestly, especially when visiting religious sites. Respect local practices and be polite in interactions.

Photography: Always ask for permission before taking photos, particularly of people or in restricted areas.

2. Stay Hydrated and Safe

Hydration: Egypt's climate can be very hot and dry, so drink plenty of bottled water. Avoid drinking tap water unless it's confirmed safe.

Food Safety: Eat at well-established restaurants and avoid street food if you have a sensitive stomach. Use hand sanitizer and avoid raw foods.

3. Currency and Payments

Local Currency: The Egyptian Pound (EGP) is the local currency. Carry some cash for small purchases, but credit and debit cards are widely accepted in hotels and major restaurants.

Bargaining: Bargaining is common in markets and some shops. Approach it with a friendly attitude and be prepared to negotiate.

4. Safety and Security

Travel Insurance: Ensure you have comprehensive

travel insurance that covers health, theft, and cancellations.

Local Laws: Be aware of and follow local laws and regulations. This includes respecting restrictions on certain activities and substances.

5. Communication

Language: While English is commonly spoken in tourist areas, learning a few basic Arabic phrases can be very helpful.

Emergency Contacts: Keep emergency numbers handy, including local police, medical services, and your country's embassy or consulate.

6. Transportation

Local Transport: Use reputable taxis or ride-sharing apps like Uber or Careem for safe and reliable transportation. For longer distances, consider booking trains or flights in advance.

Driving: If renting a car, be aware of local driving laws and road conditions. Driving in Egypt can be chaotic, so exercise caution.

7. Health Precautions

Vaccinations: Check with your healthcare provider about recommended vaccinations and health precautions for travel to Egypt.

Medical Care: Familiarize yourself with local medical facilities and have the contact details of a local doctor or hospital.

8. Connectivity

SIM Cards and Wi-Fi: Consider purchasing a local SIM card for affordable mobile data and calling. Many hotels and cafés offer free Wi-Fi.

9. Planning and Flexibility

Plan Ahead: Research and plan your itinerary, but also allow flexibility for spontaneous activities and rest.

Local Advice: Don't hesitate to ask locals for recommendations or directions. They can often provide valuable insights.

10. Enjoy the Experience

Immerse Yourself: Take time to enjoy Egypt's rich history, culture, and natural beauty. Engage with local traditions, try new foods, and make lasting memories.

Stay Positive: Traveling in a new country can have its challenges, but maintaining a positive attitude will enhance your experience.

By following these tips and staying informed, you can make the most of your trip to Egypt, ensuring a memorable and enjoyable experience.

THE END!!!

Printed in Great Britain
by Amazon